Taxat
Specialised C
and Prof

Taxation of Specialised Occupations and Professions

Seventh Edition

Tim Good BA (Oxon), ACA
The Professional Training Partnership

Updated by Sarah Bradford
Write Tax Ltd.

CCH

Wolters Kluwer UK Ltd
145 London Road
Kingston upon Thames
Surrey KT2 6SR
Tel: 0870 777 2906
Fax: 020 8247 1184
E-mail: customerservices@cch.co.uk

© 2004 Wolters Kluwer UK Ltd

ISBN 1 84140 490 X

All rights reserved. No part of this publication may be reproduced or transmitted in any form or by any means or stored in any retrieval system of any nature without prior written permission, except for permitted fair dealing under the Copyright, Designs and Patents Act 1988 or in accordance with the terms of a licence issued by the Copyright Licensing Agency in respect of photocopying and/or reprographic reproduction. Application for permission for other use of copyright material, including permission to reproduce extracts in other published works shall be made to the publisher. Full acknowledgement to author, publisher and source must be given.

No responsibility for loss occasioned to any person acting or refraining from action as a result of any material in this publication can be accepted by the author or publisher.

Crown copyright material is reproduced with the permission of the Controller of HMSO and the Queen's Printer for Scotland.

British Library Cataloguing-in-Publication Data

A catalogue record for this book is available from the British Library.

Typeset by J&L Composition, Filey, North Yorkshire
Printed in Great Britain by Clays Ltd, St Ives plc

Preface

This is the seventh edition of *Taxation of Specialised Occupations and Professions*. Since the publication of the sixth edition in 2003, there have been a number of developments of relevance to the subject matter, as well as a raft of new legislation and case law.

Following on from ITEPA 2003, the Tax Law Rewrite Project has given us the rewritten PAYE regulations, the Income Tax (Pay As You Earn) Regulations 2003 (SI 2003 No. 2682), which replace the Income Tax (Employments) Regulations 1993 (SI 1993 No. 944). The book reflects the regulations as they now stand.

In consequence of the rewritten legislation on earnings and pensions embodied in both ITEPA 2003 and the new PAYE regulations, the Revenue have rewritten their guidance manual covering this area of tax law. The material is now contained in the Employment Income Manual (EIM), which updates and replaces the Schedule E manual. The EIM comprises a useful source of guidance both to the legislation and to the Revenue's application and understanding of the law.

As far as new legislation is concerned, the Finance Act 2004 provides plenty of food for thought. Of particular interest is the new regime for subcontractors, which is to be introduced from 2006. The legislation is the culmination of an extensive period of consultation and it is hoped that the new regime will relieve much of the administrative burden inherent in the current one.

The Finance Act 2004 also makes a number of changes to the rules governing relief for European travel expenses of MPs and other representatives so as to mirror the House of Commons' procedure for reimbursing such expenses that came into force in February 2004.

The first three editions of this book were written by Brian Laventure of Grant Thornton and the subsequent three by Tim Good of the Professional Training Partnership. I am indebted to my predecessors for the basic structure of the text, which I have amended and updated as necessary so as to reflect current law and practice. I am also indebted to the CCH editorial team for the editorial work on this edition.

Sarah Bradford
WriteTax Ltd
October 2004

List of Abbreviations

Please note the following abbreviations which appear in the seventh edition of Taxation of Specialised Occupations and Professions.

Reference:	Abbreviated to:
Article	Art.
Capital Allowances Act 2001	CAA 2001
Capital Gains Tax	CGT
Corporation Tax	CT
Finance Acts (of various years)	FA [year]
Income and Corporation Taxes Act 1988	ICTA 1988
Income Tax (Earnings and Pensions) Act 2003	ITEPA 2003
Inheritance Tax	IHT
Inheritance Tax Act 1984	IHTA 1984
National Insurance	NI
National Insurance Contributions	NICs
Regulation	reg.
Schedule	Sch.
Section	s.
Social Security (Contributions and Benefits) Act 1992	SSCBA 1992
Taxes of Chargeable Gains Act 1992	TCGA 1992
Taxes Management Act 1970	TMA 1970

Contents

	page
Preface	v
List of abbreviations	vii
Table of cases	xxiii
Table of statutes	xxxi
Table of statutory instruments	xxxix
Table of Revenue documents	xli

1	**Introduction**			1
	1.1	What is a profession?		1
	1.2	Vocation		3
	1.3	Profession carried on abroad		3
	1.4	Overseas partnerships		4
	1.5	Carrying on business in the UK		5
	1.6	Carrying on a profession in the UK		5
	1.7	UK representatives of non-residents		6
		1.7.1	Definition of UK representative	6
		1.7.2	General rule for the obligations and liabilities of UK representatives	7
		1.7.3	Obligations and liabilities are limited where the UK representative is independent of the non-resident	7
		1.7.4	An independent agent can retain and recover monies due	8
		1.7.5	A partnership can be the UK representative of a non-resident	8
	1.8	Effect of change of residence		8
		1.8.1	Income tax	8
		1.8.2	Capital gains tax	9
	1.9	Employments		10
	1.10	Personal service companies		10
	1.11	Current year basis of assessment		11
	1.12	Cash or earnings basis		11
	1.13	Generally accepted accounting practice basis		12
		1.13.1	Catching-up charge	12
		1.13.2	Spread and cap	13
		1.13.3	Relief for any initial double charge	15

		1.13.4	New barristers	15
		1.13.5	Partnerships	16
		1.13.6	Valuation of work in progress	17
	1.14	Tax Faculty guidance on work in progress valuations		18
	1.15	Professional employments		19
	1.16	Trusteeships		20
	1.17	Payment of tax under Schedule D, Cases I and II		20
	1.18	Expenses		20
	1.19	Companies and professions		22
	1.20	Service companies		24
	1.21	Overseas work and companies		25
	1.22	Interest		26
2	**Creative artists**			27
	2.1	Copyright		27
	2.2	Gifts of copyright		28
		2.2.1	Sale of copyright by estate	29
	2.3	Income or capital		29
	2.4	Categories of creative artists for tax purposes		29
		2.4.1	Non-professional creative artists	30
		2.4.2	Casual authors	31
		2.4.3	Professional authors	31
	2.5	Post-cessation receipts		32
	2.6	Deductions		32
	2.7	Losses		33
	2.8	Effect of changes of residence		33
	2.9	Income spreading provisions (up to 5 April 2001)		34
	2.10	Income averaging provisions (from 6 April 2000)		36
	2.11	Public lending right		38
	2.12	Painters and sculptors		38
	2.13	Disposals of works of art subject to capital gains tax and inheritance tax		38
	2.14	Taxation of awards		39
		2.14.1	General principles	39
		2.14.2	Taxation of awards and bursaries made by the Arts Council	40
	2.14	Pension arrangements		42
3	**Entertainers**			43
	3.1	One profession: basis of assessment		43
	3.2	Overseas work		44
	3.3	Withholding of foreign tax at source		45
	3.4	Foreign entertainers visiting the UK		45

	3.5	'Slavery' contracts and service companies	48
	3.6	Entertainers and anti-avoidance legislation	50
	3.7	Capital sums received by entertainers	50
	3.8	Capital allowances	51
	3.9	Employment or a profession?	52
		3.9.1 Tax purposes	52
		3.9.2 National Insurance purposes	53
	3.10	Freelance workers in the film and allied industries	61
	3.11	Investigation of entertainers' income by the Inland Revenue	68
	3.12	Loans	69
	3.13	Tax returns	69
	3.14	Expenses	70
	3.15	Subsistence and travelling expenses abroad	73
	3.16	Travelling expenses in the UK	73
	3.17	Subsistence expenses in the UK	74
	3.18	Clothing	74
	3.19	Medical expenses	75
	3.20	Other expenses	75
	3.21	Groups' tax treatment	76
	3.22	'Angels'	76
	3.23	Pensions and retirement	78
	3.24	Musicians: sale of instruments	79
4	**Stockbrokers and market makers**	**81**
	4.1	Rules of the Stock Exchange	81
	4.2	Incorporation	81
	4.3	Golden handcuffs	82
	4.4	Period of accounts	82
	4.5	'Bear and bull excesses'	82
	4.6	Returns	85
	4.7	Dividend income and profits and losses on sales of securities	85
	4.8	Borrowing and lending securities	86
	4.9	Market maker's position on purchase of own shares by company	87
	4.10	Interest received	88
	4.11	Interest paid	88
	4.12	Unclaimed dividends	88
	4.13	Stock Exchange attachés and clerks	89
	4.14	Expenses of members of the Stock Exchange	89
	4.15	Capital gains returns	90
	4.16	Anti-avoidance provisions	90

Contents

		4.16.1	Dividend stripping	90
		4.16.2	Bond washing	91
	4.17	Special forms of investments		92
		4.17.1	Traded options	93
		4.17.2	The financial futures market	94
	4.18	Traded options and the financial futures market: capital gains tax treatment		95
	4.19	The Alternative Investment Market (AIM)		95

5 **Lloyd's underwriters** — 97
  5.1 General — 97
  5.2 Sources of income and gains — 97
  5.3 Underwriting account — 98
  5.4 Earned or unearned income — 98
  5.5 Reinsurance to close — 99
  5.6 Losses — 100
    5.6.1 PAYE relief for losses (Lloyd's Market Bulletin Y3027) — 100
  5.7 Stop-loss policies — 101
  5.8 Interest paid — 102
  5.9 Capital gains: general — 102
  5.10 Syndicate capacity auctions — 103
  5.11 Member's Agent Pooling Arrangements — 103
  5.12 Capital gains tax position on retirement or death — 104
  5.13 Inheritance tax — 104
    5.13.1 Bank guarantees and business property relief — 105
    5.13.2 Secured assets and business property relief — 107
  5.14 Special Reserve Fund — 107
  5.15 Retirement annuity and personal/stakeholder pension premiums — 108
  5.16 Subscriptions and other expenses — 108
  5.17 Foreign taxes paid and double taxation relief — 110
    5.17.1 US tax — 110
    5.17.2 Other — 111
  5.18 Non-resident Names — 111
  5.19 Accrued income scheme — 112
  5.20 Premiums trust funds: stock lending — 113
  5.21 Husband and wife — 113
  5.22 Corporate membership — 114

6 **Temporary visitors to the UK** — 117
  6.1 Employees — 117
  6.2 Residence position — 117

		6.2.1	Year of arrival or departure	117
	6.3		Remittance	118
	6.4		Place of performance of duties	119
	6.5		Domicile	119
	6.6		The payer of the income	119
	6.7		Dual employment contracts	120
		6.7.1	A salutary tale	121
	6.8		Corresponding payments relief	122
	6.9		Travel expenses	123
	6.10		Requirements of employee and employer	124
	6.11		The North Sea	125
		6.11.1	Returns by North Sea employers	125
		6.11.2	*Clark v Oceanic Contractors Inc*	125
		6.11.3	Divers	127
		6.11.4	Expenses	128
		6.11.5	The Norwegian sector	129
	6.12		Visiting professors or teachers	129
	6.13		Visitors for education	130
	6.14		All visitors: investment income and capital gains	130
	6.15		Capital gains	131
	6.16		Inheritance tax	132
	6.17		Departure from the UK	133
	6.18		National Insurance contribution	133
		6.18.1	Reciprocal UK and EU arrangements	134
		6.18.2	Reciprocal UK and USA agreement	134
		6.18.3	Reciprocal UK and Israeli agreement	135
7	**Members of the clergy**			**137**
	7.1		General principles	137
	7.2		Self assessment and PAYE procedures	138
	7.3		National Insurance contributions	139
	7.4		Types of income that are taxable	139
	7.5		Exemptions	141
		7.5.1	Treatment of vicarage, manse or other church property occupied by the clergy	141
		7.5.2	Statutory property expenses	142
		7.5.3	Other property expenses	143
		7.5.4	Property expenses of higher-paid clergy and directors of church charities	143
		7.5.5	Reimbursement of property expenses	145
	7.6		Expenses	146
		7.6.1	Rent	146
		7.6.2	Maintenance expenditure	146

Contents

		7.6.3	General expenses	146
		7.6.4	Expenses of unpaid appointments	150
		7.6.5	Removal expenses	150
	7.7	Second residences		150
	7.8	Benefits in kind		151
		7.8.1	Cars	151
		7.8.2	Car fuel	151
		7.8.3	Beneficial loans	152
	7.9	Income of contemplative religious communities and their members		152
	7.10	Evangelists		153
	7.11	Income of vocation under Schedule D, Case II		154
8	**Members of the diplomatic service and other Crown servants working abroad**			155
	8.1	Place of performance of duties		155
	8.2	Exempt allowances		155
	8.3	Other income and capital gains		156
	8.4	Tax-free investments		157
	8.5	Personal allowances		157
	8.6	Tax credits		158
	8.7	UK residences		158
		8.7.1	Capital gains tax	158
		8.7.2	Job-related accommodation	158
	8.8	Officials employed by the European Union in Brussels		159
9	**Doctors and dentists**			163
	9.1	Doctors		163
	9.2	Consultants		163
	9.3	Expenses of consultants		163
		9.3.1	Property expenses	163
		9.3.2	Motor expenses	164
	9.4	Agreement between Department of Health and Inland Revenue on certain expenses		164
		9.4.1	Car allowances	164
		9.4.2	Removal and associated expenses	165
		9.4.3	Excess travelling expenses	166
		9.4.4	Emergency call-out expenses	167
		9.4.5	Assisted travel scheme	167
		9.4.6	Journey between home and headquarters	167
		9.4.7	Late night duties	167
		9.4.8	Uniforms	167
		9.4.9	Telephone expenses	167

		9.4.10 Fees and subscriptions to professional bodies	168
	9.5	Practice accounts	168
		9.5.1 Conference expenses	168
	9.6	General practice	169
	9.7	Self assessment guidance for doctors	170
	9.8	Further matters on GPs' affairs	175
		9.8.1 Superannuation	175
		9.8.2 Partnership changes	175
		9.8.3 Notional rent allowance	176
		9.8.4 Personal awards	176
		9.8.5 Hospital appointments	177
		9.8.6 'Ash cash' and sundry fees	177
		9.8.7 Salaried partners	177
		9.8.8 Best accounting date	178
		9.8.9 Personal expenses claim	178
		9.8.10 Retired doctors	179
	9.9	Expenses in connection with *pro bono* work	180
	9.10	Superannuation deductions	180
	9.11	Dentists	181
		9.11.1 Associates	183
		9.11.2 Partnerships	183
		9.11.3 Goodwill	184
	9.12	General case law relating to doctors and dentists	184
10	**Practising barristers, barristers' clerks, judges and solicitors**		**185**
	10.1	Barristers	185
		10.1.1 Cash basis	185
		10.1.2 Inducement receipts	186
		10.1.3 Expenses	187
	10.2	Barristers' clerks	189
	10.3	Judges	190
		10.3.1 Recorders (including circuit and deputy circuit judges)	190
	10.4	Solicitors	191
		10.4.1 Bank interest, etc. received	191
		10.4.2 Interest received on behalf of clients	192
		10.4.3 Interest paid by or through a solicitor	193
		10.4.4 Temporary loans and guarantees	193
		10.4.5 Office holders	194
		10.4.6 Is the engagement in a related area?	195

11		**Members of Parliament, Members of the Scottish Parliament, Members of the Welsh Assembly and Members of the Northern Ireland Legislative Assembly**	197
	11.1	General taxation position	197
	11.2	Additional costs allowance	198
	11.3	Car allowance	198
	11.4	Other travel (by taxi, train or air)	199
	11.5	European travel expenses	200
	11.6	Overnight expense allowances	200
	11.7	Staffing allowance	201
	11.8	Other incidental expenses	201
	11.9	Pension and retirement arrangements	202
	11.10	Other income	203
	11.11	MPs' secretaries and research assistants	203
	11.12	Members of the European Parliament	203
		11.12.1 Salaries	203
		11.12.2 Travel and subsistence allowances	203
		11.12.3 Deduction for expenses	204
		11.12.4 Terminal grants	205
	11.13	Members of the House of Lords	205
12		**Merchant navy and aircrew personnel**	207
	12.1	General principles	207
	12.2	Non-resident seafarers	207
		12.2.1 Not resident and not ordinarily resident	207
		12.2.2 Not resident but ordinarily resident	208
	12.3	Foreign seafarers	208
	12.4	UK residents: 100 per cent deduction	208
		12.4.1 100 per cent deduction	214
	12.5	Definitions	214
	12.6	Administration	215
	12.7	Salvage awards	215
	12.8	Uniform allowances	216
	12.9	Travelling and subsistence allowance	216
		12.9.1 Deduction for provision of own food	217
		12.9.2 Bedding and protective clothing provided for trawler crews	217
	12.10	'Residence' of seafarers	217
	12.11	Employment outside UK territorial waters	217
	12.12	Place of performance of duties	218
	12.13	Flat-rate expenses deduction	218
	12.14	Seafarers' PAYE	218
	12.15	Merchant Navy reservists	219

		12.16	Aircrew	220
			12.16.1 Residence position	220
			12.16.2 Expenses	221
			12.16.3 Free travel, etc	221
13		**Members of the UK armed forces**		**223**
	13.1		Place of performance of duties	223
	13.2		Residence position	223
	13.3		Extra cost of living abroad	223
	13.4		Travel facilities	224
	13.5		Entertaining expenses	224
	13.6		Exemptions in respect of allowances	224
	13.7		Hotel expenses	225
	13.8		Annual subscriptions to a headquarters mess central fund	225
	13.9		Uniform allowances	225
	13.10		PAYE and the armed forces	226
	13.11		Reserve and auxiliary forces	226
			13.11.1 Employee share schemes and called-up reservists	227
	13.12		Pensions	227
	13.13		War widows' pensions	229
	13.14		Employment after leaving services	230
	13.15		Capital gains tax and residences	230
	13.16		Holders of the Victoria Cross, etc	230
	13.17		Death on active service	231
	13.18		Exemption from IHT on death: *ex gratia* payments to Britons held prisoner by the Japanese	231
14		**Publicans holding tied houses, hoteliers and guest-house proprietors**		**233**
	14.1		Publicans: basis of assessment	233
	14.2		Exclusivity agreements	233
	14.3		Termination payments	234
	14.4		Expenses	235
	14.5		Hotels: own consumption adjustments	237
	14.6		Hotels: date on which trading commences	237
	14.7		Capital expenditure	238
	14.8		Plant and machinery	238
	14.9		Furnished lettings: allowances for wear and tear	240
	14.10		Hotel building allowances	242
	14.11		Dilapidations	242
	14.12		Residences	242

Contents

		14.13	Guest-houses and roll-over relief	243
		14.14	Income from furnished holiday lettings	243
		14.15	PAYE	245
15	\multicolumn{3}{l	}{**Credit traders, hire purchase transactions, pawnbrokers, moneylenders**}	247
		15.1	General	247
		15.2	Credit traders	247
			15.2.1 Provisions	247
			15.2.2 Valuation of debts	248
		15.3	Hire purchase business	248
		15.4	Pawnbrokers	250
		15.5	Moneylenders	251
			15.5.1 Allocation of principal and interest	252
			15.5.2 Cessation	253
16	\multicolumn{3}{l	}{**Persons in receipt of foreign pensions**}	255
		16.1	Remittance basis	255
		16.2	Arrears of pension	256
		16.3	Pensions paid by Crown Agents	257
		16.4	Pensions paid to victims of Nazi persecution	258
		16.5	Double tax agreements	258
		16.6	Foreign invalidity benefits	258
		16.7	Foreign war pensions	259
		16.8	Foreign social security payments	259
17	\multicolumn{3}{l	}{**Sportspeople**}	261
		17.1	Basis of liability	261
		17.2	Subventions, grants and gifts	261
		17.3	Sponsorship and endorsement fees	262
		17.4	Appearance, participation and performance fees	262
		17.5	Visiting sportspeople	262
		17.6	Use of partnership or company	263
		17.7	Service company documentation	263
		17.8	Foreign companies	264
		17.9	Withholding taxes	264
		17.10	Expenses	264
			17.10.1 Abroad	264
			17.10.2 In the UK	264
		17.11	General principles on liability of various receipts	265
		17.12	Footballer's benefit matches	268
		17.13	Operation of PAYE	269
		17.14	Amateur sportspeople	269

	17.15	Signing-on fees	272
	17.16	Payments for winning	273
	17.17	Jockeys	273
	17.18	Pension schemes	273
18	**Persons in receipt of gratuities**		275
	18.1	General	275
	18.2	Tips	275
		18.2.1 Retirement gratuities	275
		18.2.2 PAYE on tips	275
		18.2.3 National Insurance contributions	277
	18.3	Other gifts	278
	18.4	Prizes	279
	18.5	Long-service awards	280
	18.6	Awards under suggestion schemes	280
	18.7	Third party awards	281
19	**Insurance agents**		283
	19.1	Categories of agent	283
		19.1.1 Exclusive agents	283
		19.1.2 Other agents	284
	19.2	Casual insurance commission	285
	19.3	Commission receivable on indemnity terms	296
20	**Trawler crew, river and sea pilots**		299
	20.1	Introduction	299
	20.2	Employed or self-employed?	299
		20.2.1 Trawler crew	299
		20.2.2 Share fishing	299
		20.2.3 English ports	300
	20.3	Retirement age	301
	20.4	Special clothing	301
	20.5	Capital allowances	302
		20.5.1 Free depreciation	302
		20.5.2 'Depooling'	303
		20.5.3 Roll-over claims	303
	20.6	Partnerships	304
		20.6.1 Partnership changes	304
		20.6.2 Partnerships including a company	305
	20.7	River and sea pilots	305
		20.7.1 General	305
		20.7.2 Compensation payments by Trinity House	306

21	**Private schools, higher education institutions, teachers, etc.**		307
	21.1	Definition of a charity	307
	21.2	Public schools	307
	21.3	Effect of charitable status	308
	21.4	Investment income	310
	21.5	Gift Aid	310
	21.6	Payment of school fees in the case of separated parents	311
	21.7	Capital allowances	311
	21.8	Academics, teachers, etc	311
		21.8.1 National Insurance contributions	318
		21.8.2 Taxation of bursaries, scholarships, etc	321
		21.8.3 Meals and entertaining	322
		21.8.4 Capital allowances	323
		21.8.5 Remission of school fees	324
		21.8.6 Research costs	325
		21.8.7 Conference and course expenses	325
		21.8.8 Travel expenses	326
		21.8.9 Books, subscriptions and special clothing	328
		21.8.10 Study allowances	329
		21.8.11 Living accommodation	330
		21.8.12 Other services	330
		21.8.13 Residences	331
		21.8.14 Other income of teachers	331
		21.8.15 Director of non-profit-making company	332
		21.8.16 Study leave overseas	332
22	**Inventors and persons holding patent rights**		333
	22.1	Expenses: general	333
	22.2	The law of patents	333
	22.3	Income tax position on expenses	334
	22.4	Treatment of receipts	334
		22.4.1 Capital sums	334
		22.4.2 Death	335
		22.4.3 Non-residents	335
	22.5	Incorporation of business	335
	22.6	Capital allowances	337
	22.7	Royalties	337
	22.8	Deduction of tax	338
	22.9	Foreign patents	339
	22.10	Earned income	339
	22.11	Spreading provisions	339
	22.12	Know-how	339
	22.13	Trade marks and designs	341

	22.14	Case III and trade marks	342
	22.15	Capital or income	342
	22.16	Fees and expenses	343
23	**Subcontractors**		**345**
	23.1	Tax deduction scheme	345
	23.2	Background	346
	23.3	IR35 and the construction industry: ESC C32	346
	23.4	What is a 'contractor'?	347
	23.5	What is a subcontractor?	348
	23.6	What type of 'construction' is within the scheme?	349
	23.7	Who qualifies for a 'gross certificate'?	350
		23.7.1 The business test	350
		23.7.2 The compliance test	350
		23.7.3 The turnover test	351
	23.8	Certificates and procedures	353
	23.9	Registration cards (CIS4)	353
	23.10	Subcontractor's tax certificate (CIS6)	354
	23.11	Construction tax certificate (CIS5)	355
	23.12	Employment status	356
	23.13	Expenses	366
	23.14	New scheme from 6 April 2006	368
24	**Local councillors and members of Government boards**		**369**
	24.1	Reimbursed expenses	369
	24.2	Attendance allowances	369
	24.3	Expenses	370
	24.4	Guidance note prepared by the Association of Local Councillors	370
	24.5	Office or profession	372
25	**Farmers (including market gardeners) and owners of commercial woodlands**		**375**
	25.1	One trade	375
	25.2	Losses	376
	25.3	Stocks	378
	25.4	Herd basis	385
	25.5	Partnership changes and the herd basis	388
	25.6	Averaging	389
		25.6.1 Tax credits	391
	25.7	Capital allowances	392
	25.8	Agricultural buildings allowances	392
	25.9	Revenue receipts and payments	394

Contents

25.10	Partnerships and joint ventures		399
25.11	Capital gains tax		401
	25.11.1	Hold-over relief	401
	25.11.2	Roll-over relief	402
	25.11.3	Tenancies	403
	25.11.4	Retirement relief	405
25.12	'One estate' election (up to 2001–02)		407
25.13	Quotas		408
	25.13.1	Milk	408
	25.13.2	Potatoes	412
	25.13.3	Hops	412
25.14	Ostrich 'farming'		413
25.15	Foot and mouth disease		415
	25.15.1	Interest	415
	25.15.2	Stocktaking valuations	415
	25.15.3	Compensation for slaughter of animals	416
	25.15.4	Herd basis	416
	25.15.5	Extra Statutory Concession B11	417
	25.15.6	Increases in the number of mature animals caused by foot and mouth	417
	25.15.7	MAFF aid package	418
	25.15.8	Agricultural buildings allowances	419
	25.15.9	Furnished holiday letting	419
	25.15.10	Access to IHT/CGT exempt properties	420
	25.15.11	Waivers of rent	420
	25.15.12	Appeal funds	420

Index   *423*

Table of Cases

Entries refer to paragraph numbers not page numbers

Albon v IRC [1998] STI 1600 ....16.1
Alloway v Phillips [1979] STC 452 ....2.4.1
Anderton v Lamb (1980) 55 TC 1 ....25.11.2
Andrew Grant Services Ltd v Watton [1999] STI 260 ....1.20
Andrews v King [1991] STC 481 ....25.9
Anise Ltd & Others v Hammond SpC 364 (24 March 2003 reported
   at [2003] STI Issue 18) 4.12
Ansell v Brown 23.5.01 [2001] STI Issue 22 ....17.10.2
Aplin v White (1973) 49 TC 93 ....1.22
Atkinson v Dancer [1988] STC 758 ....25.11.4
Australian Mutual Provident Society v Chaplin (1978) 18 ALR 385 ...23.12

Baird (George A), Executors of v CIR 1990) *Country Landowner*,
   September 25.11.3
Ball v Johnson (1971) 47 TC 155 ....18.4
Baxendale v Murphy (1924) 9 TC 76 ....1.16
Beare v Carter (1940) 23 TC 353 ....2.1, 2.4.1
Bennett v Ogston (1930) 15 TC 374 ....15.5.2
Bentleys, Stokes and Lowless v Beeson (1952) 33 TC 491 .....1.18, 14.4
Bentley v Pike [1981] STC 360 ....6.15
Bhadra v Ellam [1988] STC 239 ....9.3.2
Billam v Griffith (1941) 23 TC 757 ....2.1
Birkenhead School Ltd v Dring (1926) 11 TC 273 ....21.2
Bispham v Eardiston Farming Col (1919) Ltd (1962) 40 TC 322 .....25.1
Blackburn v Keeling EWCA Civ. 1222 ....5.6.1
Black Nominees v Nicol (1975) 50 TC 229 ....3.6
Blake v London Corporation (1887) 2 TC 209 ....21.2
Bloom v Kinder (1958) 38 TC 77 ....18.3
Bowden v Russell and Russell (1965) 42 TC 301 ....21.8.7
Boyd Line v Pitts [1986] ICR 244 ....20.2.1
Bray v Best [1989] STC 159 ....6.10
Brighton College v Marriott (1925) 10 TC 213 ....21.3
British Legion, Peterhead Branch Remembrance and Welcome Home
   Fund v CIR (1953) 35 TC 509 ....21.3
Bruce of Donington (Lord) v Aspden [1981] STC 761 ....11.12.2

Table of Cases

BSC Footwear Ltd (formerly Freeman, Hardy & Willis Ltd) *v* Ridgway
 (Inspector of Taxes) (1969) 47 TC 495 at 524 .... 19.3
Bucks *v* Bowers (1970) 46 TC 267 .... 4.7

Caillebotte *v* Quinn [1975] STC 265; (1975) 50 TC 222 ...... 3.17, 17.10.2,
 23.13
Caldicott *v* Varty (1976) 51 TC 403 .... 8.1
Calvert *v* Wainwright (1947) 27 TC 475 .... 18.2
Cardinal Vaughan Memorial School Trustees *v* Ryall (1920) 7 TC 611 ... 21.2
Carnaby, Harrower, Barharn and Prykett *v* Walker (1970) 46 TC 561 ... 18.3
Carson *v* Cheyney's Executors (1958) 38 TC 240 .... 2.4.3, 2.8
Carter *v* Sharon (1936) 20 TC 229 .... 6.14
Chambers (GH) (Northian Farms) Ltd *v* Watmough (1956) 36 TC 711 .. 25.7
CIR *v* Aken [1990] STC 497 .... 1.1
CIR *v* Biggar (W Andrew) [1982] STC 677 .... 25.9
CIR *v* Brander and Cruikshank (1971) 46 TC 574 .... 10.4.5
CIR *v* British Salmson Aero Engines Ltd (1938) 22 TC 29 .... 22.7
CIR *v* Falkirk Ice Rink Ltd [1975] STC 434 .... 7.10
CIR *v* Francis West (1950) 31 TC 402 .... 20.2.2
CIR *v* Hang Seng Bank Ltd [1990] STC 733 .... 1.5
CIR *v* Livingston (1927) 11 TC 538 .... 15.5
CIR *v* Longmans Green & Co Ltd (1932) 17 TC 272 .... 2.1
CIR *v* Maxse (1919) 12 TC 41 .... 1.1
CIR *v* Pemsel (1891) 3 TC 53 .... 21.1
CIR *v* Peter McIntyre Ltd (1927) 12 TC 1006 .... 1.19
CIR *v* Scottish & Newcastle Breweries Ltd (1982) 55 TC 252 ..... 14.8
CIR *v* Vas [1990] STC 137 .... 6.12
Clark, LON/82/338, February 1983 (1370) 14.1
Clark *v* Oceanic Contractors Inc [1983] STC 35 .... 6.11.2
Clark *v* Perks and other appeals [2001] BTC 336 .... 12.4
Coates *v* Arndale Properties Ltd [1984] STC 637 .... 4.16.1
Colquhoun *v* Brooks (1889) 2 TC 490 .... 1.3
Conn *v* Robins Bros Ltd (1966) 43 TC 266 .... 14.8
Constantinesco *v* R (1927) 11 TC 730 .... 22.7
Cooke *v* Beach Station Caravans Ltd (1974) 49 TC 514 .... 14.8
Cooke *v* Blacklaws (1984) 58 TC 255 .... 9.12
Cooper *v* Blakiston (1908) 5 TC 347 .... 7.4, 7.10
Copeman *v* William Flood & Sons Ltd (1941) 24 TC 53 .... 1.19
Corbett *v* Duff (1941) 23 TC 763 .... 17.11
Cordy *v* Gordon (1925) 9 TC 304 .... 14.5
Cottle *v* Coldicott [1995] SSCD 239 (Sp C 40) 25.13.1
Crossland *v* Hawkins (1961) 39 TC 493 .... 3.6
Curtis Brown Ltd *v* Jarvis (1929) 14 TC 752–753 .... 2.6

Table of Cases

Davies v Braithwaite (1933) 18 TC 198 .... 2.8, 3.1, 3.9.1
Davies v Presbyterian Church of Wales [1986] 1 All ER 705 .... 7.1
Davis v Harrison (1927) 11 TC 707 .... 17.11
Davis v Powell (1976) 51 TC 492 .... 14.3, 25.11.3
De Beers Consolidated Mines v Howe (1906) 5 TC 198 .... 1.4
Dickenson v Gross (1927) 11 TC 614 .... 25.10
Dollar (t/a I J Dollar) v Lyon (1981) 54 TC 459 .... 25.9
Donnelly v Williamson [1982] STC 88; [1981] STC 563 ...... 6.11.4, 17.13,
21.8.8
Down v Compston (1937) 21 TC 60 .... 1.2
Drummond v Austin Brown (1984) 58 TC 67 .... 14.3
Duff v Williamson [1973] STC 434; (1973) 49 TC 1 .... 9.12, 21.8.2

Edwards v Clinch [1981] STC 617; (1981) 56 TC 367 .... 10.2, 24.5
Edwards v Warmsley Henshall & Co (1967) 44 TC 431 .... 21.8.7
Elson v Prices Taylors Ltd (1963) 40 TC 671 .... 15.4
Ereaut v Girls' Public Day School Trust Ltd (1963) 15 TC 529 .... 21.2
Evans Medical Supplies Ltd v Moriarty (1957) 37 TC 540 .... 22.12
Evans v Richardson (1957) 37 TC 178 .... 13.6

Fall v Hitchen (1972) 49 TC 433 .... 3.9.1
Faulks v Faulks [1992] 15 EG 82 .... 25.13.1
Figael Ltd v Fox [1992] STC 83; [1990] STC 583 .... 14.15, 18.2.2
Finsbury Securities Ltd v Bishop (1966) 43 TC 591 .... 4.16.1
Fox (the Honourable Myra Alice Lady) (Deceased), Executors of
(1991) Lands Tribunal, 31 July 25.11.3
Friedson v Glyn-Thomas (1922) 8 TC 302 .... 7.6.5
Fry v Burma Corporation Ltd (1930) 15 TC 113 .... 1.8.1, 2.8
Furniss v Dawson [1984] STC 153; (1984) 55 TC 324 ...... 3.5, 17.7, 17.11

Gittos v Barclay (1982) 55 TC 633 .... 14.14
Glantre Engineering Ltd v Goodhand (1982) 56 TC 165 .... 17.15
Glasson v Rougier (1944) 26 TC 86 .... 2.1
Gold Coast Selection Trust Ltd v Humphrey (1948) 30 TC 209 ...... 17.14
Gold v Inspector of Taxes; HCB Ltd v Inspector of Taxes [1998]
STI 1362 .... 1.20
Graham v Green (1925) 9 TC 309 .... 1.2
Graham v White (1971) 48 TC 163 .... 8.1
Grainger & Son v Gough (1896) 3 TC 462 .... 1.5
Grant v Watton [1999] STI 260 .... 1.20
Greater London Council v Minister of Social Security [1971] 2 All
ER 285 .... 3.9.2
Griffiths v Jackson [1983] STC 184; (1983) 56 TC 583 .... 14.14

xxv

Table of Cases

Griffiths *v* Mockler (1953) 35 TC 135 ....13.7
Griffiths *v* Pearman (1982) 56 TC 583 ....14.14

Haig's (Earl) Trustees *v* CIR (1939) 22 TC 725 ....2.4.1
Hall *v* Lorimer 66 TC 349 ....23.12
Hall *v* Lorimer [1993] STI 138 ....3.10
Hamerton *v* Overy (1954) 35 TC 73 ....9.2
Handley Page Ltd *v* Butterworths (1935) 19 TC 328 ....22.15
Hardcastle and another (Executors of Vernede deceased) *v* IRC SpC 259 [2000] STI 45 ....5.13
Harrison (JP) (Watford) Ltd *v* Griffiths HL [1962] 2 WLR 909 ......4.16.1
Heaton *v* Bell (1969) 46 TC 211 ....21.8.5, 25.9
Henderson *v* Karmel's Executors (1984) 58 TC 201 ....25.11.3
Herbert *v* McQuade (1902) 4 TC 489 ....7.1
Higgs *v* Olivier (1952) 33 TC 136 ....3.7
Hillyer *v* Leeke (1976) 51 TC 90 ....7.6.3
Hobbs *v* Hussey (1942) 24 TC 153 ....2.4.1
Horton *v* Young (1971) 47 TC 69 ....6.11.3, 23.13
Housden *v* Marshall (1959) 38 TC 233 ....2.4.1
Household *v* Grimshaw (1953) 34 TC 966 ....2.4.3
Howson *v* Monsell (1950) 31 TC 529 ....2.4.3
Hugh *v* Rogers (1958) 38 TC 270 ....19.2
Humbles *v* Brooks (1962) 40 TC 500 ....1.18, 21.8.10
Hume *v* Asquith (1969) 45 TC 251 ....2.2

IRC *v* Gardner Mountain and D'Ambrumenil (1945) 29 TC 69 ....19.3
IRC *v* Mallender and others (Executors of Drury-Lowe deceased) [2001] STI 12 ....5.13

Jarrold *v* Boustead (1964) 41 TC 701 ....4.3, 17.11, 17.15
Jarvis *v* Curtis Brown Ltd (1929) 14 TC 744 ....2.8
Jay's the Jewellers Ltd *v* CIR (1947) 29 TC 274 ....15.4
Jeffrey *v* Rolls-Royce Ltd (1962) 40 TC 443 ....22.12
Jennings *v* Barfield and Barfield (1962) 40 TC 365 ....10.4.4
Jones *v* Wright (1927) 13 TC 221 ....1.16

Kneen *v* Martin (1935) 19 TC 33 ....1.8.1

Lavery *v* MacLeod [2001] STC (SCD) 118 ....12.4
Lawrence *v* CIR (1940) 23 TC 333 ....2.2
Law Shipping Co Ltd *v* CIR (1924) 12 TC 621 ....14.8
Lewis Emanuel & Son Ltd *v* White (1965) 42 TC 369 ....4.18
Lewis *v* CIR (1933) 18 TC 174 ....20.6.2

Table of Cases

Lindsay v CIR (1953) 34 TC 289 ....25.8
Lomax v Newton (1953) 34 TC 289 ....13.7
Lupton v F A and A B Ltd (1971) 47 TC 580 ....4.16.1
Lush v Coles (1967) 44 TC 169 ....13.11

McGregor v Adcock (1977) 51 TC 692 ....25.11.4
MacKenzie v Arnold (1952) 33 TC 363 ....2.4.3
MacKinlay v Arthur Young McClelland Moores & Co [1989] STC 898 ...1.18
McMenamin v Diggles [1991] STC 419 ....10.2
Mallalieu v Drummond (1983) 57 TC 330 ....3.18, 7.6.3, 10.1.3
Mannion v Johnston [1988] STC 758 ....25.11.4
Market Investigations Ltd v Minister of Social Security [1969] 2 QB
  173 ....3.10, 23.12
Mason v Innes (1967) 44 TC 326 ....2.2, 2.13, 3.5
Massey v Crown Life Insurance Co [1978] ICR 590 ....23.12
Midland Sinfonia Concert Society Ltd v Secretary of State for Social
  Services [1981] ICR 454 ....3.9.2
Mills v CIR (1974) 49 TC 367 ....3.6
Mitchell and Edon v Ross (1961) 40 TC 11 ....1.15, 9.2
Monthly Salaries Loan Co Ltd v Furlong (1962) 40 TC 313 ....15.5, 15.5.2
Moore v Griffiths (1972) 48 TC 338 ....17.16
Moorhouse v Dooland (1954) 36 TC 1 ....17.11
Morley v Tattersall (1938) 22 TC 51 ....4.12, 15.4
Munby v Furlong (1977) 50 TC 491 ....7.6.3, 10.1.3
Murray v Goodhews [1978] STC 207; (1977) 52 TC 86 ....14.3, 18.3, 20.7.2

National Provident Institution v Brown (1921) 8 TC 452 ....6.14
Nerva v United Kingdom (ECHR) 18.2.3
Nethermere (St Neots) Ltd v Gardiner (1984) ICR 612 ....23.12
Newsom v Roberston (1952) 33 TC 452 ....10.1.3
Newstead v Frost (1980) 53 TC 525 ....3.2
Nolder v Walters (1930) 15 TC 380 ....12.16.2
Norman v Golder (1945) 26 TC 293 ....3.19
Northend v White & Leonard and Corbin Greener [1975] STC 317;
  (1975) 50 TC 121 ....1.22, 4.10
North v Spencer's Executors (1956) 36 TC 668 ....9.12
Notham v Cooper [1975] STC 91 ....16.4

Odeon Associated Theatres Ltd v Jones (1973) 48 TC 257 ......14.8, 15.5.2
Odeon Associated Theatres Ltd v Jones (Inspector of Taxes) (1970)
  48 TC 257 at 273 ....19.3
Ogilvie v Kitton (1908) 5 TC 338 ....1.3
O'Leary v McKinley [1991] STC 42 ....17.11

xxvii

Table of Cases

Oppenheimer *v* Cattermole (1975) 50 TC 159 ....16.4
Osborn *v* Sawyer (1933) 18 TC 445 ....9.12
Owen *v* Elliott [1990] STC 469 ....14.12

Padmore *v* CIR (1987) 62 TC 352 ....1.4
Parikh *v* Sleeman [1990] STC 233 ....9.3.2, 9.5.1
Partridge *v* Mallandaine (1886) 2 TC 179 ....1.2
Paterson Engineering Co Ltd *v* Duff (1943) 25 TC 43 ....22.13
Pattison *v* Marine Midland Ltd [1984] STC 10 ....15.5.2
Pepper *v* Hart (1993) 65 TC 421 ....12.16.3, 21.8.5
Phillips *v* Hamilton and Macken *v* Hamilton SpC 366 19.5.03 [2003]
  STI Issue 23 ....23.13
Plumbly and Others (PRs of Harbour) deceased *v* Spencer CA [1996]
  STC 677 ....9.8.3
Plumbly *v* Spencer [1996] STI 1079 ....25.11.4
Pook *v* Owen (1969) 45 TC 571 ....9.3.2, 9.4.4, 17.13, 21.8.8
Prince *v* Mapp (1969) 46 TC 169 ....3.17
Pritchard *v* Arundale (1971) 47 TC 680 ....4.3, 17.15
Purchase *v* Stainer's Executors (1952) 33 TC 367 ....2.4.3

Ready Mixed Concrete (South East) Ltd *v* Minister of Pensions and
  National Insurance [1968] 2 QB 497 ....23.12
Reed *v* Clark [1985] STC 323; (1985) 58 TC 528 ....2.8, 3.1
Reed *v* Nova Securities Ltd [1985] STC 124 ....4.16.1
Reed *v* Seymour (1927) 11 TC 625 ....17.11
Re Shine, ex parte Shine [1892] IQB 522 ....3.9.2
Rex *v* City of London Commissioners, ex parte Gibbs 24 TC 221 ......9.11
Richart *v* Lyons & Co Ltd [1989] STC 665 ....25.9
Ricketts *v* Colquhoun (1925) 10 TC 118 ....10.1.3, 19.1.1, 21.8.8
Riley *v* Coglan (1967) 44 TC 481 ....17.15
Robertson *v* CIR (SpC 309) [1997] SSCD 282 ....19.3
Robson *v* Dixon (1972) 48 TC 527 ....6.4, 12.16.1
Rogers *v* CIR (1879) 1 TC 225 ....12.2.2

St John's School (Mountford and Knibbs) *v* Ward [1975] STC 7;
  (1974) 49 TC 524 ....14.8, 21.7
Sargent *v* Barnes (1978) 52 TC 335 ....9.11, 9.12
Saywell *v* Pope (1979) 53 TC 40 ....25.10
Scottish Provident Institution *v* Allen (1903) 4 TC 409 and 501 ....6.14
Seldon *v* Croom-Johnson (1932) 16 TC 740 ....1.1, 9.11, 10.1
Sharkey *v* Wernher (1955) 36 TC 275 ....2.2, 14.4
Shilton *v* Wilmshurst [1991] STC 88 ....17.11
Shiner *v* Lindblom (1960) 39 TC 367 ....3.7

Sidey v Phillips [1987] STC 87 ....21.8.14
Simpson v John Reynolds & Co (Insurances) Ltd [1975] STC 271;
    (1975) 49 TC 693 ....14.3, 18.3, 20.7.2
Slaney v Starkey (1931) 16 TC 45 ....7.4
Slattery v Moore Stephens [2003] STI Issue 32 ....6.7.1
Smart v Lincolnshire Sugar Co Ltd (1937) 20 TC 643 ....2.14.1
Spencer (James) & Co v CIR (1950) 32 TC 111 ....15.4
Sports Club (1), Evelyn (2), Jocelyn (3) (Appellants) v HMIT [2000]
    SpC 00253 ....17.11
Stephenson v Payne, Stone, Fraser & Co (1968) 44 TC 507 ....1.20
Stokes v Costain Property Investments Ltd (1984) 57 TC 688 ....14.7
Sturge (John & E) v Hessel [1975] STC 573 ....22.12
Symons (Inspector of Taxes) v Weeks [1983] STC 195 at 237 ....19.3

Taylor v Dawson (1938) 22 TC 189 ....2.4.3
Thomsons (Carron) Ltd v CIR [1976] STC 317 ....22.12
Turner v Cuxon (1888) 2 TC 422....................................7.1

Union Cold Storage Co Ltd v Adamson (1931) 16 TC 293 ....25.10

Vaughan-Neil v CIR (1979) 54 TC 223 ....4.3, 10.1.2, 17.15
Vestey v CIR (1979) 54 TC 503 ....3.2

Waddington v O'Callaghan (1931) 16 TC 187 ....25.10
Wain's Executors v Cameron [1995] STC 555 ....2.13
Walls v Sinnett [1987] STC 236 ....21.8.14
Warner Holidays Ltd v Secretary of State for Social Services [1983]
    ICR 440 ....3.9.2
Warner v Prior SpC 353 30.1.03 [2003] STI issue 7 ....21.8.8
Watkis v Ashford Sparkes & Harward [1985] STC 451; (1985) 58 TC
    468 ....1.18, 3.17
Way v Underdown (No 2) [1975] STC 425 ....19.2
White v G and M Davies [1979] STC 415; (1979) 52 TC 597 ......3.7, 25.9
White v Higginbottom (1982) 57 TC 283..........................7.6.3
Wicks v Firth [1983] STC 25 ....18.4
Wigmore v Thomas Summerson & Sons Ltd (1926) 9 TC 577 ....4.16.2
Willingale v International Commercial Bank Ltd [1978] STC 75 .....15.5.2
Wimpy International Ltd v Warland [1988] STC 149; (1988) 61 TC
    51 ....14.8
Wing v O'Connell [1927] IR 84 ....17.17
Withers v Nethersole (1948) 28 TC 501 ....2.1
Wolf Electric Tools Ltd v Wilson (1969) 45 TC 326 ....22.12

Table of Statutes

Entries refer to paragraph numbers not page numbers

1872	Pawnbrokers Act (c. 93) 15.4		s. 16 ....3.13
1890	Partnership Act (c. 39) 25.13.1		s. 18 ....10.4.2
			s. 21, (2)–(4) 4.6
1907	Limited Partnership Act 1.1		s. 25 ....4.15
1925	Law of Property Act (c. 20) 25.8		s. 33 ....12.4
			(2) 12.4
			(2A) 12.4
1927	Moneylenders Act (c. 21) 15.5.1		s. 42 ....12.4
			s. 78 ....10.4.3, 10.4.2
1933	Moneylenders Act (Northern Ireland) ...15.5.1		s. 87 ....3.4
			s. 98 ....4.6
1938	Trade Marks Act (c. 22) 22.13		s. 118 ....1.7.1
		1971	Courts Act (c. 23) 10.3.1
1948	Agricultural Holdings Act (c. 63) 25.11.3		Fire Precautions Act (c. 40)
			s. 5(4) 14.8
1949	Registered Designs Act (c. 88), s. 3 ....22.13		s. 10 ....14.8
1956	Copyright Act (c. 74) 2.1		Mineral Workings (Offshore Installations) Act 12.4
1964	Continental Shelf Act (c. 29) 12.5	1972	European Communities Act (c. 68) 25.9
	s. 1(7) 6.11		
	Diplomatic Privileges Act (c. 81) 8.3	1973	Finance Act (c. 51) s. 38 ....6.11.2
1967	Agriculture Act (c. 22), s. 27 ....25.9		Sch. 15 para. 2(b) ...6.11.1
		1974	Consumer Credit Act (c. 39) 15.4, 15.5.1, 15.5
1968	Agriculture (Miscellaneous Provisions) Act (c. 34) 25.11.3		s. 21 ....15.5
			Finance Act (c. 30) 16.1
	Capital Allowances Act (c. 3), s. 45 ....14.8		s. 24 ....6.10
1970	Taxes Management Act (c. 9)	1977	Finance Act (c. 36) 12.4
			Patents Act (c. 37) 22.2
	s. 8 ....6.10, 12.4	1980	Finance Act (c. 48) ...4.17.1

xxxi

Table of Statutes

1981	British Nationality Act (c. 61), s. 1(3) 16.3	
	Supreme Court Act (c. 54) 10.3.1	
1983	Finance Act (c. 28) 3.23	
	Pilotage Act (c. 21), s. 15(1)(i) 20.7.1	
	Value Added Tax Act (c. 55)	
	Sch. 1 para. 1A 14.1	
	Sch. 6 Note 1 to Group 1 ....25.11.3	
1984	County Courts Act (c. 28) 10.3.1	
	Finance Act (c. 43) 6.15	
	s. 48(6) 25.13.1	
	Inheritance Tax Act (c. 51)	
	s. 30 ....2.13	
	s. 105	
	(1)(a) 25.13.1	
	(3) 14.14	
	s. 110 ....25.13.1	
	s. 154 ....13.17	
	s. 157 ....6.16	
	s. 267	
	(1)(b) 6.16	
	(2) 6.16	
1985	Finance Act (c. 54) 5.9	
1986	Agricultural Holdings Act (c. 5), s. 60 .....25.11.3	
	Tax Reform Act 5.17.1	
1987	Finance (No 2) Act (c. 51), s. 81 ....4.18	
1988	Copyright, Designs and Patents Act (c. 48) 2.1, 22.2, 22.13	
	ss. 213–216 ....22.13	
	s. 265 ....22.13	
	Finance Act (c. 39) 25.9	
	Income and Corporation Taxes Act (c. 1)	
	s. 6(4)(b) 1.19	

s. 7(2) 4.5
s. 11 ....6.11.2
s. 13A 2.2
s. 18 ....16.1
  (1)(a)
    (ii) 1.1
    (iii) 1.1, 2.4.1, 5.18
  (3) 2.2
s. 19 ....24.5
  (1) 17.11
s. 26 ....25.12
s. 33 ....25.2
s. 53(1), (2) 25.1
s. 59(1) 9.11, 10.4.2, 19.2
s. 65
  (2) 16.1, 16.2
  (3) 1.18
  (4) 16.1
s. 74 ....25.15.11
  (1)(f) 22.16
    (a) 1.18
    (b) 14.4
    (j) 15.3
    (p) 22.7
s. 80 ....3.15
s. 83 ....22.3, 22.16
s. 85A 2.10
s. 96 ....25.6
s. 103 ....2.5
  (3)(b) 2.5
s. 104 ....1.1, 2.5
  (1) 2.5
s. 109 ....2.9
  A 9.8.10
s. 110 ....1.12
s. 110A 2.8, 3.1
s. 112 ....1.4
s. 113 ....20.6.1, 25.5
  (1) 9.11, 25.5
  (2) 25.5
ss. 114, 115 ....25.10

Table of Statutes

s. 117	1.1	(b)	4.11
(2) and (3)	1.1	s. 347B	21.6
s. 118	1.1	s. 348	2.2, 4.5
s. 118ZB	1.1	(1)	3.22
s. 129	5.20	(2)(a)	22.7
s. 132(2)	12.16.1	s. 349	2.2, 4.5, 10.4.3, 22.14
s. 145	6.16, 21.8.1	(1)	3.22
s. 146	6.16, 21.8.1	(b)	22.7
ss. 153–168	21.8.1	s. 350	10.4.3, 22.14
s. 154	21.8.5	s. 353	4.11
s. 155(2)	21.8.1	s. 380	1.1, 2.7, 3.1, 4.13, 5.6, 25.2
s. 156	21.8.5		
s. 160	1.20	s. 381	2.7, 5.6, 14.1, 20.6.1, 25.2
(1)	1.20		
(5)(a)	1.20	(1)	14.1
s. 162	5.22	(4)	25.2
s. 163	21.8.1	s. 383	25.2, 25.8
s. 167(5)	7.5.4	s. 384	3.1, 25.2
s. 192	9.12	s. 385	3.1, 4.13, 5.6
s. 192A(3)	12.4	(4)	1.22, 5.6
s. 193(1)	3.2	s. 388	5.6
s. 198	24.4	s. 393A(1), (3)	25.2
(1)	23.13	s. 397	25.2
(1A)	23.13	(10)	25.2
s. 203	6.11.2	s. 401	14.6, 17.14
s. 205	12.4	s. 419	1.20
(4)	12.4	(2)(a)	1.20
s. 231(3A)	2.2	s. 466	16.4
s. 242	4.16.1	s. 503	14.9, 14.14
s. 263C	4.8	s. 504	14.14
s. 278	8.5, 8.8	s. 505	21.3
s. 313	3.7	s. 521(6)(b)	22.5
s. 314	6.11.3	s. 524	
s. 331	21.8.2	(1)	22.4.1
s. 332(2), (a)	7.4	(2)	22.4.1
s. 335		(3)	22.4.3
(1)	12.2.1	(4)	22.4.3
(2)	12.16.1	s. 525	
s. 336	6.2.1	(1)	22.4.2
s. 337	1.8.1	(2)	22.4.2
s. 338	4.5	s. 526	
(3)		(1)	22.3
(a)	22.7	(2)	22.3

Table of Statutes

1988	Copyright, Designs and Patents Act — *cont.*		
	s. 527 ....22.11		s. 703 *et seq* 4.16.1
	s. 528(2) 22.3		s. 704 ....4.16.1
	s. 529 ....22.4.1, 22.10		s. 714(2) 5.19
	s. 530 ....6.11.3, 22.12		s. 731 *et seq* 4.16.2
	s. 531(4), (5), (6) 22.12		s. 736A 4.5
	s. 532(5) 22.12		s. 737 ....4.5
	s. 533		s. 739 ......1.21, 3.2, 6.16
	(1) 22.2, 22.7		s. 740 ....3.2
	(2) 22.4.1		s. 743(3) 6.16
	(3) 22.4.1		s. 768 ....25.1
	(4) 22.7		s. 775 ....1.21, 3.5, 3.6,
	(7) 6.11.3, 22.12		3.7, 4.3, 17.6
	s. 534 ......2.4.1, 2.9, 2.12		s. 776 ....21.3
	(4)(b) 2.9		s. 794(2)(bb) 5.18
	(7) 2.9		s. 832(1) 21.3
	s. 535 ....2.9		s. 833, (4) 1.22
	(8) 2.9		(c) 4.7
	s. 536 ....2.8		s. 835, (6) 22.9
	s. 537 ....2.11		Sch. 4A 2.10
	s. 537A 22.13		Sch. 5 ....25.4, 25.5
	(1), (2), (3) ...22.13		para. 1, (1) 25.3
	s. 537B 22.13		para. 2(3) 25.5
	s. 538 ....2.12		para. 3(10) 25.4
	s. 539 ....3.4		para. 6 ....25.15.4
	s. 555 ....3.4, 17.5		para. 8(5) 25.15.6
	s. 556 ....3.4, 17.5		Sch. 7 para. 7(b) 1.20
	s. 557 ....1.6, 3.4, 17.5		Sch. 12 ....12.4
	s. 558 ....3.4, 17.5		para. 5 ....12.4
	s. 577 ....8.2, 14.4		Sch. 12A
	(10) 14.4		para. 2(1) 23.13
	s. 585(2) 16.2		para. 4 ....23.13
	s. 607 ....20.7.1		para. 5(1)
	s. 617 ....13.12		(a) 23.13
	s. 623(2) 4.7		(b) 23.13
	s. 629 ....11.9		Sch. 13 ....4.5
	s. 634		Sch. 16 ....4.5
	(2) 20.3		Sch. 23A 4.5, 4.8
	(3) 3.23	1989	Finance Act (c. 26)
	s. 644(2) 4.7		s. 91 ....5.20
	s. 659A(1) 4.17.1		s. 178 ....7.5.1
	s. 663 ....1.19	1990	Capital Allowances Act (c. 1)
			s. 27 ....7.6.3

	s. 77 .... 4.2		s. 163 .... .25.11.4
	s. 141 .... .25.12		(2) 25.11.4
	s. 153 .... .9.8.9		(a) 25.11.4
	Courts and Legal Services Act (c. 41) ... 10.3.1		(b) 25.11.4
	Finance Act (c. 29) 3.14		(3)(a) 25.11.4
	Legal Services Act 10.3.1		(4) 25.11.4
1991	Finance Act (c. 31)		(a) 25.11.4
	s. 55 .... .4.16.2		s. 164 .... .25.11.4
	s. 72 .... .2.7, 25.2		(6) 25.11.4
1992	Social Security Contributions and Benefits Act (c. 4)		s. 165 ...... .1.8.2, 1.19, 2.2, 4.2, 17.6, 22.5
			s. 207 .... .5.20
	s. 2(2)(b) 21.8.1		s. 222 .... .10.1.3, 14.12, 21.8.10
	s. 19A 3.9.2		
	Taxation of Chargeable Gains Act (c. 12)		(8) 7.7, 8.7.2, 8.7.1, 14.12, 21.8.13
	s. 10 .... .1.7.1, 1.8.2		
	(1) 5.18		s. 223 .... .14.12
	(5) 1.2		s. 242 .... .25.11.2
	s. 17(2) 25.13.1		s. 249 .... .25.9
	s. 21 .... .22.15		s. 256 .... .21.3
	s. 25 .... 1.8.2		s. 258 .... .2.13
	s. 35 .... .25.13.1		s. 262 .... .2.13
	s. 38(1)(a) 25.13.1		s. 263B 4.8
	s. 42 .... .25.13.1		s. 271 .... .4.17.1
	(2) 25.13.1		s. 275(1) 6.15
	s. 50 .... .9.8.9		Sch. 6 .... .25.11.4
	s. 52(4) 25.13.1		para. 10 .... .25.11.4
	s. 53 et seq 25.13.1		para. 12(2) 9.8.3
	s. 55 .... .25.13.1		Sch. 7 .... .25.11.1
	s. 115 .... .4.18	1993	Finance Act (c. 34) 5.1
	s. 120(5) 25.11.2		Pt. V, Ch. III 5.1
	s. 143 .... .4.18		s. 76 .... .9.4.2
	s. 144 .... .4.17.1		s. 179B 5.22
	s. 145 .... .4.17.1		Sch. 20A 5.22
	s. 146(1)(b) 4.17.1	1994	Finance Act (c. 9) 5.1
	s. 152(8) 19.1.2		Pt. IV, Ch. V 5.1
	ss. 152–158 .... .25.13.1		Value Added Tax Act
	s. 154 .... .19.1.2		Sch. 9, Grp. .... .12 21.3
	s. 155 ..... .15.13.2, 25.13.1, 25.13.2		Sch. 19, Grp. ...... .12 21.3
		1995	Finance Act (c. 4) 1.7, 20.5.3
	s. 162 .... .1.19, 4.2, 17.6		s. 125 .... .1.4

xxxv

1995	Finance Act — *cont.*		s. 279	14.10
	s. 126		ss. 361–390	25.8
	(2)	1.7.1	Finance Act	2.10
	(5)	1.7.5	s. 107	25.15.1
	(6), (7)	1.4	2002	Finance Act (c. 36),
	(8)	1.7.1		Sch. 22, para. 11, 12 .. 10.1.1
	Sch. 23		2003	Finance Act, s. 136 ..... 1.10
	paras. 1–3	1.7.2		Income and
	para. 4	1.7.3		Corporation Taxes
	para. 6	1.7.4		Act, s. 336	11.12.2
	para. 7	1.7.3		Income Tax (Earnings
1996	Finance Act (c. 8)	20.5.3		and Pensions)
1998	Finance Act (c. 36) 3.2, 10.1.1			Act 3.1, 3.9.1, 3.9.2,
	s. 39	25.12		3.10, 6.10, 6.11.2,
	s. 42	1.1, 1.14		8.1, 9.8.5, 9.8.7,
	s. 43	10.1.1		9.11, 10.1, 10.3,
	(2)	10.1		11.1, 12.2.2, 12.3,
	(3)	10.1.1		17.11, 19.2, 24.2, 24.3
1999	Finance Act (c. 16) 11.1,			s. 5	24.5
	23.7.3			s. 15 .... 8.1, 13.1, 17.11
2000	Finance Act 5.5, 5.18,			s. 21	6.6, 6.11
	9.11.1			s. 22	6.3, 6.7
	Limited Liability Partnerships			s. 23	6.6
	Act	1.1		s. 25 ....6.7, 6.11, 8.1, 13.1
2001	Capital Allowances Act			(1)	12.4
	s. 7	25.7		s. 26	6.3, 6.7
	s. 15			s. 27	6.7, 8.1
	(1)(i)	19.1.1		s. 28	8.1, 13.1
	(3)	14.9		(4)–(8)	8.1
	s. 25	14.8		s. 40	12.1
	s. 27	14.8		(2)	12.12
	s. 35			(4)	
	(1)	14.8		(a)	12.4
	(2)	14.8		(b)	12.4
	s. 36	19.1.1, 21.8.4		(5), (c)	12.4
	s. 62	20.5.3		s. 41	6.11
	ss. 83–89	14.8		ss. 63–69	19.2
	s. 127	20.5.1		s. 65	7.6.3
	s. 128	20.5.1		s. 82	11.4
	ss. 135–136	20.5.3		s. 86	12.16.3
	ss. 176–204	14.7		s. 99	7.5.1, 7.5.4
	s. 266	22.5, 25.1		s. 102	7.5.1
	s. 271	14.10		s. 106	21.8.11

s. 121	7.8.1	s. 336	1.18, 9.2, 9.4.9, 11.12.2, 12.15, 13.5, 13.7, 13.11, 21.8.3, 21.8.6, 21.8.8, 24.4
s. 149	7.8.2		
(3)	7.8.2		
s. 151	7.8.2		
s. 175	7.8.3, 9.4.2		
s. 203	21.8.12	s. 337	12.13, 23.13
s. 216	21.8.15	s. 338	
s. 230	7.6.3	(2)	23.13
s. 248	14.4	(3)	23.13
s. 250	21.8.2	s. 339(5)	23.13
s. 264	21.8.3	s. 351	7.5.3, 7.5.4, 7.5.5
ss. 271–289	6.9, 9.4.2	(1)	7.6.3, 7.6.4, 7.6.5
s. 271	8.2	(2)	7.6.1
s. 273(2)(a)	7.6.5	s. 352	3.14
ss. 279–285	9.4.2	s. 368	13.9
s. 281	21.8.8	s. 370	3.15
s. 284	9.4.2	s. 371	3.15
s. 287	8.2	s. 378	12.4
s. 290	7.5.2	s. 390	6.8
(2)	7.5.3	s. 401	11.12.4
s. 291	11.12.4	s. 403	11.12.4, 17.11
s. 292	11.2, 11.6	s. 575, (2)(c)	16.2
s. 293	11.6	s. 613, (3)	16.2
s. 295	11.4	s. 615	16.3
s. 296	13.4	s. 617	16.3
s. 297	13.8	s. 638	13.16
s. 298	13.11	s. 639	13.13, 16.7
s. 299	8.2, 13.3	s. 640	13.13
s. 313	7.5.4	s. 641	13.12
s. 314	21.8.11	s. 655	16.6
s. 315	7.5.4, 21.8.11	s. 677	16.8
s. 317	14.4, 21.8.3	s. 681	16.6, 16.8
(4)	14.4	2004 Finance Act	6.7
s. 321	18.6	Ch. 3	23.14
s. 323	18.5	s. 144	5.22
(2)	18.5	Sch. 25	5.22

Table of Statutory Instruments

1972	SI 1972 No. 238	14.8
1974	Lloyd's Underwriters (Tax) Regulations (SI 1974 No. 896), reg. 7	5.16
1975	Income Tax Reserve and Auxiliary Forces Regulations (SI 1975 No. 91)	13.11
1978	Categorisation Regulations (SI 1978 No. 1689)	
	reg. 2(2)	21.8.1
	reg. 5, Sch. 6 para. 3	21.8.1
	Sch. 1	
	para. 5	3.9.2
	Pt. 1 para. 4	21.8.1
	Double Taxation Relief (Taxes on Income) (Hungary) Order (SI 1978 No. 1056)	6.12
	Social Security (Categorisation of Earners) Regulations	3.9.2
1979	Social Security (Contributions) Regulations (SI 1979 No. 591), reg. 19(1)(c)	14.15
1980	Double Taxation Relief (Taxes on Income) (United States of America) (Dividends) Regulations (SI 1980 No. 568)	3.3
	Art. 17	17.5
	Art. 18(2)	16.5
	Art. 20A	6.12
1984	Categorisation Amendment Regulations (SI 1984 No. 350)	
	reg. 1(2)	21.8.1
	reg. 2	21.8.1
	reg. 4	21.8.1
1985	Double Taxation Relief (Taxes on Income) (Norway) Order (SI 1985 No. 1998), Art. 31A	6.11.5
1987	Income Tax (Entertainers and Sportsmen) Regulations (SI 1987 No. 530) 1.6, 3.4	
	reg. 11	3.4
1988	The Set-Aside Regulations SI 1988 No. 1352	25.9
1989	The Set-Aside (Amendment) Regulations SI 1989 No. 1042	25.9
1990	Income Tax (Building Societies) (Dividends and Interest) Regulations (SI 1990 No. 2231)	19.2
	The Set-Aside (Amendment) Regulations SI 1990 No. 1716	25.9
1992	Income Tax (Dividend Manufacturing) Regulations (SI 1992 No. 569) 4.5, 4.16.2	
	SI 1992 No. 34	4.5

Table of Statutory Instruments

1993	Income Tax (Employments) Regulations (SI 1993 No. 774),	
	reg. 48	25.9
1998	The Social Security (Categorisation of Earners) Amendment	
	Regulations SI 1998 No. 1728	3.9.2
	reg. 5	3.9.2
1999	The Social Security (Categorisation of Earners) Amendment	
	Regulations SI 1999 No. 3	3.9.2
2001	Social Security (Contributions) Regulations (SI 2001 No. 1004)	
	reg. 115	12.4
	Sch. 3, Part X, para. 5	18.2.3
	The Social Security Amendment (Capital Disregards)	
	Regulations (SI 2001 No. 22)	13.18
	UK/USA Double Taxation Convention 2001	
	Art. 14(2)	6.6
	Art. 16(1)	1.6
	Art. 18	16.5
2003	Income Tax (Pay As You Earn) Regulations (SI 2003	
	No. 2682)	18.2.2
	Pt. 7 Ch. I	24.2
	reg. 100	18.2.2
	Social Security (Categorisation of Earners) (Amendment)	
	Regulations (SI 2003 No. 736)	3.9.2
	Tax Credits (Residence) Regulations (SI 2003 No. 654)	8.6

Inland Revenue documents

Entries refer to paragraph numbers not page numbers

Booklets
Booklet CA 26 . . . . 21.8.1
Booklet FEU50 . . . . 3.4
Booklet IR 14/15. . . . . 23.6
Booklet IR 40 . . . . 23.7.2, 23.7.1
Booklet IR 150 . . . . 25.15.11,
    25.15.9
Booklet IR 480 . . . . 6.9, 21.8
Booklet IR 490 . . . . 3.16
Business Economic Note 19 . . 25.3,
    25.14
    para. 7. . . . . 25.15.2

Capital Allowances Manual,
    para. 31800 . . . . 25.7

Employment Income Manual
EIM 03002 . . . . 21.8
EIM 70200 . . . . 12.8
Employment Status Manuals
ESM 0111. . . . . 21.8.1
ESM 1000 . . . . 21.8
ESM 1091 . . . . 21.8
ESM 4500 . . . . 21.8
ESM 4503 . . . . 21.9
ESM 4504. . . . . 21.8.1
ESM 7230. . . . . 21.8.1
Extra-statutory Concessions
ESC A9 . . . . 9.10, 9.11
ESC A11. . . . . 6.2.1
ESC A25 . . . . 8.1
ESC A29 . . . . 25.6
ESC A37 . . . . 1.15
ESC A60 . . . . 25.9
ESC A61. . . . . 7.5.3

ESC A63. . . . . 21.8.2
ESC A64. . . . . 21.8.2
ESC A66. . . . . 9.4.7
ESC A94 . . . . 3.22
ESC A103. . . . . 13.11.1
ESC B5 . . . . 25.2
ESC B6 . . . . 25.9
ESC B7. . . . . 9.8.9
ESC B10 . . . . 7.9
ESC B11 . . . . . 25.9, 25.15.5, 25.15.3
ESC B47 . . . . 14.9
ESC B55 . . . . 25.2
ESC C4 . . . . 21.3
ESC C32 . . . . 23.3
ESC D22. . . . . 25.11.2
ESC D26. . . . . 25.11.2
ESC F20. . . . . 13.18

Help Sheets
Help Sheet IR 205 . . . . . . 12.1, 12.4
Help Sheet IR 224. . . . . 25.5
Help Sheet IR 229. . . . . 9.7
Help Sheet IR 231. . . . . 9.7
Help Sheet IR 234. . . . . 2.10
Help Sheet IR 303. . . . . 3.4
Help Sheet SA101MLA
    (Notes) 11.1
Help Sheet SA101M
    (Notes) 7.2
Help Sheet SA101MP
    (Notes) 11.1
Help Sheet SA101MSP
    (Notes) 11.1
Help Sheet SA101WAM
    (Notes) 11.1

Inland Revenue documents

Inland Revenue Memorandum
  TS40/1990 .... 21.8.4
Interpretations
Revenue Interpretation 46
  (August 1993) 22.12
Revenue Interpretation 52
  (August 1993) 14.2
Revenue Interpretation 173
  (June 1997) 25.5

Leaflets
Leaflet IR 20 .... 6.13
  paras. 38 and 39 .... 6.4
Leaflet IR 25 (1977), page 16 ... 6.8
Leaflet IR 56/NI39 .... 21.8
Leaflet IR 180 .... 23.1

Press Releases
Press Release (29 October
  1987) 20.2.3, 25.13.2, 25.13.1
Press Release (11 July 1988)
  (1988) STI 578 .... 25.13.1
Press Release (12 April
  1989) 21.8.2
Press Release (29 May
  1991) 25.9

Statements of Practice
SP A3 .... 1.14, 10.1.1
SP A27 .... 1.13.1, 1.14
SP 5/81 .... 25.9
SP 10/84 .... 6.15
SP 4/85 .... 25.9
SP 1/86 .... 14.8
SP 4/86 .... 21.8.2
SP 9/86 .... 1.11
SP 9/87 .... 14.10
SP 3/90 .... 25.3
SP 14/91 .... 4.18
SP 17/91 .... 6.2.1
SP 4/97 .... 19.2

Chapter 1   Introduction

1.1 What is a profession?

Most of the chapters of this book are concerned with the taxation position of individuals carrying on professions or vocations, as opposed to trades or employments. What constitutes a profession is not defined in the Taxes Acts, but in *CIR v Maxse* (1919) 12 TC 41, Scutton LJ said:

> '... it seems to me as at present advised that a "profession" in the present use of language involves the idea of an occupation requiring either purely intellectual skill, or of any manual skill controlled, as in painting and sculpture or surgery, by the intellectual skill of the operator....'

Most cases which turned on whether an individual was carrying on a profession were concerned with excess profits duty and excess profits tax, as there were exemptions from these taxes in respect of the carrying-on of a profession if the profits were dependent wholly or mainly on personal qualifications: the word 'profession' did not broadly include activities connected with the making of contracts of a commercial nature. For the purpose of assessment, professions are now subject to the same basic rules as trades and are included with trades in the general charging section of Sch. D (Income and Corporation Taxes Act 1988 (ICTA 1988), s. 18(1)(a)(ii) and (iii)). However, whilst the same person can carry on more than one trade, anyone who is practising a profession in whatever capacity is exercising one continuing profession subject to tax under Sch. D, Case II, unless any activity is an employment. Thus in *Seldon v Croom-Johnson* (1932) 16 TC 740 it was held that a barrister who had taken silk was still carrying on the same profession. This is important, as discussed later in this chapter, when an individual carrying on a profession changes his or her country of residence.

The Inland Revenue guidance on the distinction between a trade and a profession includes the following (at IM 115c).

> 'The word "trade" is not comprehensively or generally defined in tax law although some activities, such as an adventure or concern in the nature of trade, are specifically included. Trade therefore takes its ordinary meaning which normally involves commercial operations by the trader who provides goods or services to his customers in exchange for a reward. Whether a trade exists in any given circumstances is a question to be decided on the facts of the case... Neither "profession" nor "vocation" has any statutory definition and

they, too, take their ordinary meanings. A profession, historically, meant the three learned professions of the church, medicine and the law but today the term goes much wider and normally involves some substantial exercise of intellectual skill ... The difference in practice causes few problems and it is rarely necessary to debate the point when a taxpayer is clearly carrying on one or the other. If the question is at issue then it has to be decided on the facts of the case (as with the meaning of trade).'

A profession is still liable to tax even if it is associated with elements of illegality, such as the 'oldest profession' — prostitution. In the case of *CIR v Aken* [1990] STC 497 the taxpayer appealed against Case I assessments raised on her because prostitution was not trading. Whether or not assessments could have been raised under Case II, the court held that as a general principle a trade did not cease to be such for the purposes of the Taxes Acts because it was illegal. Consequently, the same principle no doubt applies to a profession or vocation. More recently it was reported in August 2003 that a cannabis grower had paid income tax on the profits of his illegal business. He was nevertheless jailed for four and a half years and subjected to a confiscation order.

One distinction which is relevant from a taxation viewpoint is between a freelance professional activity liable to tax under Schedule D, Case II, and a professional employment liable to tax under the employment income rules of the Income Tax (Earnings and Pensions) Act 2003 (ITEPA 2003). This distinction is referred to in **1.9** and in **Chapters 3, 9 and 24**.

The main divergence between trades and professions occurred historically in the practical application of the rules of assessment because of the differing ways in which the accounts of individuals carrying on professions could be drawn up, as opposed to those of individuals carrying on trades (for instance, the recognition of the 'cash basis' or other forms of 'conventional basis' of drawing up accounts in the post-cessation receipts legislation, which was most usually met in professional accounts (ICTA 1988, s. 104)). Finance Act (FA) 1998, s. 42 now requires all businesses to compute their taxable profit 'in accordance with generally accepted accounting practice' and the cash basis has been withdrawn for accounting periods beginning after 6 April 1999 (although the cash basis still remains available to barristers in the early years of their profession: see **1.13.4**).

More recently the distinction between a trade and a profession has been revived in the context of specific tax legislation. For many years it has been the case that a loss arising from a trade carried on by a limited partnership established under the Limited Partnership Act 1907 can only be used by limited partners against total income under ICTA 1988, s. 380 up to a maximum of their capital contributions and undrawn profits (s. 117(2) and (3)). No such restriction applies where the loss arises from a profession carried on by the limited partnership.

An analogous position applies in the case of a limited liability partnership (LLP) established under the Limited Liability Partnerships Act 2000. ICTA 1988, s. 118ZB operates to extend the provisions of ICTA 1988, ss. 117 and 118 to members of LLPs that carry on a trade. The limit for relief claimed by members of LLPs is the amount they have subscribed to the LLP together with any further amount that they have undertaken to contribute in the event that the LLP is wound up. No such restriction applies where the loss arises from a profession carried on by the LLP.

1.2 Vocation

The word 'vocation' has a very wide general meaning and is similar to a calling. It means the way in which an individual passes his or her life (*Partridge v Mallandaine* (1886) 2 TC 179). It has been held that bookmakers, jockeys and land agents are engaged in vocations. However, the winnings of a golf professional on bets on his own matches were held not to be earnings of a vocation (*Down v Compston* (1937) 21 TC 60). Also, an individual whose sole means of livelihood was betting on horses from his house was held not to be carrying on a vocation, and so was not liable to tax on his betting winnings (*Graham v Green* (1925) 9 TC 309).

If an individual is exercising a vocation, there is no special treatment for tax purposes.

The main point for the purposes of taxation is whether a vocation is carried on with a view to profit, or whether a calling does not seek to make a profit, as is claimed by some evangelists (see **7.10**).

Professions and vocations are specifically included in provisions relating to the liability to capital gains tax of non-residents carrying on business in the UK through a branch or agency (Taxation of Chargeable Gains Act 1992 (TCGA 1992), s. 10(5)).

1.3 Profession carried on abroad

Where a trade or profession is carried on partly abroad, it is still assessed under Cases I and II.

Introduction

Where a trade or profession is carried on wholly abroad, it constitutes a foreign possession and is assessed in accordance with the rules of Schedule D, Case V (*Colquhoun v Brooks* (1889) 2 TC 490). A trade is treated as carried on wholly abroad only if no element of control or supervision as well as no other business activity takes place in the UK (*Ogilvie v Kitton* (1908) 5 TC 338). Clearly, in the case of an individual resident in the UK who carries on a profession not in partnership, this is practically impossible to achieve.

1.4 Overseas partnerships

A share of partnership profits of an individual resident in the UK is assessed under Case V where the partnership is managed and controlled abroad, insofar as the profits relate to activities carried out abroad (ICTA 1988, s. 112 as amended by FA 1995, s. 125). Any UK-based activities are assessable under Sch. D, Cases I and II under the normal rules relating to non-residents trading in the UK, subject to the protection of any double tax agreement. Therefore, unlike an individual carrying on a trade or profession on his or her own, a partnership can give rise to income assessable in the hands of a UK-resident partner under Sch. D, Cases I or II and Case V, provided it can be shown that management and control are exercised from abroad. This usually entails having a number of partners who are not resident in the UK — the tests as to where management and control are located being the same as for companies (see *De Beers Consolidated Mines v Howe* (1906) 5 TC 198 and *Padmore v CIR* (1987) 62 TC 352). Therefore a UK-resident individual who has professional earnings arising abroad may be able to receive them as Case V income by entering into such an overseas partnership with non-resident individuals or possibly a non-resident company. The point is discussed in **Chapter 3** in connection with entertainers.

The main advantage in receiving Case V income of this nature as against Case II income is if the individual is not domiciled in the UK, in which case the Case V income is liable to UK income tax only on a remittance basis. It may be advantageous to fall within Cases I or II so that more favourable loss relief is available. However, Case V income can sometimes benefit from relief under a double tax treaty.

Under FA 1995, s. 126(6), where a business (carried on by a partnership which includes non-resident partners) is carried on in the UK through a branch or agency, the branch or agency is treated as the UK representative of each non-resident partner.

Under FA 1995, s. 126(7), where a business is carried on in the UK by a partnership which includes both resident and non-resident partners, the partnership is treated as the UK representative of each non-resident partner. The partners are thus jointly liable for the tax payable by the non-resident partners on their shares of the partnership profit.

1.5 Carrying on business in the UK

Generally, an individual who is not resident in the UK is liable to UK income tax only on any profits derived from trading activities within the UK. There is extensive case law on the subject which, broadly speaking, indicates that an individual is treated as trading in the UK if he or she negotiates and makes contracts in the UK (*Grainger & Son v Gough* (1896) 3 TC 462). This principle was reaffirmed in *CIR v Hang Seng Bank Ltd* [1990] STC 733 PC.

1.6 Carrying on a profession in the UK

The position with regard to the carrying on of a profession is rather more obscure. The circumstances in which a visitor to this country is or is not resident here for tax purposes are dealt with in **Chapter 6**. Strictly, however, anyone performing a professional service or engagement in the UK is exercising a profession in the UK, and so is liable to income tax under Schedule D, Case II. Where there is a double tax agreement, visitors performing independent professional services, who stay for less than six months and have no fixed base in the UK, are not liable to UK tax. However, where agreements give such exemption for professions, there is often an exclusion for public entertainers, musicians and athletes from their personal activities, as in the case of the double tax treaty with France.

In certain agreements, exemption is equally excluded for the remuneration of such entertainers and athletes as employees, even where they are employed by a company having no permanent establishment in the country in which the performance is given. Thus the double tax treaty with the USA (UK/USA Double Taxation Convention 2001 which came into force on 31 March 2003) taxes entertainers no matter how they receive their income. It specifically allows (Art. 16(1)) the country in which musicians, athletes and entertainers perform to tax them, except where gross earnings are small (less than $20,000 or its sterling equivalent per annum). The absence of a fixed base and the length of stay are not relevant. If the income of the musician, athlete or entertainer is paid to a related person or company, even if not resident in the country where the musician performs, the income is still taxed.

Introduction

To help collect any tax strictly due, tax can be withheld at source on income paid to entertainers and sportspeople visiting the UK, or individuals connected with them, in respect of any activity of the entertainer and sportsperson within the UK (ICTA 1988, s. 557 and Income Tax (Entertainers and Sportsmen) Regulations 1987 (SI 1987 No. 530)). The detailed operation of these provisions is discussed in the relevant chapters, but it is clear that the law envisages any professional activity carried out in the UK as potentially liable to tax here.

In practice the likelihood of being assessed on any professional earnings arising in the UK is probably increased where someone has been resident in the UK at some time. If an individual ceases to be resident here, but continues to carry on his or her profession here as well as abroad, and cannot rely on the protection of a double tax agreement, the Inland Revenue doubtless require the UK income to be self assessed.

1.7 UK representatives of non-residents

The FA 1995 introduced rules for taxing the UK liabilities of non-residents on their UK representatives under Schedule D, Cases I and II. These rules define clearly:

- who is liable to UK tax;
- who is responsible for complying with the tax obligations, and
- the nature and extent of those obligations.

The rules define the obligations and liabilities of the UK representatives of non-residents and apply to both non-resident individuals and companies.

1.7.1 Definition of UK representative

Under the 1995 rules the 'UK representative' of a non-resident is defined (FA 1995, s. 126(2) and (8)) as the branch or agency through which the non-resident carries on any trade, profession or vocation.

'Branch or agency' means 'any factorship, agency, receivership, branch or management' (Taxes Management Act 1970 (TMA 1970), s. 118).

Where a branch or agency is a UK representative, it is responsible for complying with the tax obligations arising from its activities. That is:

- the profits of the trade, profession or vocation of the non-resident carried on through the branch or agency;
- income from property or rights which are used by, or held by or for it, and
- capital gains chargeable on non-residents under TCGA 1992, s. 10.

1.7.2 General rule for the obligations and liabilities of UK representatives

The general rule under FA 1995, Sch. 23, paras 1, 2 and 3 is that UK representatives are jointly responsible with the non-resident for all the tax obligations and liabilities in relation to the trade, profession or vocation carried on through the branch or agency.

This joint responsibility extends to all matters relating to the assessment of tax, and to the collection and recovery of tax. For example, it extends to all the mechanisms of self assessment, including: notification of chargeability; the obligation to make a return and self assessment; liability to make interim and final payments of tax; and liability to surcharges, interest and penalties in connection with those obligations and liabilities.

Either party can discharge the obligations and liabilities arising. Equally, any acts or omissions of the UK representative are treated as acts or omissions of the non-resident (but see also SAT 2 paras 7.31–7.33 in relation to tax offences).

Where the trigger for an obligation or liability is the receipt of formal notification, then the obligation or liability falls only on the UK representative once it has received the relevant notification (or a copy).

1.7.3 Obligations and liabilities are limited where the UK representative is independent of the non-resident

Where the UK representative is an independent agent of the non-resident, its obligations to provide information are limited to ones within its competence to act for the non-resident (FA 1995, Sch. 23, paras 4 and 7).

'Independent agent' is defined at FA 1995, Sch. 23, para. 7. The definition is based on that used in the OECD Model Tax Convention and UK double taxation agreements. Broadly, to be an 'independent agent', the agent must be both legally and economically independent of the non-resident.

Introduction

The rules recognise that, where the UK representative is an independent agent, the agent may not be able to provide complete information about the affairs of the non-resident. The agent is therefore required to provide any information requested – for example, a return – to the best of its knowledge and belief after taking all reasonable steps to obtain the information. The non-resident remains responsible for completing or correcting the information where necessary.

However, the non-resident can correct any error or omission made by the UK representative provided the non-resident did not know about it or participate in it.

1.7.4 An independent agent can retain and recover monies due

UK representatives who are independent agents of non-residents are entitled to retain out of the non-resident's monies amounts sufficient to meet UK tax liabilities (FA 1995, Sch. 23, para. 6).

1.7.5 A partnership can be the UK representative of a non-resident

A partnership can be the UK representative of a non-resident (FA 1995, s. 126(5)). This occurs, for example, where a non-resident trades in the UK through the agency of a UK partnership (of which he or she is not a member). In such circumstances the UK partners are jointly liable, as the UK representative, for the tax payable by the non-resident.

1.8 Effect of change of residence

1.8.1 Income tax

If an individual carrying on a profession becomes resident here, it does not necessarily follow that the commencement rules of assessment will operate (*Kneen v Martin* (1935) 19 TC 33). Similarly, when the person ceases to be resident, the cessation rules may not apply, unlike the position with a company (ICTA 1988, s. 337). It is a question of fact when a source of income first arises. Thus an actor will not change his or her profession by coming to live in the UK. The same point applies where the same trade continues to be carried on by an individual who becomes resident in the UK and the trade was partly carried on in the UK before the period of residence began, so that the trade has been assessed before under Sch. D, Case I (*Fry v Burma Corporation Ltd* (1930) 15 TC 113).

The relevance of the continuity of the profession now lies in the creation and use of overlap relief under the current year basis.

1.8.2 Capital gains tax

Problems can also arise in relation to capital gains tax on a change of residence in respect of an asset used in a profession, for instance a property or goodwill.

If an individual disposes of, say, professional goodwill whilst resident or ordinarily resident in the UK, he or she is liable to capital gains tax. If he or she disposes of the asset having left the UK but not before ceasing to carry on the profession in the UK – for instance, goodwill sold with a professional practice – he or she is still liable to capital gains tax.

If an individual becomes temporarily non-resident (ie is out of the UK for less than five years), then any disposal of UK-situated assets is liable to capital gains tax.

However, if a disposal takes place in a year of non-residence, TCGA 1992, s. 10 may render non-residents liable to UK capital gains tax on disposals of UK-situated assets used for the purposes of a trade carried on in this country through a branch or agency. There is not normally any exemption from liability under double tax treaty arrangements.

Anti-avoidance provisions tax any capital gain of a non-resident for such an asset at the time it ceases to be used for the purposes of the trade, profession or vocation carried on in the UK, or when it is transferred abroad (TCGA 1992, s. 25) — for example, the goodwill of an architectural practice transferred to an offshore location. Thus, if the profession carried on by a non-resident in the UK ceases, and after the year of cessation property formerly used for the profession is sold, there is now a liability to UK tax on the basis of the market value at the date of cessation of the profession. Non-residents used to be able to avoid such a liability by selling in a year of assessment after the profession ceased to be carried on in the UK. It still seems possible, however, for an individual carrying on a profession to separate the profession from, say, the property in which it is carried on whilst still resident here – for instance by incorporating the business using the relief afforded by TCGA 1992, s. 165 for assets transferred to the company — and then in a year after ceasing to be resident to sell the property free of capital gains tax.

Introduction

There are now similar restrictions on roll-over relief where a non-resident reinvests in assets which are not chargeable assets — for example where a non-resident carrying on a profession here sells a UK asset used for that profession and reinvests in an overseas asset. Roll-over relief is not available in such situations.

1.9 Employments

Note that professional activities can be carried on within the ambit of an employment. This distinction is discussed in greater detail in connection with entertainers (**Chapter 3**) and doctors (**Chapter 9**). In connection with professions and the demarcation between Sch. D and employment, it was reported (*Tax Journal*, 26 September 1991) that Specialeyes plc won an appeal before a Special Commissioner on the question of whether locum ophthalmic opticians were employees or self-employed. The Special Commissioner decided that 'the agreed terms (on which the locums dealt with Specialeyes) reflected the parties' belief that the locums were independent contractors carrying on their own business'. This decision could have far-reaching effects in other professions where self-employed staff are used on a freelance basis. The main advantages of being assessed under Sch. D, rather than under the employment income rules are the rules for assessing profits, the deferment of the actual payment of tax and the greater opportunity for claiming expenses against profits.

1.10 Personal service companies

Since 6 April 2000 legislation has applied to counter the use of personal service companies by individuals who provide their services through intermediaries. The so-called IR35 legislation originally applied only where services were provided to other businesses. However, FA 2003, s. 136 extended the scope of the legislation to domestic workers, such as nannies or butlers, who provide services through an intermediary (usually a service company). The legislation is extremely wide-ranging and affects a large number of professionals and other workers who have set up such companies to avoid employment status. Such individuals should perhaps revert to sole trader status provided that they can satisfy the self-employment criteria. Carrying on the trade or profession through a partnership does not protect the individual from the intermediaries legislation. Under the legislation the intermediary has to account for PAYE and National Insurance (NI) on notional remuneration unless actual PAYE has been accounted for on payments to the worker.

1.11 Current year basis of assessment

It is outside the scope of this book to examine the current year basis of assessment in detail. Where appropriate, the rules are referred to in the context of the specific profession concerned.

Partnerships are commonly used in carrying on a profession. The complication for tax purposes is in establishing whether, when a partnership is formed from an amalgamation of two professional businesses, or an existing partnership splits into two or more successor businesses, there has been a cessation or a commencement, or whether there has been a continuation of an existing business. What constitutes continuation of a business or succession to a business is sometimes very difficult to determine — for instance where a new solicitors' practice is established from the merger of two existing practices.

The Inland Revenue have set out their views in Statement of Practice 9/86 on partnership mergers and demergers. Basically, on a merger the continuation basis can usually apply, but on a demerger this facility is unlikely because there is normally no succession to part of a trade or professional business.

Sometimes, where an individual is in an employment and also starts up a professional activity — for instance a teacher writing for publication — the Inland Revenue press for the freelance professional earnings to be assessed under Sch. D, Case VI until it is established they are sufficiently regular and sustained to constitute the carrying on of a profession.

This approach should be resisted where possible as it means that the period of low profit is assessed on an actual basis and, if there is a loss, it is available only to carry forward against future Case VI income.

1.12 Cash or earnings basis

The profits of a partnership are computed using the normal rules under Sch. D, Cases I and II which require the 'earnings basis' as described in ICTA 1988, s. 110. However, individuals and partnerships were, until 1999, permitted to prepare accounts instead 'on a cash basis or on a conventional basis such as bills issued or work completed which is neither full "earnings" nor pure "cash"'.

Barristers are, perhaps, affected more than any other profession, as their fees may not even be billed until several years after the work is completed and many of their client firms are notoriously slow at making payments. However,

Introduction

other professions that benefited from cash basis accounts for tax purposes include solicitors, accountants, tax consultants, architects and surveyors.

Some professionals operated a true cash basis, with no inclusion of debtors or work in progress at all. Others operated a hybrid or halfway house scheme with, perhaps, inclusion of debtors based on fees billed at the year end, but with no calculation of work in progress. This was known as the 'conventional basis'. No doubt there are other variations, including the calculation of limited work in progress based on recorded staff time only, but without any addition for administrative overheads. This regime came to an abrupt and painful conclusion in 1999.

1.13 Generally accepted accounting practice basis

New rules were introduced with effect from 1999–2000. Professions and vocations previously on a 'cash' or 'conventional' basis were required to change to a 'true and fair view' basis in that year (amended in 2002 to a 'generally accepted accounting practice' basis) and any amounts that might otherwise escape tax on the change of basis were subject to a one-off 'catching-up' charge.

1.13.1 Catching-up charge

The catching-up charge is taxable over ten years of assessment, normally starting with 1999–2000.

The catching-up charge for any year except the last is 'capped' by charging tax on one-tenth of the total amount subject to the charge or ten per cent of the normal profits of the business, whichever is the smaller.

In calculating the catching-up charge a deduction can be made for any net double charge which can be shown to have arisen when the firm originally moved from the earnings basis to a cash or conventional basis.

New barristers (advocates in Scotland) can remain on the cash basis for the first seven years of practice, at which point they must move to the earnings basis with the catching-up charge outlined above.

The catching-up charge is allocated to partners by reference to their shares for each of the ten years over which the catching-up charge is spread.

Normally the catching-up charge is calculated at the accounting date in 1999–2000. If there is more than one accounting date in 1999–2000, the earliest date is used. If there is no accounting date in that year, then there is a deemed accounting date of 6 April 1999. These possibilities can arise where accounts are drawn up for periods shorter or longer than 12 months.

The first computation on the earnings basis is normally for the 12 months ending on the accounting date in 2000–01. The debtors, creditors and work in progress used to calculate the catching-up charge at the end of the previous period will form the opening earnings basis figures.

Professionals can no longer move to a cash or conventional basis under Statement of Practice A27. New barristers (advocates in Scotland) can still use a cash or conventional basis for the first seven years of practice (see **1.13.4**).

1.13.2 Spread and cap

The catching-up charge is spread over ten tax years. The amount chargeable each year except the last is the smaller of one-tenth of the total charge; and 10 per cent of the 'normal' profit.

For a sole practitioner the catching-up charge is taxable over the ten tax years 1999–2000 to 2008–09. The catching-up charge for any of the first nine years is nil if the normal profit for that year is nil or there is a loss. In the final year there is no limit; so the charge for that year is the balance.

The charge is made under Sch. D, Case VI and so is not liable to Class 4 National Insurance Contributions (NICs). Existing Case II losses can be set against the charge. The charge is 'net relevant earnings' and therefore pensionable (but there is no special treatment of any pensions cap). It is not possible to set 'overlap relief' against the catching-up charge.

The usual payment on account rules will operate. The operation of the payment on account rules normally means that the first payment was on 31 January 2001 with any final charge payable on 31 January 2010.

The ten-year spread and ten per cent cap apply automatically but the taxpayer can opt to pay the whole catching-up charge at once or in such greater amounts as he or she specifies (which may be beneficial in certain loss situations).

Introduction

The 'normal' profit is the amount chargeable to tax as professional income for the tax year of the practice to which the catching-up charge relates. It is the profit apart from the catching-up charge and before capital allowances adjustments. It follows that the 'normal' profit for the first year is the cash or conventional basis profit. Subsequent 'normal' profits are on the earnings basis.

Where a sole practitioner ceases to practise the ten-year spread continues, but there is no ten per cent profits cap (because there are no longer any profits).

Example 1.1

Angela is an accountant on a 'bills delivered' basis without work in progress and an accounting date of 30 April. She prepared her accounts for tax purposes to 30.4.99 on this basis. At this date she had completed work worth £10,000 that she had not yet billed, and uncompleted work in progress with a cost for tax purposes of £20,000. She had also issued an interim bill for £2,000 for work that remained uncompleted at 30.4.99. The client paid the £2,000 in March 1999. The work was completed in May 1999, when the fee was regarded as 'earned' for accountancy purposes.

Angela's accounts for the year ending 30.4.00 must be on the 'true and fair view' basis by virtue of FA 1998, s. 42. Thus they include 'opening' and 'closing' figures for debtors, creditors and work in progress in accordance with generally accepted accounting practice. In particular, those accounts have 'opening' figures which include the £10,000 in debtors, the £20,000 in work in progress and the £2,000 as a payment in advance, with no corresponding 'closing' figures for the previous year.

The amount of her adjustment is therefore a positive figure of:

£10,000 + £20,000 − £2,000 = £28,000.

Without the adjustment charge the debtors of £10,000 and the work in progress of £20,000 are not taxed. For example, the debtors are not taxed under the cash basis regime because nothing was paid in that period; and they are not taxed under the earnings basis regime because they earned before this period started. So they are added in arriving at the Case VI charge. The £2,000 interim payment, however, is deducted to avoid a double charge. The £2,000 interim payment is taxed as part of the professional profits of both the year to 30.4.99 and the year to 30.4.00. The payment was made in the first of these years (which is on the cash basis) and earned in the second (which is on the earnings basis). But the double charge is eliminated by deducting £2,000 from the adjustment charge otherwise taxable under Case VI. (If the £2,000 was

Generally accepted accounting practice basis

> the only item in the adjustment computation, it would yield a Case II deduction, instead of a reduced Case VI charge.)
>
> Angela is entitled to spreading, so the adjustment, unless she elects otherwise, is charged as income for the tax years 1999–2000 to 2008–09 inclusive. The amount charged for each of the first nine years, again unless she elects otherwise, is the smaller of £2,800 and ten per cent of her taxable professional profits (before capital allowances) for that year. For 2008–09 any remaining uncharged amount is charged to tax.
>
> If Angela ceases business in 2003–04 then for 2004–05 to 2007–08 (ie the remaining four of the first nine years) the amount charged will be £2,800. The ten per cent profit cap no longer applies since there are no longer any profits.

1.13.3 Relief for any initial double charge

Under the old regime a professional (apart from a barrister) could not use the cash or conventional basis for the first three tax years. When the cash basis was subsequently adopted, receipts or expenses could enter into the tax computation twice: once in the earnings basis period and again in the cash or conventional basis period. In some cases the opposite could happen and receipts or expenses could drop out of any assessment. Where this has happened any net aggregate amount which can be shown to have been doubly taxed may be deducted in arriving at the catching-up charge. Such a double charge cannot arise in the case of barristers because they were able to use the cash basis from the outset.

1.13.4 New barristers

New barristers face an especially difficult time because they must practise on their own from the outset; they cannot begin at the Bar as employees. In recognition of this, new barristers are permitted to remain on the cash basis until the seventh anniversary of the start of their practice. Then they must change to the earnings basis and meet the catching-up charge in the way described above; that is, with the charge spread over ten years and limited to ten per cent of the normal profits for the first nine of those years.

The seven-year period starts when the barrister is first available for fee generating work.

Introduction

1.13.5 Partnerships

The catch-up charge is allocated to each partner by reference to their partnership share for each year that there is a catching-up charge (Method 2).

The one-tenth and ten per cent limits for the first nine years apply at the partnership level and leave a net Case VI charge for allocation to the partners.

The Case VI charge for the partnership as a whole for the first year is allocated to the individuals who were members of the partnership:

- during the 12 months ending on the date the catching-up charge is calculated, and
- who will use the profit-sharing arrangements for that 12–month period.

For later years the same approach is used except that the allocation uses the 12 months ending on the anniversary of the catching-up date which falls into the tax year. This is so even if the accounting date for the partnership changes.

Each partner remains liable for his or her share of the catching-up charge only for the period up to the date they leave the partnership. Anyone joining the partnership during the ten-year spreading period becomes liable for the share of the charge allocated to them from then on.

If the partnership business ceases altogether, those who were partners in the period immediately prior to the date of cessation continue to be liable for the charge over the remainder of the ten-year spreading period. The ten per cent profit cap will not apply because there are no longer any partnership profits.

As in the sole practitioner case, the partnership could opt to pay more than the capped and spread payment (see **1.13.2** above). All partners have to give notice before this can happen.

> ### *Example 1.2*
>
> Boris & Co. are a partnership of solicitors, with an accounting date of 30 June. Thus their last accounts on an 'old' basis were to 30.6.99, and the adjustment was calculated as at that date; suppose that it is £100,000. The partners are entitled to spreading from 1999–2000 to 2008–09 inclusive.

Generally accepted accounting practice basis

> For 1999–00 the instalment of £10,000 is apportioned according to the profit-sharing arrangements for the year ended 30.6.99. For 2000–01 the next £10,000 is apportioned according to the profit-sharing arrangements for the year ended 30.6.00. This use of 30 June continues even if the partnership accounting date changes.
>
> Thus, for example, the adjustment instalment for 2003–04 is charged on those (and only on those) who were partners at some time during the year ending on 30.6.03, and in accordance with their profit-sharing arrangements for that 12-month period.
>
> Now suppose the partnership is dissolved on 31.12.04 and the business comes to an end. For 2004–05 the apportionment is, as before, according to the profit-sharing arrangements for the year ended 30.6.04. For the remaining years, however, the apportionment is according to the profit-sharing arrangements for the period from 1.7.04 to 31.12.04.

1.13.6 Valuation of work in progress

The Inland Revenue allow various methods of recognising work in progress, since generally accepted accounting practice permits more than one method of arriving at the adjustment for work in progress in particular circumstances.

The carrying forward of only the direct costs is generally acceptable to the Revenue, but the addition of appropriate overheads is preferable. In some circumstances, generally accepted accounting practice may permit the application of the sophisticated approach to long-term contract work in progress in SSAP 9, but this is less likely to apply to professional partnerships.

In terms of identifying the cost, inspectors are instructed as follows:

> 'Those professionals who carry forward work in progress at its cost may use different valuation methods. Commonly the unbilled work of each productive employee or partner is identified from their time records. Next the elements of the cost of those jobs are identified. Some costs may be specifically identified in the valuation (see disbursements, below). Generally, however, the elements of cost to be included are subsumed into valuation rates for each productive employee and partner. Broadly, these valuation rates are arrived at by firstly identifying the applicable costs for the accounting period. Next, the valuation rates per hour are calculated by taking into account each individual's actual or estimated chargeable hours during the period excluding any profit element. These applicable costs may include:

Introduction

- the direct employee and subcontract labour costs (wages and NI) incurred on producing the work in question;
- disbursements. These are (unrecovered) expenses paid out on behalf of clients. They are normally identifiable and subject to a separate charge on the client's bill;
- sometimes the notional cost of the partner or principal engaged on the work in question, but see below; and
- a proportion of the overhead costs attributable to the work performed. Because of considerations of consistency and the "industry practice" of most professions, it is unlikely that generally accepted accounting practice would provide administrative overheads must be included.'

Sometimes the notional cost of the partner or principal engaged on the work in question is taken into account in arriving at the work in progress. If the accounts are prepared on the basis of carrying forward the costs of work in progress including the notional cost of partners' time then those notional costs should not be included for tax purposes. That is because no deduction for their cost is claimed in the profit and loss account.

But the accounts may be prepared on a long-term contract basis so that profits and losses on contracts are recognised during their currency. In such cases the partners' time costs may be a factor taken into account in measuring those profits or losses, but notional costs are not simply being carried forward. If so, an adjustment in respect of partners' time should not be made in the tax computations.

1.14 Tax Faculty guidance on work in progress valuations

The ICAEW Tax Faculty has published a guidance note (*Tax Technical Release 30/98,* November 1998) on determining the value of work in progress for professional firms, following FA 1998, s. 42 and the withdrawal of SPs A3 and A27 with effect from 2000–01.

The exercise requires the application of appropriate accounting standards. This includes the Financial Reporting Standard for Small Enterprises (FRSSE) which applies to a small partnership or sole practitioner (no two of the following limits breached: turnover not more than £2.8 million, assets not more than £1.4 million, employees not more than 50).

SSAP 9 requires a valuation at the lower of cost and net realisable value. There is no cost if the sole practitioner or partners are the only fee earners. Overheads relating to a sole practitioner's time can also be ignored.

Further, staff overheads for a sole practitioner are likely to be immaterial and can therefore be ignored. For a two-, three- or four-partner firm, they may well be immaterial depending on the partner-to-staff ratio. In larger firms a proportion of overhead costs should be included, but at the smaller end of the scale a 'rough and ready' approach is acceptable.

Net realisable value is relevant both where fees are contingent at the balance sheet date and also where recovery of work in progress values is in doubt. In the first case, eg 'no-win, no-fee' litigation, if the contingency has been satisfied when the accounts are prepared, then the cost of work in progress should be recognised; otherwise the value is nil, since there is still a reasonable chance the firm will recover nothing. If a fixed fee has been quoted, work in progress should not exceed that fee, less the estimated costs to completion.

The guidance note discusses more complex cases, such as situations where the client's position is precarious, where work in progress does not exist (eg an author who has not yet got a publishing contract) and where the contract constitutes long-term work in progress.

The note annexes draft instructions to be included in the Inspectors' Manual. These emphasise that the Revenue do not expect increased enquiries into valuations of work in progress as a consequence of the changes. Different firms in the same business may value work in progress on different bases — there is always an element of judgement and the accounting concept of materiality is relevant. If, however, the matter comes to enquiry, there should be a thorough fact-finding exercise.

1.15 Professional employments

A professional activity which is an office or employment falls within the ambit of the employment income rules (*Mitchell and Edon v Ross* (1961) 40 TC 11). In certain cases, where an individual exercises his or her profession in the course of being a director of a company, the Inland Revenue allow by concession the directors' fees paid for such professional services to be included in a Sch. D assessment on a partnership where the partner brings those fees into the partnership. This happens most commonly with solicitors and accountants (Extra-statutory Concession A37). Otherwise the demarcation is strictly observed between sources of professional income liable under Sch. D, Case II and those where an office is held, or where there is a master-and-servant relationship which falls within the employment income rules. In the case of employment income, the basis of assessment is the emoluments received in the year of assessment.

1.16 Trusteeships

A professional person, such as a solicitor, who is a trustee and is authorised under the trust deed to charge for his or her services, has to bring sums so received into the Case II computation for tax purposes (*Jones v Wright* (1927) 13 TC 221). This situation, however, should be distinguished from an annual payment given as remuneration to a trustee as such, and not in a professional capacity, which was held to be within Case III (*Baxendale v Murphy* (1924) 9 TC 76).

1.17 Payment of tax under Schedule D, Cases I and II

Under self assessment income tax is payable by two payments on account on 31 January in the relevant year of assessment and 31 July following the year of assessment, with any final liability due on the 31 January following the year of assessment. The payments on account are calculated as one-half of the total liability for the previous year of assessment. The way in which self-employed taxpayers pay their tax under self assessment represents a considerable cash flow advantage compared with the PAYE system which operates in respect of income liable to tax under the employment income rules.

1.18 Expenses

Expenses allowable in arriving at Sch. D, Case I and II profits are expenses of a revenue nature which in addition do not fall foul of any specific prohibition: the main one being that they must not fall to be disallowed as 'not being money wholly and exclusively laid out or expended for the purpose of the trade or profession' (ICTA 1988, s. 74(a)). Note that it is specifically provided that the same rules apply to trades and professions assessable under Schedule D, Case V as those applicable to Sch. D, Cases I and II, where the overseas trade or profession is carried on by an individual ordinarily resident and domiciled in the UK (ICTA 1988, s. 65(3)).

Two tax cases illustrate the limits of this rule in relation to a profession. In the case of *MacKinlay v Arthur Young McClelland Moores & Co.* [1989] STC 898 removal expenses of a partner borne by the firm which had asked the partner to move to another office were disallowed as being a personal expense of the partner, even though the move was designed to benefit the firm. Thus, there was a dual purpose to the expenditure.

In *Watkis v Ashford Sparkes and Harward* [1985] STC 451 the expenses of partners' working lunches were disallowed on the duality of purpose test, whilst expenses of a partners' conference were allowed on the basis that the hotel expenses were indivisible.

This prohibition has been the subject of many tax cases and should be contrasted with the comparable rule allowing expenses to be set against employment income where the requirement is that the expenditure should be incurred wholly, exclusively and necessarily in the performance of the duties of the employment (ITEPA 2003, s. 336).

Many cases have emphasised that the rule applicable to employment expenses must be construed narrowly so as to exclude, for instance, expenses peculiar to the situation of the particular employee and only to allow those applicable to each and every holder of the office or employment. In addition, the expenses must be incurred in the course of the employment so that, for example, the cost of attending an educational course, if it is not a condition of service, is unlikely to be allowed as an employment expense (*Humbles v Brooks* (1962) 40 TC 500). By contrast, provided the subject matter is relevant to the trade or profession so that the primary purpose of the expense is to further the commercial interests of the trade or profession, it will be allowed even if there is some incidental personal benefit (*Bentleys, Stokes and Lowless v Beeson* (1952) 33 TC 491). However, if the private benefit is more than merely incidental to the business purpose, there is a duality of purpose and the expenses would not be incurred wholly and exclusively for the profession. This does not mean that expenditure cannot be apportioned to extract a business element from a total, for instance where household expenses are higher than they would otherwise have been because of an individual's business. In that situation some of the total telephone charges have been incurred wholly and exclusively for the purposes of the business.

Under self assessment any allowable expenses incurred personally by partners must be included in the partnership tax return and not dealt with in the tax returns of the individual partners.

Introduction

1.19 Companies and professions

Can a company carry on a profession? If a profession can be carried on only by an individual or individuals holding the requisite professional qualifications (as in the case of solicitors, accountants and doctors), it cannot be carried on by a company (*CIR v Peter McIntyre Ltd* (1927) 12 TC 1006). But, as that case shows, a company can carry on a professional business, and thus it is thought can, in the case of most professions, be used to hire out the individual's professional services.

Is such a professional business a trade where the same business carried on by an individual would be the exercise of a profession? The point is not academic. Although the charge to corporation tax extends to all income, certain corporation tax provisions (principally those relating to losses) refer only to trades, and a trade for corporation tax purposes includes a vocation but not a profession (ICTA 1988, s. 6(4)(b)). Therefore if a company can carry on a profession, any loss relief is apparently concessionary, although it is inconceivable that the Inland Revenue would take this point. Because of higher rates of income tax, in the past many individuals carrying on professions have formed companies to deal with some or all of their professional activities. Thus an actor might form a company to exploit all his or her earnings or only those earned abroad. However, corporation tax at 19 per cent on the first £300,000 of taxable profit and capital gains tax on the remaining 81 per cent now produce little more than a cash flow advantage over an individual's top rate of 40 per cent on any income. Therefore, the advantage of a company now is that on retained earnings it suffers lower rates of tax than the top rate of income tax. Assuming that the personal service company legislation does not apply, consideration should be given to the formation of a company through which some of the professional activities can be carried on.

Generally, where earnings are very high, a company is still a useful vehicle for retaining earnings. Bear in mind that where an individual carries on a profession, there is often an element of goodwill. On incorporation of all or part of the business, a capital gain arises on the transfer of the right to future income or goodwill to the company. There are two methods of incorporation which avoid this charge.

1. Utilise the relief available under TCGA 1992, s. 162, where all the assets of the business except cash have to be transferred to the company. To the extent that the assets are transferred in exchange for shares in the company, any chargeable gains are then rolled over into these shares. By concession, any trade liabilities taken over are not treated as cash consideration paid by the company for this purpose.

2. Utilise the hold-over relief available under TCGA 1992, s. 165. This does not require all of the assets to be transferred to the company and is particularly suitable for the incorporation of part of the business (for instance, its overseas activities). The company takes on a reduced base value for any chargeable assets acquired.

Additionally, a company can employ an individual's spouse as a director and thus there is a greater facility for paying more earned income to, for example, a wife than would be the case if she were merely employed as a secretary. The payment, however, should not manifestly exceed the commercial rate for the duties performed, otherwise the excess is disallowed to the company (*Copeman v William Flood & Sons Ltd* (1941) 24 TC 53).

Companies can also have shareholders liable at a lower rate of tax than individuals. For instance, shares in the company could be issued to trustees of an accumulation and maintenance settlement in favour of the individual's children. If dividends are paid by the company and accumulated in the settlement, they are taxed at 25 per cent. If the small companies' rate of 19 per cent applies (as is usually the case), the same corporation tax is payable whether profits are retained or distributed.

If the settlement is made by the child's grandparents, income can be paid out for the child's maintenance and be treated as the child's income for tax purposes. Although a repayment claim can no longer be made in respect of the tax credit attached to any dividend paid to the child, if the dividend is within the child's personal allowance and basic rate band it is received effectively tax free. This form of settlement is a very attractive way of paying school fees. Note that income paid out for the child from a settlement by the parent is aggregated with the parent's income and is therefore ineffective.

Also, trading companies often still provide better pension arrangements for their directors than those which are provided under the retirement annuity and personal pension provisions for individuals with non-pensionable earnings. This arises from the fact that whereas there is an upper limit (ICTA 1988, s. 663) on allowable contributions by an individual, no such limit operates in respect of a company's contributions to fund a director's or employee's pension, provided the ultimate pension does not exceed two-thirds of final earnings from the company, normally now at least 20 years' service has been given, and the pensions cap is not exceeded. Note that a new regime is introduced by the FA 2004 with effect from 6 April 2006. This contains transitional arrangements that must be registered by (it is currently believed) 5 April 2009. Advice should be sought on the impact (if any) of these changes.

1.20 Service companies

Sometimes part of an individual's activities are transferred to a company, or a service company is set up to provide services and charges for a fee based on its costs plus a percentage of profit. The service charge must be based on the cost of services provided in the relevant period (*Stephenson v Payne, Stone, Fraser & Co.* (1968) 44 TC 507) and must not be excessive. Otherwise it falls to be disallowed in the individual's trading profit computation as not satisfying the 'wholly and exclusively' test. What is reasonable is what an outside concern would charge to provide the same services.

There is also an increasing tendency for individuals who would otherwise receive employment income subject to PAYE from a variety of sources (for instance where they hold directorships of several companies) to form their own personal service company which contracts with the relevant employer for the services of the individual. Provided the arrangements are properly entered into, the fees paid to the service company should not be subject to PAYE, which is levied only on what is paid out to the director of the personal service company by way of remuneration. Advantages include flexibility in being able to enter into individually-tailored pension arrangements, the ability to retain earnings, and to have the spouse as a director of the personal service company. From 6 April 2000, however, the new anti-avoidance legislation requiring personal service companies to account for PAYE on notional remuneration could well apply to this sort of arrangement.

In any event, care needs to be taken over the contractual arrangements between the individual and the service company, as the outcome of a recent case involving an estate agent clearly illustrates.

In *Grant v Watton* and *Andrew Grant Services Ltd v Watton*, both [1999] STI 260, Mr Grant was an estate agent. He formed a company of which he was director and controlling shareholder. That company provided services to Mr Grant's estate agency for a fee. There was no written agreement for the services. The accounts of the estate agency included a management charge, with a corresponding figure appearing in the profit and loss account of the company.

The Revenue assessed the estate agency under ICTA 1988, s. 160(1) from 1986 to 1989 on the basis that Mr Grant had received the benefit of a loan in the form of credit from the company. The Revenue assessed the company under s. 419 in respect of the years 1987 to 1994 as a close company which had made a loan to Mr Grant as a participator. The assessment was on an amount equal to such proportion of the loan as corresponded to advance corporation tax for the financial year in which the loan was made. Mr Grant and the company appealed unsuccessfully to the Special Commissioner (SpC), the case being reported as *Gold v Inspector of Taxes; HCB Ltd v Inspector of Taxes* [1998] STI 1362. Mr Grant and the company then appealed. The Revenue cross-appealed against the SpC decision as to the date on which credit was extended for the purposes of ICTA 1988, s. 160.

The High Court held that there was no evidence of agreement governing the time when payment was to be made by Mr Grant for the services provided by the service company. There was a running account. The issue with regard to the assessment related to the true construction of s. 160(5)(a) that 'loan' includes any form of credit. There was no authority on the meaning of the words, which were of wide and general meaning. The court considered that whether credit had been granted was a question of fact. Mr Grant had argued that the service company provided services as a continuous supply which was complete only at the end of the year so that there was no liability, and no credit extended, until the end of the year. That did not fit the facts. There was no agreement that the company should provide services for a year. Mr Grant had therefore received credit from the service company for the purposes of s. 160. The appeals of Mr Grant and the service company were dismissed.

The question when credit was extended was also one of fact. *Prima facie* the services were rendered from day to day, as found by the commissioner. The court agreed with the commissioner that liability under s. 160 was not excluded by Sch. 7, para. 7(b).

Section 419 applied, *inter alia*, where the relevant person had incurred a debt to the close company within s. 419(2)(a). That section could apply where a debtor became legally committed to future expenditure even if unascertained. Mr Grant incurred a debt to the service company for the purposes of s. 419. The company's appeal failed. The cross-appeal by the Revenue was allowed.

1.21 Overseas work and companies

The rules for employments, but not for Schedule D trades and professions, used to allow the possibility of a 100 per cent deduction for earnings attributed to work overseas, and it was sometimes advantageous to form a company to employ the individual to carry out overseas work which would otherwise be part of his or her trading or professional activities fully liable to UK tax. However, the 100 per cent deduction was abolished in 1998 and since then the overseas earnings are tax-free only if the individual is non-resident at the relevant time.

Introduction

Companies cannot be used to convert income into capital gains on a short-term basis. Where the company is formed to exploit the earning capacity of an individual and it accrues income at a lower rate of tax than that which would have been suffered by the individual, and the shares are then realised for a capital sum which represents no more than those earnings, the capital sum is likely to be taxed as income under Sch. D, Case VI (ICTA 1988, s. 775). Specific reference is made to this provision in more detail where appropriate.

In considering any scheme for minimising UK tax on overseas income in the hands of an individual ordinarily resident in the UK, it is also important to consider whether there is any likelihood that the Inland Revenue will set aside the arrangements and tax the income as the individual's own income under the very wide-ranging anti-avoidance provisions concerning transfers of income abroad in ICTA 1988, s. 739. For this reason many arrangements for such individuals make use of a UK-resident company so that the section cannot apply.

1.22 Interest

Numerous attempts have been made to claim interest and other investment income as earned income that is immediately derived from the carrying-on of the profession (ICTA 1988, s. 833(4)). In the case of both estate agents (*Aplin v White* (1973) 49 TC 93) and solicitors (*Northend v White & Leonard and Corbin Greener* [1975] STC 317), this claim has failed. A limited exception is mentioned in **Chapter 4**. This is now relevant for enabling the income to be used for retirement annuity and personal pension purposes as being relevant earnings; note that from 6 April 2006 the provisions of FA 2004 will alter this position. Such interest might nevertheless be treated as trading profit for the purposes of loss relief under ICTA 1988, s. 385(4), although it is unlikely that professionals in receipt of such interest would have losses that they needed to relieve.

Chapter 2   Creative artists

2.1 Copyright

To appreciate the taxation position of artists and writers, it is necessary to consider the nature of copyright and the methods of exploiting it.

Copyright is a form of property that confers protection from unlawful reproduction or performance of artistic works. Copyright owners alone have a right to exploit or to grant to others the right to exploit the work in the various ways open to them. The copyright normally exists for 70 years after the death of the author. Copyright covers literary works, dramatic and musical works, artistic works (paintings, sculptures, drawings, engravings and photographs), films and records. So far as British copyright is concerned, the Copyright, Designs and Patents Act 1988 – and for works created prior to commencement of the 1988 Act the Copyright Act 1956 – permits the various rights of reproduction or publishing not only to be licensed but also to be assigned separately from each other. The owner can thus exploit copyright broadly in one of three ways.

1. Assign it in respect of all or any one or more of the rights in it (for instance, for a period of time within the life of the copyright or in relation to any one or more of the territories covered by it) in consideration of a lump sum.

2. Grant in consideration of a lump sum a licence or an interest in the copyright: that is, the copyright is retained but permission is granted to do certain things that would otherwise infringe the copyright — for instance, to reproduce a book in paperback form.

3. Receive royalties for the use of the copyright by someone else.

Only sums received under 3 are income in the hands of a person who is not a professional author. A professional author, for whom copyright is part of his or her circulating capital, is taxed under Sch. D, Case II on anything received for the exploitation of copyright (*Glasson v Rougier* (1944) 26 TC 86, and *Billam v Griffith* (1941) 23 TC 757).

What constitutes a copyright 'royalty' has been the subject of numerous tax cases. As was said in the leading case of *Withers v Nethersole* (1948) 28 TC 501, if a sum is arrived at by reference to the number of times something is used or reproduced, it is likely to be a royalty as opposed to a payment for the acquisition of the property itself or any of the rights attaching to it. Because Miss Nethersole had given up her profession many years previously and made a partial assignment of her copyright as opposed to a licence to use it, this was 'a sale of property by a person who is not engaged in the trade or profession of dealing in such property, and the proceeds of such a sale is . . . untaxable capital'. See also *CIR v Longmans Green & Co. Ltd* (1932) 17 TC 272 and *Beare v Carter* (1940) 23 TC 353.

2.2 Gifts of copyright

Copyright is important for another reason. Until 2000–01 professional authors liable under Sch. D, Case II on their income were invariably assessed on a cash basis. As well as providing flexibility on time receipts and thus income, the cash basis meant that no account was taken of stock and work in progress in their accounts. In any event, it was decided in *Mason v Innes* (1967) 44 TC 326 that authors do not have stock in trade and so copyright can be given away without attracting the sort of charge applicable to an ordinary trader giving away stock under the principle established in *Sharkey v Wernher* (1955) 36 TC 275. This means effectively that any such gift, although potentially attracting inheritance tax, does not give rise to income tax. The withdrawal of the cash basis does not affect this novel method of avoiding tax on the gift of copyright.

A gift of copyright can also attract relief from capital gains tax under the holding-over gains provisions on gifts of business assets in the case of a professional author (TCGA 1992, s. 165). Therefore, if the copyright is given away before it has proven value or is assigned in works still in preparation, as is possible under the Copyright Acts, this provides a useful means of spreading income around a family at no cost in terms of inheritance tax if it is a potentially exempt transfer and with no capital gains tax. A copyright may, for instance, be settled on accumulation and maintenance trusts for the benefit of an author's children. However, bear in mind that once the right to royalties is assigned by the author, the royalties become annual payments taxable usually under Sch. D, Case III on the recipient under ICTA 1988, s. 18(3) and, therefore, should be paid under deduction of tax under ICTA 1988, ss. 348 and 349 (*Hume v Asquith* (1969) 45 TC 251).

In one case, *Lawrence v CIR* (1940) 23 TC 333, royalties accruing to a charitable trust from the works of T. E. Lawrence were assessable under Case VI although they were still regarded as annual payments. If the assigned royalties derive from a foreign publisher under a foreign contract, they are assessable under Case V. Therefore, the author should not assign royalties on their own to a company, otherwise he or she is converting earned income into investment income of an investment company which could be regarded as a close investment-holding company (ICTA 1988, s. 13A).

The small companies' rate is not available to such a company. Before 6 April 1999 the Inland Revenue could also deny repayment of the tax credit attaching to any dividend paid by the company selectively to shareholders who are not liable to tax (such as minor children), or dividends utilising special classes of shares or waivers by other shareholders (ICTA 1988, s. 231(3A)). Since 6 April 1999 the tax credit on such dividends is in any event non-repayable.

2.2.1 Sale of copyright by estate

As copyright normally continues only for 70 years following the author's death, any right sold after 20 years is exempt from capital gains tax as it is a wasting asset since its life will then be less than 50 years.

2.3 Income or capital

It is important to establish for tax purposes whether a sum of money received in connection with a work of art is income or capital and, if it is income, the correct taxation treatment of that income for the purposes of allowing expenses.

In March 2001 the Inland Revenue published a *Technical Note: Reform of the taxation of intellectual property*. The proposals included the adoption of an accounts-based system of taxing copyrights for both authors, etc. and for investors. Such a change would be disadvantageous in the majority of cases. In the event, it was only companies that were affected by changes to the rules for taxing intellectual property (adopting an accounts basis from 1 April 2002).

2.4 Categories of creative artists for tax purposes

Authors and other producers of works of art fall into three broad categories for tax purposes.

2.4.1 Non-professional creative artists

Category 1 includes those who have not produced any work before and have not produced any subsequent work, at least on a regular and organised basis, such as politicians writing their memoirs. They are clearly not carrying on a profession. Any manifestly income payments they receive, such as royalties, are assessed under Sch. D, Case VI on the receipts basis (and treated as earned income for investment income surcharge purposes). It may be possible to spread these sums for assessment purposes (ICTA 1988, s. 534).

Problems can arise over the allowance of certain expenses against any such income, as in strictness many of the expenses, such as the cost of materials, travelling and research, may be incurred on preparatory work or in producing an income earning asset and thus be either capital expenditure or incurred in a year before income first arises. The special relief for pre-trading expenditure under which it is deemed to be incurred on the first day of trading is extended to professions and vocations, but not to casual income assessable under Case VI. In practice, the Inland Revenue usually allow more than the current revenue expenses incurred in the fiscal year in which the first payment is received. However, to avoid having to rely on concessions, defer as much as possible of any expenditure until the fiscal year in which income first arises, or alternatively negotiate an advance payment of royalties to cover such expenses.

Any lump sum received for an outright sale of the copyright or associated rights is capital (*Beare v Carter*) and falls within the capital gains tax provisions; but, of course, any revenue expenditure is not then allowable in arriving at any such capital gains tax liability. The sum is capital on the principles expounded in the case of *Earl Haig's Trustees v CIR* (1939) 22 TC 725, under which lump sums received for exploitation of a person's personal property protected by copyright, which involve alienation of some of the rights attaching to the property, are capital sums where the person is not a professional author.

In the above case, materials from the diaries of Earl Haig were incorporated in a book written by an outside author with the profits of the work being shared between the author and Earl Haig's estate. It was held that this constituted the sale of a valuable part of the property itself. The trustees were in fact free to make such other use of the diaries as they could so that there was no outright assignment of the publishing rights in them, but the reasoning in the case was that little further use could be made by the trustees of the diaries so that effectively their capital asset had been destroyed.

Not all lump sums received by someone who is not a professional writer are capital, and what is being paid for has to be carefully analysed to see if there is a disposal outright of intellectual property. The case of *Alloway v Phillips* [1979] STC 452 illustrates this. In this case, the wife of one of the Great Train Robbers sold her story to a national newspaper, and was assessed under Case VI on the sum she received. The court upheld the assessment apparently because nothing akin to the disposal of copyright was involved, but she made a profit of an income nature out of the contract with the newspaper. The fact that she was not resident at the time did not protect her from liability as the contract was with a British newspaper, and therefore the source of the profit was property in the UK under ICTA 1988, s. 18(1)(a)(iii). A professional author who is not resident and carries on writing wholly abroad should not similarly be caught for the reasons mentioned at **2.8**.

This decision followed two earlier cases where there was in essence a performance of services rather than a sale of copyright by someone who was not a professional author. Thus in *Hobbs v Hussey* (1942) 24 TC 153 a series of newspaper articles gave rise to profits assessable under Case VI, although they were the only literary activity of the cricketer, on the basis that although there was an implicit sale of copyright involved, it was a case essentially of a performance of services. Similarly, in the case of *Housden v Marshall* (1959) 38 TC 233 the taxpayer provided information for articles ghosted by a journalist and was assessed under Case VI.

2.4.2 Casual authors

Category 2 includes those who exploit their artistic talents on a casual basis. Their earnings of an income nature (fees, commissions, royalties, etc) are also assessed under Case VI, but there is usually sufficient recurrence of income to cover expenses (which are more likely not to be preparatory expenses if the income is recurring) and is thus treated as deriving from one continuing source and there being not merely one work or project under consideration. Any deficiency in this instance is carried forward against future Case VI income.

Any sums for the sale of the property in the work remain capital on the same basis as in category 1.

2.4.3 Professional authors

Category 3 covers professional authors, etc, who are taxed on all their receipts as income liable under Sch. D, Case II, including lump sum receipts from the sale of copyright or royalties (*MacKenzie v Arnold* (1952) 33 TC 363; *Household v Grimshaw* (1953) 34 TC 966; *Howson v Monsell* (1950) 31 TC 529). Equally, advance royalties receivable, unless they are returnable and are in the nature of a loan, are assessable when received (*Taylor v Dawson* (1938) 22 TC 189).

It was established from the cases of *Purchase v Stainer's Executors* (1952) 33 TC 367 and *Carson v Cheyney's Executors* (1958) 38 TC 240 that in whatever form earnings reached an author, they were either taxable as professional income under Case II or not liable to income tax at all. This meant that anything received after cessation of the profession escaped income tax liability altogether until the post-cessation receipts legislation was enacted.

2.5 Post-cessation receipts

Anything earned before cessation is now caught either by ICTA 1988, s. 103 or s. 104. Section 103 catches anything due to the author by the time of cessation but not received until afterwards, and s. 104 catches any professional earnings receivable after cessation but not brought into profits on the earnings basis before cessation. (Abolition of the cash or conventional basis of accounting normally means that s. 104 is no longer relevant.) Note that ss. 103 and 104 do not apply to lump sums received after death by the personal representatives of an author as consideration for the assignment by them of the copyright (ICTA 1988, ss. 103(3)(b) and 104(1)). Such sums are liable to capital gains tax subject to a deduction for any opening value brought into the author's estate for inheritance tax purposes.

2.6 Deductions

In computing liabilities under Case II or Case VI the allowable deductions may include the reasonable expenses of producing the literary, etc. works and the expenses, including agents' commission, incurred in putting them on the market. Where the assessment is under Case VI, it should be described as, for example, 'literary earnings'. It was held in *Curtis Brown Ltd v Jarvis* (1929), 14 TC 752–753 that the rules of Cases I and II should normally be followed, so far as they are applicable.

2.7 Losses

The advantage of being classed as a professional author is that any loss incurred is available to offset against other income of the same or following year under ICTA 1988, s. 380 (or carried back under ICTA 1988, s. 381 if incurred in the first four years) or against capital gains under FA 1991, s. 72, as opposed to being a Case VI loss which is available only against Case VI income. The Inland Revenue therefore generally resist any attempt to claim Case II treatment by someone who has another main source of earned income until it is shown there is a profit-seeking motive, and the work is sufficiently sustained and combined with systematic attempts to market the completed works as to indicate a profession is being carried on. Care should be taken not to be too zealous in seeking such Case II treatment in case the losses that are claimed for set off become in future years substantial profits. Whilst the person who is assessed under Case VI on any income has an opportunity to realise a capital gain on the sale of any copyright, the professional author does not have this opportunity.

2.8 Effect of changes of residence

Whether a person is a professional author or assessable under Case VI and liable to capital gains tax, that person may still receive substantial sums free of UK tax if he or she ceases to be resident and ordinarily resident in the UK. If a person not carrying on a profession ceases to be resident and ordinarily resident in the UK before signing a contract to sell the copyright, he or she is exempt from capital gains tax on the sale proceeds. It used to be possible to avoid capital gains tax in this way by a period of temporary non-residence, but it is now necessary to become non-resident for at least seven tax years before being exempt from capital gains tax. A professional author does not cease to carry on a profession by going to reside abroad but merely carries on the same profession in a different country (*Davies v Braithwaite* (1933) 18 TC 198 and *Fry v Burma Corporation Ltd* (1930) 15 TC 113). Thus, if authors can defer receiving substantial sums of income until after the accounting period ending in the year in which they cease to be resident and, provided they continue to carry on their profession abroad, in the final year of residence they are assessed on the current year's earnings and the high earnings should escape UK tax.

The same principle applies if an author spends one year completely outside the UK, accompanied by his or her family, and receives high income in that year and continues writing abroad, following the principles established in the Dave Clark case (*Reed v Clark* [1985] STC 323).

However, authors should ensure that they do not retain any fixed base in the UK from which they continue to write and publish such work in the UK, as even if they are regarded as residents of another country under the relevant double tax treaty, such treaties do not normally exempt from tax professional earnings of non-residents if they derive from activities carried on from a fixed base in that country. Such income is in most cases still liable to UK tax as Case II income.

In any event, changes in residence status will trigger a deemed commencement or cessation for the purposes of assessing business profits under ICTA 1988, s. 110A.

Authors should not suffer UK tax at source on copyright royalties as, following the decisions in *Jarvis v Curtis Brown Ltd* (1929) 14 TC 744 and *Carson v Cheyney's Executors*, these are part of their professional receipts and not income from property. Therefore ICTA 1988, s. 536, which provides for deduction of tax at source from royalties paid to those whose usual place of abode is outside the UK, should not be applicable as the royalties will have lost their identity as royalties and become part of the continuing professional receipts of the author who is carrying on his or her profession abroad, rather than be derived from the copyright as an independent asset. For their own protection, the payers are advised to obtain the Inland Revenue's confirmation before making such payments without deduction of tax. This interpretation of the law was confirmed in a Parliamentary answer (*Hansard* Vol 791 Col 31).

2.9 Income spreading provisions (up to 5 April 2001)

Where a receipt ranks as income of an artist, sculptor or writer, it is dealt with more generously than that of other professions where income can also arise unequally between one year and another.

A contract for royalties is between the author and the publisher, not the reading public, and in the case of an established writer the contract with the publisher often provides for advances on account of royalties and the royalties themselves can be paid by the publisher at intervals to suit the author. Thus, where a person produces a new book and the commercial success of each book is assured, a flexible form of continuing contract with the publisher avoids a concentration of income.

However, the position is different in the case of the author who receives a disproportionately large sum for one work or whose income is irregular because he or she writes more intermittently. To ensure that income is spread in such circumstances, a measure of relief is provided under ICTA 1988, s. 534. The author may claim that the payment should be spread back over two years (if the work took between 12 and 24 months to produce) or over three years (if the work took more than 24 months to produce). This deemed receipt is brought into the accounts for the purposes of computing the Case II profit of that year. The relief is given to an author of a literary, dramatic, musical or artistic work. A company formed to exploit an author's literary work cannot claim, as authorship can be attributed only to an individual or individuals.

The relief also applies to royalties, except where they are receivable more than two years after the first publication of the work (ICTA 1988, s. 534(4)(b)). In the case of royalties the relief is appropriate only where an amount on account of or in satisfaction of royalties is received in one sum. This relief is thus given to someone who is not a professional author in receipt of royalties which are bunched together.

The provision generally is operative only where an amount is received in respect of one identifiable work rather than a series of separate novels, etc for which payment is received on completion of the last one (ICTA 1988, s. 534(7)).

To cover the different situation of the professional author who may be past the peak of earning capacity, s. 535 provides that spreading may be claimed where such a person sells for a lump sum residual copyrights in his or her works which have been before the public for not less than ten years. Such a receipt is usually brought into the profits for a single year and even if it came in as a post-cessation receipt after discontinuation of the profession, it still attracts liability in a single year subject to any relief by reference to the author's age under ICTA 1988, s. 109. To avoid this situation, where the copyright in such works is assigned or an interest in the copyright is granted for a period of more than two years but less than six years, a claim may be made for the receipt to be spread forward from the date of receipt by dividing it by the number of years for which it is granted, and deeming it to be received in equal instalments over the period. Where the assigned or granted period is six years or more, the receipt is similarly spread forward over a maximum of six years.

If, exceptionally, the author is not treated as carrying on a profession but is assessed on such sums under Case VI, or where the sums are treated as post-cessation receipts assessable under Case VI, any deductible expenses are allowed exclusively against the amount to be spread (ICTA 1988, s. 535(8)).

Creative artists

As this relief is limited to cases where the first occasion on which the work or reproduction of it is published, performed or exhibited, is not less than ten years before assignment, etc it is important for the author to wait for the expiry of this period before contracting to receive such a sum.

Under self assessment a claim for income spreading under ss. 534 or 535 must be made within the 12 months after 31 January following the tax year in which the income arises. Where the income is spread backwards under s. 534, the increase in the taxable income of the earlier tax years does not affect the payment on account for later years. Rather the tax on the spread income continues to be tax of the year in which the income arises, albeit calculated by reference to the earlier year. Where, however, the income is spread forward under s. 535 the relevant amount is treated as taxable income in each of the later tax years.

2.10 Income averaging provisions (from 6 April 2000)

FA 2001 replaced the income spreading provisions (see **2.9**) with a simpler system that allows creative artists to average their profits over consecutive years. The new rules are contained in ICTA 1988, s. 85A and Sch. 4A.

The system is similar to the one that already exists for farmers (see **Chapter 25**).

Under this system individual taxpayers (whether sole proprietors or partners) can make a claim to average the profits of two or more consecutive years of assessment if those profits are:

- derived from a trade, profession or vocation whose profits are mainly earned from creative activities, and
- the profits are taxable under either Case I or II of Sch. D.

An averaging claim can be made if the profits of the lower year are less than 75 per cent of the profits of the higher year. The first years that can be averaged are 2000–01 and 2001–02.

An individual may use averaging for profits earned from a qualifying trade, profession or vocation.

A trade, profession or vocation is 'qualifying' if the taxpayer's profits from it are derived wholly or mainly from qualifying creative works created (or intended to be created) by the taxpayer personally, or, if activity is carried on in partnership, by one or more of the partners personally, and the profits are chargeable to income tax under Case I or II of Sch. D.

'Creative works' are defined as literary, dramatic works or designs. In *Help Sheet IR234* the Inland Revenue state that artistic works includes paintings and sculptures but not works of craft such as furniture.

The phrase 'intended to be created' is included to cover the case where an author receives an advance before a work is written.

The new rules apply to people with income from trades or professions. Like the rules for farmers, they do not apply to the years in which the source of income commenced or ceased. They do not apply to isolated receipts dealt with under Case VI of Sch. D.

As with the previous reliefs for backwards spreading, claims are made in the return for the later of the two years concerned and are given effect by adjusting the tax liability of that later year. The time limit is the finality date for the return for the later year which is equivalent to the present time limit for backwards spreading claims.

The new rules allow people who qualify to average their profits for consecutive tax years.

Example 2.1

An author's profits are:

Year 1   £3,000

Year 2   £45,000

In the first of these years the author might have unused allowances and in the second she might be liable to tax at the higher rate of 40 per cent. Averaging would result in the tax bill being computed as if the profits were £24,000 each year so the personal allowances would all be used and the higher rate liability would be eliminated.

By contrast with the old spreading rules there is no requirement that the claimant must have taken more than 12 months to create the work.

Spreading of income receivable before 6 April 2001 is not affected by the new rules.

It is possible to apply the spreading rules to income arising in 2000–01 and then also to average that year under the new rules with 2001–02.

If the author or artist makes a claim (from April 2003) for tax credits, the income for tax credit purposes will include the Sch. D, Case I profits disregarding any averaging claims. Thus in the example above the author could be entitled to a significant amount by way of tax credits in Year 1 but only a minimal amount (or none at all) in Year 2.

2.11 Public lending right

The provisions relating to copyright royalties comprising returns by payers, post-cessation receipts, averaging or spreading reliefs and deduction of tax where the owner is resident abroad, also apply to cover payments of royalties made to authors in respect of the borrowings of their books from public libraries (ICTA 1988, s. 537).

2.12 Painters and sculptors

Section 538 of ICTA 1988 provided a companion relief to s. 534 for those who dispose of their works outside the copyright field or work on a commission or fee basis — for example painters or sculptors where the copyright normally belongs to the person commissioning the work. The only difference is that the relief is available even if the actual work sold took less than 12 months to create, provided it is one of a number of works of art for an exhibition which took more than 12 months to complete. This relief is repealed for payments receivable after 5 April 2001. From that date, the rules outlined above for creative artists apply equally to painters and sculptors (see **2.10**).

2.13 Disposals of works of art subject to capital gains tax and inheritance tax

It is worth noting in conclusion that, in the case of the disposal of a chattel such as a tangible work of art, or books, papers and documents other than by a professional artist or author, capital gains tax is payable only where the proceeds exceed £6,000 (TCGA 1992, s. 262). There are also exemptions from inheritance tax (Inheritance Tax Act 1984 (IHTA 1984), s. 30) and capital gains tax (TCGA 1992, s. 258) for gifts of works of art which are held to be of national importance and provided certain conditions are met. Since, on the basis of the case of *Mason v Innes* a charge to income tax cannot arise on the gift of a work of art, these exemptions from capital gains tax and inheritance tax may, where the professional artist donates a work to a museum or gallery, make the gift free of all taxation.

It was held in *Wain's Executors v Cameron* [1995] STC 555 that the proceeds of sales by authors of manuscripts are Case II receipts. However, works such as diaries might be capital assets.

In any event, note that the Capital Taxes Office generally resist the granting of business property relief on personal copyrights on the basis they are not part of a 'business', but stem from a vocation which does not have a sufficiently commercial motivation behind it. This is now of course particularly relevant when 100 per cent relief from inheritance tax may be at stake.

2.14 Taxation of awards

2.14.1 General principles

The Inland Revenue seem to have changed their policy towards taxation of artists and authors in receipt of *ex gratia* payments from the Arts Council and other patrons. This doubtless reflects a considerable increase in the size of these awards since the previous arrangement was concluded, whereby the Inland Revenue did not seek to tax such awards provided that they were unsolicited and that the award did not represent payment for work to be carried out by the recipient.

However, the Inland Revenue seem no longer prepared to provide a blanket agreement, and will look at each award on its merits. On this basis, the fact that such payments are entirely gratuitous would not prevent their forming part of the taxable receipts of the donee's profession or vocation. Cases such as *Smart v Lincolnshire Sugar Co. Ltd* (1937) 20 TC 643 could enable the Inland Revenue to sustain an assessment where the awards were intended artificially to supplement the artist's professional receipts.

Although the Inland Revenue have lost a case before the Special Commissioners where they attempted to tax the winner of the Whitbread Award, this may not deter them from taxing other awards made by firms to publicise their good names as patrons of the arts. It is understood, however, that the MAN Booker Prize will remain unchallenged, presumably because it is considered to be awarded as a mark of honour to the individual. In particular, unsolicited awards from such bodies as charitable trusts in memory of famous individuals should be claimed as exempt from tax on the basis they are personal awards to an individual and usually not part of any commercial arrangement with the author. It appears, for instance, that it has been agreed that awards made by the Airey Neave Memorial Trust to authors are not taxable. Similarly, the Nobel Prize for Literature is not taxable.

2.14.2 Taxation of awards and bursaries made by the Arts Council

The Arts Council and the Inland Revenue have agreed on the tax treatment of awards and bursaries which the Council makes to artists, writers, photographers, musicians and performing artists. Agreement of the tax treatment of the awards, etc. does not impinge on the rights of appeal against an assessment to tax on any individual receipt of an award or bursary.

Arts Council awards and grants fall into two broad categories. Awards in respect of training schemes, or to enable creative artists to devote time to research and development are non-taxable. Grants afforded in respect of specific non-training projects are taxable.

Awards and bursaries made by the Arts Council fall to be treated for tax purposes in the following categories.

Category A Awards and bursaries chargeable to tax

1. Direct or indirect musical, design or choreographic commissions and direct or indirect commissions of sculpture and paintings for public sites.
2. The Royalty Supplement Guarantee Scheme.
3. The contract writers' scheme.
4. Jazz bursaries.
5. Translators' grants.
6. Photographic awards and bursaries.
7. Film and video awards and bursaries.
8. Performance art awards.
9. Art publishing grants.
10. Grants to assist with a specific project or projects (such as the writing of a book) or to meet specific professional expenses such as a contribution towards copying expenses made to a composer, or to an artist's studio expenses.

Category B Awards and bursaries not chargeable to tax

1. Bursaries to trainee directors.
2. In-service bursaries for theatre directors.
3. Bursaries for associate directors.
4. Bursaries to people attending full-time courses in arts administration (the practical training course).
5. In-service bursaries to theatre designers and bursaries to trainees on the theatre designers' scheme.
6. In-service bursaries for administrators.
7. Bursaries for actors and actresses.
8. Bursaries for technicians and stage managers.
9. Bursaries made to students attending the City University arts administrative courses.
10. Awards, known as the Buying Time Awards, made, not to assist with a specific project or professional expenses, but to maintain the recipient to enable him or her to take time off to develop personal talents. These at present include the following awards and bursaries: Theatre Writing Bursaries, Awards and Bursaries to composers, Awards and Bursaries to painters, sculptors and print makers, Literature Awards and Bursaries.

The Arts Council can make both a grant in A 10 and an award in B 10 to an individual and, in such a case, part only of the sum received by the individual concerned is treated as taxable. However, it is agreed in relation to these cases that if the expenditure incurred by the individual in connection with the matters covered by the A 10 grant and the B 10 award exceeds the amount of the A 10 grant, the excess up to and including the amount of the B 10 award is regarded as covered by the B 10 award, and to this extent is not allowable as a deduction in arriving at taxable profits. The remainder of any of the expenditure is subject to the normal Sch. D expenses rules.

The Inland Revenue will follow these arrangements (whilst the law remains as it is) in cases involving awards both for future assessments and in settlement of appeals now open. The Arts Council will, in making future awards, inform the recipient of the category applicable for tax purposes.

Note that this agreement was published in relation to awards current in September 1979. Further types of award have been instituted since this, so contact the Arts Council for details of the taxation treatment of any such award.

Creative artists

2.14 Pension arrangements

There is a special pension scheme for authors: refer to the Writers' Guild Scheme for details. In particular, it copes with the problems of uneven earnings and early retirement.

Chapter 3 Entertainers

3.1 One profession: basis of assessment

An entertainer is assessed to income tax, in accordance with the level and return of his or her activities, in one of the following ways.

1. If carrying on an unpaid vocation, or hobby, and only charging for expenses, and there is no contract of or for services, the entertainer is unlikely to be assessed at all. He or she is also unlikely to be able to claim any form of loss relief if expenses exceed income.

2. If, although making a more realistic charge than the entertainer in 1 above, he or she does not make a living from performance but derives earnings from, say, casual club work, the Inland Revenue are likely to require that a self assessment is made under Sch. D, Case VI, to avoid any loss claims under ICTA 1988, s. 380. Alternatively, the Inland Revenue may accept that the entertaining amounts to a Sch. D, Case II source but will allow the carry forward of losses under ICTA 1988, s. 385 only against earnings from the same source as it amounts to an uncommercial professional activity (ICTA 1988, s. 384).

3. There may be a specific employment contract, for example a musician's contract with an orchestra. Alternatively, the entertainer may be director of his or her own service company. In such cases, the entertainer is assessed under ITEPA 2003 (employment income) in respect of remuneration from the company.

4. Most full-time professional entertainers are assessed under Sch. D, Case II. They are deemed to carry on one profession for tax purposes (see *Davies v Braithwaite* (1933) 18 TC 198), even if their activities are partly carried on outside the UK in the year in question. But see **3.9.1** below regarding entertainers who are working under standard Equity ('Esher') contracts.

This means that, if actors or singers cease to be UK-resident, their profession does not cease although they may no longer be within the scope of UK tax. Thus, in *Reed v Clark* (1985) 58 TC 528, the singer Dave Clark escaped tax on his previous year's earnings by residing in Los Angeles throughout the year 1978/79. As he neither resided in the UK in 1978/79, nor exercised his profession at any time in the UK in that year, there was no head of charge to tax on those earnings (which would otherwise have been assessed in 1978/79), nor was there a discontinuance of his profession in 1977/78.

However, changes in residence status will today trigger a deemed commencement or cessation for the purposes of assessing business profits under ICTA 1988, s. 110A.

3.2 Overseas work

If actors have a material amount of overseas work, but remain resident and ordinarily resident in the UK, it used to be advisable to form a company to employ them for such work, so that they had, separately from their profession, an employment with the company, the duties of which could be performed abroad. They could then have claimed the 100 per cent deduction in respect of remuneration from that source, provided that they had performed those duties outside the UK for a qualifying period of at least 365 days (ICTA 1988, s. 193(1)). Unfortunately, the 100 per cent deduction was abolished in the FA 1998, so it is no longer as beneficial to set up a non-resident company through which to route the overseas work.

If using a non-resident company, its retained income is probably caught by ICTA 1988, s. 739, unless commercial reasons can be found for its formation abroad (for instance, the involvement of a local manager in the equity of the company). Some agents have a company, often based abroad, which specialises in organising the foreign earnings of such people as film and pop stars. To distinguish such an employment, a separate 'slavery' contract should be drawn up between the entertainer and the company, indicating the areas of work for which the company contracts and the relationship between the entertainer and the company in respect of such work. Where a jointly-owned company cannot be used, the accumulated earnings escape s. 739 only if the shares are held in trust for the benefit of the star's family: the star and his or her spouse must be excluded from all benefit under the settlement. In that instance, as established in *Vestey v CIR* (1979) 54 TC 503, s. 739 cannot apply. Instead, the beneficiaries, whilst they are resident in the UK, are taxed under ICTA 1988, s. 740 on any payment to them out of the trust that represents the accumulated earnings. Thus UK tax can be deferred, or eliminated altogether if the beneficiary ceases to be ordinarily resident here before receiving the payments. However, extreme caution should be exercised and specialist advice sought before such an arrangement is undertaken. There are few cases where an entertainer can circumvent both ICTA 1988, ss. 739 and 740.

Another way of isolating foreign earnings was used in the case of *Newstead v Frost* (1980) 53 TC 525. An overseas partnership was formed to receive the US income of the television personality, David Frost. It was held that his share of the profits constituted a separate source of income assessable under Sch. D, Case V. Such a separate source would not, however, attract the foreign earnings deduction from 6 April 1986, so is no longer tax-effective for those with a UK domicile.

3.3 Withholding of foreign tax at source

Entertainers may also have local tax withheld on payments to them for their overseas work, if they are not resident in the country in question. Where there is a double taxation agreement, this usually excludes them from any exemption from local tax at source.

In the case of the revised US/UK double taxation agreement, the provisions go further. Payments to UK-resident companies employing an actor may also be subject to such withholding tax: so care needs to be taken when arranging entertainers' affairs, to make sure that full credit is allowed for any foreign tax suffered against any UK tax liability. Thus if tax is withheld on a payment to a UK company, sufficient profits need to be left in charge to UK corporation tax, and not drawn out by way of remuneration, to obtain full relief for the withholding tax.

Note that where UK-resident entertainers are liable to foreign tax on a foreign tour, notification may be made to the UK Inland Revenue under the relevant double taxation agreement provision on the exchange of information.

Further information can be found in the 1987 OECD Report, *The Taxation of Income Derived from Entertainment, Artistic and Sporting Activities* issued by the Committee on Fiscal Affairs, obtainable from HMSO.

3.4 Foreign entertainers visiting the UK

With effect from 1 May 1987, ICTA 1988, ss. 555–558, and regulations drawn up thereunder (Income Tax (Entertainers and Sportsmen) Regulations 1987 (SI 1987 No. 530)), changed the rules concerning the calculation of the amount assessable on non-resident entertainers, and introduced a withholding tax scheme.

Entertainers

From 1 May 1987, any person making a payment (to any person) that is connected directly or indirectly with the UK activities of a non-resident entertainer is obliged to deduct UK basic rate income tax at source. The regulations empower the Inland Revenue to enter into arrangements with payers and artists, so a reduced or nil rate of tax is applied if the Inland Revenue are satisfied that an overpayment of tax would otherwise arise.

Applications to enter into such arrangements must be made, at least 30 days prior to the date of payment, to the Inland Revenue Foreign Entertainers' Unit at the following address: St John's House, Merton Road, Bootle, Merseyside L69 9BB Tel: (0151) 472 6488, fax: (0151) 472 6483.

A return of any connected payments, together with payment of the tax due, is made by the payer on a quarterly basis. Withholding tax need not be deducted where the total aggregate payments by a payer to any individual payee do not exceed £1,000 in a tax year. A useful Revenue booklet FEU50 deals with many of the practicalities in an easy-to-read fashion.

The scheme also applies to 'transfers', ie benefits in kind, facilities provided, loans and transfers of rights. In such cases, the amount of withholding tax is calculated by grossing up the cost of providing the 'transfer' at the basic rate of income tax, and applying the appropriate rate of withholding tax to that gross figure. The grossing up of such transfers results in higher tax being paid than if an equivalent amount was paid to the entertainer in cash.

Under the provisions of ICTA 1988, s. 555 and the Income Tax (Entertainers and Sportsmen) Regulations, an agent, sports promoter, etc. situated in the UK (the payer) is required to:

- deduct income tax at the basic rate from all relevant payments made to a non-resident entertainer or sportsperson (the payee). Such a payment may be made either directly to the payee or indirectly — for example, through a company controlled by the payee. Where the Revenue decides, a lower rate of tax may be deducted in individual cases;

- determine the cash value of any asset, such as a motor car transferred to the payee instead of or in addition to a cash payment, and treat that amount as the net sum from which tax has already been deducted, and account for the tax due on the grossed-up figure, and

- send to the Revenue a return of payments made to payees within a return period (see below), together with payment of any tax deductible within 14 days of the end of the return period.

The return periods end on:

- 30 June;
- 30 September;
- 31 December, and
- 5 April.

Regulation 11 of the 1987 Regulations provides for an assessment to be made on the payer if tax on payments to payees has not been properly accounted for on a return, or the payer has failed to pay tax due as shown by a return.

Interest is chargeable under TMA 1970, s. 87 where tax is paid late.

Payment of tax deducted by the payer is treated as a payment on account of the tax assessable on the payee, any overpayment being repaid to the payee in the normal way.

The definition of 'connected payments' (see above) is widely drawn to include sponsorship advertising and endorsement fees, but excludes payments derived from the proceeds of record sales. Such payments of royalties, including those in respect of compact discs and cassettes, are separately liable to withholding tax under the provisions of ICTA 1988, s. 539. Payments derived from the sale of video recordings are not excluded from the definition of 'connected payments', so withholding tax is chargeable. It may be possible to arrange payments so that some of the amount escapes the liability to withholding tax. For example, if an entertainer is also the director of a production, withholding tax should apply only to payments in respect of the performance as entertainer and not to his or her activities as director.

After the end of the tax year in which the relevant activity took place, the artist makes a return of taxable income and, where applicable, claims repayment of any excess tax withheld. Taxable income is calculated in the same way as under Sch. D, Cases I and II. The Inland Revenue have published Help Sheet IR303 to assist non-resident entertainers and sportspeople to complete the non-residence pages of the self assessment tax return.

Income received by certain third parties may also be attributed to and taxed on the entertainer. This treatment applies in the following circumstances:

- where the recipient is directly or indirectly controlled by the entertainer;
- where the recipient is not resident in the UK and is taxed at 25 per cent or less in the country where he or she is resident for tax purposes;

- where the payment is made to a trust of which, under the UK anti-avoidance legislation, the entertainer is regarded as the settlor, and
- where there is an arrangement in force between the recipient and the entertainer, whereby it is reasonable to suppose that the entertainer may be entitled to an amount not substantially less than the amount of the profit generated by the payment.

This legislation applies to non-resident sportspeople in the same way as it does to non-resident entertainers.

3.5 'Slavery' contracts and service companies

Entertainers often set up their own service companies, to which all earnings and royalties accrue. Typically, entertainers contract to devote the whole of their working time and professional skill to the interests of the company, and agree not to work for any other party; they agree to obey the directions of the company, or any third party to whom their services are loaned. They vest all rights in their work in the company, including copyright in products associated with their work (for example, photographs and the right to use their name, etc. on any products).

Entertainers must always give due weight to the commercial benefits or otherwise of incorporation, and these vary according to the type of entertainer, eg incorporation is probably of more commercial value for a pop star than for a West End actor.

The tax considerations are much the same as those for other businesses.

1. When individuals incorporate their business, their self-employed activities cease. There is an extended basis period for the final year of assessment, although this is compensated for by overlap relief (however, in some cases inadequate overlap relief results in high unexpected or unwanted tax liabilities).

2. Corporation tax rates are always lower than the higher rate of income tax, but any remuneration drawn from a company is subject to income tax. However, there is some scope for regulating the flow of remuneration from a company and so smoothing out major fluctuations in earnings and, therefore, in tax rates. From 6 April 2004, income paid out in dividends to non-corporate shareholders is subject to a minimum corporation tax rate of 19 per cent.

3. As employees of their own company, entertainers are subject to tax on or of their earnings from the company but if, as self-employed individuals, they are abroad for a whole tax year, they are not taxed for that year.

4. There is no longer any ceiling on employers' National Insurance Contributions (NICs). A self-employed entertainer would have to meet only Class 2 and 4 contributions. However, dividends do not attract NICs contributions.

5. There may be capital gains tax complications on incorporation.

In 1969, legislation (now ICTA 1988, s. 775) was introduced to counteract schemes under which entertainers, especially pop stars, attempted to avoid income tax by selling their services to a company in exchange for shares in the company and fixed remuneration. Care needs to be taken on incorporation not to assign valuable copyrights to the company in exchange for shares, otherwise a Sch. D, Case VI charge arises, equal to the value of the copyrights. Instead, the copyrights should be gifted to the company, making use of the *Mason v Innes* case (1967) 44 TC 326, thereby avoiding income tax on such a gift.

The Inland Revenue have challenged the one-man service company, either on *Furniss v Dawson* principles ((1984) 55 TC 324), or as a settlement, so that all accumulated earnings are attributed to the star and taxed on him or her as income. As a safeguard, a genuine commercial structure should be set up, and the earnings used where possible to acquire other businesses. If the personal service company (IR35) legislation applies to such a company, then the intermediary will have to account for PAYE and National Insurance (NI) on notional remuneration unless actual PAYE has been accounted for on payments to the individual. Clearly, such legislation has had an adverse effect on the use by entertainers, as well as other individuals, of their own one-man company.

In any event, it is essential that no corners are cut and that contracts are actually made with the service company through its sole employee. Where personal contracts are later ratified by the company and where payments due under personal contracts are paid to the company, the Inland Revenue could successfully challenge the use of the company. The correct procedure is much easier to follow where there is an agent to negotiate all contracts on the entertainer's behalf.

Entertainers

3.6 Entertainers and anti-avoidance legislation

Entertainers do not enjoy the reliefs given to writers, sculptors, etc which enable them to average their earnings for taxation purposes. Many schemes, therefore, have been devised so as to mitigate the incidence of high rates of income tax on those earnings. These have become of less interest since the top rate was reduced to 40 per cent.

In the case of *Mills v CIR* (1974) 49 TC 367, a company contracted to receive the earnings of the actor Hayley Mills from making films for the Walt Disney Studios, and all the shares of the company were settled on trust for Miss Mills until she attained her majority. The income was received by the company, on which it paid tax, and was then paid to the trust in the form of dividends. It was intended that these dividends be accumulated free of surtax, and paid out to Miss Mills as capital on her majority. The court held that Miss Mills was a settlor of the trust, as well as being the beneficiary, and that therefore the income of the trust must be treated as hers.

The lesson to be learned from this case, and from the case of *Crossland v Hawkins* (1961) 39 TC 493, is that, where shares of a company exploiting an entertainer are held by a settlement, extreme care needs to be taken to ensure that the entertainer cannot be regarded also as a beneficiary under the settlement, as he or she is always regarded as the settlor for tax purposes. The result is to cause any dividends to be assessed on the settlor as his or her income. It follows that no income must be paid out for the maintenance or education of under-age children of the settlor, as this is simply treated as part of his or her income.

In *Black Nominees v Nicol* (1975) 50 TC 229, a complicated tax avoidance scheme failed in an attempt to convert the future earnings of the actor Julie Christie into a capital sum in her hands, and the sum received was held to be income. The conversion of future earnings into a capital sum is now caught by ICTA 1988, s. 775, and any scheme that purports to exploit the earnings capacity of individuals by putting a capital sum at their disposal is also likely to be caught by s. 775.

3.7 Capital sums received by entertainers

An example of a sum that was received by an actor and held not to be income was a payment made by a film company to the actor Laurence Olivier for entering into a covenant not to act in, produce or direct any film for any other person for a specified period (*Higgs v Olivier* (1952) 33 TC 136). However, it is unwise to place much reliance on this case, as the decision does not appear to have general application. The case is not in line with a whole series of other compensation cases which indicate that, where a sum is to compensate for a temporary loss of earnings rather than to compensate for the complete destruction of the business, it is a revenue receipt. Nor was the decision followed in *White v G and M Davies* (1979) 52 TC 597, where EC payments to farmers to stop selling milk products were held to be trading income. A payment such as the one to Laurence Olivier should now be caught by ICTA 1988, s. 313, but only if made to an employee.

Unlike professional authors, actors can in fact realise a capital sum if the sum is not directly a return for their own professional work. For instance, in one case, an actor bought the film rights in a novel for £1,700, intending to treat this as an investment to compensate him for loss of earnings; however, he had to sell the film rights to × Productions Ltd because otherwise that company would not make the film. The actor starred in the film and received a salary and share of the profits from it. However, the profit on the sale of the film rights was held to be capital because it was not part of an actor's profession to dispose of copyright, and so he was realising an investment (*Shiner v Lindblom* (1960) 39 TC 367).

Although such sums should escape ICTA 1988, s. 775, see **3.22** below for the situation where entertainers also back their own show financially.

3.8 Capital allowances

Musicians may claim capital allowances in respect of their score libraries and musical instruments. Musicians need a substantial library of music, transcriptions, tapes, records and translations, and strictly, the initial cost of building up the library is a matter for capital allowances, although it may be possible to negotiate with the inspector a revenue allowance for replacements on a 'renewals' basis. The problem with claiming capital allowances on instruments is that their market value often appreciates. Many musicians like to keep their instruments when they retire so claims to capital allowances may eventually result in a substantial balancing charge, without any sale proceeds to pay the tax arising. In such circumstances, with professional income substantially reduced if not nil, the musician may be forced to sell the instrument.

3.9 Employment or a profession?

3.9.1 Tax purposes

The decision in *Davies v Braithwaite* (see **3.1** above) made it clear that a series of engagements, although each relates to a specific play or film, should not normally constitute a series of employments within ITEPA 2003. However, if a person is contracted to a company for several films, or is a permanent member of a touring company, it can be more difficult to resist the contention that the entertainer is in an employment, on the basis that a master-servant relationship exists, as in the case of the ballet dancer who worked for Sadler's Wells (*Fall v Hitchen* (1972) 49 TC 433).

The dancer in *Fall v Hitchen* was engaged under a standard 'Esher' contract, the type of contract approved by Equity. In 1989, the Inland Revenue notified the acting profession that, from 6 April 1990, they intended to assess as employment income those earnings from work performed under standard Equity contracts, quoting the decision in *Fall v Hitchen* as authority for this approach. At the same time, they announced that all existing performers who had been treated as self-employed for the three years ended 5 April 1990 would continue to be assessed under Sch. D if they so wished.

However, in 1993 two actors, Alec McCowen and Sam West, appealed to the Special Commissioners and successfully argued that their income from standard Equity theatre contracts did not fall to be taxed as employment income. The decisions were given in public and accordingly they can be openly referred to, but they are not binding on other bodies of commissioners. The Revenue did not pursue these cases to the High Court.

It is clear from these contrasting cases that the terms of the contract may not be decisive by themselves, and in the case of artistic workers, such as theatrical performers/artists, the way in which they generally carry on their profession also needs to be considered.

In *Fall v Hitchen*, Mr Hitchen was engaged for a minimum period of about six months 'to rehearse, understudy, play and dance as and where required by the Manager'. Both Mr West and Mr McCowen, however, were engaged to play a specific role in a specific play for the run of a play or a shorter fixed period. Also, both Mr McCowen and Mr West had a variety of engagements in different media (film, television, radio and theatre), consecutively and sometimes concurrently.

The type of engagement undertaken by Mr McCowen and Mr West is now much more typical of the profession than that undertaken by Mr Hitchen in 1969. These days it is comparatively unusual for a performer/artist to be engaged to play parts as and when cast in a series of different plays or other productions. The typical performer/artist is likely to have a whole series of separate engagements in different media making up his or her professional working life, commonly interspersed with periods without paid work between the end of one engagement and the commencement of another.

Other case law supports the view that, for theatrical performers/artists, independence from a particular regular paymaster may indicate that individual contracts are not contracts of employment, even though the *prima facie* view based on the particular terms of the particular engagement may suggest otherwise.

Accordingly, Sch. D assessment of a performer's/artist's earnings is normally appropriate. The sort of engagement where the employment income rules apply and PAYE is appropriate is more likely to be where a performer/artist is engaged for a regular salary to perform in a series of different productions over a period of time, in such roles as may be from time to time stipulated by the engager, with a minimum period of notice before termination of the contract, as was Mr Hitchen in *Fall v Hitchen*. This applies, for example, to permanent members of some orchestras and permanent members of an opera, ballet or theatre company. The employment income rules and PAYE apply in these cases regardless of the receipt by the performer/artist of other income correctly chargeable under Schedule D.

3.9.2 National Insurance purposes

For NI purposes, members of certain well-known orchestras were found by the courts to be self-employed (eg *Midland Sinfonia Concert Society Ltd v Secretary of State for Social Services* [1981] ICR 454), whereas in the case of *Warner Holidays Ltd v Secretary of State for Social Services* [1983] ICR 440, holiday camp entertainers were found to be employees.

The Contributions Agency has, with the encouragement of British Actors' Equity, long taken the view that entertainers engaged under Equity contracts are employees liable to Class 1 NICs. Following advice which confirmed that they had no legal authority to depart from the true legal position, the DSS issued a press release on 15 July 1998 explaining that they had been wrong all along and those who had incorrectly paid Class 1 NICs could now claim a refund. Meanwhile, to secure continuing entitlement to state benefits for entertainers, regulations were introduced to deem them to be employees for NIC purposes (SI 1998 No. 1728).

These regulations contained a self-destruction mechanism — reg. 5 provided that they ceased to have effect on 1 February 1999. From the above press release it seems that the Government intended to align the tax and NIC position of entertainers in the longer term. Presumably it was intended that appropriate consultation could be undertaken, final policy decisions made, new regulations drafted and implemented, and new guidance issued for those engaging entertainers, in the space of a six-month period during which all the officials involved in the process were preparing to deliver themselves up to the Inland Revenue. Just in time, in regulations which took effect on 31 January 1999 (SI 1999 No. 3), the DSS managed to revoke reg. 5, thus allowing a consultation period for the new rules which may if necessary be infinite, without causing 'resting' actors to starve.

It is tempting to think that when the temporary-but-now-permanent new regulations were drafted, the authors were determined to maintain the trend towards insanity represented by these rules. The definition of 'entertainer' is not too remarkable, ie 'a person who is employed as an actor, singer or musician or in any similar performing capacity'. Nor is it surprising that anyone who is employed under a contract of service or in an office with emoluments chargeable to tax under ITEPA 2003 is excluded (ie those who are employees are liable to Class 1 NICs under normal rules). Self-employed entertainers are then deemed to be employees for Class 1 NIC purposes, but not if their remuneration '(disregarding any payment in kind) does not consist wholly or mainly of salary'.

As is usual in NIC legislation it is necessary to unscramble a number of negatives in the wording. The effect is that if you are a self-employed entertainer you are caught for Class 1 NICs only if, ignoring payments in kind, you are paid wholly or mainly by salary. No special definition of salary is provided. It is quite possible that the words were simply lifted from the similar rules for ministers of religion in the Categorisation Regulations 1978 (SI 1978 No. 1689), Sch. 1, para. 5, which use the expression, 'wholly or mainly of stipend or salary'. Presumably, it was assumed that not many actors get stipends. However, the regulations were probably drafted in blissful ignorance of the way words are used in the acting profession. As is clear from the decisions in the *McCowen and West* appeals, '. . . In theatrical contracts the reward to the actor is normally called "salary" whereas in TV and film the word used is "fee"'.

Revised special NIC rules

IR *Tax Bulletin* Issue 65 June 2003 contained important details of the current NIC position for entertainers. Following the commissioners' case of *McCowen and West*, the Revenue accepted that most performers/artistes in the entertainment sector were engaged under contracts for services and were therefore assessable under Sch. D. This carried the corresponding disadvantage that the majority of entertainers would not receive universal title to contributory benefits. In order to treat the majority of entertainers as employed earners for NIC purposes, while continuing self-employment treatment for certain 'key talent' stars, regulations in 1998 created a Class 1 NIC liability for entertainers whose earnings consisted 'wholly or mainly of salary'. However, very few actors were paid in this way and therefore the 1998 regulations did not achieve the object of bringing most entertainers into Class 1. This is because it had become the usual practice for the majority of entertainers to receive as part of their remuneration package pre-purchase payments as compensation for the loss of future repeat fees and rights and royalties worth many times the salary element.

Therefore, the Social Security (Categorisation of Earners) (Amendment) Regulations 2003 (SI 2003 No. 736) were introduced, with effect from 6 April 2003: instead of a 'wholly or mainly' salary test, those entertainers whose remuneration includes any element of salary are treated as employed earners, with liability for Class 1 NIC on all earnings from the engagement (including rights payments).

The entertainer would remain self-employed and liable to Class 2 and Class 4 NIC only where the payment is a fee for the production, not a salary, which would have to be made clear in the contract.

Where an entertainer is engaged through the agency of a third party, the producer of the entertainment in respect of which the payments of salary are made is treated as the secondary contributor — though this does not override the effect of the intermediaries legislation (IR 35): where an entertainer provides his or her services to a client through a personal service company it is the latter which is the secondary contributor.

There are some exceptions: session musicians and session singers, generally engaged through Musicians Union approved contractors and whose earnings were not previously subject to Class 1 NIC, are exempted from the 2003 Regulations.

The 1998 regulations led to some entertainers being wrongly categorised as employed earners because their remuneration did not consist 'wholly or mainly of salary'. It may therefore be that for an appropriate period between 17 July 1998 and 5 April 2003 contributions have been paid in error and refund claims are now invited.

The Inland Revenue have published *Guidelines on the Special NIC Rules for Entertainers* that contain the following extract.

'SECTION A: THE SOCIAL SECURITY (CATEGORISATION OF EARNERS) (AMENDMENT) REGULATIONS 2003

1. The new regulations from 6 April 2003 reflect the fact that instead of a 'wholly or mainly' salary test, those entertainers[2] whose remuneration includes any element of salary, as defined below, will be treated as employed earners.

Once subject to the regulations there will be liability for Class 1 NICs on all earnings from the engagement (including rights payments.)

2. The new regulations are aimed at reflecting the NICs position of entertainers prior to July 1998, when there was a distinction between entertainers treated as self-employed and those treated as employed, based on the terms and conditions of their engagements. The vast majority of entertainers are engaged on the basis of payments of salary, but a small proportion of 'Key Talent' performers are paid a fee for an engagement not dependent on the time worked.

3. Where the payment is a fee for the production, not a salary — and this would have to be made clear in the contract — the entertainer will remain self-employed for NICs purposes and liable to Class 2 and Class 4 NICs.

4. For the avoidance of doubt the position with regard to liability for Class 1 NICs on rights payments after the initial contract payments have taken place is that:

    - If the initial payment was not subject to NICs because no salary element was included in the remuneration then any subsequent rights payments would not be subject to Class 1 NICs either;

    - If there was a liability for Class 1 NICs on the initial payment because any part of that payment satisfies the definition of salary then any subsequent rights payments will also be subject to Class 1 NICs.

5. 'Salary' is defined in the new regulations which requires that the following four of the five tests[1] which formed the basis of the previous legislation described in the introduction to these notes need to be satisfied:

- made for services rendered;
- paid under a contract for services;
- where there is more than one payment, payable at a specified period or interval; and
- computed by reference to the amount of time for which work has been performed.

6. The third bullet point includes those entertainers engaged on a single day or two day engagement. This means that the policy intention of ensuring that the regulations apply to film extras and walk-on parts is achieved. The last bullet point ensures that Key Talent artistes are excluded, as they will be contracted to appear in productions for which their remuneration is not directly calculated according to the period of weeks or months they are assigned to the production. Such an arrangement will be exceptional.

7. The legislation also includes provisions which amend paragraph 10 of Schedule 3 to the Social Security (Categorisation of Earners) Regulations 1978 to ensure that where an entertainer is engaged through a third party (an agency) the secondary contributor is treated as the producer of the entertainment in respect of which the payments of salary are made. However, this does not override the effect of the Intermediaries legislation (IR35) which states that where an entertainer provides his services to a client through a personal service company it is the latter which is the secondary contributor.

8. In accordance with the Revenue's policy intention Session Musicians and their deputies, who are generally engaged through Musicians Union approved contractors and their earnings were not previously subject to Class 1 NICs, are excepted from the new regulations.

9. Where there is evidence that entertainers are paid a salary but the contract is being framed in such a way as to treat the payment as a fee in order to avoid Class 1 NICs the Inland Revenue will investigate such arrangements and seek to collect any unpaid Class 1 NICs due as a result of these investigations.

Further Information

10. If engagers have any questions about the status of their workers in the light of the new legislation or any individual wishes to query their status they should contact their local Inland Revenue office. Engagers and

Entertainers

workers in the TV Industry should ring the TV Industry Unit on 0161 261 3255.

SECTION B: ARRANGEMENTS FOR CLAIMING REFUNDS OF CLASS 1 NICS PAID IN ERROR

Who can claim refunds

1. The 1998 Regulations have led to some entertainers being wrongly categorised as employed earners because their remuneration did not consist 'wholly or mainly of salary' and therefore any primary or secondary Class 1 contributions which have been paid in relation to entertainers on the footing that they were employed earners may have been incorrectly paid. There is provision under National Insurance legislation for the return of contributions which have been paid in error and refund claims will be invited for appropriate periods between 17 July 1998 and 5 April 2003.

2. The restriction on refund claims to 2 years provided for in section 19A of the Social Security Contributions and Benefits Act 1992 will be waived for the purposes of this exercise until further notice.

3. However, individuals can choose not to have their primary contributions refunded, but to let them count instead towards their Additional Pension (AP) entitlement, as if they had been correctly paid. This does not prevent the engager from seeking a refund of the wrongly paid secondary contributions or the individual notifying the Revenue that they wish to claim a refund before they reach pension age.

4. Primary Class 1 NICs refunded to entertainers will be reduced by the amount of any Class 2 and 4 contributions which were due from them as self-employed earners, and of any contribution based Jobseeker's Allowance paid on the basis of the incorrect Class 1 contributions.

How to make a claim

5. An engager or entertainer who considers that Class 1 NI contributions may have been incorrectly paid between 17 July 1998 and 5 April 2003 can apply for a refund. Claims for all tax years should be submitted together. Anyone who wishes to do so in the belief that workers previously treated as employed earners should have been regarded as self-employed should write to:

National Insurance Contributions Office,
Refunds Group, (Erroneous 4)
Room BP1001
Benton Park View,
Newcastle upon Tyne
NE98 1ZZ

Employment or a profession?

Alternatively they should telephone Refunds Group on 084591 54042 [calls will be charged at BT local rates]

Claim forms will be available on request from the beginning of July 2003 and Refunds Group will begin dealing processing applications shortly after that.

6. As an alternative to the written application form engagers may find it more convenient to submit claims for refunds by CD Rom or floppy disk. Engagers should indicate which method they prefer.

What we need to know from you

7. Please give as much information as possible when making a claim i.e. Full name of individual/ Stage Name (where appropriate)/ NI NO/ Date of Birth/ Correct address. You will also be required to declare:

   i. All Basic and Rights Payments made in each tax year for which a claim is made.

   ii. Total earnings on which NICs were deducted and total amount of NICs paid.

   iii. Amounts of employer's and employee's contributions.

   iv. The type of contract under which the individual has been engaged; if it is either of the standard BBC/Equity, ITVA/Equity or PACT/Equity contracts then, subject to IR audit requirements, no other documentary evidence of payment will be required. Contracts and/or invoices will be required in all other cases.

If information is incomplete or incorrect

8. We will be unable to proceed with your claim and you will be asked to provide the additional information.

What happens when we receive your claim

9. On receipt the claim will be registered and if sufficient information is supplied, all secondary Class 1 NICs confirmed as erroneously paid will be refunded. All claims will be dealt with in the order they are received and will be processed as soon as possible. Employees named on the claim form whom, as a result of previous refund action have already notified the Inland Revenue that they did not wish to claim a refund of primary NICs, will not be contacted but applications will be accepted from those individuals who choose not to allow their wrongly paid contributions to remain on their NI record. Please note that claims for refund of primary Class 1 NICs from individuals will not be processed until the bulk of the refund claims from engagers have been processed.

Entertainers

How do I know if I am entitled to claim a refund?

10. If Class 1 NICs have been paid between 17 July 1998 and 5 April 2003 in respect of entertainers whose remuneration does not satisfy the 'wholly or mainly of salary' criteria in the 1998 regulations then the engager is entitled to apply for an immediate refund of those contributions. For example remuneration made up of 60% Rights Payments and 40% Salary would not be 'wholly or mainly of salary' and there would have been no liability for Class 1 NICs. However, Class 1 NICs were properly payable in cases where, at the time of the engagement, it was known that the salary element of the remuneration exceeded any residuals. There is less certainty in cases where the salary exceeds the fee element at the time of the engagement but further royalty and residual payments are made as and when they arise resulting in the rights payments ultimately exceeding the salary level. Revenue is seeking legal advice on this issue and a further announcement will be made soon as to whether claims for refunds can be made on this basis.

11. The following table should help you decide whether or not the various elements of remuneration under any of the standard BBC/Equity, ITVA/Equity or PACT/Equity contracts satisfy the case law definition of salary (see [above]):

Type of payment	*Salary/Rights payment*
Engagement fee	Salary or Rights payment depending on contract type
Attendance days	Salary
Standby days	Salary
Holiday pay	Salary
Overtime	Salary
Additional use fee	Rights payment for pre-purchase
Retainer	Salary — to ensure services available when needed
Royalty	Rights payment — at each sale of programme
Residual	Rights payment — either pre-purchase or at each sale
Option fee	Rights payment — to ensure an engager has priority use of an entertainer's services

12. If you are in any doubt about the categorisation of entertainers you have engaged or you are an entertainer yourself and wish to query your own

position then contact your nearest Inland Revenue office and ask to speak to a member of the Status team. Enquiries about entertainers engaged by TV Broadcasting Companies should be made to the TV Industry Unit on 0161 261 3255.

Notes

1   There is no statutory definition of the word 'salary'. Remuneration does, however, have to have all of the following characteristics to be regarded as 'salary':

- It is paid for services rendered or to be rendered
- It is paid under some contract or appointment
- It is computed by reference to time worked
- It is payable at a specified time or at specified intervals
- It is paid for regular work

The above statements are based on the cases of *Re Shine, ex parte Shine* [1892, 1 QB 522] and *Greater London Council v Minister of Social Security* [1971, 2 All ER 285]

2   Entertainer is defined in the Social Security (Categorisation of Earners) Regulations 1978 as a "person employed as an actor, singer or musician or in any similar performing capacity." This includes such professions as dancers, voice-overs and walk-on parts. TV presenters and news reporters are not regarded as entertainers for the purposes of the legislation.'

3.10   Freelance workers in the film and allied industries

As a result of discussions with various representative bodies in the industry, the Inland Revenue consider that a number of such workers, such as studio hands and people operating cameras and lights, are engaged under contracts of service, either written or oral, and should be assessed to employment income under ITEPA 2003. However, they have also accepted that a number of workers engaged in the industry are self-employed. These mainly comprise people exercising professional and technical skills on one production, for instance the producer or director, and people engaged for special effects.

In June 2003, the Inland Revenue published *Film and Television Industry Guidance Notes 2003 edition* (updating the 2001 edition) and have stated that the following are normally to be regarded as self-employed for tax purposes in the film industry:

Entertainers

- advance rigger — where the contract requires substantial provision of equipment;
- animal handler;
- animation director;
- animation production co-ordinator;
- animator — where the work is performed other than on premises provided by the engager and the contract requires substantial provision of equipment;
- animatronic model designer;
- art director;
- assistant art director — where the work is performed other than on premises provided by the engager;
- assistant costume designer — where the work is performed other than on premises provided by the engager or the contract requires substantial provision of materials;
- associate producer — except where engaged primarily for general research;
- auditioner;
- background artist — where the work is performed other than on premises provided by the engager;
- camera operator — where the contract requires substantial provision of equipment;
- cameraperson — where the contract requires substantial provision of equipment;
- casting director;
- chaperone/tutor;
- choreographer;
- composer;
- construction manager — where the contract requires substantial provision of equipment;
- continuity — where script breakdown is an integral part of the contract;
- contributor — where payment is made on a per contribution basis;

Freelance workers in the film and allied industries

- co-producer;
- costume designer — where the work is performed other than on premises provided by the engager or the contract requires substantial provision of materials;
- cricket scorer;
- director;
- director of photography;
- dressmaker — where the work is performed other than on premises provided by the engager;
- editor;
- executive producer;
- fight arranger;
- film stylist;
- first assistant director;
- gaffer — where the contract requires substantial provision of equipment;
- graphic artist — where the work is performed other than on premises provided by the engager;
- graphic designer — where the work is performed other than on premises provided by the engager;
- grip — where the contract requires substantial provision of equipment;
- hairdresser — where the contract requires substantial provision of equipment (including wigs), or 50 per cent or more of the work is performed other than on premises provided by the engager;
- head of art department;
- head of department rigger — where the contract requires substantial provision of equipment;
- language assessor — where used on an occasional basis to check style and delivery of foreign language broadcasts;
- lettering artist — where the work is performed other than on premises provided by the engager;
- lettering designer — where the work is performed other than on premises provided by the engager;

Entertainers

- lighting cameraperson — where responsible for designing lighting or photography;
- lighting director — where responsible for designing lighting or photography;
- line producer;
- location manager — where the contract requires provision of facilities by the worker;
- make-up artist — where the contract requires provision of a standard make-up kit by the worker, or 50 per cent or more of the work is performed other than on premises provided by the engager;
- matron;
- model camera — where the contract requires substantial provision of equipment;
- model designer — where the contract requires provision of equipment and materials by the worker and 50 per cent or more of the work is performed other than on premises provided by the engager;
- model maker — where the contract requires provision of equipment and materials by the worker and 50 per cent or more of the work is performed other than on premises provided by the engager;
- modeller;
- musical arranger — where the work is performed other than on premises provided by the engager;
- musical associate;
- musical copyist — where the work is performed other than on premises provided by the engager;
- musical director;
- musical score reader;
- nurse;
- photographic stylist;
- post production supervisor;
- printer — where the work is performed other than on premises provided by the engager;

Freelance workers in the film and allied industries

- producer production accountant — where the contract requires provision of relevant facilities by the worker;
- production assistant — where script breakdown is an integral part of the contract;
- production buyer;
- production designer;
- production manager;
- production supervisor;
- property master — where the contract requires substantial provision of equipment (including props);
- property hand — where the contract requires substantial provision of equipment (including props);
- provider of occasional information — embraces tip-offs, racing tips, news, sports news and similar information;
- publicist;
- scenic artist — where 50 per cent or more of the work is performed other than on premises provided by the engager;
- scenic designer — where 50 per cent or more of the work is performed other than on premises provided by the engager;
- script reader — where the work is performed other than on premises provided by the engager;
- script supervisor — where script breakdown is an integral part of the contract;
- scriptwriter — excluding reporting scripts;
- sculptor;
- senior floor manager;
- set decorator — where the contract requires set design performed other than on premises provided by the engager;
- set dresser — where the contract requires set design performed other than on premises provided by the engager;
- sound maintenance engineer — where the contract requires substantial provision of equipment;

Entertainers

- sound mixer — where the contract requires substantial provision of equipment;
- sound recordist — where the contract requires substantial provision of equipment;
- special effects supervisor — where the contract requires provision of necessary equipment by the worker;
- special effects wireperson — where the contract requires provision of necessary equipment by the worker;
- specialist researcher — where the worker has either an existing profession outside of the film industry (academic, legal adviser, doctor, etc.) or specialist knowledge of the programme content to be researched and the worker is engaged for a specific project and the worker is not a regular contributor;
- sport statistician;
- stage manager — where the contract requires substantial provision of equipment (including props);
- stills photographer — where the contract requires provision of all cameras by the worker;
- story writer — excluding news reporting;
- storyboard artist — where the work is performed other than on premises provided by the engager;
- stylist — film or photographic styling;
- tracer — where the work is performed other than on premises provided by the engager;
- transcript typist — where the work is performed other than on premises provided by the engager;
- translator — where the work is performed other than on premises provided by the engager;
- transport manager — where vehicles are provided by the worker;
- tutor;
- video technician — where the contract requires substantial provision of equipment;

- wardrobe — where the work is performed other than on premises provided by the engager or the contract requires substantial provision of materials;
- warm-up;
- wigmaker — where the work is performed other than on premises provided by the engager, and
- wireperson — where the contract requires provision of necessary equipment by the worker.

Of course each case must be considered on its own facts, as determined in *Hall v Lorimer* [1993] STI 138. In this important reversal for the previous Inland Revenue approach to employment status it was held that a freelance vision mixer was not an employee of the various production companies for whom he worked. The circumstances of this case merit consideration.

The work of a freelance vision mixer is a skilled editing job, involving the selection of television camera shots taken from different angles coming up on screen in front of him. Mr Lorimer normally worked in a studio provided by the production company and supplied no equipment of his own. In 1985 he left full-time employment to go freelance, registering for VAT and setting up an office at home. He also engaged an accountant. In a four-year period he worked for more than 800 days on 580 engagements for 30–40 different companies. He hired no staff but on six occasions provided a substitute with the consent of the relevant production company. All the work was conducted at the studios which provided all the equipment. Mr Lorimer had no financial risk on a particular project, but could lose money if a client became insolvent or failed to pay an invoice. His appeal against the Inland Revenue's assessment under Sch. D, Case I was upheld both by the Special Commissioner and by the High Court.

The Crown had made an important concession not previously made, namely that tax could not be charged under Sch. E (ie on employment income) on Mr Lorimer's profits on the six occasions when a substitute had been provided. However, the Court of Appeal agreed with the Crown that this had no significant bearing on the proper classification of the other 574 engagements. The Special Commissioner's conclusion was one of mixed fact and law which could be disturbed on appeal only if either the commissioner had misdirected himself in law, or the true and only reasonable conclusion on the facts found by him was inconsistent with his determination. In such cases there was no single path to a correct decision. The tests of self-employment suggested by the Crown based on the decision in *Market Investigations Ltd v Minister of*

Social Security [1969] 2 QB 173 were not necessarily apposite in this case. These were:

- control by the production company of the time, place and duration of any given engagement;
- he provided no equipment;
- he hired no staff;
- he ran no financial risk save those of bad debts and inability to find work;
- he had no responsibility for investment in or management of the programme making, and
- he could not profit from the manner in which he carried out individual assignments.

However, the question of whether the individual was in business on his own account would typically be of little help in the case of a person carrying on a profession or vocation, eg a self-employed author, actor or singer. Here one should rather bear in mind the traditional distinction between a servant and an independent contractor, where what is significant is the extent to which the individual is dependent on or independent of a particular paymaster for the financial exploitation of his or her talents. In any case, the *Market Investigations* case criteria were not intended to be an all-purpose definition of employment. The most significant facts here were that the taxpayer customarily worked for 20 or more production companies per year and that the vast majority of his assignments lasted only for a single day.

Accordingly, the Court of Appeal could not accept that the commissioner's conclusion was inconsistent with the facts found, nor that his conclusion had been reached on a basis of a misunderstanding of the law. The Crown's appeal was dismissed and leave to appeal to the House of Lords was refused.

3.11 Investigation of entertainers' income by the Inland Revenue

The Inland Revenue are aware that the local press is a useful source of information on entertainers, as clowns, magicians, discos, etc. usually advertise their services. In holiday areas especially, regular entertainment guides are published and these can assist in checking the extent of local entertainers' activities. Districts have the assistance of the Taxes Information District Office (TIDO) at Cardiff, which receives all 46P slips (return of entertainment and publishing payments), retains a master index of such notifications, and distributes slips giving information on payments over a certain figure to districts. Bringing the entertainer within the ambit of PAYE is an easier way of combating tax evasion.

The use of standard profit ratios is generally accepted by the Inland Revenue as not applicable to entertainers, as expenses vary widely between various artists. On the receipts side, as a check, the Inland Revenue may ask to see the agent's statements of gross fees and commission deducted, and any diary of engagements. Agents' commission can vary between 10 and 15 per cent of fees; in some cases another agent or someone specialising in obtaining bookings – 'a booker' – may bring the engagement to the notice of the agent and also receive a commission. In the case of a star, the work of the agent may be done by a full-time manager and, in this situation, it is difficult to resist the contention that the manager is an employee of the star.

3.12 Loans

Not all 'loans' or 'advances' are taxable. Sometimes, to promote rising stars, a promoter loans money to entertainers to enable them to live and to meet promotion expenses. If such a loan is repayable, it is not taxable. Non-repayable advances of fees or royalties are, however, assessable when received, even if they are recouped against future royalties.

3.13 Tax returns

TIDO sends those 46P slips that show fairly substantial sums to the tax district dealing with the affairs of the payees (see **3.11** above). Where entertainers' tax returns appear to show discrepancies (for instance, between outgoings or accumulated capital and known income), the inspector may attempt from time to time to reconcile the professional receipts shown in the entertainers' accounts with the amounts shown as paid to them in the 46P slips. This may be difficult as the payers may use different accounting dates from the entertainers. Some larger payers are also notoriously inefficient and may return the same payment more than once. However, if the discrepancies appear significant and continue over two or more years, the inspector may enquire into the entertainers' tax returns.

Therefore, it is imperative that entertainers inform their tax advisers of all fees that are likely to be returned by the payer under TMA 1970, s. 16. Also ensure that the entertainer has disclosed casual receipts, such as receipts for opening shops and fees paid by persons who, in practice, are not required to render a 46P return.

The Inland Revenue may enquire about the following which entertainers sometimes do not disclose:

- rehearsal fees, which are often paid in cash;
- casual expenses for subsistence made by show managers;
- general expense reimbursement;
- cash payments made on tour in respect of small stage shows and local summer seasons;
- payments in cash by clubs;
- fees for articles in magazines and newspapers;
- 'repeat' fees, where paid through Equity. Equity often acts as a clearing house for payments to artists, for instance, where the artist has no fixed address. Also fees for the extension of a tour;
- TV and film repeat fees;
- commercial radio fees, and
- payments in cash by advertising agencies.

3.14 Expenses

The distinction between self-employment and employment is important in the consideration of the expenses that can be claimed. Expenses of entertainers are often a source of contention with the Inland Revenue. The importance of being assessed under Sch. D, wherever possible, cannot be over-emphasised. Expenses allowable against employment income are confined to what is wholly, exclusively and necessarily incurred in the performance of the duties of that employment. This at once excludes all the general expenses of promoting and preserving the person's standing in the profession and, in particular, prevents a claim for travelling expenses to and from the entertainer's home and place of work. It would also prevent a deduction for agents' fees, but for ITEPA 2003, s. 352 (introduced by FA 1990). This allows a deduction from employment income for agents' fees paid to licensed agents (including co-operative societies acting as such agents) up to a maximum of 17.5 per cent of earnings for the tax year. Provisional relief may be obtained through the PAYE coding.

Expenses

Note that such agents' fees do not reduce relevant earnings for personal pension purposes.

Generally, contributions to expenses as part of a promoter's package to a performer should be brought in as income and the actual expenses claimed whether he or she is assessed under Sch. D or to employment income.

Expenses allowable under Sch. D, Case II have only to satisfy the test of being 'wholly and exclusively incurred' for the purposes of the profession. A list of expenses that in most cases can be claimed against Sch. D, Case II income is reproduced by kind permission of Equity, and is as follows:

- agent's/manager's fees and commission;
- secretarial services for keeping books and records, answering fan mail and dealing with enquiries;
- travelling and subsistence on tour if supporting a permanent home;
- make-up;
- hairdressing;
- wardrobe and props;
- laundry and cleaning of wardrobe and props;
- renewal, replacement and repair of wardrobe and props;
- travelling and expenses attending interview and auditions;
- gratuities to dressers, call boys, doormen, make-up girls;
- postage for business letters, fan mail;
- business stationery;
- tuition and coaching for dancing, singing, speech;
- professional publications, eg *Radio Times* and *TV Times*, *The Stage*, *PCR*;
- records, cassettes, scripts, sheet music;
- theatre and cinema tickets;
- Equity subscription;
- accountant's fees;
- legal charges for debt recovery, contract disputes;
- photographic sittings and reproduction;

Entertainers

- advertising, eg *Spotlight* and agency books, and
- maintenance of instruments and insurance.

The business proportion of the following is generally allowed:

- telephone;
- hire of television and video together with licence payment, and
- motor expenses.

In addition, the following may be incurred and a case established with the Inland Revenue for an appropriate deduction:

- chiropody (mainly ballet dancers);
- physiotherapy;
- cosmetic dentistry, and
- trichological treatment.

Where capital items are acquired for business purposes the Inland Revenue will consider claims for capital allowances. These are given at the rates of 40 per cent in the first year and then 25 per cent of the cost less allowances already given on a reducing balance. A claim may be made for:

- motor car;
- answerphone;
- office furniture and equipment;
- video recorder and television, and
- musical equipment and instruments.

An appropriate percentage will be disallowed to cover private use.

It must be emphasised that this list has not been agreed with the Inland Revenue. It therefore has no force in any argument with the Inland Revenue except by reference to the fairness and equality of treatment promised in the Taxpayers' Charter. A similar list of expenses, appropriately modified, is available from Incorporated Society of Musicians.

3.15 Subsistence and travelling expenses abroad

Entertainers who are resident and ordinarily resident in the UK and have set up a company to employ them solely in respect of their overseas work benefit under ITEPA 2003, ss. 370 and 371, relating to travel expenses. They are not taxed on any travel expenses that are reimbursed and that relate to journeys to take up or return from such an employment. The journeys can be between any place in the UK and the place of performance of the overseas duties. If entertainers are abroad for 60 days or more, which is quite likely for, say, a theatrical tour, they are not taxed on the travel expenses of two outward and return journeys in a tax year by spouses and/or children visiting during the period of overseas work.

Entertainers who do not have a separate company for overseas work but are nonetheless employed by their own company and perform only some of the duties of their employment in the UK, are not taxed on travel expenses in respect of all outward and return journeys between the UK and the place of performance of the overseas duties, provided the duties can be performed only overseas and the journeys are made solely for that purpose. Again, entertainers must be resident and ordinarily resident in the UK.

Note that in both cases the expenses must be reimbursed by the employer. This is presumably designed to introduce a measure of control but this is likely to be theoretical rather than real where the entertainer controls the employer company.

Similar reliefs are available, under ICTA 1988, s. 80, for a self-employed individual who is UK-domiciled or, if a British subject or Irish citizen, who is ordinarily resident in the UK and carrying on a profession or vocation wholly outside the UK. Certain travel and accommodation expenses are allowed as Sch. D, Case V deductions. These expenses would not otherwise be allowable as a deduction in arriving at income assessable under Sch. D, Case V.

3.16 Travelling expenses in the UK

The Inland Revenue contend that, where a person works regularly at one theatre or in one area, the work base is the theatre and not the actor's home. This may be the situation where, exceptionally, an actor is working more or less permanently on long runs in the West End, and lives in the suburbs. However, an actor performing a particular engagement in the West End followed by work elsewhere, and certainly an actor on tour, should be regarded as

Entertainers

operating from his or her own home. In the latter case, the actor has no centre of activity and travelling expenses from home may be allowed.

Even where the actor is working regularly within a certain area, in practice the extra travelling and other expenses that are incurred over normal costs, for instance on taxis, should be allowed.

Actors assessed to employment income should refer to Inland Revenue booklet IR 490 for the tax treatment of travelling and subsistence expenses.

3.17 Subsistence expenses in the UK

Meals and accommodation expenses should be allowed without difficulty, if the travelling expenses are also allowable. The Inland Revenue contend that lunches are not allowable, except where a person is on location or on a short tour. In this, the Inland Revenue have the backing of the decision in *Caillebotte v Quinn* (1975) 50 TC 222, and of the decision in *Watkis v Ashford Sparkes & Harward* (1985) 58 TC 468, where solicitors were disallowed the cost of lunches in working hours. The Inland Revenue are also particularly hard on subsistence expenses on a long engagement, where the artist has no home. Where someone has a home, subsistence is normally allowed in full.

Some inspectors may also allow claims for expenses incurred in going to the cinema or theatre for professional purposes, rather than for personal pleasure. However, no deduction is allowed for the cost of providing business entertainment, such as the cost of a meal for other actors, agents, etc though it may be possible to establish that the meal was incidental to the main purpose of a longer meeting to research a new role, etc.

The Inland Revenue dispute the allowance of an expense it if includes an element of personal choice, or benefit that is more than incidental to the main purpose of the expenditure. Thus, where a draftsman who played the guitar partly as a hobby and partly for payment cut his finger and had to pay for an operation, the payment was held not to be wholly and exclusively laid out for the purposes of his vocation (*Prince v Mapp* (1969) 46 TC 169).

3.18 Clothing

There is usually no difficulty obtaining a tax deduction for theatrical costume and clothes. Clothes bought specifically for an audition should similarly qualify. The decision in *Mallalieu v Drummond* (1983) 57 TC 330 is not thought to affect this position. The most common areas of difficulty are off-stage clothing and general expenses of keeping in the public eye, such as attendance at premieres for professional purposes. The public nature of the profession usually means that the Inland Revenue concede a deduction for limited reasonable claims. However, the cost of ordinary clothing that is also worn outside the theatre is subject to some restriction for private use, even where it is necessary for, say, TV personalities or actors to buy particularly expensive clothing for their public image. Whenever possible expense claims should be categorised as 'costumes' rather than as 'clothes'.

3.19 Medical expenses

Claims for medical expenses are generally disallowed (see *Norman v Golder* (1945) 26 TC 293). The cost of most treatment, even cosmetic treatment, will be resisted, as will sauna and health club fees. The 1989 VAT Tribunal case involving the actor Anthony Anholt (LON/89/487) may, however, provide some support for such claims if the health and fitness of an actor is a specific requirement of an ongoing professional role. In Mr Anholt's case this arose from his role in the TV series 'Howard's Way'.

3.20 Other expenses

Coaching and training costs incurred to improve performance are normally allowed.

The cost of tickets provided for publicity or advertising to others is allowable as a deduction. Such costs should be distinguished from those incurred to provide 'entertainment' for others. The inspector may also disallow the cost of tickets provided for actors themselves, if duality of purpose can be proved. Thus it is easier to justify the cost of tickets if family and friends do not accompany the entertainer and where the 'research' motive can be shown to over-ride any other reason for viewing the show or film. Similarly, the Inland Revenue resist claims for the costs of a TV licence, or of hiring a TV set or a video, unless those assets can be shown to be of use in the exercise of the profession. Even then the deduction will probably be restricted to take account of private use.

However, it is often possible to claim part of the household expenses as relating to professional use, eg for learning lines or music practice.

3.21 Groups' tax treatment

Groups pose special problems, especially if the Inland Revenue contend that they carry on business as a partnership. This can lead to complications on ownership of instruments, and copyrights where songs have been written by only one or two members of the group. For these reasons, and because of the tendency of groups to split up, it is normally advisable for each group member to have his or her own service company which in turn has an agreement with a central company owned by all the group members. The central company will deal with third parties on behalf of the group and distribute all its profits to the individual members' companies. The particular functions carried out by the central company will vary from group to group.

In the case of casual and less well-established groups, the Inland Revenue normally accept that each member of the group is a self-employed individual for the sake of expediency, and to avoid the complications of the partnership division rules.

For practical accounting purposes the group is treated as a joint venture, so income and expenditure of the joint activity are recorded and annual joint venture statements are prepared. Profits or losses are allocated to each member. Each member maintains his or her own self-employed records (comprising a share from the joint venture plus, in some cases, other composing or performing work) which are the basis of his or her own annual accounts submitted to the Inland Revenue.

3.22 'Angels'

Theatre angels are people who put up money to finance a theatrical production. If the show is successful their money is first repaid, and then they receive a share in any profit. If the show is a failure they may lose not only the possibility of a profit but also part or all of their original investment.

Profits from a production for a particular year are amounts received which do not represent the repayment of the investment. Losses can be computed only when there is no further prospect of a return from the investment.

Unless the angel uses Extra-statutory Concession (ESC) A94, the treatment of profits and losses is as follows.

1. Profits are liable under Sch. D, Case III.
2. There is no income tax relief for losses.
3. Losses may attract capital gains tax loss relief.
4. If an angel works in a trade or profession within the theatre then, depending on the facts, his or her activities as a backer may be part of that trade. But this is not the case for most angels.

Capital gains tax losses are of no use unless the angel has chargeable gains. So, where an angel backs various productions, the strict treatment may result in profits being liable to income tax with no relief for losses.

Under ESC A94, UK resident angels can set losses from one show against profits from another. The concession operates by applying the Sch. D, Case VI rules to profits or losses arising to UK resident angels from theatre backing. So losses may be offset against other Case VI income of the year concerned, or carried forward and set off against later Case VI income.

The purpose of the concession is to allow offsetting of losses in this way, not to allow expenses which might be allowed if the income were, in law, liable under Sch. D, Case VI.

Where the concessionary treatment is given, the loss will not also qualify as a capital loss.

The concessionary Case VI treatment does not change the true Case III nature of the payments. Payers of sums chargeable under Case III have a right to deduct tax if the payment falls within ICTA 1988, s. 348(1) and an obligation to deduct tax if the payment falls within ICTA 1988, s. 349(1). All payments by incorporated payers fall within s. 349(1). According to the terms of the concession, the Inland Revenue will not insist on deduction of tax from payments to theatre angels for their theatrical investments if their usual place of abode is in the UK. Payers may, however, exercise the right to deduct tax if they wish.

The place of abode is a practical test which the payer can apply; the payer is not likely to know the residence status of the recipient for tax purposes.

Entertainers

Theatre angels who are not resident in the UK may be able to obtain authority for tax not to be deducted from payments made to them in respect of their theatrical investments, if they are resident in a country which has a double taxation agreement with the UK which contains an Other Income article. Claims from non-residents for repayment of UK tax and/or applications from nonresidents for exemption from deduction of UK tax should be sent to the Inland Revenue Financial Intermediaries and Claims Office (International), Fitzroy House, PO Box 46, Nottingham NG2 1BD.

3.23 Pensions and retirement

In the case of pop singers who are employed by a company, the Pension Schemes Office sometimes allow a pension scheme to be set up to give them a pension (at age 40) of 15/60ths of their final earnings, subject to the earnings cap, etc. The FA 1983 contained provisions giving the Inland Revenue power to approve similar retirement annuity contracts for individuals who, because of the exceptional nature of their work, are likely to retire early (for instance pop stars and professional sportspeople). This brings the law and practice for retirement annuities into line with that for equivalent occupational pension schemes.

The following is a list of agreed early retirement ages for entertainers:

Profession	*Retirement age*
Brass instrumentalists	55
Dancers	35
Singers	55
Trapeze artists	40
Circus animal trainers	50

Note, however, that the personal pension rules in ICTA 1988, s. 634(3) provide for a lower retirement age of 50, whatever the occupation, although under FA 2004 this will increase to 55 from 6 April 2006. An even lower retirement age for particular occupations is still possible under the personal pension rules. It remains unclear what impact (if any) FA 2004 will have on these provisions.

3.24 Musicians: sale of instruments

Taxation on the proceeds of sale of valuable musical instruments can pose problems for musicians (see **3.8** above). A concession allowing roll-over relief on the disposal of a musical instrument was too difficult to sustain and has now been discontinued. Retirement relief would however have been due for disposals before 6 April 2003, provided that the normal conditions for the relief are met. Retirement relief is not available for disposals after 5 April 2003. Business asset taper relief will normally be available for disposals since 6 April 1998.

Chapter 4 Stockbrokers and market makers

4.1 Rules of the Stock Exchange

There are a number of rules laid down by the Stock Exchange governing the constitution of firms and the way members can carry on business. Certain of these rules are relevant in considering the taxation treatment of stockbrokers and market makers.

It is of course possible for a limited company to trade as a market maker or broker. Where the company is limited, a solvency margin is required. The company may carry out business like a firm as a sole corporate trader or, if it is unlimited, in partnership with individuals.

It is also possible for a partnership to use a company as a service company.

4.2 Incorporation

Many stockbrokers and market makers are wholly owned by a financial institution, and have been taken over and their functions amalgamated into one securities dealing concern. Prior to takeover, the firm will be incorporated. Depending upon the circumstances, capital gains tax relief is claimed on the incorporation, particularly in respect of chargeable gains accruing on the goodwill of the firm. The provisions of TCGA 1992, ss. 162 or 165 give the necessary relief.

Section 162 gives the company a base value equal to the current market value of the assets acquired. Section 165 may be appropriate when not all of the assets of the business are being transferred, although in this connection if the whole trade has not been transferred to the company an election under the Capital Allowances Act 2001 (CAA 2001), s. 266 (transfer of plant and machinery at tax written down value) may not be accepted. The effect of s. 165 is that by first incorporating the company with a small capital subscribed for in cash by the partners, the base value of goodwill in the company is relatively low. The base cost of shares in the company is also negligible. There are, however, stamp duty savings as against the other method.

4.3 Golden handcuffs

Arrangements for the sale of the company's shares typically involve the use of 'golden handcuffs' — deferred consideration under which part of the payment is deferred and is dependent on the principal serving a minimum number of years as a director of the company. The consideration is usually given in the form of deferred loan stock redeemable at the end of the period. Provided this consideration clearly refers to it relating wholly to the individual's share of goodwill of the firm, it should not be taxed as employment income under ITEPA 2003 or under ICTA 1988, s. 775 (capital sums derived from the earning power of an individual).

However, ordinary 'golden hello' payments offered to individuals to join such financial services companies stand little chance of being taxed as anything other than Schedule E income, as no asset is being given up — such as the loss of a right to practise at the Bar or as a chartered accountant or the loss of amateur status (as in the cases of *Vaughan-Neil v CIR* (1979) 54 TC 223; *Pritchard v Arundale* (1971) 47 TC 680; and *Jarrold v Boustead* (1964) 41 TC 701).

4.4 Period of accounts

Firms sometimes draw up accounts to end on the same Stock Exchange account each year rather than on the same day. This day may vary by as much as a fortnight from one year to the next but, in practice, the accounts are treated as the profits of one year for taxation purposes (including ranking as an accounting period for corporation tax purposes).

4.5 'Bear and bull excesses'

Sometimes it is necessary for market makers to 'manufacture' a dividend if they have insufficient dividends from sellers of stock to pass on to purchasers of stock who have bought *cum dividend*. This can happen, bearing in mind that they may find they have to buy stock which has gone *ex dividend* to satisfy previous purchases *cum dividend*. This is termed a 'bear excess'.

The rules of the Stock Exchange stipulate that they should, in those circumstances, make 'a payment in lieu of a dividend' and this is regarded as income of the recipient for tax purposes. To guard against loss of tax to the Inland Revenue because no income tax or (before 6 April 1999) advance corporation tax will have been accounted for in such circumstances, they are regarded as making an annual payment on which income tax would be accounted for under ICTA 1988, ss. 348 or 349 and which is deductible against total income (ICTA 1988, s. 737).

The reverse position, namely where they receive more dividends than they have to account for, is referred to as a 'bull excess'. It is considered that such income should form part of their trading income which has already borne tax at the basic rate.

The position of corporate market makers is slightly more complex in relation to these transactions because of the need to segregate franked and unfranked investment income. The practice, however, is as follows.

1. The bull or bear excess for an accounting period should be ascertained separately in respect of unfranked and franked investment income.
2. For the purpose of ICTA 1988, Schs. 13 and 16, and of taking into account the relevant income tax, tax credit or (before 6 April 1999) advance corporation tax attributable to dividend excesses, a bull or bear dividend excess arises on the last day of an accounting period and should be included only in the final return on Form CT61 relating to that period.
3. The gross amount of an unfranked bull excess is regarded as unfranked investment income in the normal way and credit for the income tax suffered allowed as a credit against the corporation tax for the accounting period (ICTA 1988, s. 7(2)).
4. The gross amount of an unfranked bear excess is treated as a charge and allowed as a deduction from total profits (ICTA 1988, s. 338). The amount of income tax appropriate to the excess is payable under ICTA 1988, Sch. 16.
5. A franked bull excess plus the tax credit attributable thereto was treated as franked investment income and excluded from the corporation tax computation and was available for deduction from franked payments in arriving at the advance corporation tax payable in respect of qualifying distributions.
6. A franked bear excess was regarded as a qualifying distribution in respect of which no deduction was allowable for corporation tax purposes and in respect of which advance corporation tax was payable.

Market makers sometimes contract to sell more stock than they can purchase by normal delivery date. In practice, the stock is delivered late to the buying broker but, if the sale is made before the end of their accounts and the purchase is made after, they could be taxed on a gross sum without a deduction

Stockbrokers and market makers

for the liability to purchase the stock. In the circumstances, an adjustment is made to the accounts by creating a liability or reducing their stocks.

There are now often additional complex arrangements between financial concerns, for instance for the borrowing and lending of securities (as to the tax treatment of which see **4.8** below), satisfying a particular demand by one market maker for securities he or she does not have, and for passing dividends and interest through the market because several transactions take place in securities purchased *cum dividend*. The provisions on manufactured dividends and interest (in ICTA 1988, s. 737) cover such complexities. *Inter alia*, the provisions distinguish the position of a non-UK company market maker from a UK company market maker. They provide for a specific legal framework for the UK company market maker as opposed to the practice described above in relation to such manufactured UK dividends and interest in relation to withholding tax on overseas manufactured dividends. The latter would arise in respect of overseas dividends and interest such as on a quoted Eurobond that would normally have been paid through a UK paying agent to a UK resident person (the latter provisions are further covered in detailed regulations).

This legislation is in ICTA 1988, s. 736A and Sch. 23A. Broadly, manufactured dividends and interest are treated in the same way as their real counterparts as far as accounting for tax on them is concerned. The position of such manufactured payments in relation to all the various concerns, including non-residents, which are now involved in securities dealing on the Stock Exchange are also dealt with.

Regulations for dividends (the Income Tax (Dividend Manufacturing) Regulations 1992 (SI 1992 No. 569)) and for interest (SI 1992 No. 34) apply for quarterly return periods ending on or after 22 March 1992 for dividends and from 30 June 1992 for interest.

The regulations govern accounting for tax on manufactured dividends on UK equities paid or payable on or after 25 February 1992. These include:

- administrative arrangements for accounting for tax on manufactured dividends;
- arrangements to remove certain disadvantages which UK branches of non-resident companies which are Stock Exchange market makers or LIFFE members would otherwise suffer compared with UK-resident companies in the same position, and

- provisions ensuring that the tax treatment of manufactured dividends paid by LIFFE members in the ordinary course of their business are not disadvantageous.

4.6 Returns

The Revenue can obtain information from market makers concerning transactions giving rise to such excesses of payments of interest and dividends over receipts for interest and dividends, where the excesses are treated as annual payments by the market maker. The Revenue may serve a notice requiring market makers to make available such books, accounts and other documents in their possession or power as are specified in the notice, for the purpose of obtaining details of the beneficial owners of the income in question (TMA 1970, s. 21(2)).

The Revenue may also serve a notice on brokers requiring similar information from them (TMA 1970, s. 21(3)). Brokers' records may give more information than market makers' on such dealings with market makers on behalf of their clients. Similarly, where people acting on behalf of others who are not brokers, have received income from or paid income to market makers (for instance, have sold *cum dividend* and have passed on income to a market maker, or have bought *cum dividend* and received the income from a market maker), they may be required to give details of the person on behalf of whom they are acting (TMA 1970, s. 21(4)).

The Revenue cannot exercise their powers under TMA 1970, s. 21 in relation to transactions in any year of assessment ending more than six years before the service of the notice. There are penalties for default in complying with such a notice (TMA 1970, s. 98).

4.7 Dividend income and profits and losses on sales of securities

Where the proceeds of sale of any investments are taken into account in computing profits or gains of a trade, the income from those investments is not investment income for tax purposes. A similar provision operates for a close company. However, in the case of stockbrokers and market makers, the Inland Revenue have resisted Case I treatment for profits and losses on private sales of securities, and therefore the treatment of dividend income is as earned income except in the following situations.

1. Where market makers buy and sell in their own market, that is the shares in which the market maker specialises. Any dealings outside their own market are treated as private transactions falling under the capital gains provisions.
2. In the case of brokers, where the dealings are directly connected with their business as brokers, for instance arbitrage transactions consisting of the purchase of shares in one market and selling them at a higher price in another market where brokers act as principals on their own account.
3. Again, if brokers underwrite an issue of shares, or there is an error in carrying out clients' instructions, they may hold stock on their own account arising out of their business as brokers.

The Inland Revenue rely on *Bucks v Bowers* (1970) 46 TC 267, in which a partner in a merchant bank attempted to claim earned income relief on investment income arising from securities in which dealings took place by the partnership. It was decided that the income from the securities was not 'immediately derived from the carrying on of a trade' and thus not earned income (ICTA 1988, s. 833(4)(c)).

The point appears now to be relevant only in relation to what are net relevant earnings for retirement annuity and personal pension purposes (ICTA 1988, ss. 623(2) and 644(2)) and thus may become academic once the provisions of FA 2004 come into force from 6 April 2006.

4.8 Borrowing and lending securities

Sometimes market makers borrow from and lend securities to another market maker who is short of stock or to create an active market, and the debt is repaid with securities of the same kind. Similarly, market makers may enter into stock lending arrangements whereby they acquire the necessary stock from institutional holders on terms which require them to return equivalent securities later. If such borrowing and lending takes place in circumstances where the lending market maker parts with the legal interest in the securities and is subsequently repaid in other securities of the same kind, an occasion of charge strictly arises under Sch. D, Case I or under the capital gains provisions, depending upon the circumstances on the criteria mentioned above.

TCGA 1992, s. 263B provides that for stock lending arrangements entered into on or after 1 July 1997 all acquisitions and disposals of securities under the arrangement are to be disregarded for the purposes of capital gains tax.

'Securities' includes UK equities (shares), UK securities (UK debt securities — essentially company and Government loan stocks), and overseas securities (both shares and debt securities), as defined in ICTA 1988, Sch. 23A.

Generally a borrower will sell or otherwise dispose of the securities he has borrowed and repay the loan with other securities. In this case the shares sold are deemed, for the purpose of any question regarding their acquisition by the borrower, to be the shares with which he repaid the loan. This ensures that their cost for capital gains purposes is the cost of the replacement securities.

If it becomes apparent that the borrower will fail to return the securities, the borrower is deemed to acquire them at that time and the lender to dispose of them. If the securities have by then been sold by the borrower they are, in any question regarding their acquisition, identified as the ones acquired at this point.

It is possible that the securities borrowed under the loan arrangement might be redeemed by the company that originally issued them. In this case the lender may require the borrower not to return the shares but to pay it an amount equal to the proceeds of redemption. If this happens then the lender is deemed by s. 263C to have disposed of the securities for the redemption proceeds. If the borrower has retained the shares to redemption then he is deemed not to dispose of them on redemption. If instead the borrower has previously sold the shares then their cost is deemed to be the amount paid to the lender.

4.9 Market maker's position on purchase of own shares by company

There are special rules involving market makers where a quoted company purchases its own shares in the market. The individual shareholder, who may not be aware that the company is purchasing his or her shares, sells them to the market maker and qualifies for capital gains tax treatment. The market maker, when selling them to the company, pays tax on the difference between the price paid and the price actually received from the company. A market purchase by the quoted company through a market maker, as opposed to an off-market purchase, thus enables the investor to obtain capital gains tax treatment whilst leaving the market maker in a neutral position on the transaction.

4.10 Interest received

It is understood that the treatment of interest is more liberal in practice than that of dividend income. Interest debited or credited to a client's account is treated as part of the Case II profits, and overnight interest on the investment of purely temporary surpluses of working capital is equally left in the Case II computation — but interest arising in other circumstances is treated as investment income. This treatment was reinforced by the case of *Northend v White & Leonard and Corbin Greener* [1975] STC 317; (1975) 50 TC 121 which confirmed that interest on monies held on client accounts by solicitors is assessable under Case III.

4.11 Interest paid

Any interest paid to a member of the Stock Exchange may be allowed to the borrower, if he or she satisfies the various rules for eligibility for tax relief for individuals (ICTA 1988, s. 353).

This applies whether the interest can be regarded as annual interest, that is, broadly because the loan has some degree of permanence and is capable of exceeding a year, or is short interest.

Similarly, companies may obtain relief for such interest as a Case III deficit where it cannot be regarded as a trading expense — for instance, where it is paid by an investment company or is paid by a trading company on a loan used to acquire an investment (ICTA 1988, s. 338(3)(b)).

4.12 Unclaimed dividends

Unclaimed dividends sometimes arise to brokers, for instance where a buyer's broker fails to claim the amount on a purchase *cum dividend*. These receipts are not income of the broker as he or she holds them as trustee on the basis of the principle in the case of *Morley v Tattersall* (1938) 22 TC 51. The more recent case of *Anise Ltd & Others v Hammond* SpC 364 (24 March 2003 reported at [2003] STI Issue 18) may also be relevant. The companies received excess payments under some standing orders, the error of either the customer or the customer's bank. The commissioners found as a fact that the overpayments were not received as part of the trading activities of the companies. Accordingly, the sums were not received as trading receipts. The commissioners could see no basis for taxing the overpayments when they were transferred from creditor's account to profit and loss account: that was a purely internal transaction and no trading asset was created. Even if, in the course of time, the overpayments became irrecoverable under the Limitation Act, that did not mean that they arose directly from the companies' trading activities; the issue was when the receipts became trading receipts. Whether or not the receipts could, for other purposes, be regarded as assets or some other kind of income, they had not been received as part of the companies' trades and therefore had not been and did not become trading receipts. The point of principle was therefore determined in favour of the companies.

4.13 Stock Exchange attachés and clerks

Attachés and clerks are attached to a single firm and may be full members of the Stock Exchange, but are not partners in a firm or directors of a company. They introduce clients to firms and are paid a proportion of the stockbroker's commission. They are usually responsible for a proportion of the bad debts of any clients they introduce depending upon the proportion of the commission they receive. The same rules apply for treating their income from investments as earned income as for stockbrokers. If they are taxed as employees under ITEPA 2003, losses exceeding their remuneration cannot be allowed under the normal employment expenses rules and where the person is an office holder, as opposed to just an employee, they are not strictly allowable under ICTA 1988, s. 380 either. However, in practice, where bad debts exceeding their remuneration arise, through defaults of clients, they are allowed in all cases under s. 380; but in employment cases, such losses cannot be carried forward under ICTA 1988, s. 385.

The relationship of the attaché with the particular firm determines whether he or she is assessable as an employee or as self-employed — for instance, whether the attaché is supplied with office accommodation and required to attend regularly at the office. If so, he or she is assessable as an employee under ITEPA 2003. Clerks are nearly always assessed as employees; the few who are assessed as self-employed under Sch. D are likely to be members acting as authorised clerks who carry out transactions on behalf of and in the names of their principals.

4.14 Expenses of members of the Stock Exchange

There are certain specific expenses which are peculiar to members of the Stock Exchange.

1. Subscription: A member's entrance fee is not allowable but the annual subscription is.
2. Stock Exchange Compensation Fund: Contributions to this fund are allowable in full. Receipts from this fund in respect of securities disposed of by a hammered broker and not accounted for, are subject to capital gains tax.
3. Stock Exchange Benevolent Fund: Contributions to the Benevolent Fund, which is to alleviate distress among ex-members of the Stock Exchange, are treated as donations and not allowed. Contributions to the Clerks' Benevolent Fund are allowed because they are for the benefit of employees.

4.15 Capital gains returns

For the purposes of obtaining particulars of chargeable gains, stockbrokers, but not market makers, may be required to make a return giving particulars of transactions carried out by them in the course of their business during the period specified in the notice, and in particular detailing the parties to the transactions, the number or amount of the shares concerned and the amount or value of the consideration (TMA 1970, s. 25).

4.16 Anti-avoidance provisions

There are numerous anti-avoidance provisions in the Taxes Acts that relate to transactions in securities involving dealers in securities such as market makers. They are designed to take away any tax advantage arising from dealings in the securities. It is outside the scope of this book to discuss these provisions in detail, but insofar as they affect the potential tax liabilities of share dealers such as market makers, mention is made of the more important of them.

4.16.1 Dividend stripping

The most wide-ranging is ICTA 1988, s. 703 *et seq*. Circumstances A and B of s. 704 are aimed at the share dealer. In particular s. 704, Circumstance A, deals with the situation where, in connection with the purchase and sale of securities, a person receives an abnormal amount by way of dividend which is relieved in some way (for instance against losses).

This covers 'dividend stripping', where a person buys shares to procure the payment of such a dividend so that the tax credit can be utilised in one of the ways mentioned in the section to obtain a tax advantage. For instance, the effect of the company being stripped in this way may be to create a trading loss on the sale of the securities which might otherwise be set against the abnormal dividends received under ICTA 1988, s. 242. Alternatively, there might be other losses which could be set against the abnormal dividend. This type of short-term dealing transaction was considered in *Harrison (JP) (Watford) Ltd v Griffiths HL* (1962) 40 TC 281 and was reaffirmed in the Court of Appeal as creating in certain circumstances such a trading loss in *Reed v Nova Securities Ltd* [1985] STC 124, but not in *Coates v Arndale Properties Ltd* [1984] STC 637. Both of these cases concerned transactions turning a loss for capital gains purposes into a trading loss by appropriating an asset within a group to trading stock. In the former case, the trade was held to be a genuine one. There were, however, other cases decided which suggest that a loss which arises entirely from dividend stripping transactions which are carried out for fiscal motives, is simply not a trading loss at all for tax purposes. The main cases reaching this conclusion are *Finsbury Securities Ltd v Bishop* (1966) 43 TC 591 and *Lupton v F A and A B Ltd* (1971) 47 TC 580. It is, therefore, likely that market makers who are engaged commercially in share dealing would be caught under the specific legislation in s. 704 and any tax advantage would be nullified as they would be carrying on a genuine trade of share dealing.

Section 704, Circumstance B, also concerns *inter alia* a share dealer who seeks to relieve a loss produced by a fall in the value of securities which is caused by the payment of a dividend in respect of the securities. No relief is given whether the dividend is abnormal or not. This extends Circumstance A to cover any situation where there is such a connection between the payment of a dividend of any amount and the loss.

4.16.2 Bond washing

Section 731 *et seq* of ICTA 1988 are designed to prevent the obtaining of a tax advantage from 'bond-washing'. This occurs where there is an arrangement for the purchase of securities *cum dividend* and their sale *ex dividend* within a short period of time. The legislation refers to six months after which the legislation cannot bite or one month if it can be shown broadly there was no tax avoidance motive.

The one-month rule also applies now where securities such as shares are bought or sold using options exercised within one month (FA 1991, s. 55).

A tax repayment is then sought on the loss against the dividend or interest received. This trading loss is computed in the case of a dealer in securities on the principle established in *Wigmore v Thomas Summerson & Sons Ltd* (1926) 9 TC 577 under which the cost of the securities includes any accrued interest element, thus giving rise to a trading loss to set against the interest. Such a loss is restricted in the case of ordinary dealers in securities by broadly the amount of accrued interest in the purchase price.

Note that the accrued income scheme does not apply to dealers in securities if the disposal falls to be taken into account in computing their trading profits. Hence the legislation in s. 731 is still potentially relevant to dealers in securities as the old case law applies to compute the trading loss in such circumstances.

However, market makers who are members of the Stock Exchange are specifically exempted from this legislation and are thus subject to no adjustment in respect of such dealings in securities, provided they are bought in the ordinary course of such business. As it is against the rules of the Stock Exchange to indulge in this sort of systematic bond washing, market makers should not in practice be affected by this legislation.

Similarly, dealers in Eurobonds and managers of unit trust schemes are exempt from the legislation if they are acting in the ordinary course of their business, and there are regulations exempting prescribed clearing houses or a member of a prescribed class or description of a prescribed recognised investment exchange if the subsequent sale is after the date to be prescribed and in the ordinary course of business. The Dividend Manufacturing Regulations 1992 extended the exemption from this legislation to principal traders as well as market makers on LIFFE. As with the stock lending reliefs, there are prescribed limitations to restrict the exemption to hedging transactions and transactions entered into as a result of the exercise of options. This covers members of the new body set up to regulate traded options and futures contracts.

4.17 Special forms of investments

The tax treatment of certain types of specialised investments often dealt with by stockbrokers on their own account have been the subject of discussion between the Stock Exchange and the Inland Revenue.

4.17.1 Traded options

A traded option gives the right to buy or sell a particular share at a pre-established price over a given period. An option to buy a share is known as a 'call' option and one giving the right to sell a share is known as a 'put' option. A traded option can be bought and sold in the market, almost as if it were a share, so that if, for instance, investors guess wrong about the movement in the price of a share in which they buy a traded option, they can decide to cut their loss and sell rather than let the option lapse through time and thus lose the whole of the 'premium' or price paid for the option. The writer of the option is effectively the other side of the transaction in which an investor buys an option. Holders of some XYZ plc shares, for instance, might take the view they were more likely to fall than rise over the next seven months and would be quite happy to get 330p for them. If they 'write' a XYZ plc 330p July call option at 11p premium, they get an immediate 11p per share which they pocket. If they are right and the option expires worthless, that is the end of the matter. If they are wrong and the share price rises to the point where they are 'exercised', they sell the shares at 330p and thus obtain in total 341p for them.

It is possible to cover risks as an investor in traded options by reducing that risk through writing call options for premiums or fees.

The traded options market is part of the Stock Exchange and has 'market makers' much like the market in shares. These market makers are in fact normal market making firms which operate in shares as well and effectively create a market in the options by bringing together writers of options and investors.

Dealers in traded options on UK equities, whether or not they are market makers, may be faced with an obligation to deliver securities on which they have entered into options contracts. Tax relief is allowed on stock borrowed by such dealers to hedge positions in options or to enable stock to be delivered on the exercise of an option. The limitations for non-market making principal traders (who can choose whether or not to deal in a particular option) are more restrictive than those for market makers (who have to deal and who therefore require a more flexible regime). Nevertheless, the limitations in each case recognise the need to hedge, and to maintain a hedge against options positions.

Prior to the FA 1980, only options to subscribe for shares were not treated as wasting assets, but following pressure from the Stock Exchange, similar treatment was afforded to traded options (TCGA 1992, s. 146(1)(b)). Therefore, if as is usual, the option is abandoned or sold, the full cost is allowable in computing a loss for capital gains tax purposes. If shares are acquired in pursuance of the option, the normal rules apply and the cost of the option and the shares are rolled into one and the option cost is treated as part of the larger transaction (TCGA 1992, s. 144). There are, however, special rules to distinguish the cost of the option and the cost of the shares for indexation purposes so that the costs are treated for these purposes as incurred when they are payable as if they were separate assets (TCGA 1992, s. 145).

The rules on the 'writing' of options, that is, selling such options to others, work in reverse to those for the acquirer of the option. The fee or premium for writing the option is simply liable to capital gains tax if the option lapses. If it is exercised and the underlying shares have to be sold at the option price, the whole operation is lumped together and the cost of the shares is compared with the sale proceeds of both the option and the shares in establishing the writer's tax position. Under the rules of the markets, a writer can extinguish the obligation with the purchaser to sell or buy the underlying security if the option is exercised, by buying back in other markets an option identical to the one that has been written. If the person who has granted the traded option closes it out in this way by acquiring a traded option of the same description, the disposal involved in closing out the original option is disregarded for capital gains tax purposes. Any costs of acquiring the second option are added to any existing costs of the grantor for this purpose (TCGA 1992, s. 148). Market makers include their turn in their trading profits as it is a normal transaction in a specialised market so far as they are concerned.

Pension funds are exempt from capital gains tax on dealings in traded options as they are on futures contracts (ICTA 1988, s. 659A(1) and TCGA 1992, s. 271).

4.17.2 The financial futures market

The London International Financial Futures Exchange (LIFFE) (now part of the traded options market) was set up by a group of bankers and brokers familiar with trading commodities for delivery at future dates. The Exchange enables investors to buy and sell contracts for the future delivery of a range of currencies and fixed interest securities, such as bank deposit certificates (called Euro dollar or Sterling time deposits) or gilts or fixed interest securities, at a future date with the price agreed at the time of the deal. The market operates in a way similar to the Stock Exchange with standard contracts to buy and sell being traded. Some member firms of the Stock Exchange have shown interest in the market and acted for clients in respect of such futures transactions. The market has attracted the wealthy speculator although it has a stronger appeal for financial institutions and companies who wish to have a hedge against unexpected fluctuations in exchange and interest rates.

4.18 Traded options and the financial futures market: capital gains tax treatment

Transactions in commodity or financial futures or traded options on a recognised exchange are treated as capital in nature unless they are regarded as profits or losses of a trade (TCGA 1992, s. 143). Section 81 of FA (No. 2) Act 1987 extended this treatment to other transactions in futures and options. Case VI treatment, which derived from the old case law, no longer applies to such transactions, and unless the hallmarks of trading are present as discussed in the case of *Lewis Emanuel & Son Ltd v White* (1965) 42 TC 369, capital gains tax treatment applies. Most individuals are taxed under the capital gains tax rules, as are majority of companies, unless they are hedging a trading situation or have an existing financial trade or embark on the activity in a sufficiently organised way as to constitute trading. This matter is discussed in detail in Statement of Practice 14/91. For capital gains tax purposes, contracts which do not run to delivery are regarded as unconditional contracts to acquire the underlying asset, and are therefore subject to the normal rules of identification.

Where a contract runs to delivery, the tax treatment ignores the financial futures or options transactions and treats it as a method of buying or selling what is actually delivered. The LIFFE's gilt contracts enjoy exemption if the contract runs to delivery. Consequently, to ensure symmetry of tax treatment for futures and underlying cash markets, TCGA 1992, s. 115 exempts LIFFE's gilt futures and options contract from capital gains tax.

4.19 The Alternative Investment Market (AIM)

The Alternative Investment Market replaced the Unlisted Securities Market (USM) and has become increasingly popular for companies which do not want a full quotation for their shares but require a market for their shares. As it has a number of tax advantages for the investor, it is appropriate to mention them in this chapter.

The tax advantages must be weighed against the commercial disadvantage which can arise from the fact that because companies need only float off as little as ten per cent of their shares on the AIM, there are chronic shortages of stock which can lead to unrealistic ratings for particular shares.

Stockbrokers and market makers

Joining the AIM has no impact on close company status so that investors can obtain tax relief on borrowings to purchase shares in a close company, some of whose shares are traded in the market, provided of course that the other conditions for such relief are satisfied.

Inheritance tax business property relief is also available on the shares, whereas no relief is due on quoted shares.

An unquoted company whose shares are traded on the market can purchase its own shares and the shareholder may be able, if fulfilling the other conditions, to obtain capital gains tax treatment from such a disposal. This treatment is not possible for a quoted company except through a sale in the market to a market maker.

Income tax relief is available for losses on an investment in such a company's shares as this extends to losses on unquoted shares subscribed for in trading companies.

Chapter 5 Lloyd's underwriters

5.1 General

The rules for taxing Lloyd's underwriters were substantially altered by FA 1993 and FA 1994 with effect for 1994 and later underwriting accounts. In anticipation of the introduction in 1996–97 of self assessment, the basis of assessing profits or losses of an underwriting account was changed from the corresponding basis to the distribution basis.

On the distribution basis profits or losses are assessable in the tax year in which they are declared.

Names can underwrite on either an individual or corporate basis.

The rules governing the taxation of individual Names are found in FA 1993, Pt. V, Ch. III and those governing corporate Names in FA 1994, Pt. IV, Ch. V.

5.2 Sources of income and gains

An underwriting member ('Name') of Lloyd's receives income and gains from various sources. These comprise all or some of the following:

- underwriting profits;
- syndicate investment income in respect of invested premiums;
- interest and dividends from investments forming the Name's Lloyd's deposit, Special Reserve Fund or any other personal reserve fund;
- capital appreciation in respect of investments acquired with the syndicate's premium income;
- capital gains arising on disposals of investments forming the Name's Lloyd's deposit, Special Reserve Fund and other personal reserve funds, and
- amounts to be included in the 'total income' of the Name in respect of withdrawals from the Name's Special Reserve Fund.

The amount of a Name's share of underwriting profits, syndicate investment income and capital appreciation in respect of investments acquired with the syndicate's premium income, is all agreed with the Inland Revenue, HM Inspector of Taxes, City F.

The measure of profits, income and gains in the first, second and fourth bulleted items above is the Name's share of the underwriting account, year ended 31 December. The other sources are calculated on a normal fiscal year basis (ie from 6 April to 5 April in the following year).

Each individual underwriter sends his or her personal self assessment tax returns to the inspector in West Yorkshire Personal Tax Unit, which is now the General Claims District for most individual UK-resident Names (ie the district that deals with the Name's main source of income).

5.3 Underwriting account

The underwriting account coincides with the calendar year and includes underwriting profits or losses, syndicate investment income and capital appreciation/depreciation (both realised and unrealised). An account normally remains open for two years following the end of the year of account. If there are outstanding claims two years after the end of an account and these claims can be quantified, then the account is closed by reinsurance. Hence the 2001 underwriting account was not closed until 31 December 2003 and, during the two-year 'open' period, premiums, claims, investment income and gains were received or paid which in fact related to 2000 account transactions. The profits or losses for the 2001 account (closed 31 December 2003) were declared in 2004 and are therefore taxable in 2004–05. The underwriting profit is assessed under Schedule D, Case I, on an 'actual' basis, with no apportionment or application of the commencement or cessation provisions. Thus the underwriting profit, syndicate investment income and investment appreciation for the 2001 account will be assessable as income or capital gains of the fiscal year 2004–05.

5.4 Earned or unearned income

With effect from the 1993 account onwards, the underwriting profits of all Names have been treated as earned income. Previously, the income of 'non-working' names was treated as unearned income. This distinction is relevant for the order of set-off of losses and the ability to pay retirement annuity or personal pension premiums.

From those relevant earnings are deducted not only the gross amount of any special reserve transfer but also underwriting losses incurred in earlier years which have not yet been off set against relevant earnings to determine net relevant earnings of the year.

5.5 Reinsurance to close

The premium paid at the end of the underwriting account to reinsure any outstanding liabilities in the following account is normally deducted in arriving at the syndicate profit for the earlier account. In accounting terms the reinsurance to close can be viewed as a provision deferring profits from an earlier period to a later period. The reinsurance to close premium is deductible for tax purposes only to the extent that it does not exceed a fair and reasonable assessment of the value of the liabilities in respect of which it is payable. This assessment is made on the basis that the person who receives the premium makes neither a profit nor a loss on the transaction. It is not therefore surprising that the Inland Revenue challenge the amount of the reinsurance to close (RITC) premium, and in recent years this caused some difficulty in the agreement of a Name's tax affairs.

The Revenue had thought that for tax purposes a syndicate should calculate its profits on the footing that only a best estimate of its liabilities – which might reflect an element of discounting and which might be less than the RITC premium paid to reinsure those liabilities – would be allowed. But, in a tax appeal heard in 1999, the General Commissioners for the City of London decided that the Revenue's understanding of the law was erroneous. Having taken legal advice, the Revenue decided not to challenge this ruling. Instead new regulations were made under FA 2000.

For the 2001 and later accounting periods, if a deduction turns out to have been significantly greater (more than five per cent) than the discounted cost of the claim, an amount equivalent to interest is charged, to reverse the tax advantage gained by the excessive deduction. Equally, an amount representing interest is repaid to the insurer (subject to the five per cent threshold) if the tax deduction is shown to have been too low. The new rules do not apply to most individual Lloyd's Names so long as their participation in syndicates is below a minimum level (four per cent).

If part of the premium in respect of a member of a syndicate is disallowed for tax, that part is also ignored in calculating the tax liability of that continuing member of the syndicate who receives the premium. Where a member leaves a syndicate he or she receives a full deduction for the premium payable at the close of the last account for which he or she is a member. In consequence, the continuing members are taxed in full on that premium.

5.6 Losses

Relief for an underwriting loss is available as for any other trading loss (for example, under ICTA 1988, ss. 380, 381, 385 and 388). The underwriting loss is calculated after the inclusion of any withdrawal from the Special Reserve Fund.

Under s. 380 the underwriting loss is set against the total income of the Name in the same tax year and/or the previous tax year. Thus an underwriting loss for the 2001 account (taxable in 2004–05) can be set against total income of 2004–05 and 2003–04. If relief is claimed under ICTA 1988, s. 385 carrying a loss forward against future underwriting profits, Lloyd's investment income on deposits and reserves is regarded as underwriting profit available for set-off under s. 385(4).

Terminal loss relief under ICTA 1988, s. 388 normally takes the final year of assessment as the year during which the result of the final account of the last open syndicate year is distributed. A Name who resigns as at 31 December 2003 (thus making the 2003 account his last underwriting account) would expect all of his syndicates to close at 31 December 2005. The results would be declared and distributed in the summer of 2006 and the final year of assessment will be 2006–07. But if there is a delay in releasing the deposit, the final year of assessment is the year during which the result of the final account of the last open syndicate year is declared and this could result in a restriction on the availability of terminal loss relief. The Chairman of the ALM Tax Advisers Group confirms the problem and advises that the only solution would be for the Name in question to buy his way out of any run-off syndicates.

5.6.1 PAYE relief for losses (Lloyd's Market Bulletin Y3027)

The Revenue will give provisional relief for Lloyd's losses of the 2000 year of account in members' 2003–04 PAYE codings. This applies to all Lloyd's losses of income tax year 2003–04, including movements on earlier years' run-offs and non-syndicate income and expenses.

Members who wish to claim relief in their codings will have to provide evidence that relief will be due and that they will be able to show title to it at some time in 2003–04. Members should therefore complete and send the calculation sheet to the Revenue's West Yorkshire Personal Tax Unit together with their claims.

This represents a change from the Revenue's approach as reported in previous *Market Bulletins*. Those Bulletins reported that members would have to wait until 1 January 2004 before their 2000 year of account losses could be taken into account in the tax coding system. The change brings forward the time at which the Revenue will give relief in the PAYE system.

This accords with the Court of Appeal judgement in *Blackburn v Keeling* [2003] EWCA Civ 1222.

The taxpayer was a Lloyd's Name. He anticipated that he would have losses in May 2003 to be declared for the 2003 underwriting year and therefore relevant to the 2003–04 year of assessment. In February 2002 the taxpayer wrote to the inspector asking him to amend his 2002–03 PAYE code to take account of his losses. The inspector refused, on the grounds that the losses were not yet established. The General Commissioners and the High Court allowed the taxpayer's appeal and the Revenue appealed to the Court of Appeal.

The right to income tax relief was conferred by ICTA 1998, s. 380. The relief was triggered where the taxpayer 'sustained a loss' in a year of assessment. Losses declared in May 2003 were 'sustained' in the year of assessment 2003–04. That loss could be used on a claim made for that purpose, to give relief in either 2003–04 itself or in the preceding year 2002–03. It was clear that in February 2002, when the claim was made, and in July 2002, when the commissioners considered the matter, there was as yet no right to the relief, since the losses had not yet been 'sustained'. The Revenue's appeal therefore succeeded.

5.7 Stop-loss policies

If an underwriter effects a personal 'stop-loss' or reinsurance policy, the premiums on the policy are an allowable deduction in computing taxable underwriting profit. If insurance money is received by the underwriter as a result of a claim under the policy, the amount received is included as a trading receipt for the year of assessment that corresponds to the underwriting account in which the loss arose. Thus a stop-loss recovery in respect of a loss for the 2001 account is treated as a trading receipt for 2004–05.

If the stop-loss recovery is subsequently repaid (for example because the Name receives compensation for some of the relevant loss) then the recovery payment is deductible as an expense of the relevant year.

5.8 Interest paid

Interest paid by a Name in respect of the following loans is allowable:

- loans raised to fund losses;
- loans raised to finance the Lloyd's deposit;
- loans raised to finance cash calls, and
- loans raised to finance stop-loss premiums.

Tax relief on such interest is given by reference to the date of payment. For example, interest paid in the year to 31 December 2004 was allowed for 2004–05.

5.9 Capital gains: general

Investment appreciation arising from the premiums trust fund (syndicate investments) is based on the gains allocated to an underwriting year of account and, since the 1994 account, such gains are included in the Schedule D, Case I computation. The computation of gains/losses includes both realised and unrealised gains and losses and proceeds as follows:

	£	£
Value of assets held at year end		x
Add:		
Sales in the year (proceeds)		x
		x
Less:		
Value of assets held at start of year	(x)	
Purchases in the year (cost)	(x)	
		(x)
Appreciation		£x

The resulting gain or loss is then allocated, in accordance with the normal rules and practices of Lloyd's, to the account of the year of valuation and to the two preceding accounts ('the open years'). In computing both the realised and unrealised gains or losses, the appropriate adjustment is made in respect of exempt gains or losses relating to Government securities and qualifying corporate bonds, the advantages of which have been greatly diminished by the accrued income provisions introduced by FA 1985 (see **5.19** below).

Capital gains arising from all Lloyd's funds other than the premium trust fund (that is, the Special Reserve Fund, personal reserve fund, etc) are returnable by the Name personally. The Name should self-assess such gains in the usual way and they are computed on the basis of realised transactions during the fiscal year, with capital gains tax payable under the normal self assessment rules.

5.10 Syndicate capacity auctions

Since 1995 a Name has been able to sell syndicate capacity through auction and the Inland Revenue accept that the normal capital gains tax rules apply to disposals of capacity. In particular, the Inland Revenue now concede that taper relief at the business asset rate is applicable in computing the gain on a sale of capacity. Furthermore, syndicate capacity is now included in the class of assets eligible for capital gains tax roll-over relief; and a working Name retiring from Lloyd's membership should benefit from retirement relief on the gains from the disposal of syndicate capacity on or before 5 April 2003.

5.11 Member's Agent Pooling Arrangements

Two changes to the capital gains tax rules, introduced from 6 April 1999, significantly reduce the complexity of the calculations for individual members of Lloyd's and allow the tax charge to be deferred.

Members can participate in syndicates directly or through an arrangement known as a 'Members' Agent Pooling Arrangement' (MAPA) which allows members to buy into a pre-selected portfolio of syndicates.

These two changes are as follows.

1. A member who joins a MAPA is allowed to treat his or her share of the various syndicate capacities held through the MAPA as if it were a single direct holding of syndicate capacity. This substantially reduces the number of capital gains tax computations that would otherwise be needed

whenever the MAPA manager buys and sells syndicate capacity or when other members join or leave the MAPA.

2. All syndicate capacity whether held directly or through a MAPA is eligible for capital gains tax roll-over relief. This applies in relation to acquisitions or disposals of syndicate capacity on or after 6 April 1999.

Only individual members of Lloyd's and individuals who are partners in a Scottish limited partnership which is itself a Lloyd's member can benefit from these deregulatory changes. Different rules apply to corporate members of Lloyd's.

5.12 Capital gains tax position on retirement or death

When a Name ceases to be an underwriting member of Lloyd's, through resignation or death, he or she is deemed to dispose of any interest in the investments held by the syndicates in which he or she participated. No special computation is necessary in respect of a Name who retires, since he or she retires at the end of an account and the gains assessed for that account include the accrued appreciation. Under present capital gains tax rules, assets held at death do not give rise to any chargeable gain or allowable loss by reference to their deemed disposal at market value at that date. The sale by the executors of a deceased Name of syndicate capacity at auction could however give rise to a capital gains tax liability for the estate.

5.13 Inheritance tax

Business property relief of 100 per cent is given on death on the market value of a member's underwriting interest. Such an interest comprises investments forming part of the premiums trust fund, the Special Reserve Fund and Lloyd's deposits and profits for open years. The value of any property, including any securities deposited with a bank or insurance company, forming the collateral for a bank guarantee or letter of credit up to the maximum amount of the guarantee, qualifies for relief.

The other conditions for the relief have of course to be satisfied, including in particular minimum periods of ownership. However, this relief does not apply to the extent that the Name's main residence is the collateral for the guarantee. The Capital Taxes Office is of the view that the main residence cannot be an asset used wholly or mainly for the purposes of the underwriting business to qualify for relief. If instead, the underwriter raises a loan using the residence as security and applied the borrowing to purchase Stock Exchange investments for deposit at Lloyd's, entitlement to business property relief should be preserved, at least to the extent of the loan (see *IRC v Mallender and others (Executors of Drury-Lowe deceased)* [2001] STI 12).

In *Hardcastle and another (Executors of Vernede deceased) v IRC* SpC 259 [2000] STI 45 it was held that the excess of £251,900 on an estate protection plan (EPP) policy, which indemnified the Name's estate against losses arising on any account for which an underwriting result was not notified before death, was allowed as a deduction from the estate rather than, as the Capital Taxes Office had argued, reducing the value of the assets at Lloyd's that qualified for 100 per cent business property relief.

5.13.1 Bank guarantees and business property relief

Lloyd's have confirmed (*Lloyd's Market Bulletin* 23 April 2002) that where an individual member of Lloyd's provides a bank guarantee as part of his funds at Lloyd's, 100 per cent business property relief is allowed (up to the amount of the guarantee which is used or required as funds at Lloyd's).

The Revenue have confirmed that the availability of business property relief will no longer be restricted by reference to the nature of the underlying asset or assets. This used to be the case if assets backing the guarantee were not used wholly or mainly for purposes of the Lloyd's business, eg if a guarantee was secured on a main residence. However, the Revenue will treat the value of underlying assets as reduced by the amount of the guarantee for purposes of giving any other reliefs or exemptions. This is illustrated in the following examples.

> ### Example 5.1
>
> The deceased was an individual member of Lloyd's and a farmer. He has farmland (including property) worth £1 million and other assets valued at a net £1.25 million. The farmland qualifies for 100 per cent agricultural property relief.
>
> He has a bank guarantee of £400,000 which is used in his funds at Lloyd's. The bank guarantee is secured on the other assets.

On his death, the inheritance tax calculation is as follows. The valuation of the Lloyd's interest, which is covered by 100 per cent business property relief, is ignored for the purpose of this example, as are any other reliefs:

	£
Farmland	1,000,000
Other assets	1,250,000
	2,250,000

Less:

Business property relief on bank guarantee	(400,000)
Agricultural property relief on farmland*	(1,000,000)
Net estate after reliefs	850,000

*There is no reduction in the value of the farmland as the bank guarantee is not secured on it.

Example 5.2

The facts are as above except that the £400,000 bank guarantee is secured on the farmland.

The estate calculation is as follows. Again, the valuation of the Lloyd's open years and all other reliefs are ignored.

	£
Farmland	1,000,000
Other assets	1,250,000
	2,250,000

Less:

Business property relief on bank guarantee	(400,000)
Agricultural property relief on farmland*	(600,000)
Net estate after reliefs	1,250,000

*In this case, for the purpose of giving the 100 per cent agricultural property relief, the value of the farmland is reduced by the value of the bank guarantee on which business property relief is given. It is therefore £600,000 (£1 million less £400,000).

5.13.2 Secured assets and business property relief

Inland Revenue Capital Taxes have changed their view on the availability of business property relief for assets used by a shareholder in an underwriting company at Lloyd's (commonly known as a NAMECO) to support the company's underwriting bank guarantee or a letter of credit secured on a shareholder's own assets. (See *Lloyd's Market Bulletin* TAX/DC/IN/Y2840 dated 23 July 2002.)

In the past Inland Revenue Capital Taxes have allowed 100 per cent business property relief on the collateral assets (where they qualify). Inland Revenue Capital Taxes have now changed their view and consider that no business property relief is due on the collateral. The valuation of the collateral assets for inheritance tax purposes must also take into account the fact that the assets being provided as underwriting security represents negative value to the estate. This will entail valuing the open years and the likelihood of the collateral assets being drawn upon. It will also entail discounting the value of the assets to take account of the period for which they are fettered by the Funds at Lloyd's arrangements with the bank and with Lloyd's.

This ruling does not apply to cases where the assets are provided as collateral security for both an underwriting company and for personal underwriting by the shareholder. In these cases (known as interavailable funds at Lloyd's) business property relief continues to be available.

A shareholder in a NAMECO may also put up third party funds at Lloyd's for the company to use in its underwriting activity. The position for such third party funds at Lloyd's is the same as for bank guarantees and letters of credit. While business property relief is still available to interavailable assets, this is not the case where the funds are provided for the company alone.

Those who have relied on the previous view are told by Inland Revenue Capital Taxes not to continue to do so and to adjust their financial affairs. However, appropriate action will be taken on an individual basis if an inheritance tax liability arises during that transition.

5.14 Special Reserve Fund

Rules relating to the Special Reserve Fund mean that the maximum amount that can be transferred into the fund is 50 per cent of the aggregate syndicate profits for each account, subject to the condition that the value of the fund at the end of the previous account is no more than 50 per cent of the Name's premium limit.

Withdrawals from the fund must be made whenever the Name incurs overall syndicate losses. The amount of the withdrawal is the lower of the loss and the amount of the fund. The amount of any stop-loss recovery is taken into account in determining the necessary withdrawal from the fund.

Transfers into and withdrawals from the Special Reserve Fund are treated as deductible expenses or trading receipts respectively in calculating the Case I profit or loss.

The Special Reserve Fund is valued as at 31 December each year to ensure that the limit of 50 per cent of the Name's premium limit is not exceeded. Any excess must be withdrawn.

On retirement or death of a Name any balance in the Special Reserve Fund is repaid and treated as trading receipts of the final underwriting year. The overall effect of transfers into and out of the Fund is to defer tax on the underwriting profits until eventual withdrawal from the Fund.

5.15 Retirement annuity and personal/ stakeholder pension premiums

The Sch. D, Case I profit for all Names qualifies as 'relevant earnings' for the purposes of retirement annuity or personal/stakeholder pension relief. Under self-assessment the normal rules for obtaining tax relief on pension premiums apply equally to Names as to other taxpayers. The facilities to carry back premiums one year and (for retirement annuity premiums) to carry forward unused relief are particularly relevant to Names. Advice should be taken on the impact (if any) of the new regime to be introduced from 6 April 2006 by FA 2004.

5.16 Subscriptions and other expenses

Where expenses are met by the syndicate (for example contributions to the Central Fund) a relevant amount is deducted in arriving at the overall under-writing profit or loss. Other expenses, incurred personally by a Name, are allowable by reference to the actual date of payment. Amounts paid in a particular calendar year are deductible for the tax year in which the calendar year ends. Thus expenses personally met during 2003 are deductible in the tax year 2003–04.

The following list gives details of typical expenses incurred by a Lloyd's Name.

1. The annual subscription for membership of Lloyd's is allowable. It is normally paid by the underwriting agent and reflected in the underwriting profit reported.

2. The annual percentage fee charged for a bank for providing letters of credit and bank guarantees may be deducted (but not the initial arrangement fee or the cost of increasing the facility), even if the bank charges relate to a Name's personal reserve funds.

3. The subscription paid to the Association of Lloyd's Members, the pressure group formed to establish relations with Lloyd's Council and improve the format of accounts and information that Names receive, is allowable for tax relief in full. A claim can also be made for one-half of the published cost of the food and drink element in the cost of attending ALM meetings. The cost of travel to ALM regional meetings (but not those held in London) is allowed, insofar as this does not exceed the cost of travel from London to that regional meeting.

4. Litigation has been commenced by affected syndicates to recover misappropriated funds, following the investigation into certain suspended underwriters and offshore companies controlled by those underwriters. West Yorkshire Personal Tax Unit has stated that the majority of claims for relief for reasonable legal costs are allowed as an underwriting expense in the same way as stop-loss premiums of the year in which the costs are incurred. Similarly, any recoveries are taxable in the year they are received. As an allied issue, the Inland Revenue consider compensation received (less legal expenses incurred) by Lloyd's members following actions against the lead underwriters of syndicates, their syndicate managing agents or members' agents is taxable on normal principles as trading income in the year of entitlement, subject to the special two-year carry back rules for running off syndicates (under reg. 7 of Lloyd's Underwriters (Tax) Regulations 1974 (SI 1974 No. 896)) (see *Market Bulletin* of Lloyds, March 1992).

5. Because of the complexities of dealing with underwriters' tax affairs, the Inland Revenue at West Yorkshire Personal Tax Unit used to allow claims for personal accountancy fees without question against the underwriting profits of Names, up to certain limits. Under self-assessment, however, each Name determines an appropriate deduction for such fees.

6. Stop-loss premiums are treated as an expense in the Case I computation, and any recoveries are treated as trading receipts.

7. Estate protection plan premiums are deductible as a personal expense.

5.17 Foreign taxes paid and double taxation relief

5.17.1 US tax

(The following applies to UK-resident non-US Names only.)

US tax returns are submitted annually in respect of profits arising in the USA, including investment income and gains 'effectively connected' with the US business. In the past, Le Boeuf, Lamb, Leiby & MacRae have prepared consolidated US tax returns on behalf of most non-US Names. The Name's personal accountant would have supplied, through the agents, details of non-Lloyd's US income for inclusion on that return.

Under the current closing agreement with the USA, Le Boeuf's file a US return to report the Lloyd's syndicate income and gains only. If a Name has other US source income, a separate return may need to be filed by the Name's personal accountant.

Double taxation relief in respect of US federal income tax is computed individually for each Name in respect of his or her Lloyd's income and gains, and the figures are agreed between Lloyd's and the Inland Revenue. The inspector then advises the Name's personal accountant of the agreed figures. A double taxation relief report is issued by West Yorkshire Personal Tax Unit, which includes Canadian taxes paid.

Repayment of the double taxation relief due can be obtained by the Name's personal accountant on submission of a formal claim for tax credit relief.

The rules for relieving underwriting losses in the USA are different from those in the UK. Under the Tax Reform Act 1986, Lloyd's income in the USA is deemed to be 'passive' income (ie, where a taxpayer does not participate on a regular basis), and passive losses can only be set off against passive income or carried forward.

5.17.2 Other

The reports from the syndicate accountants, and also the Form LL9 received from the inspector, show foreign taxes paid. These will have been deducted as an expense in computing the Sch. D, Case I profit or loss. If there is a profit, the foreign taxes are added to the profit and are then allowed as a credit against the tax charged. If there is a loss, there is no adjustment.

In the case of working Names, the foreign taxes paid can be allowed only as a credit against the tax due on the Sch. D, Case I profit. If, however, the Sch. D, Case I liability has been reduced to nil, or to an amount less than the foreign taxes paid (eg by transfer to the Special Reserve Fund), the foreign taxes paid are allowed as allowable Sch. D, Case I expenses, and can thus create or augment a loss.

5.18 Non-resident Names

A non-resident Name is liable to UK tax in respect of any Lloyd's profits, as he or she is deemed to be carrying on a trade in the UK. Taxable profits include Sch. D, Case I profit, and income arising from investments forming the Lloyd's deposit, Special Reserve Fund, and personal reserve funds and capital gains (ICTA 1988, s. 18(1)(a)(iii) and TCGA 1992, s. 10(1)) on assets situated in the UK. Assets in the Lloyd's deposit and Special Reserve Fund situated outside the UK are deemed to be part of the UK trade. Therefore, any income arising therefrom is still deemed to arise from a UK trade.

Investments held in the Lloyd's sterling trust fund are generally situated in the UK, but any non-UK securities are considered to be situated outside the UK.

Investments held in the Lloyd's US trust fund or Lloyd's Canadian trust fund are regarded as situated outside the UK.

The syndicate accountant will provide details of the Name's share of gains arising in respect of investments situated outside the UK. Since all net gains arising to the syndicate in any year of assessment are assessed at the basic rate of income tax, it is the responsibility of the Name's personal accountant to claim any repayment due in respect of the gains that are exempt because the Name is neither resident nor ordinarily resident in the UK.

Two changes occurred in March 2000, allowing credit relief to be claimed by non-UK resident underwriters. First, UK credit relief is extended to all non-UK residents carrying on business in the UK through a branch or agency

(ICTA 1988 s. 794(2)(bb) introduced by FA 2000). This applies to all accounting periods ending on or after 21 March 2000. Accordingly, Lloyd's names resident in all other countries will be able to claim credit relief for non-UK tax paid on their Lloyd's income (subject, however, to the 'own country tax' restriction).

UK tax relief will not be given for taxes paid in the member's own country of residence. Here, only deduction relief (if applicable) will be available. The own country tax restriction will be applied to all members claiming credit relief for 1999–2000 and subsequent years on a worldwide basis. The forms CTA 1 for 1999–2000 and for subsequent years show a breakdown of foreign tax by country.

5.19 Accrued income scheme

An underwriting member of Lloyd's or of an approved association of underwriters is treated (for the purposes of the bond washing provisions) as absolutely entitled to the securities forming part of his or her premiums trust fund, Lloyd's deposit, Special Reserve Fund and any other trust fund required by the rules of Lloyd's. The accrued income scheme rules apply, therefore, in the normal way to transactions in the securities constituting the Lloyd's deposit, Special Reserve Fund and other personal reserve funds.

However, syndicate investments that are included in a premiums trust fund are deemed to be transferred and reacquired on 31 December and 1 January respectively each year, starting with a deemed acquisition on 1 January 1986. This means that the income accrued up to 31 December each year forms part of the syndicate investment income of that year, with a corresponding deduction from the first interest receipt (or accrued interest on sale) in the following year. To achieve this result, it is provided that, where an interest period straddles 31 December in any year (starting with 31 December 1986), it is deemed to be split into two interest periods — the first ending on 31 December and the second starting on 1 January.

Liability under the accrued income scheme is assessable under Schedule D, Case VI (ICTA 1988, s. 714(2)). The West Yorkshire Personal Tax Unit (has confirmed that Names' non-Lloyd's Sch. D, Case VI losses, including those brought forward from years before the accrued income scheme began, may be relieved, where possible, against accrued income forming part of their syndicate investment income. Future forms LL185 E should indicate the proportion of Sch. D, Case VI tax paid by the agent.

Where an individual dies, there is no deemed disposal by the deceased to his or her personal representatives on death. As far as personal funds are concerned, the personal representatives are liable on the basis of the deceased's acquisition details. The position regarding syndicate investments is not clear.

In practice, the Name is assessed on the share of any accrued income arising to his or her syndicates and credited to the accounts for years up to and including the year of death.

5.20 Premiums trust funds: stock lending

The stock lending provisions in ICTA 1988, s. 129 were introduced to place Inland Revenue Extra-statutory Concession B15 on a statutory basis. These provisions cover disposals giving rise to a liability under Sch. D, Case I under the accrued income scheme and to capital gains tax. The provisions were extended by FA 1989, s. 91 to Lloyd's. For the purposes of the accrued income scheme and for capital gains tax, stocks lent by Lloyd's underwriters are now deemed to remain within the premiums trust fund without giving rise to disposal and reacquisition. This does not apply to the extent that the loan extends over a year end where, as in the case of securities actually held then, they are deemed to have been sold and reacquired at the year end for accrued income scheme and capital gains purposes (see TCGA 1992, s. 207).

5.21 Husband and wife

It is important to remember the following in relation to the taxation of husbands and wives as it affects Lloyd's members.

1. If transfers of assets are made between spouses to maximise possible tax benefits, the Name must not overlook the ongoing means requirement or annual solvency test required by Lloyd's.
2. Lloyd's losses are available only against the other income of the Name and not of the spouse. They may be carried forward against future underwriting profits or related back against other income of the previous year if beneficial.
3. Syndicates are likely to produce capital losses so that the Names should retain the capacity to make personal capital gains if this is practical. The Name's capital losses are not available to set against the spouse's gains.

5.22 Corporate membership

Corporate membership of Lloyd's has been available since 1 January 1994 and an increasing number of individual Names are considering or have already converted to corporate membership.

The tax treatment of the profits of a corporate member is beyond the scope of this book.

Where an individual Name converts to corporate membership there are capital gains tax issues, depending on the conversion vehicle used. Conversion is achieved either by 'transition' or by 'interavailability' and the conversion vehicle can be either a limited company or a Scottish limited partnership. Where conversion is through transition to a limited company, the individual Name's underwriting liability is reinsured into the company and, provided the whole of the funds at Lloyd's and all syndicate capacity (if not reinsured) is transferred to the company in exchange for shares issued by the company, the Inland Revenue accepts that any gains arising are held over under ICTA 1988, s. 162.

Where conversion is through interavailability the funds at Lloyd's are retained by the Name and any income or gains arising continue to be assessed on the Name. Syndicate capacity is transferred to the conversion vehicle, but because the condition of s. 162 requiring a transfer of all of the assets of the business has not been satisfied, capital gains relief is not available.

Relief on conversion to limited liability underwriting

The Finance Act 2004 introduced new rules that make certain reliefs available where an individual member of Lloyds converts to limited liability underwriting. The rules are contained in FA 1993, s. 179B and Sch. 20A (as inserted by FA 2004, s. 144 and Sch. 25) and apply from 6 April 2004.

For the reliefs to be available the following conditions must be met.

Condition 1

- The member gives notice of his resignation from membership of Lloyd's in accordance with the rules or practice of Lloyd's;
- in accordance with such rules or practice, the member does not undertake any new insurance business at Lloyd's after the end of the member's last underwriting year, and
- the member does not withdraw that notice.

Condition 2

All of the member's syndicate capacity is disposed of by the member under a conversion arrangement to the successor company ('the syndicate capacity disposal') with effect from the beginning of the underwriting year that immediately follows the end of the member's last underwriting year.

Condition 3

Immediately before the syndicate capacity disposal:

- the member controls the successor company, and
- more than 50 per cent of the ordinary share capital of the successor company is beneficially owned by the member.

Condition 4

The syndicate capacity disposal is made in consideration solely of the issue to the member of shares in the successor company.

Condition 5

The successor company starts to carry on its underwriting business in the underwriting year that immediately follows the member's last underwriting year.

The member's last underwriting year is the underwriting year during which or at the end of which the underwriting member becomes a non-underwriting member in accordance with the rules and practices of Lloyd's.

Where the conditions are met, the member is able to carry forward underwriting losses prior to conversion and set those losses against income from the successor company, whether dividend income or otherwise, provided that the member controls the successor company and is beneficially entitled to at least 50 per cent of the share capital. For the purpose of relieving underwriting losses carried forward, the income from the successor company is treated as if it were income from the underwriting business assessable under Sch. D, Case I. A similar relief is available under a conversion arrangement to a successor partnership.

Roll over relief is available for capital gains tax purposes on the disposal of syndicate capacity and the disposal of assets forming the member's ancillary trust fund.

Chapter 6 Temporary visitors to the UK

6.1 Employees

The liability to UK tax of temporary visitors to the UK for employment purposes depends on their residence position, the place of performance of their duties, their domicile position and by whom they are paid for their duties.

6.2 Residence position

6.2.1 Year of arrival or departure

An individual's status as resident and/or ordinarily resident in the UK normally applies for the whole or for none of a particular tax year. Under Extra-statutory Concession (ESC) A11 when an individual arrives in the UK or leaves the UK he or she is resident only for the part of the tax year after arrival or before departure respectively.

An individual is always resident in the UK if spending six months or more in the UK in any tax year (ICTA 1988, s. 336). The availability of accommodation in the UK is no longer a relevant factor in determining the residence of a temporary visitor. An individual who comes to the UK to work for a period of at least two years is treated as resident here for the whole period from the day of arrival to the day of departure, whether retaining accommodation in the UK or not. Individuals are not usually regarded as having become ordinarily resident in the UK until they have been here for at least three years, unless it is clear from the outset that they intend to be in the country for three or more years, in which event they are normally treated as ordinarily resident from the date of arrival.

Ordinary residence in the UK is usually taken to mean habitual residence. It is not defined by statute.

Individuals are not normally treated as ordinarily resident if they are in the UK for less than three years. The tax year in which they become ordinarily resident depends on the circumstances. If it is clear from the date of arrival in the UK that the individual intends to be resident for more than three years, he or she is treated as resident and ordinarily resident from the outset. Otherwise the individual may become ordinarily resident from 6 April following the third anniversary of his or her arrival in the UK.

Statement of Practice 17/91 explains the determination of the ordinary residence of someone who comes to the UK not intending to stay here for three or more years. An individual with such an intention is treated as resident from the outset. In the absence of such intention, ordinary residence begins with the tax year starting after the third anniversary of arrival.

For individuals who come to the UK and, before the beginning of the tax year following the third anniversary of their arrival, either purchase a house or acquire a lease for more than three years, or change their mind as to how long they are staying, ordinary residence begins:

- from the day of arrival if one of the above occurs in the tax year of arrival, or
- from the beginning of the tax year in which one of the above events occurs.

Ordinary residence status has some significant implications; and perhaps the most important are that:

- an individual is liable to capital gains tax if either ordinarily resident or resident, and
- a UK citizen is taxable only on a remittance basis if resident in the UK but not ordinarily resident.

The definition of habitual residence can be expanded on by asking: 'where is the centre of an individual's economic activity or dependence?' Thus, it is possible for a returning expatriate to maintain economic links and a base abroad and still obtain a tax advantage from foreign earnings.

6.3 Remittance

One of the major tax consequences for non-UK domiciliaries is the operation of the remittance basis. This basis applies to:

- foreign earnings assessed under ITEPA 2003, ss. 22 or 26 (formerly Sch. E, Case III);
- foreign income assessed under Sch. D, Cases IV and V;

- capital gains on assets situated abroad, and
- inheritance tax only on UK-situated (non-excluded) property.

There is an entire industry based on tax planning for foreign domiciliaries which relies on the application of the above rules.

6.4 Place of performance of duties

Incidental duties are ignored in deciding the place of performance of duties. What constitute incidental duties depends upon the facts of each case. The time taken in relation to the duties is not conclusive (*Robson v Dixon* (1972) 48 TC 527). Reporting to one's employer, receiving fresh instructions or coming to the UK to be trained (provided it does not exceed three months in a year), are regarded as incidental duties by the Revenue (leaflet IR 20, paras 38 and 39). Note that the Inland Revenue do not accept that any duties of a UK company director can be incidental.

6.5 Domicile

Domicile is a concept of general law and it is outside the scope of this book to discuss it in detail. Broadly speaking, an individual is domiciled in the country in which he or she has a permanent home. Domicile is distinct from nationality or residence. An individual may be resident in more than one country but at any given time is domiciled in one country only. Individuals acquire a domicile of origin at birth which is normally the domicile of their father. This they retain until they acquire a domicile of choice or a domicile of dependency. A domicile of choice is acquired if they can show they have severed ties with the country of their domicile of origin, and settled in another country with the intention of remaining there permanently. A domicile of dependency occurs in the case of a minor whose domicile follows that of the individual on whom he or she is legally dependent.

6.6 The payer of the income

The relevance of the payer of the income is that most visitors are domiciled abroad and retain their foreign domicile during any stay in the UK. If they are paid by an employer who is not resident in the UK, they are taxable under ITEPA 2003, s. 21 in respect of any duties performed in the UK, and under

Temporary visitors to the UK

ITEPA 2003, s. 23 (formerly Sch. E, Case III) on a remittance basis in respect of any duties performed abroad.

To identify what part of such earnings has been remitted to the UK, s. 23 liability arises only where the aggregate of earnings paid in, benefits enjoyed in, and the earnings remitted to the UK exceeds the amount assessable under s. 21 on the above basis. The s. 23 assessment is thus restricted to the excess of the aggregate over the s. 21 assessment.

There is the further advantage that under most double tax agreements, including in particular the US/UK agreement, if an individual is paid by an employer not resident in the UK, and the remuneration is not charged to a permanent establishment in the UK, and the employee is not present for more than 183 days in the UK but is resident in the other country, he or she is exempt from UK tax (see Art. 14(2) of US/UK Double Tax TreatyConvention).

6.7 Dual employment contracts

Where an individual is either not domiciled or not ordinarily resident in the UK and has an employment, the duties of which are performed both in the UK and overseas, it may be advisable to have the employment split under two separate contracts. This enables the overseas earnings to escape UK tax providing they are not remitted to the UK. Standard dual contract arrangements need not be disclosed to the Revenue under the disclosure regime introduced by FA 2004, although more innovative arrangements should be disclosed (letter from the Inland Revenue to the CIOT). There are, therefore, three categories of foreign visitors who come to the UK to work in the UK, including designated areas of the North Sea.

1. Those who come for more than six months in a fiscal year, and are therefore resident here, and who cannot rely on any double tax treaty to modify their position. If they are paid by a UK-resident employer, either the whole of the earnings are liable to UK tax under ITEPA 2003, s. 22 (formerly Sch. E,, Case I), or the whole of the earnings referable to UK duties are liable under ITEPA 2003, s. 25 (formerly Sch. E, Case II), depending upon whether they stay long enough to be regarded as ordinarily resident as well as resident here. Any income from a separate employment with a foreign employer, where all duties are performed overseas, is liable on a remittance basis under ITEPA 2003, s. 26 (formerly Sch. E, Case III). The remittance basis also applies to the overseas proportion of earnings of a mixed employment, where some duties are carried out in the UK and

some abroad, if the employee is resident here but not ordinarily resident, and thus liable under ITEPA 2003, s. 25 (formerly Sch. E, Case II) in respect of UK duties. The overseas investment income and capital gains from the disposal of non-UK chargeable assets of an individual resident, but not domiciled, in the UK are also taxable on remittances.

2. Those who come to the UK for less than six months and have temporary rented accommodation during their stay. They are regarded as not resident here and are liable to UK tax under ITEPA 2003, s. 27 (formerly Sch. E, Case II) only on money earned for duties carried out in the UK. Where the duties of the employment are carried out partly in the UK and partly outside the UK, a split of the total remuneration is made. Note that no liability to UK tax attaches to any other income arising abroad and there is no liability to capital gains tax.

3. As in 2 whether there is accommodation retained or not, except that an individual can claim complete exemption from UK tax because of the provisions of a double tax treaty. Usually he or she must be paid by a foreign employer and the income must not be charged to any permanent establishment of that employer in the UK. The fact that a management charge may be rendered to a UK subsidiary company by its parent company in respect of services performed for it by individuals who continue to be employed by the parent company, should not mean that such remuneration is charged to a permanent establishment for this purpose.

6.7.1 A salutary tale

In the recent case of *Slattery v Moore Stephens* [2003] STI Issue 32 the High Court held that the taxpayer's accountants should have advised their client of the potential tax benefits of payment outside the UK of earnings in respect of non-UK duties.

The claimant, a non-UK domiciliary, worked for an international bank with headquarters in New York. He came to the UK to take up employment at the bank's London branch. He should have been assessed to UK tax under what was Case II in respect of UK duties and under Case III (the remittance basis) in respect of non-UK duties. Based on tax returns prepared by the defendant accountants, the claimant was given a PAYE refund by the Revenue. The defendant had prepared the returns as if the claimant was paid abroad, whereas he was being paid all his earnings by the bank in London. He was therefore not entitled to a PAYE refund and was later required to repay the tax to the Revenue plus interest. He took action against the firm.

The failure even to alert the claimant to the potential benefits of payment offshore in respect of non-UK duties fell below the standard to be expected of a reasonably careful and competent tax accountant. The court held also that the claimant too had failed in not raising with the defendant the issue which must have looked odd to him at the time, given his own understanding of the UK tax position. There was therefore also contributory negligence on the claimant's part.

6.8 Corresponding payments relief

Temporary visitors can deduct from the earnings any expenses that would satisfy normal employment income rules of allowability, and also after any payments (out of the earnings) of a corresponding nature to those that would have reduced the individual's liability to income tax if the income derived from a UK employer (for instance, payments to a superannuation scheme comparable to contributions to an approved UK scheme (ITEPA 2003, s. 390)). However, advice should be taken on the impact (if any) of the 'migrant member relief' provisions of FA 2004, effective 6 April 2006.

The Revenue have a discretion to allow such 'corresponding payment' claims, and in the exercise of their discretion will in practice require claimants to show that they have insufficient overseas income on which UK tax is not chargeable to enable them to make the payments without having recourse to the foreign earnings. Where there is some overseas income, but it is insufficient to cover the payments, relief is given on the excess. However, in the case of corresponding superannuation contributions paid out of foreign earnings, the foreign earnings are treated as reduced by the contributions whether or not there is overseas income to make the payments (leaflet IR 25 (1977), page 16) but NB the new FA 2004 regime referred to above.

The availability of capital out of which the payments could have been made is disregarded.

A payment is regarded as a corresponding payment only if it differs from a payment which qualifies for relief under UK tax rules not in substance but solely because it is made under a foreign obligation or in accordance with normal foreign practice. Examples are alimony paid under a foreign court order, interest on a loan to purchase a residence in the employee's home country, and annual contributions to a foreign pension fund which corresponds to a UK pension fund in respect of which relief on contributions is given. The amount of the relief is computed as far as possible by reference to the appropriate UK tax rules. Relief for mortgage interest and maintenance payments has not been available since 5 April 2000.

6.9 Travel expenses

Where individuals who are not domiciled in the UK are in receipt of earnings for duties performed in the UK they are, subject to certain conditions, exempt from tax in respect of certain travel expenses between their home abroad and the UK which are reimbursed by their employer. They must not have been resident in the UK in either of the two years of assessment immediately preceding the year of assessment in which the employment is taken up, nor must they have been in the UK for any purpose at any time during the period of two years ending with the time of taking up the employment. The period during which the travel facilities are allowed is of five years' duration only.

The expenses can relate to any journey from their normal home to the UK to take up or resume their employment, and vice versa. In addition, travel expenses of a spouse and children between the home abroad and the UK is exempt if the employee is in the UK for a continuous period of at least 60 days in order to perform the duties of the employment, and the journey is:

- made to accompany them at the beginning of the period;
- to visit them during it, or
- is a return journey following such a journey.

There is a restriction of two journeys to the UK and two return journeys per year.

Note that the favourable tax treatment applies to direct payments by the employer, or to travel expenses reimbursed by the employer. The employee cannot claim any personal expenditure under these heads as a deduction.

It is commonplace to find that employees, particularly of US concerns, receive substantial extra compensation payments to cover extra UK tax they have to pay over and above what they would have paid in the USA. All such allowances and benefits that would be assessed to UK tax have to be included in the foreign earnings.

Removal and relocation expenses reasonably provided in connection with a change of the employee's residence reimbursed to an employee transferred within an organisation are tax deductible against income up to a maximum of

£8,000. The legislation (ITEPA 2003, ss 271–289) defines the categories of deductible removal expenses. Employees no longer have to dispose of their home in their country of origin.

Where employees are seconded to the UK from their normal place of work abroad, it should be possible to secure exemption from UK tax for reimbursed travel, accommodation and subsistence expenses. This treatment is available only where the absence is not expected to (and does not in fact) exceed 24 months, and where employees return to their normal place of work thereafter. The situation is covered by the rules for temporary absences from a normal place of work found in Booklet IR 480. To meet the cost of upkeep of his or her home country residence without the assistance of rentals, Inland Revenue practice is to allow exemption for reasonable board and lodging expenses where an individual is on detached duty in the UK for a period not expected to exceed 12 months.

6.10 Requirements of employee and employer

Where the employer is not resident in the UK but an employee performs duties in the UK for the benefit of an individual resident here or for the benefit of an individual carrying on a trade here (for example a UK branch of a non-resident concern), the individual for whose benefit the duties are performed may be required to give the name and address of the employee to the Inland Revenue (FA 1974, s. 24). The PAYE obligations of a non-resident employer are discussed in **6.11.2** below. In addition, the employee may be required to make a return of the full amount of any earnings received whether or not UK tax is chargeable on them (FA 1974, s. 24 and TMA 1970, s. 8). This is obviously to enable the Inland Revenue to apportion on a reasonable basis the foreign earnings referrable to UK duties where the individual is liable under ITEPA 2003, s. 25 (formerly Schedule E, Case II).

Where the earnings are paid in the UK, the Inland Revenue seek to operate the normal PAYE regulations on them, although the gross figure of the earnings is very often not known until all figures of UK tax liability and other benefits are worked out.

Where the earnings are paid abroad the direct collection method is normally used, under which an assessment is raised on the employee based on the estimated amount of the earnings for the current tax year, and tax is paid in four instalments during the year. Appropriate adjustments are made when the final figures are known.

The receipts basis of assessment for employment income has not itself altered the liability to income tax under the various provisions of ITEPA 2003. However, receipts in a year after the source has ceased are liable, reversing the case of *Bray v Best* [1989] STC 159. Equally, receipts in a year before a source commences are also liable. In the case of multi-national businesses, transferring employees to and from the UK, it may be difficult to devise packages which enable payments for UK duties to escape UK tax.

6.11 The North Sea

The position of individuals working on North Sea oil and gas installations is that, irrespective of their residence position, if they perform their duties in a designated area (that is an area designated by Order in Council under the Continental Shelf Act 1964, s. 1(7)), they are treated as performing their duties in the UK (ITEPA 2003, s. 41).

Such individuals are liable to UK tax on an arising basis under ITEPA 2003, s. 25 (formerly Sch. E, Case II) if they are not resident, or not ordinarily resident in the UK, in respect of their earnings for the work they carry out in the North Sea; or under ITEPA 2003, s. 21 (formerly Sch. E, Case I) if they are resident and ordinarily resident in the UK on all their earnings.

6.11.1 Returns by North Sea employers

There are special provisions requiring licence holders employing individuals on activities carried on under the licence to give details to the Inland Revenue of any earnings or other payments made in respect of services performed in the area and the names of the recipients, so that employers cannot escape their obligations by not having a branch in the UK or a subsidiary company resident in the UK (FA 1973, Sch. 15, para. 2(b)).

6.11.2 *Clark v Oceanic Contractors Inc*

In the case of *Clark v Oceanic Contractors Inc* [1983] STC 35, the House of Lords held by a narrow majority of three to two that a non-resident employer operating in the North Sea is also liable to account for tax under the PAYE procedure on any earnings of its employees liable to UK tax.

If a non-resident company is taxed on any profits derived from activities in a designated area of the North Sea, and its employees are deemed to perform their duties in the UK when working in that area, under the special provisions in FA 1973, s. 38 it follows that the employer has an obligation to apply PAYE to such earnings.

There is, of course, no practical problem where an overseas employer has a branch in the UK. However, in the above case the respondent corporation, which was incorporated in Panama as a wholly-owned subsidiary of a US parent, maintained only a design office and platform fabrication yard in the UK. The company's activities, which extended throughout the world, included a North Sea division with its headquarters in Brussels. This division was engaged in the installation and maintenance of platforms and the laying of pipelines in both the UK and Norwegian sectors of the North Sea. Some 60 per cent of the employees engaged by the North Sea division were UK nationals, the remainder being principally citizens of the USA. Since 1973, some 40 per cent of the corporation's North Sea activities had been located in the UK sector of the North Sea. Employees' earnings were paid from Brussels in US dollars by cheques made out in Brussels and drawn on a New York bank. It was common ground that, by reason of s. 38, the corporation was liable to UK tax on profits arising from the activities of its North Sea division in the designated area, and equally employees working in this area were assessable to income tax under ITEPA 2003 on their earnings.

The Inland Revenue argued that ICTA 1988, s. 203, which governs the operation of PAYE, imposed no territorial limitation, and that the PAYE regulations also applied wherever earnings chargeable under ITEPA 2003 are paid. Oceanic submitted that s. 203 had no application to a foreign employer paying earnings from some place outside the UK.

The House of Lords ruled that the corporation was liable to apply PAYE. However, Lord Scarman dismissed the Inland Revenue assertion that the application of PAYE had no territorial limits. There was the practical impossibility of enforcing or monitoring the system against an uncooperative employer residing overseas. Therefore, some territorial limitation had to be applied. The existence of this limitation implied a 'tax presence' within the UK. The operations carried out by the corporation did disclose such a presence because of the application of FA 1973, s. 38 and it was, therefore, liable to account for PAYE.

> 'For the purposes of corporation tax, Oceanic, it is agreed, carries on a trade in the UK which includes its operations in the UK section of the North Sea. For the purposes of this trade, it employs a work force in that section whose earnings are assessable to British income tax. Finally, Oceanic does have an address for service in the UK.. . .. For these reasons, I conclude that Oceanic

by its trading operations... has subjected itself to the liability to operate Pay As You Earn.'

Lord Wilberforce similarly considered that liability arose only where an employer had a branch or agency in the UK so as to be within the provisions of ICTA 1988, s. 11.

This decision raises matters of some importance, particularly to those employers operating in the North Sea. It means that wherever there is some establishment employing labour in the UK or in a designated area, there is an obligation to apply PAYE.

6.11.3 Divers

Divers are no longer regarded as employees for tax purposes although anyone employing divers in the UK or a designated area is required to disclose details of payments made to them (ICTA 1988, s. 314). This means divers can claim all the normal expenses allowable to self-employed individuals and, if they can show that the base of their operations is their home, travelling expenses to and from the North Sea installation can be claimed on the basis of the decision in *Horton v Young* (1971) 47 TC 69.

Note that the Inland Revenue regard the cost of diving training courses as capital expenditure, as such courses put the diver in a position to earn income rather than being undertaken in the course of earning that income. In the case of employee divers, no relief is due. However, if the diver is treated as self-employed, it has been agreed between the Inland Revenue and the association of offshore diving contractors that the expenditure can be treated as expenditure on 'know-how', qualifying for relief under ICTA 1988, s. 530.

The expenditure qualifies for relief because the knowledge gained relates to 'techniques likely to assist in the working of a mine, oil well or other source of mineral deposits'. For the diver who also works on non-oil related activities there is a restriction, so that the relief given in any year is restricted with reference to the amount of s. 314 profits (basically from diving in the UK Continental Shelf in the North Sea and in the UK itself on oil related activities) and the total diving earnings for the year (for instance, from dock or harbour work or work outside the UK).

Receipts may be required to substantiate the expenditure, which can amount to over £5,000 for a saturation diving course and more than £3,500 for an air diving course.

For qualifying courses undertaken after 1 April 1986, relief is given by way of a writing-down allowance of 25 per cent per annum on the reducing balance basis.

The initial costs of basic survival and fire fighting courses are regarded as capital expenditure which does not qualify for relief under the know-how provisions in ICTA 1988, s. 533(7), but the costs of renewal courses are allowable as revenue expenditure.

6.11.4 Expenses

Difficulties have arisen concerning the allowability of expenses payments made to oil rig workers and others who live at a considerable distance from their place of work and who receive travel expenses when they go on periodic leave to visit their families from the rigs. These difficulties apply to both overseas visitors and UK nationals. As there is only one fixed base from which, in most cases, they work, all expenses are arguably expenses of travelling to and from the place of work. The amounts are not so small as to be capable of being ignored as a perquisite, which appeared to be the basis of the decision in the case of the local authority teacher, *Donnelly v Williamson* [1981] STC 563, where a mileage allowance of £13 per annum to help a teacher meet the cost of attending school functions out of hours was held to be not taxable. Neither do the payments come within the 'working rules agreements' governing the payment of travel and subsistence allowances up to certain amounts tax free to construction industry workers moving from site to site as agreed between the trade unions and the Inland Revenue.

The position is, therefore, that in strict law the amounts are probably assessable.

Consequently, ITEPA 2003, s. 305 (formerly ESC A 65) was introduced to deal with the problem. All expenses reimbursed by the employer for transfers between the mainland and the oil and gas rigs or platforms, including the journey from home to the port of transfer, are not now taxed. Where the employees have to take overnight accommodation in the vicinity of the mainland departure point, income tax is also not charged on reasonable accommodation and subsistence costs or, in the case of employees earning £8,500 or more, on the benefit of such accommodation provided at the employer's expense.

6.11.5 The Norwegian sector

Article 31A of the UK/Norway Double Tax Treaty (Double Taxation Relief (Taxes on Income) (Norway) Order 1985 (SI 1985 No. 1998) introduced special rules applicable to certain offshore activities. One of the rules states, basically, that salaries and similar remuneration derived by a resident of the UK, in respect of an employment connected with the exploration of the seabed and subsoil situated in Norwegian waters to the extent that the duties are performed in Norwegian waters, is taxable only in Norway. This rule applies only where documentary evidence is produced which satisfies the UK authorities that tax has been paid in Norway, otherwise the normal domestic laws are to apply, with double taxation relief given accordingly.

6.12 Visiting professors or teachers

In connection with visitors to the UK generally, bear in mind that it may be possible to claim exemption from UK tax on earnings in the UK under a double tax agreement, if the individuals concerned are visiting professors or teachers.

However, the wording of the agreement must be carefully studied as the case of *CIR v Vas* [1990] STC 137 illustrates. In this case the taxpayer, a Hungarian, visited the UK on three separate occasions, on each occasion to take up research appointments at the University of Newcastle. He was a resident of Hungary immediately before each visit, which did not exceed two years. He claimed exemption under the relevant article in the UK/Hungary Double Tax Treaty for each visit on the grounds that it was of less than two years' duration. The court held that no exemption was due for any period running after the expiry of two years from the date of his first visit.

Article 20A of the US/UK Double Taxation Convention is identical to the teachers article in the previous treaty and provides a two year tax exemption for UK- and US-resident professors or teachers who visit the other country for not more than two years for the purpose of teaching or engaging in public interest research at a university, college or other recognised educational institution. The exemption relates only to remuneration derived from such teaching and public interest research.

One of the conditions of receiving the exemption is that the teacher or professor may stay in the other country for only two years. If they stay longer, they will be treated in the same way as any other group of employees, and tax will be payable for the full period, starting from the first day of the visit.

6.13 Visitors for education

Individuals who come to the UK for a period of stay and education which is expected to last for more than four years are regarded as resident and ordinarily resident from the date of their arrival. If the period is not expected to exceed four years they may be treated as not ordinarily resident but this depends on whether:

- they have available accommodation here; or
- they intend to remain here at the end of their period of education, or
- they propose to visit the UK in future years after their educational visit is finished for average annual periods of three months or more. If, despite the original intention, they remain in the UK for more than four years, they are treated as ordinarily resident in any event from the beginning of the fifth tax year of their stay (leaflet IR 20).

6.14 All visitors: investment income and capital gains

Any visitors may become resident and ordinarily resident in the UK depending upon the degree of presence in the UK and their intentions as indicated above. In addition, they may ultimately acquire a new domicile of choice in the UK if they decide to make their home permanently in the UK and thus cease to be visitors.

If they become resident in the UK but remain domiciled outside the UK, they are liable on a remittance basis in respect of foreign investment income and capital gains on foreign assets. If remittances are made out of a mixed fund of capital and income, the Inland Revenue will cite *Scottish Provident Institution v Allen* (1903) 4 TC 409 and 501 as authority for the contention that the remittances are of income up to the full amount of the income content of the fund unless the taxpayer can identify remittances as having clearly been made out of specific receipts into the fund. The same principle applies to capital gains out of a mixed fund of pure return of capital invested and gains.

It is therefore advisable, where material amounts are involved, for resident visitors to operate three foreign bank accounts: one for income, one for capital gains and one limited to the return of the original capital invested in the chargeable asset.

Remittances out of a source of income which ceased before the visitor became resident are not liable to tax on the authority of the principle established in *National Provident Institution v Brown* (1921) 8 TC 452, where it was held that income cannot be assessed for a year in which the taxpayer does not possess the source. Note that a continuing source of income, assessable on a remittance basis, if income from the source has already been remitted before a period of residence, may strictly be already liable on a previous year basis under the normal rules for assessing Case V income where an individual becomes resident (*Carter v Sharon* (1936) 20 TC 229). However, in practice, for new residents the Inland Revenue do not normally claim tax on more than the income that has arisen since the period of residence began if less than such remittances.

6.15 Capital gains

The process of quantifying remitted capital gains can be quite complex, bearing in mind that the gain has first to be quantified in sterling terms by reference to the sterling equivalent at the rate of exchange ruling at the date of acquisition of the foreign currency cost of the asset and a similar equivalent of the proceeds of the sale (*Bentley v Pike* [1981] STC 360). If the gain or part of it is shown to have been remitted to the UK, the foreign currency remitted is converted at the rate of exchange at the time of remittance. If this shows a greater gain than the sterling gain on the sale of the asset, the balance has been caused by a separate foreign currency gain which is itself liable to capital gains tax.

The anomaly under which all foreign currency bank accounts of an individual resident here were treated as located in the UK for capital gains tax purposes was corrected under FA 1984. Before FA 1984, unremitted gains arising from the use of such accounts were technically liable to capital gains tax even if the holder was not domiciled here as they arose from a UK asset. Now only such accounts held at a UK branch of a bank are treated as situated here.

It seems, however, that the practice (SP 10/84) of treating all foreign bank accounts containing a particular foreign currency as one account for capital gains purposes, thus ignoring transfers between them until all debts represented by the bank accounts have been repaid to the taxpayer, does not apply to non-domiciled individuals. The text of the Statement of Practice says: 'Except in relation to an account to which TCGA 1992, s. 275(1) applies (accounts of non-domiciled individuals)'. On this basis, therefore, the capital gain is computed on any eventual remittance tracing through realisations by such transfers between accounts on a strict basis.

6.16 Inheritance tax

Applying the principles referred to above, visitors normally retain their foreign domicile and will not acquire a special fiscal domicile for inheritance tax purposes until they have been resident here for not less than 17 years out of the 20 years of assessment, ending with the year of assessment in which the transfer of value is made (IHTA 1984, s. 267(1)(b)). This is also subject in the case of a disposition on death to the provisions of any old double tax agreement made for estate duty as well as for inheritance tax which continue to operate for transfers on death and could, therefore, still mean that the individual has retained his or her foreign domicile even after 17 years of residence in the UK (IHTA 1984, s. 267(2)).

As inheritance tax imposes a charge only on assets situated in the UK which are transferred by an individual not domiciled in the UK, it is important for visitors to minimise their exposure to inheritance tax by keeping their UK estate below the threshold for inheritance tax. Thus, if an individual wishes to invest substantial amounts in UK assets potentially liable to inheritance tax, this is best done through the medium of a company incorporated outside the UK so that should the individual die, the asset passing on death is shares in a foreign company. However, bear in mind that if the investments are income-producing and the income is accumulated in the foreign company, the income being from a UK source, there may be a liability under ICTA 1988, s. 739 in the case of visitors who have become ordinarily resident in the UK. The exclusion from the section of non-domiciled individuals does not apply to UK source income (ICTA 1988, s. 743(3)).

One way of avoiding a possible inheritance tax liability on the UK residence of a non-domiciled individual has been to buy it in the name of an offshore company, so that if the individual dies while resident here, he or she does not own a UK *situs* asset. Unfortunately, the Inland Revenue now contend that the individual in these circumstances is a director of the company for Schedule E purposes and liable to tax on the annual value of the property (under ICTA 1988, s. 145), and on interest at the official rate if the property costs more than £75,000 (ICTA 1988, s. 146). The individual would also be liable on any other outgoings met by the company, subject to the usual limits.

Note that foreign currency accounts held in the UK are outside the scope of inheritance tax on death only if the individual is both not domiciled in the UK immediately before death and is neither resident nor ordinarily resident here at that time (IHTA 1984, s. 157). Therefore, a visitor who is resident in the UK at the time of death is still liable to inheritance tax on such bank balances.

6.17 Departure from the UK

Care needs to be taken with the UK tax position of investment income, especially bank and building society interest, when visitors cease to be UK-resident. Individuals ceasing to be UK-resident part way through a year of assessment are advised to close their UK deposit accounts on departure and to open new ones in an offshore location such as the Channel Islands or Isle of Man. Any interest received after the cessation of UK residence is then free of UK tax.

If the new account is opened before departure, the Inland Revenue may treat all interest on the new account arising to the following 5 April as taxable because the source was held during a period of residence.

6.18 National Insurance contributions

If individuals are ordinarily resident in the UK liability to primary Class 1 contributions arises if they are employed earners who are either resident or present in the UK.

If individuals are not ordinarily resident in the UK liability to primary Class 1 contributions also arises if they are employed earners who are either resident or present in the UK, but there is no liability for the first 52 weeks providing:

- they are not ordinarily employed in the UK;
- the employment is mainly outside the UK, and
- their employer has a place of business outside the UK.

Class 1 liability for such individuals cannot arise until after a continuous period of residence in the UK of 52 weeks has elapsed.

The employer is liable to secondary Class 1 contributions only if either resident, present or having a place of business in the UK. Where primary contributions are payable the employer may also pay the secondary contributions and deduct the primary from the employee's pay. Failing that, NICO collects the primary contributions direct from the employee.

Self-employed earners are liable to the flat rate Class 2 contributions if they are either ordinarily resident in the UK or have been resident in the UK for 26 of the last 52 contribution weeks.

Self-employed earners who are not liable to Class 2 contributions are entitled to pay Class 2 contributions voluntarily if they are present in the UK.

Self-employed earners pay Class 4 contributions if assessed under Schedule D, Case I.

6.18.1 Reciprocal UK and EU arrangements

The basic principle is that an individual should be subject to the contribution legislation of only one member state at any one time. This is normally the member state in which he or she is employed or self-employed irrespective of residence or the place of business of the employer.

Temporary employment in another member state has no effect on the individual's liability to contributions providing that:

- the temporary employment is not expected to last for more than 12 months, and
- the individual is not replacing another individual whose period of employment in the other member state has ceased.

Where individuals have more than one employment in different member states they are normally subject to the contributions legislation of the member state in which they reside.

6.18.2 Reciprocal UK and USA agreement

Under the UK and USA reciprocal agreement, no dual liability to contributions arises where an employee of an employer in one of the territories is sent to work in the other territory for a period not expected to exceed five years.

Liability in such cases continues to arise in the employer's territory.

6.18.3 Reciprocal UK and Israeli agreement

Under the UK and Israeli reciprocal agreement (covered by DSS leaflet SA14), liability to Class 1 contributions follows the place of employment irrespective of the employee's residence status or the employer's place of business or residence.

Self-employed earners are treated on the same basis.

Liability in respect of temporary postings is dealt with in the normal way as described above.

Chapter 7   Members of the clergy

7.1 General principles

Members of the clergy are usually holders of an office (not an employment — see *Davies v Presbyterian Church of Wales* [1986] 1 All ER 705) and are assessable under ITEPA 2003, s. 5 in respect of the emoluments from that office, including any profits arising from their office not paid to them by one of their employers. The same tax rules apply to ministers of all faiths, religions and denominations. Their sources of income and their expense allowances can be complicated.

For example, members of the Anglican clergy are paid by the Church Commissioners on the basis of recommendations by the Diocesan Boards of Finance. They also receive income from local sources such as wedding fees and some receive salaries as teachers or chaplains. The Church Commissioners 'top up' these local sources where necessary. A very few of the clergy receive nothing from the Church Commissioners because their benefice is sufficiently well-off to support them fully. Fees received for conducting weddings, funerals and similar services are part of the emoluments of the office. Fees received for preaching in churches not within their charge, however, are normally regarded as casual income within Sch. D, Case VI.

Other examples of clergy who are paid partly locally and partly centrally include those of the Presbyterian churches of Scotland, Wales and Northern Ireland. Ministers of independent churches and of those belonging to 'looser' associations are paid predominantly (if not entirely) locally. However, such ministers usually still receive income from sources other than their employers (ie the local congregation), such as wedding, funeral or lecturing fees — though in many cases they surrender such fees to their church.

In general, items received by the clergy from various sources are taxable where they arise by virtue of the office and without the fulfilment of any further condition on the part of the particular office holder. Thus in *Herbert v McQuade* (1902) 4 TC 489, grants made by the Queen Victoria Clergy Sustentation Fund in augmentation of the income of the benefice were held to be taxable as profits accruing from the office. In contrast, in *Turner v Cuxon* (1888) 2 TC 422, a grant paid to a particular clergyman from a religious society in recognition of past faithful service, and renewable annually on certain conditions, was held not to be taxable. The Churches Main Committee Circular 1986/10 puts it like this:

> 'If there is a legal right to receive, the gift is taxable. So there would normally be no liability in respect of a complete windfall, such as an unrestricted gift or bonus in recognition of outstanding service; but special collections at Easter or on other occasions for the minister are liable to income tax. [See **7.4** below.]'

This circular deals generally with the taxation of ministers of religion and is available from The Churches Main Committee, 1 Millbank, London SW1P 3JZ. Senior Inland Revenue officials have seen the circular and have described the notes as a reasonable guide, subject to a warning that decisions on individual claims depend upon all the facts and circumstances.

7.2 Self assessment and PAYE procedures

There is a two-page supplementary schedule for the self assessment tax return for ministers of religion. Help sheet SA101M (Notes) provides assistance in the completion of the self assessment return for ministers of religion.

PAYE applies to all office holders, including the clergy and ministers of religion. Under the PAYE system, tax due on income is calculated and collected on an ongoing basis during the tax year.

Special arrangements have been made for Catholic clergy whereby the priest calculates the tax due on any official emoluments and pays it over to the Collector of Taxes, Accounts Office, each quarter. The Church Commissioners pay the clergy monthly. They may pay non-recurring grants in certain circumstances. If this grant is the minister's only income from the Church Commissioners, tax is deducted using code 0T.

Ministers of the Church of Scotland hold offices. The Church and Ministry Department operates PAYE on stipends and such additional items as income arising from the invested proceeds of sales of glebe payments of occupier's rates on the glebe by Kirk Sessions endowments and bequests. The local church treasurer operates PAYE on payments to assistant ministers who are employed by the local congregation.

Cardiff 1 district deals with all incumbents and pensioners of the Church in Wales. The Representative Body operates PAYE on stipends, annuities and such additional items as payments representing interest on private endowments given or bequeathed in trust and, exceptionally, income from local endowments of which the Representative Body are not trustees.

7.3 National Insurance contributions

Ministers of religion engaged in pastoral or ecclesiastical duties are normally classified as employed earners for National Insurance (NI) purposes and are liable to pay primary Class 1 contributions.

Those supported mainly by gifts and offerings, rather than salary or stipend (for example, Roman Catholic parish priests), are treated as self-employed for NI purposes and are not liable for Class 1 contributions.

It was pointed out by Peter Arrowsmith in the July 2003 issue of *Taxline* that the expression 'minister of religion' is not defined in the contributions regulations. However, it has been held that such a person must be 'set apart in sacred matters and superior to the rest of the religious community, the laity'. Remunerated leaders of the 'new churches' where there is no distinction between clergy and laity would therefore not fall within the definition. Similarly, a member of the Jehovah's Witnesses would not qualify, as each Witness is termed a 'minister of God'. A Sikh priest probably does not come within the definition either, as there is no formal training for the Sikh religion.

The other arm of NIC categorisation relates to stipend or salary. If categorised as an employee, the minister must receive a stipend or salary as of right and it must be the major part (over half) of the minister's remuneration. As an Elim Pentecostal minister's salary has the last call on church funds, it is not termed as salary or stipend and such a ministry is regarded as self-employed for NIC purposes. Traditionally, this has always also been the position of Roman Catholic priests and missionary priests. It can therefore be seen that some ministers of religion will be regarded as employees for direct tax purposes, but self-employed for NIC purposes.

7.4 Types of income that are taxable

Specific items of the clergy's income that are taxable as income from that office include the following.

1. Easter offerings. It used to be general practice for the collection in Anglican churches on Easter Sunday to go directly to the parish priest. Now it is quite common for ministers to waive this right and state that the offerings will go to some other cause. The Church Commissioners then pay them more. However, some clergy still receive their Easter offerings, especially those few who receive nothing from the Church Commissioners. Such offerings were held to be taxable in the case of *Cooper v Blakiston*

(1908) 5 TC 347, as a profit accruing by reason of the office in accordance with the general principles set out in **7.1** above. Whitsun offerings to a curate are similarly assessable (*Slaney v Starkey* (1931) 16 TC 45). On occasions when two Easter Days fall in a single year of assessment the second one may be treated as falling in the following year, provided:

(a) the offerings are returned consistently on a similar basis each year thereafter, whether or not the minister continues to hold the same office, and

(b) for the year in which he or she ceases to hold office, any offerings not actually received in that year but deemed to be received in it under this arrangement are included in that year's income.

The Inland Revenue were also asked by the Church Commissioners for their opinion on the position if such collections were earmarked for a specific purpose, for instance, payment of school fees for the minister's children or wages of gardeners. As a result of this enquiry, Circular 1986/10 (see **7.1** above) gives the following view:

- if offerings are solicited on behalf of ministers, they are assessable whether they are paid to them direct or into a fund to meet their expenses (eg school fees, books), or even if they divert them to a fund from which they do not personally benefit (eg a church restoration fund), but
- if, however, ministers clearly divest themselves of the right to the offerings, eg by advance public announcement of the destination of the offerings, or by some similar notification in the church magazine, and the offerings are given in the knowledge that they are going to a fund which in no way benefits ministers, they are not assessable.

2. Grants from the Church Commissioners, including dividends and interest, for instance, from the invested proceeds of the sale of glebe.

3. Payments-in-lieu of, or in composition for, tithes (such as corn rents).

4. Fees for conducting marriages and burial services.

5. Pew rents.

6. Glebe rents.

7. Grants from sustentation and similar funds, for instance, from the Parochial Church Council or Diocesan Board of Finance. Where the grant is a reimbursement of statutory expenses in connection with the manse or vicarage, it is exempt (ICTA 1988, s. 332(2)(a)).

8. Voluntary payments by patrons or others towards the stipend.

9. Any part of the stipend borne by a lay impropriator.

10. Dividends or interest from local endowments received by the incumbent either direct or from trustees.

11. Private gifts by parishioners or church members to ministers for themselves whenever given.

12. Certain benefits in kind where the minister is 'higher-paid' (see **7.5.4** and **7.8** below).

7.5 Exemptions

There are various exemptions from income tax enjoyed by ministers of religion, as well as specific expenses that they may claim.

7.5.1 Treatment of vicarage, manse or other church property occupied by the clergy

Full-time ministers of religion are not assessable under ITEPA 2003, s. 102 on the annual value of any house provided for them to perform the duties of their office. They are treated as representative occupiers (see below) and, consequently, no benefit arises on the annual value of the premises (or in respect of any council tax paid on their behalf or reimbursed to them) (ITEPA 2003, s. 99). This exemption extends, in practice, to:

- full-time incumbents of benefices in the Church of England;

- occupiers of properties belonging to cathedral chapters;

- occupiers of properties belonging to charitable bodies such as bodies of trustees on behalf of particular denominations, and

- occupiers of property held by Diocesan Boards of Finance in trust for a parochial church council.

There are complications with part-time clergy living in Church accommodation. They have to prove that the accommodation is necessary for the proper performance of their duties, or that it is provided for the better performance of those duties. The Churches Main Committee Circular No 1986/10 indicates that the Inland Revenue do not accept automatically that there is representative occupation in all such cases.

Each case is looked at on its merits. To be exempt from liability on the annual value of any accommodation provided for them, part-time ministers must demonstrate either:

- that it is necessary for the proper performance of their duties that they should reside in the accommodation, or
- that the accommodation is provided for the better performance of the duties of their employment and theirs is one of the kinds of employment in the case of which it is customary for employers to provide living accommodation for employees (ITEPA 2003, s. 99).

This is known as 'representative occupation'.

Where a member of the clergy is not exempt, the measure of the benefit is the gross annual value for rating purposes of the accommodation provided (or the rent which the Church pays if this is greater), less any amount made good by the minister to the Church, plus an 'appropriate percentage' of the amount (if any) by which the cost (or in some circumstances the value) of the property exceeds £75,000. (The 'appropriate percentage' is determined by a formula laid down by statutory instrument, following FA 1989, s. 178, eg five per cent per annum for 2002–03.) In addition, where the provider of the accommodation meets any pecuniary liability incurred by such a part-time minister, for example heating and lighting, gardener's wages or domestic or other services, the minister is chargeable under basic employment income rules. This applies whether or not he or she is higher-paid and regardless of whether the provider meets the expenses directly or reimburses the minister. For these purposes it is irrelevant whether the accommodation is provided for the better performance of the minister's duties, unless he or she is higher-paid, in which case the special rules referred to in **7.5.4** below apply. However, where the employer actually incurs such liabilities directly no charge arises unless the minister is higher-paid.

7.5.2 Statutory property expenses

Where members of the clergy or ministers of religion hold full-time offices, and reside in a property belonging to or leased by a charity or ecclesiastical corporation, in order to perform their duties and not as lessees, the making good to the ministers, or the direct payment on their behalf, of statutory amounts payable in connection with the residence (such as water rates and in Scotland community water charge, and general service charges), is not assessable on them (ITEPA 2003, s. 290). This also covers repayments on behalf of or to the incumbent of loans made under the Clergy Residence Repairs Acts, or Glebe Loans by a parochial church council or diocese, or other payments made under the Ecclesiastical Dilapidations Measures. Where the minister lets part of the residence, the rent received is taxable in the normal way and the exemption does not extend to statutory amounts paid that relate to such parts.

7.5.3 Other property expenses

Where the charity itself incurs any expenses in providing living accommodation for ministers, these expenses do not count as part of ministers' income provided they are not 'higher-paid'. This covers the upkeep, maintenance or insurance of the residence or provision of services such as cleaning, gardening, lighting, heating, etc (ITEPA 2003, s. 290(2)). Extra-statutory Concession (ESC) A61 states that where the church or charity owns or leases a property for members of the clergy, no tax is charged on sums paid on their behalf or reimbursed for heating, lighting, cleaning and gardening expenses, although they are the contractual liability of such members because they occupy the property. Similarly, where an allowance is paid to meet such costs, the Inland Revenue do not seek to tax it except to the extent that it exceeds such costs. As this concession does not apply to the higher-paid clergy (ie those with emoluments greater than £8,500), the comments in **7.5.4** below are relevant to them.

Where full-time ministers bear any expenses in maintaining (including decorating), repairing, insuring or managing any church premises of the type referred to in **7.5.1** above, they may claim a deduction of one-quarter of the amounts involved (ITEPA 2003, s. 351).

7.5.4 Property expenses of higher-paid clergy and directors of church charities

Different rules apply where members of the clergy are in higher-paid employment or are directors.

To determine whether a member of the clergy is higher-paid, it is necessary to include everything paid to or on behalf of the minister and family, except reasonable removal expenses where the minister has to change residence to take up a new appointment, and the cost of provision of retirement pensions for the minister and any dependants. It thus includes:

- all stipends, fees and, where applicable, Easter offerings, and

- expenses reimbursed or paid on the minister's behalf including expenses which can be claimed as deductions under ITEPA 2003, s. 351, such as travelling and subsistence expenses, and
- the cost of any telephone or car running expenses if paid for by the Church authorities,

but not anything included in **7.5.2** above.

Therefore, many church dignitaries and clergy who are reimbursed heavy travelling expenses, and those with a high service allowance to cover repairs, heating, lighting and cleaning, are likely to be higher-paid, if they are not already such by virtue of their other emoluments from the same employer (see below). In determining who is higher-paid, emoluments from separate employments are not aggregated. For instance, the various emoluments of clergy who are pastors of their congregation, hospital chaplains, schoolteachers or university lecturers, are not aggregated for these purposes nor is any income of their spouse. However, all employments under the same employer are treated as a single employment as are those of connected companies, and so the emoluments therefrom are aggregated for these purposes.

Individuals are not treated as directors, for these purposes, if they are not remunerated at a rate exceeding £8,500 a year and do not have a material interest in the company (that is, broadly not more than five per cent of the ordinary share capital of the company), and if:

- their employment is as a full-time working director; or
- the company is non-profit making, or
- the company is established for charitable purposes only (ICTA 1988, s. 167(5)).

These provisions should save most, if not all, of the clergy from being held to be directors for tax purposes, for instance of church bookshops. In the case of companies limited by guarantee, which have been formed to act as trustees for various church purposes, the companies the Inland Revenue have examined come within the definition of non-profit making companies. Where this is not so, the Inland Revenue would consider the matter sympathetically to see whether some concession could be granted (Churches Main Committee Circular 1986/10).

For those who are directors or higher-paid clergy who are required to live in accommodation provided for the better performance of their duties (ITEPA

2003, s. 99 — see above), the position in respect of expenses incurred by the church or charity or reimbursed to the member of the clergy is as follows.

1. Services not subject to tax — structural alterations and additions; repairs of a kind which would be the landlord's responsibility if the premises were let (ITEPA 2003, s. 313).

2. Services which are taxable subject to a limit (see below) — heating, lighting and cleaning; internal repairs; maintenance or decoration, which are normally the responsibility of the tenant; the provision of furniture (ITEPA 2003, s. 315).

3. Services taxable without limit — all services other than those listed in 1 and 2, such as the services of gardeners and domestic services other than cleaning.

The limit in the case of services included in 2 above is ten per cent of the net amount of the emoluments of the employment. The gross amount includes everything mentioned above; the net amount is the gross amount less:

- any capital allowances, for instance on a car; allowable expenses including expenses specifically allowable to the clergy up to the one-quarter limit mentioned below (see **7.5.5**);
- contributions to an approved superannuation scheme, and
- personal pensions and retirement annuity premiums where the member of the clergy is not in a pensionable office.

Where part of the accommodation which is provided is used partly for living in and partly for the performance of their duties (for instance as an office or study), the costs of taxable services are allocated or apportioned so that members of the clergy are liable to tax only on that which relates to the living accommodation. All the other rules of assessment of benefits for directors and higher-paid employees apply to such directors and higher-paid clergy. Details of the application of these rules to some of the benefits more commonly enjoyed by ministers are given below at **7.8**.

7.5.5 Reimbursement of property expenses

It is important for higher-paid clergy that, where exemption from income tax applies, property expenses are borne directly by the charity or by specific reimbursement as, if ministers pay them out of a general grant provided to them, they can claim only a quarter of the expenses under ITEPA 2003, s. 351.

Thus the Diocesan Boards of Finance are advised, by agreement with the Inland Revenue, to divide payments into reimbursements and stipends.

7.6 Expenses

The following expenses can be claimed, where borne by members of the clergy themselves.

7.6.1 Rent

If ministers rent houses themselves, which they use mainly or substantially for the purpose of their duties as clergy or ministers, the inspector of taxes may allow up to one-quarter of the rent as a deduction (ITEPA 2003, s. 351(2)). However, where this situation arises it is usually advantageous for the lease to be in the name of the church authorities, so that the rent is payable by them and is not the minister's liability. In this situation no charge to income tax arises in respect of the rent.

7.6.2 Maintenance expenditure

Members of the clergy can also claim any expenses they bear in maintaining, repairing, insuring or managing church premises that they occupy, up to one-quarter of the total amount (for instance, payments they make under the Ecclesiastical Dilapidations Measures). This, therefore, covers the cost of decorations and property insurance. The total claim under this heading, and under **7.6.3** below in respect of similar expenditure, is subject to a ceiling of one-quarter of the total of such expenditure (ITEPA 2003, s. 351(3)).

Therefore, it is important that reimbursement of such expenses should, where possible, be made to obtain complete relief.

7.6.3 General expenses

Members of the clergy can claim any expenses they incur wholly, exclusively and necessarily in the performance of their duties (ITEPA 2003, s. 351(1)). The Inland Revenue regard this as covering any duties enjoined on ministers by law or by their ecclesiastical superiors, as well as duties arising directly from their obligations to their congregations. It may often be more convenient for some of the expenses to be borne direct by the parochial church council, or by the church stewards or trustees, as then the need to claim all the allowable expenditure does not arise unless the minister is higher-paid. They may, for example, rent the minister's telephone even though it is the minister's name which appears in the directory. Specifically, the following cover most of the types of claim likely to be met and are regarded as *prima facie* allowable.

1. The cost of stationery, postage, use of telephone, etc incurred in connection with the minister's duties.

2. Travelling expenses when visiting members of the congregation, or attending meetings of official church bodies such as presbytery, where required of ministers by law or by their superiors.

3. The cost of repair or replacement of robes actually used in divine service in accordance with church law, or by custom of the particular church. The Inland Revenue will not give an allowance other than for the basic apparel for the service. The only robes which an Anglican incumbent is by canon law required to wear are the surplice and the hood. Where it is the custom or a requirement of canon law for a cassock to be worn (such as in certain cathedrals and college chapels), the Inland Revenue also allow the cost of replacement of a cassock. The Inland Revenue also normally allow a deduction for the cost of 'dog-collars', as this is usually small. In a case before the Commissioners, a Devon vicar was successful in claiming the cost of his cloak, used mainly for funerals (see *The Times* of 22 January 1986). The Inland Revenue do not accept that this decision has general application. Nonetheless, if priests in similar rural parishes need cloaks to protect themselves from the elements during funerals, it is probably worth making a claim. The successful Devon vicar, however, did not win a claim for the cost of his shirt and dog collar, on the basic principle that he had to be clothed anyway (see *Hillyer v Leeke* (1976) 51 TC 90 and *Mallalieu v Drummond* (1983) 57 TC 330). The Inland Revenue would probably have passed the claim for the dog collar if it had not been associated with a claim for a shirt, a cloak and a computer (see point 16 below).

4. The cost of a *locum tenens* during an illness or holiday.

5. The cost of reasonable entertainment on official occasions.

6. Any stipend or payment to a curate or assistant curate, whether or not licensed to officiate within the parish.

7. Secretarial assistance, including the cost of repair or replacement of typewriters, filing cabinets, etc. and payments to a spouse to carry out such work, provided the wages are actually paid and are commensurate with the duties performed. The Free Church of Scotland, in its supplement to the Churches Main Committee Circular, recommends ministers to keep a

separate bank account for their spouses' wages and to make regular transfers to that account from their own, keeping such transfers distinguishable from housekeeping money. The sort of work for which a spouse can be paid must be distinguished from work undertaken as an active member of the church, eg as leader of a women's group, or for the organisation of Church social events.

8. Communion expenses.

9. Costs of domestic help, where necessitated by the performance of a minister's duties, for instance in cleaning, entertaining visiting dignitaries, or reasonable wages paid to a spouse for cleaning that part of the house used mainly or substantially for the purposes of the cleric's duties (see point 7 above).

10. Costs of heating, lighting, repairs or replacements of carpets or chairs applicable to the part of the house used mainly for the purposes of a minister's duties. Insofar as a cost is claimed under this heading, and could also be claimed under ICTA 1988, s. 332(3)(c) (eg rates or costs of repairs to the premises), the amount allowable cannot exceed one-quarter of the total costs. Otherwise, the proportion allowed is what can reasonably be regarded as incurred in the performance of the duties of the office.

11. Tenths, first fruits, duties and fees on presentation.

12. The costs of procurations and synodals which are usually allowed on the basis of the average amounts paid over the previous seven years.

13. The cost of repairs of chancels.

14. The purchase of books. The Inland Revenue recognise that expenditure by ministers on books purchased for actual use in the conduct of church services, or in the preparation of sermons, is incurred wholly, exclusively and necessarily in the performance of their duties. Therefore, provided the church authorities do not or would not supply the books if asked, the Inland Revenue allows a deduction for this expenditure under ITEPA 2003, s. 351(1). Books which fall within this category include the Bible, prayer books and office books such as the Book of Common Prayer. For similar reasons, the Inland Revenue allow a deduction for expenditure on books such as those given out to engaged couples or to members of confirmation, baptism, membership or Bible classes.

Where the church authorities buy ministers theological or other books that they need to fulfil their duties, or reimburse their expenditure on such books, the Inland Revenue does not normally regard the provision of the books as giving rise to a benefit, as where ministers are 'higher-paid' they can claim under ITEPA 2003, s. 351(1). However, if the church authorities simply give them a cash allowance for books, without regard to their actual expenditure, the allowance is regarded as a taxable emolument. Following the decision in *Munby v Furlong* (1977) 50 TC 491, claims may be made for capital allowances under CAA 2001, ss. 15(1)(i) and (4), 36 and 262 in respect of substantial reference books that have a useful life of more than two years. The Inland Revenue notes published with the self assessment tax return contain the following guidance: 'You can deduct the cost of books you have purchased for use in the conduct of divine service or used directly in the preparation of sermons. No deduction is available for books or periodicals you use for general background reading. However, you can claim capital allowances on substantial theological reference books'.

15. Car expenses. Members of the clergy can claim capital allowances on the proportion of the costs of their cars, and running expenses relating to official duties in the normal way. The usual practice in the Church of England is for the diocese to pay a mileage allowance (to cover the whole cost of putting cars on the road including standing charges, maintenance and depreciation). Most dioceses pay the Inland Revenue authorised mileage rates which do not give rise to taxable benefits (as laid out in ITEPA 2003, s. 230).

The tax and NIC free rates, which have applied from 6 April 2002, are as follows:

On the first 10,000 miles in the tax year	40p per mile
On each additional mile over 10,000 miles	25p per mile

Considerable amendments have also been made to the capital allowances provisions to ensure that it is not necessary for office holders to buy a car for their office in order to claim allowances based on business use if they have not used the non-taxable mileage allowances.

Where an allowance is paid, it is taken into account in determining whether ministers are higher-paid and, if they are, is taxable as an emolument unless a dispensation under ITEPA 2003, s. 65 is in force. Where the allowance is taxed ministers can claim a deduction for motoring expenses incurred wholly, exclusively and necessarily in the performance of their duties as ministers. For many ministers the vast majority of local visits have a pastoral element and it is difficult to envisage any tax inspector arguing that such visits do not meet the 'wholly and exclusively' test.

16. Apart from expenditure on a car and certain books, as detailed above, the Inland Revenue often resist claims for capital allowances on other items of plant and machinery. This attitude is supported by the decision in

White v Higginbottom (1982) 57 TC 283, where a vicar lost his claim for capital allowances on the cost of a projector and other audio-visual equipment which he used in his sermons. However, relief should be given on expenditure incurred by ministers of religion on equipment necessarily provided for use in the performance of their duties (CAA 2001, ss. 15(1)(i) and (4), 36 and 262). Claims are accepted only in respect of assets intended for permanent use in the ministry which have an expected life of two years or more. For example, capital allowances are given on a computer or word processor if it enables long-standing tasks – such as compiling and maintaining lists of church members, parish records or accounts or to issue circulars and magazines – to be carried out more efficiently (see *The Times* of 22 January 1986).

Expenditure qualifies for a 25 per cent writing down allowance on a reducing balance basis.

7.6.4 Expenses of unpaid appointments

Normally any expenses incurred on such appointments are not allowable, but in practice the Inland Revenue allow claims under ITEPA 2003, s. 351(1) for expenses, not reimbursed, necessarily incurred in the capacity of a rural dean, honorary canon, or other honorary ecclesiastical appointment (such as a Proctor in Convocation in the Church of England).

7.6.5 Removal expenses

Removal expenses may be allowed under ITEPA 2003, s. 351(1) against benefice income, but removal expenses from one ecclesiastical office to another used not to be allowed when incurred by members of the clergy (*Friedson v Glyn-Thomas* (1922) 8 TC 302). However, ITEPA 2003, s. 273(2)(a) now usually applies, under which removal expenses reimbursed by a new employer are not taxable, provided the expenses are reasonable in amount and their payment is properly controlled.

7.7 Second residences

Relief from capital gains tax is available for clergy in connection with residences owned by them in addition to official residences provided for them. Where individuals occupy job-related accommodation but intend to occupy their own house as their only or main residence, capital gains tax exemption is given on the sale of that residence in respect of periods after 30 July 1978 (TCGA 1992, s. 222(8)).

To take advantage of these provisions, members of the clergy do not have to work full time at their duties, provided that they can be regarded as representative occupiers (see **7.5.1** above). There is an exclusion for directors unless they fall into the category mentioned in **7.5.4** above, which exempts most directors who hold office with companies carrying out activities connected with a church and who occupy living accommodation belonging to the church.

7.8 Benefits in kind

7.8.1 Cars

Where a car is provided for a minister on the strict understanding, confirmed in writing, that it is not in any circumstances to be used for private travel, no tax liability arises in respect of the car, whatever the level of the minister's emoluments. However, this is normally impossible to achieve as few ministers can afford a second car for private travel. Therefore, where a car is provided, the benefit charges provided for by ITEPA 2003, s. 121 normally apply, assuming the minister is earning at a rate of £8,500 per annum or more.

7.8.2 Car fuel

Ministers provided with a car by the authorities employing them may incur a charge not only in respect of the car but also in respect of its fuel (ITEPA 2003, s. 149). The relevant provisions are widely drawn and state that fuel is provided for a car if (ITEPA 2003, s. 149(3)):

- any liability in respect of the provision of fuel for the car is discharged;
- a voucher, credit token or money (including credit cards) is used to obtain fuel for the car, or
- any sum is paid in respect of expenses incurred in providing fuel for the car.

The scale charges for fuel are drawn up on very similar lines to the car scale charges. The fuel scale charges may be reduced to nil if, in the relevant year (ITEPA 2003, s. 151):

- ministers are required to make good to the authorities providing the fuel the whole of the expense they have incurred in or in connection with the provision of fuel for their private use and they do so, or
- the fuel is made available only for business travel.

To substantiate a claim that this was the case, ministers need to keep records both of their total mileage and of their business mileage. This is clearly worthwhile if it keeps their emoluments below £8,500 or, if they are higher-paid in any event, keeps the level of these taxable benefits down. The requirements laid down to avoid a fuel scale charge also make it undesirable simply to pay a round-sum allowance towards fuel rather than specifically to reimburse fuel expenses incurred for recorded official travel. It would be particularly unwise to pay a general expenses allowance if the minister is higher-paid, as he or she might well be taxed both on the allowance and in respect of a fuel scale charge.

7.8.3 Beneficial loans

Many ministers receive loans from the church authorities that employ them. If ministers are higher-paid they may face a charge to tax in respect of the benefit from such a loan. However, if the loan does not exceed £5,000 the benefit is not taxable. Also, if the loan is for such a purpose that if obtained at arm's length the interest on it would have qualified for tax relief, no charge to tax arises (ITEPA 2003, s. 175). Examples of loans that do not give rise to a taxable benefit are loans to acquire assets used in the performance of the minister's duties. Another charge to tax can arise where a beneficial loan is released or written off in whole or in part.

7.9 Income of contemplative religious communities and their members

ESC B10 relates to the income of religious communities from the sale of produce, pottery, etc. The precise legal position as regards the title to such income which is treated by the community as belonging to a common fund is often difficult to ascertain. In practice in the case of certain orders (such as those engaged in charitable work among the poor) relief is given under the provisions relating to charities. In the case of contemplative orders and other orders which are not in law capable of being regarded as charities as they do not promote their religious beliefs among the community, a proportion of the aggregate income not exceeding a specified sum per monk or nun (as representing the amount applied for the maintenance of each individual) is regarded as his or her income for the purposes of relief from tax. Since 1995/96 the allowable figure is set at the basic personal allowance for the year. Where in any year the aggregate of the 'allowable figures' exceeds the community's income, the excess may be set against chargeable gains of that year.

7.10 Evangelists

The distinction between a personal gift and taxable income is more difficult to define where a person does not have a parish but operates on a freelance basis.

There are several well-known religious figures around the world who receive sums through the post and at gatherings which are given mainly because of the personal magnetism of the individual and his or her reputation, and do not attach to any office or services as in *Cooper v Blakiston*.

It has been accepted (in the case of one freelance evangelist at least) that personal gifts sent through the post, some from areas the evangelist has not visited recently or at all, are not assessable. They arise from a personal regard for the evangelist, an interest in the evangelist's work and a desire to contribute to his or her personal needs.

However, where sums are received, although unsolicited, in connection with specific speaking engagements, they are regarded as arising from services rendered and are assessed. Thus where someone makes a gift to an evangelist after hearing him or her preach, it is accepted as assessable.

The practice is probably conceded from the following dicta of Lord Loreburn in *Cooper v Blakiston*:

> 'In my opinion, where a sum of money is given to an incumbent substantially in respect of this services as incumbent, it accrues to him by reason of his office ... Had it been a gift of an exceptional kind such as ... a subscription peculiarly due to the personal qualities of this particular clergyman it might not have been a voluntary payment for services, but a mere present.'

It was reported in a query in *Taxation* of 21 November 1991 that the Inland Revenue were attacking the receipts of evangelists as taxable.

The general consensus of the replies was as follows.

1. Unsolicited receipts from family, close friends, other friends and acquaintances where no services are rendered, are not taxable.

Members of the clergy

2. Receipts from churches for whom the evangelist has worked are linked to services rendered and are therefore taxable.

3. Churches with whom the evangelist has previously worked is a difficult area but the receipt is probably sufficiently closely linked to services rendered that the Inland Revenue would seek to tax it. The difficulty is that there would probably be an ongoing link with that church.

4. Where gifts are received from Christian charitable trusts, it is likely that they were solicited. They might also be taxable on the basis of the decision in *CIR v Falkirk Ice Rink Ltd* [1975] STC 434 as being made to support the work of the evangelist.

5. Unsolicited gifts from individuals of whom the evangelist has no prior knowledge should not be taxable where there are no services rendered. Unsolicited gifts from churches might pose the same difficulty as point 3 as there might be the possibility of an ongoing relationship with those churches and anticipated services to be rendered.

7.11 Income of vocation under Schedule D, Case II

The Inland Revenue accept that in some cases missionaries or evangelists are assessable under Sch. D, Case II.

Taxable receipts of the vocation include any sums received in virtue of the exercise of the vocation, or that enable the missionary or evangelist to continue to exercise the vocation (for example, grants or gifts – whether solicited or not – by religious bodies, charitable trusts or individuals for the maintenance of the individual or his or her family).

Taxable receipts of the vocation do not include:

- monies given towards specific works such as the building or repair of a place of worship, in relation to which the individual acts in the capacity of a trustee;
- personal testimonials, or personal gifts (for example on marriage or for medical treatment), or
- personal gifts from parents or immediate friends.

Chapter 8 Members of the diplomatic service and other Crown servants working abroad

8.1 Place of performance of duties

Members of the diplomatic service are in a peculiar taxation position. Whilst their residence position follows the normal practice applicable to any individual, they are deemed to perform their duties in the UK for the purposes of liability to income tax under ITEPA 2003 on their emoluments. All persons who hold an office or employment under the Crown which is of public nature, and which is payable out of the public revenue of the UK, are deemed to perform their duties in the UK (ITEPA 2003, s. 28). This includes an employee of the Crown, performing duties for the Crown abroad with a foreign government, paid by a UK government authority, even if that authority recovers the salary from the foreign government (*Caldicott v Varty* (1976) 51 TC 403). The fact that the position held is technical or industrial does not make it any the less of a public nature (see *Graham v White* (1971) 48 TC 163). In practice, however, UK tax is not charged in the case of locally-engaged (as distinct from UK-based) unestablished staff working abroad who are not UK-resident if the maximum rate of pay for their grade is less than that of an executive officer in the UK Civil Service working in Inner London (ITEPA 2003, s. 28(4)–(8), formerly Extra-statutory Concession (ESC) A25).

The effect of deeming the place of performance of duties to be the UK is that, if diplomats cease to be resident (as is usual) or remain resident but not ordinarily resident, they are liable to tax under ITEPA 2003, s. 27 or s. 25 (formerly Sch. E, Case II) on the full amount of their emoluments. However, if they remain resident and ordinarily resident in the UK, they are assessable under ITEPA 2003, s. 15 (formerly Sch. E, Case I).

8.2 Exempt allowances

Emoluments for this purpose do not include foreign service allowances, where the allowance is certified by the Treasury to represent compensation for the extra cost of having to live outside the UK to perform the duties of the employment. Such allowances are specifically exempted from UK tax (ITEPA 2003, s. 299). This covers allowances for boarding school education for children and any other foreign service allowance representing the increased cost of having to live abroad to do the job in question. It also covers the cost of travel to and from the overseas location by diplomats and their families. It also seems to cover the initial cost of removal expenses to the residence abroad whereas others have to rely on the statutory relief under ITEPA 2003, s. 271 which limits tax-free relocation expenses to £8,000 (ITEPA 2003, s. 287). Such allowances are not caught by the benefits legislation (according to a House of Commons Written Answer of 6 May 1976). Other subsistence allowances, paid to diplomatic staff whilst stationed in a foreign country, are not taxable in the same way as subsistence allowances paid in the UK to home civil servants. This is based on general employment income principles, as such allowances are designed only to cover expenses incurred in the course of carrying out their duties away from base. The scales are set out in the Civil Service pay and conditions of service code.

Entertaining allowances paid to diplomats are normally taxable. However, provided diplomats spend their allowance wholly, exclusively and necessarily in the performance of their duties, they can claim under ITEPA 2003, s. 336, as ICTA 1988, s. 577 applies only to business entertainment.

The value of any living accommodation occupied abroad is not liable to income tax, on the basis that Crown servants are representative occupiers required to live in the premises to do their job properly. Any costs of maintaining any residence abroad, insofar as reimbursed, are not liable under the benefits provisions as they are part of the allowance exempt under the special provisions for allowances to cover the increased costs of living abroad.

Under most double tax agreements, civil servants are not liable to foreign tax on their remuneration (including the foreign service allowance), because it falls under the provisions relating to remuneration payable out of the Government funds of one of the contracting parties. Alternatively, in the case of diplomats, diplomatic privilege under international law should exempt them from local taxation and this again may also be specifically mentioned in the relevant double tax treaty.

8.3 Other income and capital gains

The tax position of other income and capital gains depends on the person's residence position. Note that the provision deeming the duties of the employment to be performed in the UK applies only for the purposes of taxing employment income under ITEPA 2003. Therefore, the general rules on the residence position of people working abroad still applies for other sources.

If the individual is not resident in the UK, the position on liability to UK tax on UK income, other than such as is exempt in the hands of all non-residents, is governed by international law, which effectively ensures that diplomats are not treated as a resident for fiscal purposes of the country in which the embassy is situated. Double taxation agreements usually refer to this complete exemption from local tax on all sources of income and capital gains which corresponds with the specific exemptions the UK gives (under the Diplomatic Privileges Act 1964) to foreign diplomats residing in this country. Diplomats thus cannot take advantage of any reduced rate of UK tax on UK dividends and taxed interest which is available only to those who, under the terms of agreement, are treated as residents of the country with which the double taxation agreement has been concluded. They therefore remain fully liable to UK tax on dividends, taxed interest, rents and other UK income not exempt from UK tax in the hands of a non-resident. To get over this problem, it is possible for a member of the diplomat's family who does not enjoy this complete exemption – for instance, his or her spouse – to hold the investments and become a resident of the other country for the purposes of the relevant double taxation agreement. However, the tax consequences in that other country should not be overlooked. Alternatively, it may be worth using an offshore investment company to avoid at least the higher rate of tax.

8.4 Tax-free investments

Non-resident Crown employees serving overseas are able to take advantage of tax-free investments that are normally available only to UK residents. Examples include individual savings accounts and, previously, PEPs and TESSAs.

8.5 Personal allowances

Note that, where the diplomat is not resident in the UK, a claim to personal allowances is possible. If, exceptionally, the person is not a British subject, he or she is still eligible under ICTA 1988, s. 278, as being employed in the service of the Crown.

8.6 Tax credits

A Crown servant posted overseas is treated as being resident in the UK for the purposes of determining entitlement to child tax credit and working tax credit from 6 April 2003. The partner of a Crown servant posted overseas who is accompanying the Crown servant posted overseas is also treated as being in the UK when he or she is either in the country where the Crown servant is posted or absent from that country in certain circumstances (The Tax Credits (Residence) Regulations 2003 (SI 2003 No. 654)).

8.7 UK residences

8.7.1 Capital gains tax

Difficulties have arisen for Crown servants serving overseas in respect of capital gains exemption on UK residences. Where diplomats themselves own the residence, the period of absence counts as a qualifying period. If the spouse owns the residence, there used to be a problem as the spouse was not the one in employment. ESC D3 now gives the owner exemption where either spouse is in full-time employment abroad.

Likewise, owners normally have to resume residence before selling so that the period of absence qualifies for exemption. This is not required under ESC D4 if owners are unable to resume residence because their terms of employment require them to reside elsewhere, so that they sell without resuming residence in the house. In any event, it seems that it is possible to argue in many cases that the diplomat was residing in job-related accommodation abroad so that he or she would not have to rely on any concession to obtain full relief for capital gains tax on a sale of the residence (TCGA 1992, s. 222(8)).

8.7.2 Job-related accommodation

Employees who live in 'job-related accommodation' can normally obtain capital gains tax exemption on a private residence other than the one in which they actually have to live (TCGA 1992, s. 222(8)). The Inland Revenue have confirmed that service personnel and diplomats serving overseas who extend their overseas tour beyond four years, are regarded as living in job-related accommodation for these purposes if they live in the following:

- accommodation provided by the Ministry of Defence;
- flats provided by the Foreign and Commonwealth Office, or
- officially approved hirings for which a rent allowance is payable.

Therefore, Crown servants in this position should not need to rely on any of the concessions referred to above.

8.8 Officials employed by the European Union in Brussels

Crown servants are increasingly employed by the European Union Office in Brussels. As with United Nations officials, their emoluments are subject to a special form of community tax. Emoluments (including pensions) received from the European Union are exempt from UK tax by virtue of Art. 13 of the Protocol on the Privileges and Immunities of the European Communities. Such emoluments were, up to 5 April 1990, also excluded from total income for the purposes of ICTA 1988, s. 278, which governs the granting of personal allowances to certain non-residents.

This exemption from UK tax extends to income received from the Council of Europe and the Western European Union.

However, Art. 13 deems that officials who have gone to work at the European Union Office remain resident and ordinarily resident for income tax purposes in the UK, with their dependent accompanying spouses and children, and are also domiciled in the UK for inheritance tax purposes — thus protecting them from Belgian tax on their other income. However, capital gains tax follows the normal rules of residence.

Difficulties can arise when UK officials go to the EC office from a posting abroad with, say, the Foreign Office, so that they are not resident or ordinarily resident when they start work in Brussels. The Protocol does not cope easily with this situation but it appears, as diplomats, that they can waive their right to immunity from tax including UK tax and thus come within the Protocol.

There are various other international organisations employing people where there is immunity from tax on their remuneration. Commonwealth citizens and certain other non-UK residents can now set their full UK personal allowances against UK income potentially liable to UK tax such as rents, dividends, etc (ICTA 1988, s. 278). This applies to employees of a United Nations

Members of the diplomatic service and other Crown servants working abroad

organisation (although the exemption does not extend to pensions) provided a certificate is supplied from UNO stating that during the period of employment the employee had the status of 'official' for the purposes of Section 18 (Article 5) of the General Convention of the Privileges and Immunities of the UN, dated 13 February 1946.

Other organisations where the emoluments are treated in the same way are:

- Food and Agricultural Organisation (FAO);
- International Civil Aviation Organisation (ICAO);
- International Labour Organisation (ILO);
- International Maritime Consultative Organisation (IMO);
- International Telecommunications Union (ITU);
- Universal Postal Union (UPU);
- World Health Organisation (WHO);
- World Intellectual Property Organisation (WIPO), and
- World Meteorological Organisation (WMO).

Exemption depends upon completion of the appropriate certificate, the terms of which are advised in each case by the Inland Revenue in the case of the following organisations:

- Central Treaty Organisation (CTO);
- Council of Europe (COE);
- Customs Co-operative Council (CCC);
- Inter-commission for the International Trade Organisation (ICITO);
- International Atomic Energy Authority (IAEA);
- North Atlantic Treaty Organisation (NATO);
- Organisation for Economic Co-operation and Development (OECD);
- South East Asia Treaty Organisation (SEATO);
- United Nations Childrens Fund (UNICEF), and
- Western European Union (WEU).

Officials employed by the European Union in Brussels

Further guidance on the tax treatment of Crown employees (for example, civil servants, diplomats, members of the armed forces) may be obtained from HMIT Public Department 1, Ty-Glas Road, Llanishen, Cardiff, Wales CF14 5XZ (tel: 029 2032 5048).

Chapter 9 Doctors and dentists

9.1 Doctors

The tax position of doctors depends on whether they are consultants or general practitioners, and whether they are self-employed – as in the case of the latter or in the case of many non-National Health Service consultants – or employed, as in the case of consultants, in respect of NHS earnings.

9.2 Consultants

Income received by a self-employed consultant from private practice is assessable under normal Sch. D, Case II principles. However, a consultant may hold an employment post in the private sector. Full-time NHS consultants are within the employment income rules of ITEPA 2003 and subject to its restrictive rules for expenses claims (see ITEPA 2003, s. 336 and *Hamerton v Overy* (1954) 35 TC 73). Similarly, part-time sessional payments by the relevant paying authority are assessable as employment income, and ITEPA 2003, s. 336 again applies to expenses claims.

A clear distinction must always be drawn between employment and self-employment income. In *Mitchell and Edon v Ross* (1961) 40 TC 11 it was established that expenses incurred in relation to the office of NHS consultant and disallowed against employment income, are not allowable as expenses of earning the profits of the profession taxable under Sch. D, because the employment and self-employment codes are mutually exclusive. However, there is a choice of treatment for some expenses, such as professional subscriptions.

9.3 Expenses of consultants

9.3.1 Property expenses

The practice proportion of property expenses should be claimed by a self-employed consultant, but bearing capital gains tax in mind. A 'points' basis for the garage/s, first floor and upstairs rooms (distinguishing practice rooms, common areas and private rooms), gives a sound base for the proportion of rates, repairs, insurances, etc. It may be difficult for consultants holding employment posts to obtain a deduction for such expenses against their employment income; however, it may be possible to claim on the basis of contributions to the additional costs incurred.

9.3.2 Motor expenses

When claiming a deduction for motor expenses, bear in mind that home to base (ie main commitment) hospital is private mileage. The case of *Pook v Owen* (1969) 45 TC 571 involved reimbursed travelling expenses for the part-time hospital appointment of a medical practitioner. As the appointment involved being on standby duty at certain times, the duties were treated as commencing from the time of leaving home, and the reimbursed expenses were therefore not assessable. Such circumstances can arise with doctors on call from outside the hospital, where advice is given before starting the journey and responsibility is taken from that time (but see **9.4.4** below concerning emergency call-out expenses). Two cases involving doctors that illustrate the principles involved are *Bhadra v Ellam* [1988] STC 239 and *Parikh v Sleeman* [1990] STC 233.

9.4 Agreement between Department of Health and Inland Revenue on certain expenses

The Department of Health and the Inland Revenue have reached an agreement in respect of the taxability of certain allowances paid to NHS staff, including consultants, under Whitley Council agreements or by direction of the Secretary of State. This agreement (ref: HC(78)39 of November 1978) covers the taxation position on all allowances paid to NHS staff, including car allowances.

9.4.1 Car allowances

The Inland Revenue have agreed a fixed, taxable amount in respect of each individual who travels a prescribed number of miles in his or her own car on business for the employing authority during one income tax year. However, regular car users travelling in excess of 3,000 miles per annum on health authority business are not subject to tax on their allowances. The normal scale benefits apply in respect of private use of cars allocated to doctors by health authorities, if they are in higher-paid employment.

Agreement between Department of Health and Inland Revenue on certain expenses

Volunteer drivers can also use the authorised mileage rates to calculate the profit on mileage allowances they receive from hospitals, social service agencies and other voluntary organisations.

9.4.2 Removal and associated expenses

Employees (but not partners) who are offered relocation packages by their new or existing employers are entitled to a statutory exemption from tax on removal expenses and benefits, up to a maximum £8,000 in total.

The exemption was introduced by FA 1993, s. 76, and is now found in ITEPA 2003, ss. 271–289.

The relief applies where the employer meets or reimburses removal expenses or provides removal benefits.

Scope of the legislation

Only qualifying removal expenses and benefits are exempt. To be qualifying, expenses and benefits must be eligible (see below) and satisfy certain conditions. These conditions are as follows.

1. The employee must change his or her main residence as a result of:
   (a) starting a new employment;
   (b) a change of duties of employment, or
   (c) a change of location of employment. Note that this does not require an employee to dispose of his or her former residence, merely to change main residence. What constitutes an employee's main residence is a question of fact.

2. The new main residence must be within a reasonable daily travelling distance of the new normal place of work.

3. The old residence must not be within a reasonable daily travelling distance of the new normal place of work.

   The legislation does not define a 'reasonable daily travelling distance'. It is a matter for common sense, taking into account local conditions, and may depend on either or both travelling time or distance.

4. The expenses must be incurred, or benefits provided, before the end of the year of assessment following the one in which the employee starts the new job. It does not matter when the employee moves to his or her new

home. The Inland Revenue have the power to extend this time limit by one or more complete tax years if it seems reasonable so to do.

Eligible expenses and benefits

Eligible expenses and benefits are grouped into six categories:

- disposal or intended disposal of old residence;
- acquisition or intended acquisition of new residence;
- transportation and storage of domestic belongings;
- travelling and subsistence for employee and family;
- replacement domestic goods for new property, and
- interest on bridging loans made by third parties.

The specific items which fall within each category are set out in the detailed lists of removal expenses and benefits in ITEPA 2003, ss. 279–285.

Additional relief for in-house bridging loans

Employer-provided cheap or interest-free bridging loans are chargeable under the usual rules for beneficial loans (ITEPA 2003, s. 175). However, some relief may be available if the employee, after the relevant time limit, has part of the £8,000 exemption still unused. For instance, if an employee were reimbursed total removal expenses of £6,000, and given an interest-free bridging loan by his or her employer, there would be £2,000 of unused exemption to convert into a reduction in the charge on the bridging loan.

ITEPA 2003, s. 284 contains the calculation used to reduce the beneficial loans charge.

PAYE arrangements

To help employers operate the rules they are obliged to apply PAYE to cash payments made to employees which relate to qualifying expenses paid above the £8,000 ceiling.

9.4.3 Excess travelling expenses

Reimbursement of excess travelling expenses following a change of base hospital is taxable, except where a change of residence is involved, when reimbursement of travelling expenses may be exempt as part of removal expenses.

9.4.4 Emergency call-out expenses

In spite of *Pook v Owen*, travelling expenses for emergency call-out to the normal place of employment are regarded as taxable, except in the circumstances mentioned in **9.3.2** above.

9.4.5 Assisted travel scheme

This allowance is taxable, as it covers partial reimbursement of the costs of getting to the hospital.

9.4.6 Journey between home and headquarters

Where doctors, normally based at one place, use their cars to visit other places in the course of their duties, and are reimbursed mileage costs within the limit of 'base to places visited and return plus 20 miles', the allowance for actual mileage on duty is not taxable; nor is the 'plus' element.

9.4.7 Late night duties

Night duty allowance and meal allowances are taxable. See however ITEPA 2003, s. 248 (formerly Extra-statutory Concession (ESC) A66) which gives some relief to individuals in an employed capacity.

9.4.8 Uniforms

The provision of uniforms, overalls and protective clothing, or an allowance to buy them, is not taxable. However, the Inland Revenue regard allowances to cover the cost of ordinary, everyday clothing ('mufti') given to staff who work in psychiatric hospitals, as taxable, even if the clothing is worn only on duty. The normal rules for calculating the taxable amount apply. The use of mufti owned by the health authority and retained at the hospital for use only on duty is taxable only in the case of higher-paid employees, subject to exemption where the amounts involved are negligible.

9.4.9 Telephone expenses

Where the employee is the subscriber, any payment by the health authority is taxable under basic employment income rules, as the employer is meeting the employee's pecuniary liability. Where the employing authority is the

Doctors and dentists

subscriber, payment of telephone rental and other charges is taxable only when the employee is higher-paid. All cost of calls in the performance of the employment are allowable in the normal way under ITEPA 2003, s. 336.

9.4.10 Fees and subscriptions to professional bodies

Recurrent annual subscriptions are allowed but initial registration fees, if required, are not allowable under normal employment expenses rules.

9.5 Practice accounts

The accounts of partnerships of self-employed consultants should show the practice proportion of expenses and depreciation, less monies received from the relevant paying authority for inter-hospital and domiciliary visits. Depreciation is added back and the practice proportion of capital allowances claimed in the normal way. Under self assessment it is essential that the partnership tax return reflects any allowable expenses incurred personally by the partners.

9.5.1 Conference expenses

Conference expenses often cause problems. In practice, the costs of attending conferences and courses are allowed where the basic requirements of any business claim are satisfied. It is helpful, however, to quote regional health authority approval of the course, whether or not the regional health authority makes a contribution to expenses. The usual argument against allowability by the Inland Revenue is that the conference expenses are incurred in order to increase the consultant's knowledge and skills, and are therefore incurred to enable doctors to carry on their profession better, rather than incurred wholly and exclusively for the purposes of that profession. Not surprisingly, the Inland Revenue take more convincing where the conference is held outside the UK (*Parikh v Sleeman*), and even more so where the doctor's spouse also attends. Similarly, the expenses of training for some new area of medical practice, if borne by doctors to equip them to do something quite different from their existing work, could be disallowed as the primary objective is self-improvement. This applies for instance to course fees of someone seeking to become a psychotherapist where the purpose is to qualify to carry out treatment in that field.

9.6 General practice

The move towards 'group practice' continues, as does the concentration in purpose-built premises, instead of surgeries that form part of a doctor's residential property. Where practices are carried on from a private house, the same considerations apply in relation to expenses and capital gains tax as for self-employed consultants (see **9.3.1** above).

Where there is a health centre, at which a number of doctors or group practices are given facilities for reception and practice rooms with common access to other NHS disciplines (eg district and community nursing, minor surgery facilities, maternity clinics, child psychology, etc), each doctor or group practice pays an inclusive rental figure and special arrangements are made for telephone costs.

For anyone advising GPs, it is essential to obtain a copy of the NHS 'Red Book' — *Statement of Fees and Allowances Payable to General Medical Practitioners in England and Wales* (available on the internet at *www.nhs.uk/redbook*). This gives details of the various allowances and conditions of doctor's contracts. It is also important to read *Medeconomics* and other medical finance journals.

There may be three 'tiers' of expenses for partners in a general practice, as follows.

1. The normal expenses of running the practice and the common surgery premises reflected in the partnership accounts.

2. Sometimes doctors meet the costs of the surgeries to which they are attached, and separate claims are made for the same basis period.

3. Almost invariably, personal expenses and capital allowances are claimed by individual doctors for motor expenses and, frequently, for subscriptions, the costs of a surgery provided at their private residence, upkeep of personal surgical equipment, etc. Again, the claims are related to the normal practice basis period.

Spouses can, therefore, be remunerated by the partnership, or by the individual doctors, provided that the remuneration is actually paid and is commensurate with the duties performed.

Individual partners often take personal loans from the G.P.F.C. (now owned by Norwich Union), and interest paid is deducted in the second or third 'tier' of expenses, as appropriate. Interest so claimed in respect of the premises should not restrict capital gains tax retirement relief.

9.7 Self assessment guidance for doctors

The Inland Revenue have published a self assessment help sheet (IR 231) to assist in the completion of tax returns for doctors. The text is reproduced below.

> 'This Help Sheet gives advice about the calculation of business profits that is of particular relevance to doctors and medical practitioners.
>
> For a partnership it explains how to return details of:
>
> - expenditure incurred by a partner on behalf of the partnership (in boxes 3.51 to 3.63 of the Partnership Tax Return)
> - capital allowances claimed by the partnership on a vehicle (or other asset) owned by a partner (in boxes 3.14 to 3.21 of the Partnership Tax Return)
> - and, where appropriate, how such items are then reflected in the allocation of partnership profit between the partners.
>
> For both individuals and partnerships there is a reminder of the guidance on preparing medical accounts contained in the Department of Health's 'Red Book'.
>
> More general guidance on the completion of the Standard Accounts Information section of the Tax Return can be found in *Help Sheet IR229: Information from your accounts,* available from the Orderline.
>
> **CALCULATION OF PARTNERSHIP PROFITS**
>
> The rules for calculating the taxable profit made by any business, reflect the sources of income making up that business. And where, for example, a medical practice is carried on in partnership, that practice is a single source for tax purposes, regardless of the number of partners entitled to share the profits of the practice.
>
> It follows that the Partnership Tax Return for any business must contain all the information required to calculate the taxable profits arising from that business in any accounting period. This includes any claims (such as capital allowances) that must be taken into account when calculating the taxable profits.
>
> It also follows that individual partners are not entitled to make any adjustments to the amount of partnership profit allocated to them for a particular accounting period. For example, the entry that a partner makes in box 4.7 of the Partnership Pages of the personal Tax Return is the share of profit allocated to that partner in the Partnership Statement for the relevant accounting period.

TREATMENT OF EXPENDITURE INCURRED BY A PARTNER ON BEHALF OF THE PARTNERSHIP

The Partnership Tax Return for any business must contain all the information relevant to the calculation of the taxable profits arising from that business including any expenses incurred by a partner on behalf of the partnership. **It is not possible for individual partners to make supplementary claims, whether for expenses or capital allowances, in their own Tax Return.** This is because expenditure incurred by a partner only qualifies for relief if it is made 'wholly and exclusively' for the purposes of the partnership business. And the only legal basis for giving relief for any such expenditure is as a deduction in the calculation of the profits of the partnership business.

Similarly, the only legal basis for giving relief for expenditure that qualifies for capital allowances is as a deduction in the calculation of the profits of the partnership business (unless there is a formal leasing agreement between the partner and the partnership, when the allowances will be due against the leasing income).

However, this does not mean that any legitimate expenditure incurred by a partner — that is, any expense that would be allowable if met from partnership funds — can only be relieved if it is formally included in the partnership accounts. Nor does it mean that capital allowances can only be claimed on vehicles, or other assets, that feature in the partnership accounts.

Providing that:

- any expenditure, or claim to capital allowances, is correctly calculated for tax purposes, and
- records relevant to those calculations are made and kept *as if* the expenditure, or assets, were part of the partnership accounts

the Inland Revenue will accept entries in the relevant sections of the Partnership Tax Return which, though based on the partnership accounts, include adjustments for such expenditure, or allowances. But once the adjustments have been made the expenditure will be treated, for all practical purposes, as if it had been included in the partnership's accounts.

Where partners' personal expenses have been included in arriving at the figure of net taxable profit or loss and those expenses have not been included in the partnership's accounts either:

- a corresponding adjustment should be made to the net profit figure in box 3.112 of the Partnership Tax Return, **or**
- the accounts figure should be entered in box 3.112 and a reconciliation given in the 'Additional information' box on page 3 of the Partnership Tax Return.

For the year ended 5 April 2004

Doctors and dentists

Example 9.1

Doctors John, Hook and Feelgood carry on a Health Centre practice in partnership together. Their partnership agreement requires profits to be shared 50:30:20 but each partner is entitled to an adjustment for any expenditure incurred on behalf of the partnership. No other 'fixed adjustments' are due.

The partnership accounts for the 12 months to 31 December 2003 include entries for:

Employee costs	£24,000
Premises costs	£12,000
Motor expenses	£7,500

The capital allowances due on the practice vehicles are £3,750.

The three doctors bear the full running costs of their own private cars, although the vehicles are used in the practice.

For the 12 months to 31 December 2003 the running costs attributable to the practice were:

John	Hook	Feelgood
£4,000	£2,400	£1,900

Capital allowances are due (based on separate pools and adjusted for private usage) as follows:

John	Hook	Feelgood
£1,750	£1,420	£460 (balancing allowance on car disposed of)
		£3,000 (new car)

In addition, Dr John runs a small satellite surgery at home which is part of the partnership practice. Although the practice bears some of the costs directly Dr John incurs some costs himself. These are:

Proportion of home running costs	£1,500
Wife's wages and pension payments	£8,000

Entries in the 2003–04 Partnership Tax Return

When completing the Trading Pages of the Partnership Tax Return for 2003–04 the following composite entries are required:

Employee costs	£24,000 + £8,000 = £32,000 in box 3.51
Premises costs	£12,000 + £1,500 = £13,500 in box 3.52

Motor expenses	£7,500 + £4,000 + £2,400 + £1,900 = £15,800 in box 3.55	
Capital	£3,750 + £1,750 + allowances on £1,420 + £460 + motor cars £3,000 = £10,380 in box 3.70	

The net taxable profit (box 3.73) returned by the partnership for the 12 months to 31 December 2003 was £120,000. This is allocated between the partners as follows:

Step 1: adjust for expenditure incurred by individual partners

Net taxable profit	£120,000	
Add back	motor expenses	£8,300
	capital allowances	£6,630
	surgery costs	£9,500
Profit to be shared before individual adjustments		£144,430

Step 2: allocate profit between the partners

	Totals	John (50%)	Hook (30%)	Feelgood (20%)
Profit before individual adjustments	£144,430	£72,215	£43,329	£27,886
Motor costs	(£8,300)	(£4,000)	(£2,400)	(£1,900)
Capital allowances	(£6,630)	(£1,750)	(£1,420)	(£3,460)
Surgery costs	(£9,500)	(£9,500)	0	0
Net share of taxable profit	£120,000	£56,965	£39,509	£23,526

When completing the Partnership Statement for 2003–04 the following entries are required:

> £120,000 in box 11 (the total profit from this source)
>
> £56,965 in the corresponding profit share box for Dr John
>
> £39,509 in the corresponding profit share box for Dr Hook
>
> £23,526 in the corresponding profit share box for Dr Feelgood.

CORRESPONDING ADJUSTMENTS IN THE APPORTIONMENT OF TAXABLE PROFIT BETWEEN THE PARTNERS

Some partnership agreements, generally those relating to medical practices, provide that any expenditure incurred by a partner on behalf of the partnership, or any capital allowances due on assets owned by a partner, should be taken into account when the net profit of the practice is shared between the partners. Where this is the case the Inland Revenue accepts that it is appropriate for a corresponding adjustment to be made in the allocation of net taxable profit between the partners, to ensure that a partner receives the benefit due under the partnership agreement.

This adjustment will be equivalent to the expenditure incurred by the partner on behalf of the partnership, or to the amount of the capital allowances attributable to the vehicle (or other asset) owned by the partner but used in the partnership business.

Any such adjustments are analogous to 'fixed profit adjustments' for 'salary' or 'interest on capital' and should be identified as such in the Partnership Statement for the relevant accounting period.

DEPARTMENT OF HEALTH GUIDELINES ON THE COMPLETION OF THE ACCOUNTS OF MEDICAL PRACTICES

Each year the Inland Revenue carries out a survey of the income and expenses of medical practitioners on behalf of the Department of Health and the General Medical Services Committee of the BMA. The information from this survey is used to work out a ratio of expenses (including capital allowances) to income, which in turn is used to calculate the level of the profession's reimbursable expenses.

The Department of Health publishes the 'Red Book' which contains detailed guidance on the treatment of different items of income and expenditure in the accounts of medical practitioners. Of particular importance is the treatment of expenditure that is met either directly, or indirectly, by a Health Authority. This is because the treatment adopted influences the ratio of expenses to income derived from the annual survey.

Two key principles are identified in the 'Red Book':

- where a revenue expense (such as medical supplies, premises running costs, staff costs, or motor running costs) is met directly, or indirectly, by a Health Authority then
    - **the expense should be reported as the gross cost, and**
    - **the amount met directly, or reimbursed to the practice at a later date, should be reported as income.**

The amounts should not be set off, one against each other (so that only the net cost appears in the accounts)

- by contrast, where the practice receives a grant for capital expenditure (for example, computer equipment) **only the net cost of the capital asset should be reported in the practice accounts. Similarly, any capital allowances due should be calculated using the net capital cost.** (GPs and their advisers should refer to the 'Red Book' for the special rule precluding GPs from obtaining tax relief for any capital expenditure part-funded by an Improvement Grant from the Health Authority.).

Whether you are in practice on your own, or with others, it is in everyone's interest that the annual survey carried out by the Inland Revenue is as accurate as possible. Therefore, you should ensure that the figures you enter in your Tax Return follow the detailed guidelines set out in the 'Red Book'.

9.8 Further matters on GPs' affairs

All expenses should be shown gross, ie before reimbursement of expenses by the relevant paying authority.

9.8.1 Superannuation

Superannuation payments are added back in the practice tax computations and should therefore be claimed on the personal tax returns. Relief is available on an 'actual' basis as a deduction from the assessable profits.

9.8.2 Partnership changes

Although it is the simplest method, time-apportionment of profits should not be used, unless changes take place on 1 April which is the pay review date. An increase or decrease in the number of partners can have a marked effect on the level of profitability, due to extra/lower practice allowances. Instead, therefore, there should be a strict allocation of income to each partner, in order to arrive at his or her share on a change. It is unusual for goodwill to be valued by doctors, although not by dentists. It is a criminal offence for a doctor to sell goodwill (although not for a dentist).

9.8.3 Notional rent allowance

Notional rent or cost rent allowance is paid by the relevant paying authority, where the surgery is owned by one or more doctors. This allowance is part of the remuneration of the GP from the NHS, in return for using premises that he or she owns in treating NHS patients.

Where actual rent is paid by a practice to a partner who owns the surgery there may be a restriction in respect of retirement relief. Under TCGA 1992, Sch. 6, para. 12(2) an asset held on which rent is received is disqualified from the retirement relief provisions and consequently a rented property would not attract relief (although the recent case of *Plumbly and Others (PRs of Harbour deceased) v Spencer CA* [1999] STC 677 appears to overturn this long-standing presumption if the practice ceases at the time the surgery is sold). However, Statement of Practice D5 allows a measure of relief equal to the individual partner's share of the rent. A larger fraction of the asset may qualify for relief if the rent charged is clearly less than market rent.

An alternative arrangement would be not to treat the rental payment as a credit to the individual doctor but as partnership income, which is then reflected as an appropriation of profit to the owning doctor. It is true there is no landlord/tenant relationship between the parties and the family practitioner committee, and the 'cost rent' (as it is called) is merely a contribution by the family practitioner committee towards the financing costs of providing premises which recognise the effective subsidy which the partners are making to the health service by providing facilities for NHS patients. However, this treatment should avoid capital gains tax retirement relief problems and maximise relevant income for the purposes of retirement annuity premiums or personal pension payments. The same considerations apply where one doctor owns the premises and the partners pay rent. It is in fact better for that doctor to waive the rent and receive a higher share of partnership profits.

9.8.4 Personal awards

These are taxable and are paid for seniority, postgraduate training, study leave, vocational training, etc. Grants are also paid for training a trainee GP. Whether these are kept personally or are to be treated as partnership income must be agreed among the partners. If the award is not included in the partnership accounts, it must be shown in the doctor's personal tax returns.

9.8.5 Hospital appointments

Where one or more members of a partnership hold a hospital appointment, the partners should decide whether the income from the appointments is to be kept personally, or to be treated as income of the partnership. The agent should try to obtain an NT (nil tax) coding on salaries going to the partnership, although not all inspectors of taxes will agree to this, and practice varies from one tax district to another. If an NT coding is not given, then it is necessary to deduct in the tax computations the income assessable as employment income under ITEPA 2003 on the individual partner and to make an equalising adjustment in the allocation of partnership profits.

9.8.6 'Ash cash' and sundry fees

Some doctors receive payments, often in cash, for signing cremation certificates. Other sundry fees are often received from insurance medicals, lecturing, air-call duties and similar sources. The Inland Revenue Special Compliance Office examines records of such payments, particularly those kept by crematoria, and a number of investigations into the tax affairs of doctors and consultants have followed, resulting in substantial claims for tax, interest and penalties. A record of these fees should be kept and disclosed to the Inland Revenue on the annual tax return. The Inland Revenue have also enquired into questionnaire completion fees paid to doctors and consultants by market research organisations acting for pharmaceutical companies.

9.8.7 Salaried partners

Some partners who are genuinely self-employed are allocated 'salaries' under the partnership agreement. These are added back in arriving at the partnership Sch. D, Case II profit and are then taken into account in apportioning that assessment among the partners. However, there are some partners who actually receive a salary and no more, and who therefore fall within the scope of the employment income rules in ITEPA 2003.

These latter arrangements are to be avoided, as there is a danger of such partners being treated as assistants by the family practitioner committee, with a consequent loss in partnership allowances. It is better, therefore, to let such individuals have a low share of profits, with a guaranteed minimum share.

9.8.8 Best accounting date

Historically, the best accounting date for tax purposes is probably 30 June, the end of the first NHS quarterly period. However, for practical purposes under the current year basis, 31 March, which is the end of the NHS financial year (pay is reviewed each 1 April), creates least problems concerning tax on partnership changes and the complications of overlap relief.

The information on GPs' income and expenses supplied by inspectors of taxes (see the last section of help sheet IR 231 in **9.7** above) is from a sample of returns drawn only from those doctors whose accounting year ends between 1 January and 5 April in the year in question. To ensure that as representative a sample as possible is used, the BMA has urged GPs to use an accounting date within this period if they can.

9.8.9 Personal expenses claim

Allowable personal expenses should be included in the completion of the standard accounts information on the partnership tax return. Such personal expenses will typically include the following.

1. Motor cars — motor car expenses should be claimed in the 'third tier' of expenses (see **9.6** above). It is advisable to avoid the complications of leasing cars.

2. Spouse's pension — pension provision can be made by the employing partnership or the individual partner as appropriate.

3. Practice use of home — a supplementary practice allowance is paid by the relevant paying authority for 24-hour cover, which is a useful argument if household expenses relating to the practice area are challenged by the inspector. The claim should include a proportion of the following:

    (a) rent and water (not council tax);
    (b) light and heat;
    (c) insurance — buildings and contents;
    (d) domestic help;
    (e) garden (maintenance of approach to the front door);
    (f) window cleaning, and
    (g) structural repair.

    To ensure that the expenses are allowed, it is recommended that there be a plate outside the house, and a telephone directory entry or a private number available through the surgery.

Capital gains tax is unlikely to be a problem, unless there is exclusive use of part of the house for the purposes of the practice. Even then, retirement relief (until 5 April 2003), roll-over and/or hold-over relief should cover any potential charge. However, note the comments in **9.8.3** above in connection with retirement relief, where premises are owned by one individual partner. Also, it is necessary to withdraw from the practice ('withdrawal' includes 'partial withdrawal'), to claim relief from gains on individually-owned property. A '24-hour retirement' for pension purposes is not sufficient. A reduction, as opposed to an outright disposal, in partnership share is enough, but to what extent is not clear. Each case is judged on its facts but a restoration of the full partnership share shortly after the disposal is likely to prejudice the position.

4. Accountancy fees relating to claims in this 'third tier'.
5. Professional subscriptions and journals, including the subscription to the British Medical Association.
6. Local charitable and similar donations (see ESC B7).
7. Overseas conferences — it is necessary to be ready here for an Inland Revenue challenge, on the grounds of duality of purpose.

Sometimes part of the costs of works of improvement to surgery premises can be financed by improvement grants from the relevant paying authority. A condition for obtaining a grant is often that the expenditure cannot qualify for tax allowances and a declaration to that effect has to be signed by the doctor. The claiming of such expenditure therefore follows normal tax rules, namely capital expenditure on plant and machinery elements must be reduced to the extent it is met by way of grant (CAA 2001, s. 532). Equally, no expenditure subject to such a subsidy can be taken into account for capital gains purposes (TCGA 1992, s. 50).

Note that where a doctor's surgery is at home, any mortgage interest referable to the business part of the house can be claimed for tax relief as a business expense.

9.8.10 Retired doctors

Fully-retired doctors should be able to obtain tax relief on relevant payments, eg medical defence subscriptions, under ICTA 1988, s. 109A (post-cessation receipts).

9.9 Expenses in connection with *pro bono* work

A doctor recently suffered a Revenue investigation. The doctor spent part of his time in private practice and the remainder working unpaid at a special clinic for patients with a limited command of English. The Revenue wanted to disallow all the expenses directly attributable to the *pro bono* work and a substantial proportion of his general professional expenses. The Revenue's argument was that only expenses incurred in the course of a profit-making activity are allowable for tax purposes.

A substantial amount of money was at stake, as the Revenue wanted to reopen prior years and even charge a penalty. Indeed, the doctor was fearful that he might have to sell his house to pay the tax.

A compromise was eventually reached after two long and difficult meetings with the Revenue (and a substantial amount of work by the accountant who waived his own fees for the investigation). The compromise reduced the tax bill to manageable proportions. The outcome, however, was the finding by the doctor that his willingness to take a substantial amount of *pro bono* work had produced an unexpected tax bill.

9.10 Superannuation deductions

Superannuation deductions are made by all the paying authorities for fees or remuneration originating in the NHS.

The NHS takes as pensionable earnings the gross payments, other than direct reimbursements, by the relevant paying authority to doctors, less an approximation of the amount that the GP typically spends by way of expenses. For dentists only, there is a maximum, adjusted annually, on this pensionable earnings figure. GPs pay six per cent of their pensionable earnings by way of contributions to the NHS and these should be claimed by reference to the year of payment.

The availability of retirement annuity premium relief relative to private practice income and other non-pensionable earned sources is governed by ESC A9. GPs who are employed in the NHS, and are taxed under Schedule E, merely pay their six per cent to the statutory scheme. A GP is self-employed, but, most unusually, is required to be a member of a sponsored superannuation scheme. This unusual circumstance naturally calls for special arrangements, and these are set out in detail in ESC A9. As the rules are very specific, the GP's taxation advisor should consult them, and no attempt is made to paraphrase them here. However, the Inland Revenue have confirmed that, for the purposes of applying this concession, it is necessary to aggregate the whole of a doctor's medical earnings including any assessable in respect of a separate wholly private sector practice carried on his or her own.

Doctors can purchase 'added years' of superannuable service, payable quarterly, to increase service to a maximum of 40 years at age 60 and thus increase benefits due. Tax relief is available only if the instalments do not exceed nine per cent of NHS earnings at the time payments commence. Where premiums towards a retirement annuity are also being paid, concessions are available to prevent an inequity, and details of the arrangement can be obtained from the Pensions Schemes Office.

A doctor or dentist may claim relief for NHS superannuation contributions and personal/stakeholder pension contributions (ESC A9) along the same basis as applies for retirement annuity relief.

However, because the earnings cap applies to the calculation of net relevant earnings for personal/stakeholder pension purposes, relief for the personal/ stakeholder pension contributions must be calculated by subtracting the deemed NHS earnings from the total net relevant earnings or the earnings cap, whichever is the lower amount.

The Inland Revenue have also confirmed that under the personal/stakeholder pension arrangements it is possible to choose the statutory relief for personal/stakeholder pension premiums calculated by reference to total Schedule D earnings, and forgo concessional relief for contributions to the NHS scheme on a year-by-year basis. The doctor who claims the statutory relief in one year may, therefore, revert to claiming relief on the NHS contributions on a non-statutory basis in a later year. It appears that such an election can also be made for the immediately preceding year of assessment where personal/stakeholder pension premiums are related back one year.

The provisions of FA 2004, which come into force from 6 April 2006, are likely to have an impact on all of these arrangements and advice should be sought.

9.11 Dentists

Dentists who are not employed within the NHS by a health authority but who provide general dental services are chargeable under Sch. D, Case II on their professional receipts. Dental practitioners may be included in the General Dental List only if they undertake to provide a general dental service as a

Doctors and dentists

principal. In consequence, a dental surgery may serve a number of dentists, each responsible professionally as a principal, with the common services, receptionists and nursing staff for the surgery being provided by one of the dentists. The contract between the dentist providing the common services and the other dentists working on the premises may be either a contract for services or a contract of employment.

Note that there is a standard form of agreement, approved by the British Dental Association, for dentists practising as principals in premises run by another dentist. Where this agreement is used and its terms followed, the income of dentists working in the practice is assessable under Schedule D, Case II and not to employment income under ITEPA 2003.

Dentists, like doctors, have NHS patients and private patients. Where there are earnings from both sources, Inland Revenue ESC A9 operates to quantify what are pensionable NHS scheme earnings, in respect of which retirement annuity premiums or personal pension premiums cannot be paid and allowed unless relief for the NHS scheme contributions is disclaimed. With dentists, however, there is a limit on the amount of pensionable earnings, which is reviewed in line with average earnings of dentists under the NHS scheme.

ESC A9 continues in relation to the personal/stakeholder pension rules which replaced the previous retirement annuity premium rules from 1 July 1988.

However, the provisions of FA 2004, which come into force from 6 April 2006, are likely to have an impact on all of these arrangements and advice should be sought.

The Inland Revenue Inspector's Manual contains the following remarks concerning dentists:

> 'A principal dentist usually has a practice, consisting of a list of patients, premises, equipment and staff. That practice, in which he exercises his professional skill, is the source of the profits to be assessed under Case II of Schedule D. As the person receiving or entitled to the income from that source, the dentist is the person chargeable (S59 (1) ICTA88). It follows that, if there is a change in the person carrying on that practice, there will be a succession and Section 113 (1) ICTA88 will apply. The position of a principal dentist with a practice in a particular area is to be distinguished from that of a professional man, such as a barrister; who can exercise his professional skills anywhere in the country; see *Seldon v Croom-Johnson*, 16 TC 740, *Rex v City of London Commissioners, ex parte Gibbs*, 24 TC 221 at p.239, and *Sargent v Barnes*, 52 TC 335. Accordingly, if a principal dentist leaves a practice in one location and moves to a practice in another location, the income from both practices must

be computed on cessation and commencement lines. The argument that a principal dentist carries on one continuous profession wherever he goes should not be accepted where he operated in established practices.

The situation is different for an associate dentist. An associate dentist has no patients of his own, usually no premises or staff and sometimes no equipment. He makes his services available to one or more principal dentists on terms which usually preclude him from retaining any of the patients as his own at the end of the engagement. As long as he is an associate dentist, he carries on one continuous profession wherever he goes. Accordingly the cessation and commencement provisions should not be applied when he moves from one associate position to another. They should however be applied if he permanently ceases to be an associate and becomes a principal dentist, either in a practice of his own or as a partner in another practice (even if he had previously worked for that practice as an associate). In many cases where an associate dentist becomes a principal dentist he will have taken over a practice previously carried on by a principal dentist. In such cases Section 113(1) ICTA 1988 will apply as there will be a succession to that practice.'

9.11.1 Associates

Dental associates are normally accepted as self-employed by the Inland Revenue. The partnership or individual dentist that engages an associate can claim the associate's remuneration as a Sch. D, Case II deduction.

When an associate is admitted into a partnership, the cessation rules apply to his or her source of income as an associate, as the associate's status changes completely and the source, as a matter of fact, ceases.

The personal service company or intermediaries legislation was introduced by FA 2000 to counter the use of personal service companies by individuals who provide their services through intermediaries to other businesses. The legislation is extremely wide-ranging and could affect a large number of professionals and other workers (including associate dentists) who have set up such companies to avoid employment status. If the intermediaries legislation does apply, then the intermediary has to account for PAYE and National Insurance (NI) on notional remuneration unless actual PAYE has been accounted for on payments to the individual.

9.11.2 Partnerships

Partnerships of dentists are usually either cost-sharing, where the dentists do not pool their fees but share premises and costs, or full profit-sharing, where income is pooled. In either case, as with GPs, there is a second tier of personal business expenses allowable against their own individual profit shares (but, for self-assessment, dealt with in the partnership return).

9.11.3 Goodwill

Advice on the value of goodwill of a dental practice should be sought from the British Dental Association, to whom many members make requests for guidance.

9.12 General case law relating to doctors and dentists

Other cases of limited interest relating to doctors and dentists are:

- *North v Spencer's Executors* (1956) 36 TC 668 — whether payments to executors after death are assessable;
- *Osborn v Sawyer* (1933) 18 TC 445 — assessability of rent and rates of a medical officer of a hospital;
- *Duff v Williamson* (1973) 49 TC 1 — assessability of a research grant paid to a doctor;
- *Sargent v Barnes* (1978) 52 TC 335 — travelling expenses of a dentist to and from a dental laboratory, where the dental laboratory was between home and surgery, were not allowed under the 'duality of purpose' principle, and
- *Cooke v Blacklaws* (1984) 58 TC 255 — 'foreign emoluments' deduction due in respect of salary paid to a non-domiciled dentist by a Panamanian company to which NHS earnings were transferred, notwithstanding that, under NHS (General Dental Services) Regulations 1973, it was the dental practitioner who was strictly entitled to the fees (see ICTA 1988, s.192).

Chapter 10 Practising barristers, barristers' clerks, judges and solicitors

10.1 Barristers

The earnings from the profession of a barrister are assessable to tax under Sch. D, Case II.

The profession is regarded as commencing when the barrister or advocate indicates availability to carry out fee-earning work (FA 1998, s. 43(2)).

A barrister's profession does not cease when he or she becomes a Queen's Counsel (*Seldon v Croom-Johnson* (1932) 16 TC 740). However, a cessation occurs when barristers take up full-time appointments (for instance as judges), assessable as employment income under ITEPA 2003, or when they retire or die prior to retirement. As with doctors, income and expenses relating to part-time employments – such as recorderships – must be strictly segregated in the relevant tax computations from the professional accounts in arriving at the income assessable under Sch. D, Case II.

10.1.1 Cash basis

Historically, barristers prepared their accounts on a cash basis, largely because they are not able to sue for fees. However, following the withdrawal of the cash basis for Sch. D taxpayers by the FA 1998, this option is now only available to new barristers.

The profits of a barrister or advocate in actual practice can be computed in accordance with the cash basis for the first seven years of practice (FA 1998, s. 43). However, the profits for accounting periods ending more than seven years after the commencement of the profession are computed on the earnings basis. For these purposes, the profession is regarded as commencing at the time that the barrister or advocate first holds himself out as available for fee-earning work.

The barrister or advocate has the option of computing profits for the first seven years on either a cash basis of an earnings basis (by reference to fees whose amount has been agreed or in respect of which a fee has not been issued). However, once a particular basis has been adopted, it must be adopted consistently (FA 1998, s. 43(3)).

Move to earnings basis

Once the first seven years have passed, profits must be computed on the earnings basis as for other Sch. D professions. As a consequence of the move, some income may be taxed twice, or some income may not be taxed at all and some expenses may be allowed twice and some expenses may not be taxed at all. The adjustments that are needed to prevent undercharging or overcharging are aggregated. Where the result is positive, known as an adjustment charge, it is charged to tax under Sch. D, Case VI in the year in which the move to the earnings basis took place.

However, an election can be made for an 'adjustment charge' over ten years (FA 2002, Sch. 22, para. 11, 12).

Where such an election is made, in each of the nine years beginning with that in which the whole amount would otherwise be chargeable to tax, an amount equal to the lower of one-tenth of the adjustment charge and ten per cent of the profits of the profession is treated as arising and chargeable to tax. For these purposes, the profits of the profession are computed without taking account of any capital allowances.

In the tenth year, the balance of the adjustment charge is taxed. If the profession ceases prior to year ten, the adjustment charge continues to be spread over the ten years, but the amount charged from the cessation to year nine is ten per cent of the adjustment charge.

An election to spread the adjustment charge over ten years must be made in writing by 31 January following the end of the tax year in question. The election can be made for any amount up to so much of the adjustment charge as has not previously been charged to tax.

10.1.2 Inducement receipts

A payment to induce a barrister to give up his or her status as a practising barrister, and to accept an appointment with an employer that precludes the barrister from continuing in practice in chambers, is not taxable as income (*Vaughan-Neil v CIR* (1979) 54 TC 223).

10.1.3 Expenses

Travel

A barrister's expenses of travelling between home and chambers are not allowable, following the decision in *Newsom v Robertson* (1952) 33 TC 452, even if part of the barrister's home is used as a study. The places where the profession of a barrister is considered to be carried on are the courts and chambers. Only travelling between the two, or between two sets of chambers, is therefore allowable.

The position on claiming expenses where there is income from an office or employment is more restrictive still. Thus the costs of a barrister's travel between chambers in London and the place of performance of his duties as a recorder in Portsmouth were held not to be allowable against employment income, where the barrister held a recordership as well as carrying on a practice in London (see *Ricketts v Colquhoun* (1925) 10 TC 118). The test of allowability was what each and every holder of the office incurred. This test excludes expenses peculiar to the circumstances of the particular holder of the office — in this instance, as recorder.

Cost of chambers

The appropriate costs of running and renting chambers, including a clerk's fees, are allowable. The Inland Revenue also allow an appropriate proportion of the costs of the home that are referable to professional use. However, where a proportion of the home expenses is claimed, the capital gains implications need to be considered before a claim is made that a specific proportion of the home is used exclusively as a study, as such a claim affects the capital gains tax private residence exemption (TCGA 1992, s. 222).

Court apparel

Generally, the costs of replacing a barrister's special court apparel are allowable. A barrister's wig and gown appear to rank as plant, following a decision before the Special Commissioners on the point, so that the initial cost of such items now qualifies for capital allowances. In *Mallalieu v Drummond* (1983) 57 TC 330, however, it was held that the cost of the ordinary dark dresses and suits with white tunics and black tights that a female barrister has to wear to appear in court, is not allowable, as the reason for buying this clothing is not only to be able to appear in court but also to provide warmth and decency.

Patent fee

The patent fee on becoming a Queen's Counsel is not allowable as a Schedule D, Case II expense because of its capital nature.

Books

The replacement of books is allowable as a Sch. D, Case II expense, as is the cost of servicing looseleaf volumes. The initial cost of a barrister's library is regarded as capital and cannot be claimed as a revenue expense. However, following the decision in *Munby v Furlong* (1977) 50 TC 491, books now rank as plant for capital allowances. With the withdrawal of the 100 per cent first-year allowance, it is probably to the barrister's advantage to adopt the 'renewals' basis outlined above, ie to disallow the original cost of the library and allow the cost of replacements as a Sch. D, Case II expense. As an alternative, the barrister may claim writing-down allowances for both original and replacement books. Where books have not been claimed as plant, because figures have been agreed before the decision in *Munby v Furlong*, it is possible, for future periods, to claim writing-down allowances on such a library on the notional written-down value.

Secretarial

In August 1994 the Inland Revenue published an interpretation on the possibility of a deduction for costs of secretarial assistance and childcare costs. The text is reproduced below:

> 'The Revenue's attention has been drawn to recent press articles which indicate that a new "concession" has been given to barristers in private practice for part of the costs of employing a nanny. The Revenue wish to make it clear that neither by law nor Revenue concession is tax relief available for a business person's own childcare costs.
>
> **The law**
>
> Expenditure is not deductible in computing the profits of a trade, profession or vocation unless it is incurred wholly and exclusively for the purposes of the business. But where an outgoing is such that a definite part or proportion of it can be identified as being wholly and exclusively expended for business purposes a deduction may be due for that part. This widely held understanding of the law has been approved by the courts.
>
> **Use of nanny to undertake secretarial duties**

A nanny may be partly employed to carry out material secretarial duties in the business of her employer. If so, a deduction may be due for that part of the costs of employing her referable (on a time basis) to those duties.

What proportion of the employment costs may be deductible in this way depends on the facts and circumstances of individual cases. But, where a district inspector handles the returns of a number of businesses carried on in an essentially similar way, he or she may decide, as a matter of local practice, to set down guidelines regarding the treatment of particular items of expenditure.

In the case of a barrister's nanny it has been reported that the local inspector has accepted that a secretarial "allowance" can be claimed. This misrepresents the position. What the inspector has done is to give an indication of the maximum deduction he would ordinarily accept.

It remains the case that no deduction at all will be due if the employee does not undertake material secretarial duties. Conversely, in a case where detailed records showed that exceptionally heavy duties were undertaken, a contention that a greater sum should be deducted would have to be considered on its merits. And in any event the figures have no application to other businesses where the need for a nanny to undertake secretarial duties may be very different.'

10.2 Barristers' clerks

Barristers' clerks occupy a unique position as they are effectively employed by a number of principals in the chambers where they work. Because of this, special taxation arrangements operate in respect of their earnings. They can account for PAYE quarterly themselves, by reference to the PAYE codes on their net receipts for the preceding quarter, after expenses and pension scheme payments. If they do not operate this system, the Inland Revenue will make quarterly 'direct collection' assessments, based on the previous year's income, excluding expenses.

The head of chambers should deal with both the employers' and employees' National Insurance Contributions (NICs) in respect of barristers' clerks. However, some senior clerks have negotiated self-employed status for National Insurance (NI) purposes, although this applies only on an individual basis. Similarly, some senior clerks have succeeded in persuading the Inland Revenue that they are self-employed for tax purposes.

Self-employed status was challenged unsuccessfully by the Inland Revenue in *McMenamin v Diggles* [1991] STC 419. This case concerned the senior clerk of

Practising barristers, barristers' clerks, judges and solicitors

a leading set of barristers' chambers in Manchester. Up to 7 October 1985 he was senior clerk under a contract of employment. Thereafter, new contractual arrangements operated with each member of the chambers, under which in return for a specified percentage of the gross income of each member, he agreed at his own cost to provide a full clerking service for each member. It was open to him to act as head clerk himself or to provide some other suitably qualified person to act as such. The point at issue was whether this occupation constituted an office. The Inland Revenue contended that, because under paragraph 26 of the Code of Conduct issued by the Bar Council every barrister had 'to have the services of the clerk of the chambers', each barrister must engage the services of a person holding the office of clerk of chambers.

In *Edwards v Clinch* [1981] STC 617 it was held that an 'office' was a continuing position, independent of the person who filled it, and occupied by successive holders. There had to be an instrument creating the office and it had to have a degree of public relevance with formality of appointment. In the *McMenamin* case, there was no obvious instrument creating an office, in no sense were there public duties, and the revised arrangements were the most convenient means of discharging the contractual obligations of the clerk.

10.3 Judges

Her Majesty's judges are assessable to employment income under ITEPA 2003 in respect of their remuneration. It is understood that the Inland Revenue have, in certain cases, allowed a deduction where judges have to maintain a study at home for the proper performance of their duties. Similarly, deductions have been agreed for a judge's law books and for maintenance of robes, wing collars and bands.

10.3.1 Recorders (including circuit and deputy circuit judges)

The Courts Act 1971, as amended by the Supreme Court Act 1981 and the Courts and Legal Services Act 1990, includes provision for the appointment (in England and Wales) of circuit judges, deputy circuit judges, recorders and assistant recorders. The Supreme Court Act 1981 provides for the appointment of deputy High Court judges. The appointments are statutory and are offices within the scope of the charge to tax on employment income. Salaries of circuit judges, which are paid by the Treasury, and fees for the other four categories, which are paid by the Lord Chancellor's Department, are subject to tax under PAYE.

The following treatment has been agreed with the Lord Chancellor's Department regarding travelling and subsistence allowances.

Recorders and assistant recorders

A recorder may be required to 'sit' anywhere in England or Wales and is regarded as holding a travelling appointment. His or her travelling and subsistence allowances are not chargeable to tax and PAYE should not be applied.

Circuit judges

Some circuit judges hold travelling appointments whilst those who do not agree with the Lord Chancellor's Department a base to be regarded as their normal place of employment. A judge in the latter category personally bears the cost of travel between home and base and no allowance is given for this expense. Where there is a travelling appointment, or where judges are required to serve away from their base, travelling and subsistence allowances are paid. These allowances are not chargeable to tax and PAYE should not be applied.

Deputy High Court and deputy circuit judges

Deputy High Court and circuit judges are regarded as holding travelling appointments. Travelling and subsistence allowances paid under this form of appointment are not chargeable to tax and PAYE should not be applied.

Deputy district judges

Deputy district judges are appointed under the provisions of the Supreme Court Act 1981 and the County Courts Act 1984 (as amended by the Courts and Legal Services Act 1990). They are regarded as travelling appointments. Travelling and subsistence allowances paid are not chargeable to tax and PAYE should not be applied.

10.4 Solicitors

10.4.1 Bank interest, etc received

Bank interest received and retainable by solicitors on the investment of clients' or their own business monies is normally assessed under Sch. D, Case III. Interest does not constitute relevant earnings for the purpose of retirement annuity or personal pension relief, but otherwise forms part of the solicitor's total income.

Solicitors' Rules (Great Britain)

Bank and building society interest on deposits of clients' money should be dealt with as follows.

1. Designated clients' deposit account. The client is entitled to the interest arising on the account, and depending on the status of the client the interest may be paid gross or net. The solicitor simply passes on the interest gross or net to the client.

2. Undesignated deposit accounts. Deduction of tax does not apply to interest on an undesignated (general) client account.

Where money is deposited into an undesignated client account the solicitor, instead of accounting to the client for the interest, pays the client a sum in lieu of interest which is assessable on the client under Case VI. The sum paid in lieu of interest is payable without deduction of tax. Such payments are regarded as the client's income and not the solicitor's. The solicitor is accordingly assessed only on the net interest retained in the year. Where the amount paid to clients exceeds the interest received the excess may be allowed as a Case II deduction.

The net interest does not constitute relevant earnings for the purposes of retirement annuity relief. Correspondingly, the interest paid to clients in respect of monies held in undesignated accounts is not allowed as a deduction in computing the profits of the practice and therefore does not reduce the profits for pension premium purposes.

The Case III assessment on the net interest retained is normally made at the same time as the Case II assessment on the profits of the solicitor's profession.

10.4.2 Interest received on behalf of clients

Solicitors are not assessed to tax under ICTA 1988, s. 59(1) in respect of mortgage interest, etc. they receive on behalf of a resident client. All such interest is passed on gross to clients, who are liable to direct assessment under Sch. D, Case III. Normal practice in Scotland is for assessments to be made on solicitors in respect of interest received by them in acting for executors or trustees.

If the client is non-resident, a solicitor who manages or controls the interest may be assessed under TMA 1970, s. 78. A solicitor who places funds in an account designated for a non-resident simply to comply with the Solicitors' Rules is not considered to have management or control of the interest. If, however, there is an arrangement with the client under which the solicitor has wider discretion to invest the client's funds, the solicitor may have management or control.

Power to require a return of particulars of items of interest paid gross is given by TMA 1970, s. 18.

10.4.3 Interest paid by or through a solicitor

Where interest is required to be paid under deduction of tax (for example, to a person whose usual place of abode is abroad), a solicitor may be charged under ICTA 1988, ss. 349 and 350 if he or she is the person by or through whom the payment is made (although normally the assessment is made on the person for whom the solicitor is acting).

Exceptionally, a solicitor may receive on behalf of a non-resident client interest paid without deduction of tax (for example, where the payer has failed to comply with ICTA 1988, ss. 349 and 350) and may then be charged under TMA 1970, s. 78.

10.4.4 Temporary loans and guarantees

Some solicitors are prepared to make temporary loans to clients to facilitate legal transactions already in train. For example, solicitors may make a bridging loan to clients who cannot pay for a new house until they have been paid for their old house, so that the purchase can proceed as planned. In some cases solicitors themselves borrow temporarily from their bank for the purpose. Interest received and paid on such temporary loans, the only purpose of which is to remove an obstacle to the progress of professional legal work, may be regarded as a professional receipt or expense of the solicitor's practice.

A loss on a temporary guarantee given by a solicitor to expedite a particular legal transaction may similarly be allowed (*Jennings v Barfield and Barfield* (1962) 40 TC 365).

In contrast, interest received by a solicitor other than on a temporary loan relating to a transaction in hand is regarded as investment income assessable under Sch. D, Case III. Thus an advance to a speculative builder, although it may generate future legal business, should not be regarded as an integral part of the professional activities. As a corollary, if the borrower fails to repay the loan, any claim to deduct the loss as an expense of the practice or as a bad debt should be refused.

10.4.5 Office holders

Where a professional in private practice holds an office the emoluments from that office are strictly chargeable as employment income under ITEPA 2003. This is so even if the duties of the office are such that they normally fall within the scope of the office holder's profession and it is held as an incident in carrying on a private practice by the holder (see in this connection *CIR v Brander and Cruikshank* (1971) 46 TC 574). The same normally applies in the case of an employment held by such an individual.

However, there are particular practical difficulties if the employment income rules were applied to the fees received by certain taxpayers in this type of situation. For example, accountants acting as company auditors or secretaries and solicitors acting as company registrars or secretaries often hold numerous such offices concurrently as an integral part of their professional practice. Similar difficulties can arise where a partner holds an office or employment and the fees are included with partnership income and pooled amongst the partners (eg a solicitor who is clerk to a body of commissioners, or a GP with a part-time NHS hospital appointment). The amount of tax payable under the rules of the different employment and self-employment tax codes is often similar in these types of situation.

In these circumstances, such fees can be treated as ordinary professional receipts within Sch. D, Case II and any expenses admissible are allowed under the rules of that Schedule. This treatment applies, however, only where all the following conditions are met:

- the duties of the office or employment (in terms of time taken) are small in relation to other practice work (of the individual or partner) which is clearly of a Sch. D nature;
- the office or employment is in a field related to the profession and particular practice concerned (see **10.4.6** below);
- in a case involving a partner, there is an agreement between the partners that the fees are included as income of the partnership and pooled for division amongst the partners — and that agreement is acted upon;
- the individual and any partners agree that the income is treated for tax purposes in this manner and agree to pay tax on the fees on that basis (where appropriate as part of the partnership profits) — written confirmation should be obtained from all concerned to this effect; and

- the fees are not derived from the directorship of a company and are small in relation to the receipts of the practice generated by the individual or partner.

10.4.6 Is the engagement in a related area?

In deciding whether an office or employment is in a related field, compare the nature of the duties of the office or employment with those of the practice conducted by the individual/partnership and of the profession concerned. For example, a solicitor who is clerk to a body of commissioners is in a field related to his or her profession and practice – but not if appointed chair of a golf club. Likewise, a GP employed as a part-time NHS hospital doctor is in a related field – but not if employed as a part-time history lecturer.

Similarly, cases involving membership of public tribunals and trusts should be reviewed on their own merits by reference to the particular facts of the appointment, practice and profession concerned. However, where a partner is involved and income from a public tribunal or trust is to be pooled amongst the partners (ie the third condition in the bullet list in **10.4.5** above is satisfied) it may be accepted that the appointment is in a related field where the partner is appointed because of general business skills or experience, rather than to provide specific input in respect of his or her own profession.

Chapter 11 Members of Parliament, Members of the Scottish Parliament, Members of the Welsh Assembly and Members of the Northern Ireland Legislative Assembly

11.1 General taxation position

Members of Parliament (MPs), Members of the Scottish Parliament (MSPs), Members of the Welsh Assembly (WAMs) and Members of the Northern Ireland Legislative Assembly (MLAs) are all on the same footing for tax purposes in relation to termination payments, certain travel and accommodation allowances, and pensions. The rules which apply to ministerial and other offices also apply to equivalent offices in the devolved administrations. Unless otherwise stated, therefore, the expenses and allowances described below in relation to Westminster arise and are dealt with in the same ways in relation to the other UK Parliaments. The relevant legislation was brought in by the Finance Act 1999.

Because of the complexity of their allowances, MPs are dealt with by a special unit of the Inland Revenue in Cardiff, which issues notes for guidance on the tax position of MPs (reissued in 1988 and subsequently updated).

Members of Parliament are required to complete the Parliament pages of the self-assessment return (SA101MP). The Inland Revenue have published helpsheets SA101MP(Notes), SA101MSP(Notes), SA101WAM(Notes) and SA101 (MLA)(Notes) to accompany the return. These are available on the Revenue website (*www.inlandrevenue.gov.uk*).

MPs are liable to income tax under the employment income rules in ITEPA 2003 on their Parliamentary salary as holders of an office. MPs are also in receipt of certain allowances principally designed to cover the expenses incurred on living away from home, travel and secretarial assistance.

Members of Parliament, Members of the Scottish Parliament etc.

Considerable detail is to be found in Factsheet M5 *Members' Pay, Pensions and Allowances* available from the House of Commons Information Office and at www.parliament.uk/parliamentary_publications_and_archives/factsheets/m05.cfm. The tax position of such allowances is set out below.

11.2 Additional costs allowance

The main allowance is the daily additional costs allowance for non-inner London members: inner London members have a London allowance, which is taxable. This additional costs allowance covers the additional costs of living away from home whilst engaged in Parliamentary duties either in London or in the MP's constituency. The allowance is not taxable (ITEPA 2003, s. 292). In consequence, claims for expenses incurred in connection with staying away from the MP's home to perform Parliamentary duties, such as the cost of meals in London, rent and the heating of a second home in London, are not taxable. This means that an MP can obtain effective tax relief on interest on a mortgage to buy a second home in London, as the allowance is calculated to allow the payment of either rent or such mortgage interest in the case of an owned property.

11.3 Car allowance

The position of car allowances is complex because the cash mileage reimbursement that the MP receives from the Fees Office includes the cost of travel between the MP's home and Westminster, or between home and constituency, which ranks for tax purposes as private travel. In strictness, the car mileage allowance paid by the Fees Office is assessable as an emolument and an expenses claim should be made. However, taking one year with another, this cash allowance seems adequately to cover both allowable running costs and depreciation. For practical purposes, therefore, the allowance is not taxed (unless the Fees Office pays an allowance on a taxable journey), nor is an expenses claim required from the MP in the average case where a member claims for an annual mileage of up to 25,000.

The rates of mileage allowance for 2004–05 are as follows:

First 20,000 miles	After 20,000 miles
57.7p	26.6p

If MPs claim for an annual mileage in excess of 25,000, the Fees Office requires detailed particulars of their journeys.

11.4 Other travel (by taxi, train or air)

Incidental travel costs in London, such as taxi fares between London rail and air terminals and Westminster, and in visiting ministers on Parliamentary business, are allowable expenses.

MPs are issued with rail and air warrants which give them free rail and air travel. Where the travel is from Westminster to the constituency, this does not rank as a benefit, because it is a facility used in the course of the performance of the duties of an office which has two places of work (Westminster and the constituency). Therefore, there is no taxable benefit in relation to such travel. However, travel from the MP's home or main home to Westminster, or between home and the constituency (where the home is neither in Westminster nor in the constituency), is taxable on the following basis.

1. Where the MP's home is not more than 20 miles in a direct line from the nearest point of the constituency boundary, a warrant for travel between home and Westminster, or between home and the constituency, is not taxable.

2. Where the home is within 20 miles' radius of Westminster, a warrant used for travelling between home and the constituency is not taxable.

3. Where the home is more than 20 miles from the nearest point of the constituency boundary, a warrant used for travelling between home and Westminster is taxable.

4. Where the home is neither in the constituency nor in London, and warrants are used for travelling between Westminster and the constituency via home, provided the journey between Westminster and the constituency can be regarded as continuous, only the excess of the value of the warrant used for the round trip over the value of a warrant for a direct journey between Westminster and the constituency is taxable.

'Continuous' for this purpose means that no more than one night is spent at the MP's home before continuing the journey, unless the journey spans a weekend, when Saturday and Sunday are disregarded. The Fees Office notifies the Inland Revenue of the private proportion.

Other private air or rail travel not connected with the performance of Parliamentary duties, for instance attending political meetings, also gives rise to a benefit. The benefit is the cost of the equivalent ticket (ITEPA 2003, s. 82). An MP's spouse and minor children can use special rail/air warrants to make 15 return journeys per calendar year by rail or air between London and the constituency, and/or between London and home. Again, this is not taxable, except to the extent that the journeys are to and from the home or principal home. The basis of the exemption for other journeys is presumably the same as the concession given for directors' spouses accompanying them on business trips, where the expenses are allowable if they can be regarded as helping directors in the performance of their duties.

No tax liability arises in respect of the provision of transport or subsistence that is made available by or on behalf of the Crown to a holder of a ministerial office or to a member of the office holder's family or household. Likewise, there is no liability to tax in respect of payments and reimbursements by or on behalf of the Crown in connection with the provision of such transport or subsistence (ITEPA 2003, s. 295).

11.5 European travel expenses

No liability to tax arises in respect of a sum that is paid to an MP, MSP, WAM or a MLA in respect of European travel expenses. European travel expenses are the costs of, and any additional expenses incurred in, travelling between the UK and a European institution or agency or the national parliament of another member state, a candidate or application country or a member state of the European Free Trade Association (EFTA) (ITEPA 2003, s. 294).

11.6 Overnight expense allowances

No liability to income tax arises in respect of an overnight expense allowance paid to a MP in accordance with a resolution of the House of Commons (ITEPA 2003, s. 292). An overnight expense allowance is an allowance expressed to be in respect of additional expenses necessarily incurred by the MP in staying away overnight from the member's main residence for the purposes of performing parliamentary duties in the London area or in the member's constituency.

Likewise, no liability to tax arises in respect of a payment that is made to a MSP, WAM or a MLA in respect of necessary overnight expenses (ITEPA 2003, s. 293). Necessary overnight expenses are additional expenses necessarily incurred by the member for the purposes of performing duties as a member in staying overnight away from the member's only or main residence in the area in which the Parliament or Assembly sits or in the constituency or region that the member respresents.

11.7 Staffing allowance

The Office Cost Allowance (OCA) was abolished in April 2003. Members who served in the previous Parliament could opt to retain their OCA entitlement until then or transfer to the Staffing Allowance. For 2003/04 the Staffing Allowance maximum is set at £64,304 (£74,985 for members with London constituencies).

The allowance is for office, secretarial and research expenses. This is taxable, but a deduction is made for the actual costs of any secretarial and clerical assistance, general office expenses and research assistance undertaken in the proper performance of the MP's Parliamentary duties. Such expenses include the normal costs of office accommodation such as rent, heat and light, including the use of part of the home as an office and the costs of repairs and renewals of office equipment. Telephone, stationery and postage costs, if not provided free, are also allowable. An MP's secretary is paid direct by the Fees Office rather than the MP receiving the salary as part of a claim for office expenses, and PAYE is operated by the Fees Office. There are also provisions for sickness benefits and superannuation contributions. Detailed claims are generally only required where claims are made in excess of the allowance.

11.8 Other incidental expenses

MPs may claim an allowance to cover various other incidental expenses, including:

- the hiring of rooms to meet constituents;
- delegation expenses with all-party Parliamentary organisations such as the Inter-Parliamentary Union or the Parliamentary Group for European Unity;
- payments for assistance on constituency work to a local agent or party organisation, and
- the extra cost of meals while travelling on Parliamentary business — see **11.2** above).

The current maximum of this allowance is £18,799, and it is increased annually in line with the Retail Prices Index.

Amongst the items that the Inland Revenue regard as not allowable are:
- any party political expenses (such as election expenses);
- extra costs of late night sittings;
- periodicals, books and newspaper cuttings, and
- overseas trips unless as part of an official all-party Parliamentary delegation.

An attempt is made to allow, in the PAYE code number of the MP, an estimate of the excess of allowable expenses over taxable allowances. To this end, an MP makes a formal claim with a signed declaration after the end of each fiscal year. With the exemption now afforded to most allowances, such coding adjustments are rarely needed.

11.9 Pension and retirement arrangements

MPs qualify for parliamentary pensions of N/40ths so there is no reason why they should also accrue retirement benefits under a former employer's scheme.

An exception is where the MP still receives remuneration from that employer.

There are special pension and retirement arrangements for MPs. Compulsory contributions (with the contribution rate now set at nine per cent of salary) to the House of Commons Members' Fund and contributions to the Parliamentary Contributory Pension Fund are treated as reducing the MP's salary for tax purposes. MPs can also purchase additional years of service reckonable for superannuation purposes, either by periodical contributions at any time during their service as MPs, or by lump sum payment effected within 12 months of election to the House of Commons.

Terminal grants to MPs made in pursuance of a Resolution of the House of Commons to a person ceasing to be an MP are treated as taxable under the 'golden handshake' legislation, and are therefore exempt up to £30,000. Such grants include severance payments equal to three months' salary as a member.

There are special provisions (ICTA 1988, s. 629) for ministers who are not participants in the Parliamentary pension schemes in respect of their extra ministerial salary over and above what is pensionable under those schemes. They can make personal pension premium payments in respect of such element of their remuneration and accordingly, may wish to seek advice on the impact (if any) of FA 2004, the pension provisions of which come into force from 6 April 2006.

11.10 Other income

Most MPs have other earned income in addition to their Parliamentary salaries. Where an MP has Sch. D, Case II income from writing on political matters, some of the expenditure on purely political research not allowed against the salary as an MP may, in suitable cases, be claimed against such income on normal Schedule D principles.

11.11 MPs' secretaries and research assistants

Pension schemes set up by Members of Parliament or the European Parliament for their secretaries and research assistants are dealt with by Public Sector Section. They are usually individual arrangements with a named MP as employer, but other types of scheme are possible. Advice should be sought on the impact (if any) of the provisions of FA 2004, which come into force from 6 April 2006.

11.12 Members of the European Parliament

11.12.1 Salaries

UK members of the European Parliament are entitled to a salary paid by HM Government which the Inland Revenue regard as taxable. Their tax affairs are dealt with by Public Department 1, Ty-Glas, Cardiff CF4 5XZ. This tax district has issued notes for guidance on the taxation of Euro MPs or MEPs.

11.12.2 Travel and subsistence allowances

The Inland Revenue now accept that the substantial expense allowances paid to MEPs are not subject to UK tax. The European Parliament pays flat-rate subsistence and travel allowances to MEPs to enable them to meet their expenses in travelling to the Parliament and its various agencies. The Inland Revenue originally argued that these allowances, being flat-rate round sums

Members of Parliament, Members of the Scottish Parliament etc.

rather than actual reimbursements, were emoluments taxable as employment income, subject to any ITEPA 2003, s. 336 claim.

The Special Commissioners referred a case on this point, *Lord Bruce of Donington v Aspden* [1981] STC 761 to the European Court of Justice. The Court ruled that Community Law prohibited the imposition of national taxes on these lump sums, unless the Inland Revenue could show that they were, in part, remuneration.

Following this ruling, the Inland Revenue no longer require MEPs to enter these allowances on their tax returns, unless they claim they were inadequate to meet the expenditure actually incurred on Parliamentary duties and that the balance was paid out of their Parliamentary salary. As ITEPA 2003, s. 336 is very restrictive, where a claim does arise, the inspector needs to examine the whole of the expenses incurred by the member under a particular heading. Tax relief is then given on the balance by which the allowable expenditure exceeds the expense allowances received or that could have been received from the European Parliament.

11.12.3 Deduction for expenses

The following principles are broadly followed by the Inland Revenue in determining whether an expense is allowable.

A deduction may be claimed by an MEP for travelling in the performance of official duties. This includes travelling within the constituency and from the constituency to the Parliament. When the MEP's home is outside the constituency, the cost of travelling between home and the constituency and between home and the Parliament is inadmissible in the same way as for members of the UK Parliament, and for home to work travel generally. If, however, an MEP travels between the Parliament and constituency via home, the cost of the direct journey between the constituency and the Parliament is admissible, provided that the journey via home is a continuous journey (ie as for Westminster MPs, that any break does not exceed one night during the week or two nights at the weekend).

MEPs can claim a deduction for other expenses incurred wholly, exclusively and necessarily in the performance of their duties. Examples of admissible expenses are:

- secretarial and clerical assistance in dealing with constituents' affairs;

- office accommodation (including the cost of a room at home set apart as an office);
- repairs to and renewals of office equipment (eg computers);
- telephone and telegram charges, stationery and postage if these are not provided free;
- hiring rooms to meet constituents (eg surgeries in the constituency), and
- payments to a local agent or party association in return for which an MEP receives help in carrying out Parliamentary work, eg clerical assistance and fixing interviews.

The following are examples of inadmissible expenses:

- literature issued for canvassing purposes;
- election expenses;
- newspapers, periodicals, books, news cutting services, etc;
- charitable subscriptions and donations;
- entertaining, including the cost of entertaining constituents;
- expenses incurred by MEPs' spouses (eg in deputising for or accompanying MEPs);
- payments to political organisations for political purposes, and
- generally, expenses which a MEP incurs not as a member of the European Parliament but as a member of a political party.

11.12.4 Terminal grants

ITEPA 2003, s. 291 applies the same treatment to such payments as that given for payments to MPs referred to in **11.9** above. They are thus only chargeable under ITEPA 2003, s. 401, subject to the £30,000 exemption in ITEPA 2003, s. 403.

11.13 Members of the House of Lords

Most members of the House of Lords receive no salary, only allowances which are not taxable. In addition, they can claim the cost of travel by public transport or car at the same mileage rate as MPs from their home to the Lords.

Members of Parliament, Members of the Scottish Parliament etc.

Ministers in the House of Lords and office holders who are members of that House receive termination payments on giving up office, subject to certain conditions. Such payments are treated in the same way as the terminal grants to MPs and MEPs (see **11.9** above).

Chapter 12 Merchant navy and aircrew personnel

12.1 General principles

The taxation of the income of aircrew and merchant navy personnel is determined by the specific provisions relating to the place of performance of their duties and their residence status (ITEPA 2003, s. 40). The position of seafarers is considered first and that of aircrew insofar as they differ from seafarers. The Inland Revenue have published notes on the tax position of seafarers together with a self assessment help sheet, IR205.

12.2 Non-resident seafarers

12.2.1 Not resident and not ordinarily resident

Seafarers may claim the above status in either of two ways.

1. If for a period which encompasses a complete income tax year they:

    (a) serve on ships with both open and close Crew Agreements (previously known as Ship's Articles) abroad and do not visit the UK at any time during the period of the Crew Agreement, thus performing all their duties outside the UK, and

    (b) do not visit the UK during the period of claim for more than an average of 90 days per annum or a total of 182 complete days in any one complete income tax year.

2. If they are employed wholly abroad, that is, do not enter British ports in the course of their engagement or engagements, for a continuous period exceeding three years (36 months) they are not resident and not ordinarily resident from the date of departure from the UK to their date of return, providing that their visits to the UK do not exceed 182 complete days in any income tax year or an average of 90 days per annum. Note that the maintenance of any place of abode in the UK is ignored in deciding a person's residence in these situations (ICTA 1988, s. 335(1)).

12.2.2 Not resident but ordinarily resident

This normally applies if seafarers are physically absent from the UK on voyages during the whole of an income tax year, but in the preceding and subsequent years visit the UK for periods which make the annual average over 90 days per annum. In a very old case, *Rogers v CIR* (1879) 1 TC 225, a Master Mariner who was absent from the UK for a complete fiscal year while his wife and family continued to live in the UK in the family house, was held to be ordinarily resident in the UK for that year.

If seafarers qualify as not resident, they are not liable to UK tax on their pay for the period of the successful claim as they are not liable under any provision of ITEPA 2003.

Any relief where a person is not resident is normally granted by repayment on a claim to The Marine Section, South Wales Area, Ty Glas Road, Llanishen, Cardiff CF14 5FP, tel: (08701) 555 445 (IR Marine Section), as the master of the vessel remains responsible for deduction of tax in accordance with the seaman's code.

12.3 Foreign seafarers

Where foreign seafarers have their home outside the UK, serve in the coasting trade or are in receipt of 'off Articles' pay (whether on ship or on shore in the UK), they are liable to tax on those earnings under ITEPA 2003. Foreign seafarers employed in the foreign-going trade as opposed to the coasting trade, who can satisfy the Inland Revenue that they normally live outside the UK and do not spend six months or more in the UK in any one year of assessment, or periods of three months per annum in any one period of four consecutive years, are not liable to UK income tax. They may claim repayment of tax deducted from their earnings in the foreign-going trade by completing Form R43(M), obtainable from any Mercantile Marine Office or the IR Marine Section.

12.4 UK residents: 100 per cent deduction

If seafarers are unable to qualify as being non resident in the UK, they may be eligible for a deduction of 100 per cent from their pay before liability to UK tax is calculated. The Finance Act 1977 provided that UK-resident seafarers and aircrew are eligible for deductions from their emoluments, despite the fact that the duties could be treated as otherwise performed in the UK under the specific legislation in ITEPA 2003, s. 25(1). Although the 100 per cent deduction has been abolished for other individuals, it is specifically continued for seafarers under ITEPA 2003, s. 378.

Deductions are available for duties treated as performed outside the UK:

- where the voyage begins or ends outside the UK (ITEPA 2003, s. 40(4)(a)), or

- where there is a part of a voyage which begins or ends outside the UK, although the whole voyage begins and ends in the UK (ITEPA 2003, s. 40(4)(b)).

Duties are treated as performed in the UK in respect of any part of the voyage which both begins and ends in the UK, or where the voyage extends outside the UK but there is no scheduled call at a foreign port (for instance a fishing boat going into the Norwegian sector of the North Sea on a voyage to and from a UK port). The UK side of the Continental Shelf is treated as part of the UK, so that voyages to North Sea installations in the UK sector do not qualify for any deduction (ITEPA 2003, s. 40(5)(c)).

For these purposes, the casting-off from a UK berth, allied to passage for the overseas port, are taken as the time of departure from the UK, and to count as a qualifying day the person must be absent from the UK at midnight. Duties performed on board ship before it actually casts off from a UK berth are not treated as performed outside the UK.

Again, a ship is regarded as arriving in the UK at the time of berthing, so that if the voyage is from a foreign port to a UK port, any duties carried out after berthing (for instance cleaning the ship) and before casting off, are not treated as performed outside the UK as at that time the vessel is not 'engaged on a voyage' beginning or ending outside the UK. However, if the voyage is from a foreign port back to the foreign port, then duties performed on the vessel whilst in the UK are treated as performed outside the UK in accordance with ICTA 1988, Sch. 12, para. 5. Seafarers must still be absent from the UK at midnight when reckoning qualifying days.

In *Clark v Perks and other appeals* [2001] BTC 336 it was held that a 'jack-up' drilling rig was a ship, so as to qualify a taxpayer for the foreign earnings deduction. So long as navigation was a significant part of the function of the structure in question, the mere fact that it was incidental to some more specialised function did not take it out of the definition of 'ship'. In the present cases it was clear as the commissioners had found that the rigs were capable of, and used for, navigation. The Court of Appeal decision (as against the High

Court decision) is consistent with the Special Commissioners' decision (in favour of the taxpayer) in Lavery v MacLeod [2001] STC (SCD) 118. In that case the decision was given in favour of the taxpayer on an *'eiusdem generis'* basis, in that the Revenue had accepted that a semi-submersible unit was a ship and it was difficult to distinguish between that and the jack-up unit. The 2001 Inland Revenue Helpsheet IR205 states:

'You can qualify for the Foreign Earnings Deduction as a seafarer if:

- you perform all your duties on a ship, or
- you perform most of your duties on a ship, and the other duties are incidental to the duties on the ship.

The word "ship" is not defined in tax law, but "offshore installations" used in the offshore oil and gas industry are specifically identified and are not regarded as "ships" for the purposes of the Foreign Earnings Deduction. The following list of "offshore installations" is given as a guide only:

- fixed production platforms
- floating production platforms
- floating storage units
- mobile offshore drilling units (both semi-submersibles and jack-ups)
- flotels.'

In *Tax Bulletin* Issue 57 (February 2002) the Inland Revenue published the following article.

'Litigation on the meaning of ship for FED purposes

On 27 July 2001, the Court of Appeal gave judgement in favour of the three taxpayers in the joined cases of Perks v Clark (HMIT), Perks v Macleod (HMIT) and Newrick & Granger v Guild (HMIT) – TL 3649. The point at issue was whether their earnings were "emoluments from employment as a seafarer" for the purpose of paragraph 3(2A) of Schedule 12 Income and Corporation Taxes Act (ICTA) 1988. If they were then they could take advantage of more generous FED provisions. "Employment as a seafarer" is defined as "employment consisting of the performance of duties on a ship (or of such duties and others incidental to them)".

During the relevant years, the taxpayers performed the duties of their employment on jack-up drilling rigs in the offshore oil and gas industry. A jack-up rig has a floating hull and retractable legs. For the purposes of drilling the legs are lowered so that the feet stand upon the seabed and the hull is jacked up so that it is clear of the water. The legs are then retracted upwards to enable the floating hull to be towed from place to place. Neither of the two rigs in these cases had a rudder or motive power. When under tow, the navigation of the rigs and their towing vessels was under the command of a towing master located on the rigs themselves and assisted by navigational equipment also located on the rigs. In addition, the rigs carried specialist equipment normally carried by ships and had to satisfy various statutory requirements commonly associated with ships.

The General Commissioners considered the line of authorities concerned with the definition of ship for the purposes of the Merchant Shipping Acts. They decided that these showed that it was sufficient for a vessel to be a ship if it was capable of and used in navigation. Both rigs were capable of and used in navigation and had sufficient of the characteristics associated with ships to be ships for the purposes of the definition in Schedule 12 ICTA 1988. Therefore, the taxpayers who worked on these vessels were entitled to FED as seafarers.

The Revenue's appeal to the High Court succeeded on the basis that the "real work" of these two jack-up rigs was to drill for oil whilst stationary with their legs resting on the seabed. Any navigation was incidental to their main purpose.

However, the Court of Appeal ruled that the judge in the High Court had not been entitled to interfere with the decisions of the Commissioners. The word "ship" was an ordinary English word and the meaning of an ordinary word in the English language was not a question of law. It was for the Commissioners to decide as a question of fact whether the statutory words applied to the facts that they had found. Their decisions were within the limits of reasonableness and the Commissioners had not misdirected themselves by considering authorities concerned with the definition of ship in the Merchant Shipping Acts.

The Court of Appeal also considered the merits of the Revenue's "real work" test. The Court found little support for the Revenue's position in the authorities. The common thread running through the cases dealing with the definition of ship in other contexts was the use of a vessel in navigation. Navigation connoted no more than ordered movement across the water. For a vessel to be used in navigation, it did not need to be self-propelled or to convey persons or cargo. Whether a vessel that was capable of navigation was a ship would depend on the extent to which it was used in navigation.

Application of the decision of the Court of Appeal – FED before 17 March 1998

The decision is now final and we have accepted that before 17 March 1998 jack-up rigs will be ships for the purposes of FED.

In the absence of a statutory definition of the word ship, our previous view was that for the purposes of FED a ship had to satisfy three conditions. These were that it had to be:

(a) capable of navigation;

(b) used in navigation; and

(c) navigation was more than incidental to its function.

It is clear from the judgement that the third of these tests is not a relevant consideration. The critical question is whether a structure is used in navigation. Provided navigation is a significant part of the function of the structure in question, the mere fact that it is incidental to some specialised function does not take it outside the definition of ship.

It is also clear that relative infrequency of navigation does not necessarily exclude a structure from the definition of ship. The Court agreed that in most cases, the categorisation of a structure should be governed by its design and capability rather than by its actual use at any time.

In addition to jack-up rigs, there may be other floating structures in the offshore oil and gas industry that are capable of satisfying the tests advocated by the Court of Appeal. We will consider such structures on the specific facts of each case. We will be revising our published guidance to reflect our changed view and in particular paragraph 33102 in the Inland Revenue's Schedule E manual.

Changes to FED effective from 17 March 1998

FED was withdrawn for all employees other than seafarers in March 1998. From 17 March 1998, s. 192A(3) ICTA 1988 excludes offshore installations within the meaning of the Mineral Workings (Offshore Installations) Act 1971 from the definition of ship for FED purposes. This means that employees who perform the duties of their employment on jack-up rigs or similar structures in the offshore oil and gas industry can no longer be regarded as seafarers and are therefore not entitled to FED.

FED claims from employees working on jack-up rigs before 17 March 1998

As we have decided to apply the Court of Appeal's decision more widely, employees who worked on jack-up rigs before March 1998 may be entitled to FED provided they satisfy all the other conditions for the deduction and are eligible to make a claim.

Open appeals against Schedule E assessments for 1995–96 or earlier or against Revenue amendments to SA returns for 1996–97 or 1997–98 can now be settled where the point at issue is whether a jack-up rig is a ship for the purposes of FED. Open SA enquiries dealing with the same point can also be settled.

A very few employees may still be in time to amend their SA returns for 1996–97 or 1997–98. However, we expect that most will be seeking to establish entitlement to FED and to obtain a repayment for closed years. FED is not claimed under Section 42 TMA or subject to the associated machinery in Schedule 1A TMA for dealing with claims outside of returns.

Those employees who have made a return and paid tax charged by an assessment (including a self-assessment) may be able to claim relief for an error or mistake in their return under Section 33 TMA. Claims for relief under Section 33 are subject to the proviso in Section 33 (2) (Section 33(2A) for 1996–97 and subsequent years) which restricts relief where the return was made in accordance with generally prevailing practice. Before 6 April 1995, we consider that there was a generally prevailing practice that jack-up rigs were not ships. Therefore, employees who did not include FED in returns made before that date are not in a position to claim relief by reason of an error or mistake in their returns.

Section 33 claims for 1996–97 and 1997–98 must be made by 31 January 2003 and 31 January 2004 respectively. The time limit for 1995–96 or earlier years is six years from the end of the year of assessment in which the assessment was made.

Employees who have not made a return for 1996–97 or 1997–98 must complete SA returns for those years. Where income has been taken into account for the purposes of PAYE, then Section 205 ICTA 1988 permits an employee to require an officer of the Board to give him a notice under Section 8 TMA 1970 to make a personal return. Section 205(4) sets out time limits so that for 1996–97 employees cannot require a Section 8 notice after 31 October 2002. The time limit for 1997–98 is 31 October 2003.

Employees without a return or assessment for 1995–96 or earlier and whose income was subjected to PAYE can no longer request a Schedule E assessment for those years. The version of Section 205 that was in force before 1996–97 gave the taxpayer five years from the end of the year of assessment to require the inspector to make a Schedule E assessment. Therefore, the time limit for 1995–96 expired on 5 April 2001.

In a number of cases, the issue of foreign earnings deduction for work carried out on jack-up rigs will have been openly addressed in the course of correspondence or discussions between the taxpayer and the Inland Revenue. If these exchanges resulted in the determination of appeals whether by the Commissioners or by agreement, then the position is final for that year and an error or mistake claim cannot be accepted so far as it relates to this issue.

More detailed guidance can be found in the Inland Revenue's Schedule E manual which lists paragraphs relevant to FED at SE33000. There is also a guidance note to assist individuals who believe that they were entitled to FED and who now wish to claim error or mistake relief. A copy of this can be obtained from your tax office.

National Insurance Contributions

We also accept that jack-up rigs will be ships for the purposes of Regulation 115 of the Social Security (Contributions) Regulations 2001. This sets out interpretation provisions in relation to "Mariners" who represent a special class of earners for the purposes of National Insurance Contributions.'

12.4.1 100 per cent deduction

Resident seafarers are entitled to relief at 100 per cent where they perform their duties of employment abroad in the course of a qualifying period which consists of at least 365 days. Time spent in the UK during this period will not debar the claim to 100 per cent relief provided that:

- it does not exceed 183 consecutive days, and
- the time spent in the UK does not exceed one-half of the period — such tests to be applied at the conclusion of each overseas visit by reference to a period stretching back to the last period of absence from the UK and any intervening visits to the UK which do not exceed the 183 consecutive days or one-half test.

12.5 Definitions

A qualifying day is defined as any day at the end of which the seafarer is outside the UK, ie at midnight (24.00 hours in the UK), whether:

- at a port outside the UK; or
- on any sea passage other than between two UK ports; or
- in connection with North Sea oil operations within the area designated under the Continental Shelf Act 1964, or
- travelling from or to the UK to join or having left a ship.

The sea passage *must* be one to or from a port outside the UK (or to or from an oil rig outside the designated area). A voyage from a port merely to carry out operations at sea which does not touch a foreign port, does not normally count.

However, voyages by tankers which end in a lightening operation are treated as voyages ending at a port. If the lightening operation takes place in UK territorial waters or within the area designated under the Continental Shelf Act 1964, the voyage is treated as if it had terminated in a UK port. If the lightening operation takes place outside these waters, the voyage is treated as if it were one to a port outside the UK.

The United Kingdom is defined for this purpose as Great Britain and Northern Ireland. Thus ports in the Republic of Ireland, Channel Islands and the Isle of Man are regarded as outside the UK. Moreover, a ship is deemed to have left the UK at the moment at which she leaves her berth or anchorage to proceed on her voyage. Equally, a seafarer travelling by air to join a ship abroad is deemed to have left the UK at the schedule time of the flight's departure. Arrival times are similarly defined.

Thus days of departure from the UK count as qualifying days, whilst days of arrival do not.

12.6 Administration

Special forms are available from Cardiff 1TSO, requesting details of on-crew agreements, names of ship and employer, and the dates of voyages and ports visited to determine the appropriate amount of the deductions.

12.7 Salvage awards

A salvage award is apportioned between the owners and the members of the crew of the salving ship on a basis which varies with the particular circumstances of each salvage. Salvage awards are fully taxable.

The award may be agreed on the salvor's behalf with the owners of the vessel, but increasingly seafarers negotiate their own settlements, sometimes through the courts.

Where an award is paid to the owners of the salving ship for distribution among the crew the owner should include each employee's share on the deductions working sheet and operate PAYE on it. Where an award is made by the courts it is usually paid over to the salvor's solicitors, and in such cases

PAYE is not operated, so an assessment under ITEPA 2003 has to be raised to collect the tax due from the individual to whom it is paid.

12.8 Uniform allowances

Allowances may be made to officers and certain ratings of the Mercantile Marine to cover the cost of upkeep of uniforms (whether or not the wearing of uniform is compulsory). The tables below show the maximum allowances agreed with representatives of the officers, etc concerned. These allowances are intended to cover all working gear and also the renewal of instruments, and are not chargeable to tax. Where only a proportion of the cost is borne by the officer, etc, the allowances paid should be restricted accordingly (Employment Income Manual EIM 70200).

1995–96 onwards.

Occupation	Passenger liners £	Cargo vessels, tankers and ferries £	Coasters (except ferries) £
Master	135	115	75
Chief Officer, Chief Engineer, Second Engineer	135	105	75
Other Officers (including Pursers and Chief Stewards*)	135	85	60

*Including Chief Purser, Chief Catering Officer and Chief Radio Officer.

12.9 Travelling and subsistence allowance

Guidelines have been agreed with the shipping industry on the taxation treatment of travelling and subsistence allowances payable to seagoing personnel of the Merchant Navy for journeys between homes and ports. Most taxpayers affected by these guidelines are dealt with by IR Marine Section.

12.9.1 Deduction for provision of own food

Seafarers engaged under an agreement which require them to 'find own food' are entitled to a food deduction of the full expense which they necessarily incur in connection with board, etc., whilst living away from home.

As circumstances vary from port to port it is not possible to agree a national flat-rate deduction but Districts may, in worthwhile cases, negotiate a local flat-rate deduction covering a particular group of employees. In negotiating such a deduction, pay regard to the average expenditure for each day of duty aboard, after taking account of leave absences, public holidays and periods when the vessel is in dry dock, etc.

No allowances are due to seafarers whose rates of pay are on a 'food found basis'.

12.9.2 Bedding and protective clothing provided for trawler crews

At a number of ports owners often supply trawler crews, other than mates and skippers, with bedding and/or protective clothing free of charge. In these cases the agreed flat-rate expenses deduction has to be restricted.

12.10 'Residence' of seafarers

The same legal principles apply in deciding the residence status of a seafarer as apply in the case of any other individual. At one time, seafarers absent on 'foreign-going service' were subject to considerations which were not necessarily applicable to persons employed abroad on land. But over the years the distinctions between seafarers and other individuals have been eroded. The rules followed in deciding the residence status of a seafarer in the main now follow the normal pattern.

12.11 Employment outside UK territorial waters

Where seafarers who are ordinarily resident in the UK leave the UK to take up employment on a ship, and their absence from the UK and their period of service includes a complete tax year, and their leave spent in the UK:

Merchant navy and aircrew personnel

- totals less than 183 days in any tax year, and
- averages less than 91 days for each tax year,

they are normally regarded as not resident and not ordinarily resident in the UK from the day following their departure to the day preceding their return.

12.12 Place of performance of duties

For various purposes, it is often necessary to know whether the duties of an employment are performed in or outside the UK. In certain circumstances duties have to be treated as performed in a particular place.

There are some special rules which apply only to seafarers, notably that duties performed on North Sea and other offshore gas and oil fields are treated as performed in the UK.

Under ITEPA 2003, s. 40(2) duties performed by any person on a vessel on a voyage not extending to a port outside the United Kingdom are to be treated as performed in the United Kingdom.

Duties which a person resident in the United Kingdom performs on a vessel or aircraft engaged on certain other voyages and flights are to be treated as performed in the United Kingdom. These voyages and flights are:

- those either beginning or ending in the United Kingdom, or
- any part of them which either begins or ends in the United Kingdom.

12.13 Flat-rate expenses deduction

A deduction is allowed for the sum, if any, fixed by the Treasury which, in their opinion, represents the average annual expenses incurred by employees in the repair and maintenance of work equipment (ITEPA 2003. s. 367). The amount of the deduction is reduced by an amount paid or reimbursed by the employer.

12.14 Seafarers' PAYE

The general PAYE regulations apply to seafarers. However, special arrangements known as the Marine Tax Deduction Scheme have been agreed between the Inland Revenue and the National Maritime Board. Their main features have been set out in the Guides issued by the Board of Inland Revenue (*Master's Guide to the Marine Tax Deduction Scheme (P7 (Master)* April 1977)).

Subject to certain exemptions for seafarers engaged in normal employment, the arrangements apply to all seafarers in the Merchant Navy. In particular the term 'Authorised Code' means any normal code given by the inspector or, if there was no such code, a code assigned to the seafarer by the Mercantile Marine Office Superintendent.

The arrangements also apply to seafarers engaged on a foreign ship who are resident in the UK. Pay includes leave pay, pay in lieu of leave, leave subsistence allowance, pay in respect of overtime, shipwreck, unemployment indemnity, and special payment while sick abroad (as defined by the National Maritime Board). Every employer paying wages to seafarers must deduct tax in accordance with the Seaman's Tables and the Seaman's Authorised Code. There are instructions for determining the code where no code notification has been received.

Normal PAYE regulations broadly apply and tax deducted from wages must be paid over not later than the 14th day of the month following the month in which the payment is made or, if the agreement with the crew terminates outside the UK, within such longer period as allowed by the Commissioners of Inland Revenue.

The administration of seafarers' tax is dealt with at The Marine Section, South Wales Area, Ty Glas Road, Llanishen, Cardiff, CF4 5FP (tel 08701 555 445).

12.15 Merchant Navy reservists

The Merchant Navy Reserve is a voluntary organisation. Reservists are paid a bounty each per year. Reservists are employees and the bounty is within the scope of employment income under ITEPA 2003.

The bounty is deemed to cover the cost of:

- one return journey a year from the reservist's home to the nominated reporting station for call-out exercise;
- one single journey to the nominated station when called out to serve (if at all), and

- any examinations, including medical examinations, required to become eligible to join the reserve.

No deduction under ITEPA 2003, s. 336 is made for the expenditure covered by the bounty since it is not expenditure incurred in the performance of the duties.

Failure to report for duty when leave of absence has not been granted is an offence punishable by a fine. These fines are not deductible for income tax purposes and the gross bounty remains chargeable.

12.16 Aircrew

Similar considerations and legislation apply to aircrew.

12.16.1 Residence position

The residence position of aircrew should be looked at in the light of the decision in *Robson v Dixon* (1972) 48 TC 527. This case concerned a British pilot employed by KLM, his base being Schiphol Airport, Amsterdam, who maintained a home in the UK from which he commuted to Amsterdam. None of the flights commenced in the UK and, of 811 take-offs and landings in the relevant year, only 38 were in the UK. He spent less than 60 days on average in the UK. He claimed to be non-resident in the UK and thus not liable to tax on his emoluments on the basis that the UK landings constituted duties incidental to the performance of the other duties outside the UK and that the employment thus was one carried on abroad, so that the maintenance of a house in the UK was irrelevant in determining his residence position (ICTA 1988, ss. 132(2) and 335(2)). The court decided that it was the nature of the duties, not the amount of time spent on them, which determined whether they were incidental, and in this case, the duties performed in the UK were the same as those performed elsewhere: therefore the pilot was held to be resident in the UK. The Inland Revenue would normally, however, disregard on *de minimis* grounds a single take-off and landing in the UK in a year, in considering whether any duties were performed in the UK by a pilot of British nationality, owning a house in the UK, who is otherwise resident abroad (*Hansard* Written Answer, 28 October 1975).

Foreign employees of foreign employers may possibly avoid being taxed under ITEPA 2003, s. 21 by claiming the protection of a double tax treaty. This may be possible even if, on the basis of *Robson v Dixon* (above), the duties were not incidental (unless the foreign employees became resident in the UK by virtue of having a place of abode here, or by virtue of the duration of their visits). Double tax treaties normally exempt foreign employees working for a foreign employer where they are not present in the UK for more than 183 days on their UK duties.

12.16.2 Expenses

The two principal items of expenditure allowable to pilots are travel expenses and uniform allowance.

Travel expenses

Following the case of *Nolder v Walters* (1930) 15 TC 380 (which concerned an airline employee who successfully claimed the extra cost of staying in hotels and incidental travelling abroad over and above the subsistence allowance he was given), any costs of staying overnight abroad not reimbursed are allowed. This is because the employment is a travelling one and therefore the duties commence at the start of the flight and do not finish until the return to the UK. Therefore, any such costs are incurred in the performance of the duties.

Uniform allowance

A deduction should be allowed for the cost of special clothing and uniforms insofar as incurred by the employee.

12.16.3 Free travel, etc

Note that perquisites such as free or reduced price travel for employees and their dependants were thought not to be taxable as they were not realisable in money or money's worth and, in the case of higher-paid employees, there was no identifiable cost to the employer which could be the measure of the benefit. The Inland Revenue have attempted to tax the value of such travel but later withdrew their proposals. Employees of airlines and their dependants are similarly specifically exempted when benefits legislation was extended to transport vouchers (ITEPA 2003, s. 86).

However, following the House of Lords' decision in *Pepper v Hart* (1993) 65 TC 421, it is clear that only the marginal cost, if any, of providing free or reduced price travel for employees or their families is strictly taxable. The Inland Revenue responded to the decision in *Pepper v Hart* by stating that the marginal cost of in-house benefits depends on each employer's particular

Merchant navy and aircrew personnel

circumstances. But, as a general guide, the Inland Revenue accept that rail or bus travel by employees on terms which do not displace fare-paying passengers involves no or negligible additional costs. Presumably the same principle applies to air and sea travel.

Chapter 13 Members of the UK armed forces

13.1 Place of performance of duties

The duties of the UK armed forces are deemed to be carried out in the UK wherever they are in fact performed (ITEPA 2003, s. 28). Thus, whether or not members of the armed forces are technically resident or ordinarily resident in the UK, their earned income, subject to certain exceptions, is fully liable to UK tax under ITEPA 2003, s. 15 or s. 25 (formerly Sch. E, Cases I or II). UK-resident status is however compensated for by the tax-free foreign service allowances that are received, and by the fact that, under international law and double taxation agreements, they are not subject to taxation in the country to which they are posted. For instance, those operating abroad under the provisions of the NATO status of forces agreement are exempt, under Art X of the agreement, from any local taxes resulting from residence or domicile in the receiving state, or on the salaries and emoluments paid to them in respect of their employment as members of the armed forces. Outside NATO, the Government always seeks to ensure that similar arrangements apply (*Hansard* Vol 135 Col 69, Written Answers, 14 June 1988).

13.2 Residence position

The residence and ordinary residence position of a member of the armed forces is determined on normal principles. However, as explained in **13.1** this is of relevance only to the tax treatment of income other than income from employment, such as investment income or income from property.

13.3 Extra cost of living abroad

If a sum is paid to Crown servants, including service personnel, as compensation for the extra cost of living abroad, and is so certified by the Treasury, the sum is exempt from UK tax under ITEPA 2003, s. 299. This is known as the foreign service allowance. This exemption covers sums paid to assist with a child's education.

13.4 Travel facilities

No charge to tax arises in respect of travel facilities provided for members of the armed forces going on or returning from leave. This covers journeys within and outside the UK (ITEPA 2003, s. 296) and extends not only to travel vouchers and warrants for particular journeys, but also to cash allowances and other payments in respect of leave travel, whether or not a warrant is available and irrespective of whether the member of the armed forces is higher-paid or not.

13.5 Entertaining expenses

Under ITEPA 2003, s. 336 the entertaining expenses incurred 'wholly, exclusively and necessarily in the performance of' their work by employees of non-trading organisations such as the civil service, the armed forces, non-trading activities of local authorities and trade unions are allowed for tax purposes.

13.6 Exemptions in respect of allowances

There are various exemptions from tax applicable to members of the armed forces in respect of allowances paid to them. These exemptions are made known to service personnel by the appropriate service pay authorities acting on Ministry of Defence regulations. Thus, for example, in common with other employments, extra subsistence allowances paid to personnel whilst temporarily posted away from base are not taxable. Note that service personnel are no different from any other taxpayers in respect of any allowances, unless they have a specific exemption from tax, as shown by a case concerning a claim that lodging allowances paid by service personnel should be free of tax (*Evans v Richardson* (1957) 37 TC 178). The allowances were held to be taxable or not under normal principles.

Thus boarding school or day school allowances paid to RAF personnel are taxable pay, but the RAF pay the tax by grossing up the allowance to cover the tax liability at the basic rate. If the grossed-up figure does not cover the tax liability, extra compensation is due to the service personnel to cover the actual tax liability, for instance where they are liable at the higher rate of tax. In that situation, however, this extra compensation is not in practice itself taxable.

13.7 Hotel expenses

In the case of *Griffiths v Mockler* (1953) 35 TC 135 a Royal Army Pay Corps officer lost a claim under what is now ITEPA 2003, s. 336 for a deduction in respect of his annual mess subscription. Similarly, in *Lomax v Newton* (1953) 34 TC 289, a Territorial Army officer failed in his claim for a deduction in respect of a share of battalion mess guests' expenditure, payments to batmen at weekend and holiday camps, the hire of camp furniture and the cost of tickets at sergeants' and other ranks' dances. The Commissioners did not accept claims in respect of mess dinners and dances. Mr Justice Vaisey disallowed all of the above items on the basis that they were expenses incurred from tradition and custom, accepted voluntarily by the officers of the unit, and containing elements of personal choice and benefit. However, the Commissioners accepted a claim for a deduction in respect of amounts paid for hotel accommodation at conferences and exercises in excess of official allowances. This decision was upheld in the High Court.

13.8 Annual subscriptions to a headquarters mess central fund

If an officer is obliged to incur such subscriptions under Queen's Regulations, they should be allowable (unlike ordinary mess subscriptions, which are not wholly incurred in the performance of military duties — see **13.7** above). However, any sums paid that the Treasury certifies to be paid in lieu of food or drink normally supplied in kind to members of the armed forces (for instance, in place of the Navy's rum allowance that was abolished in 1970) or to be payable as a contribution to the expenses of a mess, are not taxable (see ITEPA 2003, s. 297).

13.9 Uniform allowances

Officers in the armed forces may claim a deduction for expenses on uniforms, and minimum amounts are fixed in accordance with ITEPA 2003, s. 368 as being, in the opinion of the Treasury, fair equivalents of the average annual amounts which full-time serving officers are obliged to expend wholly, exclusively and necessarily in the performance of their duties. In practice, such allowances are usually obtained under a 'net pay' agreement with the Inland Revenue. Details of the allowances currently available may be obtained from the Ministry of Defence, which publishes a guide to the allowances entitled *Regulations for Army Allowances and Charges*.

Officers may claim further tax relief if a larger amount than the appropriate annual allowance is expended. However, they are required by the inspector to prove the necessity for such expenditure and to give details supported by receipted bills.

13.10 PAYE and the armed forces

There are special provisions within the PAYE regulations applicable to the armed forces. The paying unit identifies what are tax-free allowances and what is taxable pay. These provisions also provide in particular for a special Form P45 to be issued by the Ministry of Defence when a member of the armed forces leaves and enters other employment (SI 2003 No. 2682, reg. 122 to 133).

13.11 Reserve and auxiliary forces

The reserve and auxiliary forces of the Crown normally receive three different types of emolument.

1. They are paid a training and travelling allowance for attendance at evening drill and training sessions. This is intended as a reimbursement of out-of-pocket expenses and is exempt from tax (see ITEPA 2003, s. 298).

2. In consideration of their undertaking the prescribed training and attaining the required standard of efficiency, such forces are entitled, subject to the approval of the commanding officer, to an annual bounty which is also tax free (see ITEPA 2003, s. 298). Note that a bounty is exempt only if paid out of the public revenue and not by a local authority, as shown in the case of *Lush v Coles* (1967) 44 TC 169.

3. Such forces receive daily pay for all training in excess of eight hours' duration. This pay is subject to tax and also to the payment of National Insurance Contributions (NICs), if appropriate. Normally, basic rate income tax is deducted at source and a detailed pay statement is provided by the reservist's unit under special regulations for reserve and auxiliary forces (see Income Tax Reserve and Auxiliary Forces Regulations 1975 (SI 1975 No. 91)).

The only expenses which are likely to cause difficulty are those relating to uniforms and mess subscriptions. Officers normally receive a cash grant on initial commissioning, and an annual allowance for the upkeep of their kit, but if individual officers spend more on the purchase of essential items (as laid down in the scale of kit prescribed for their rank and duties), then they may properly claim relief under ITEPA 2003, s. 336. The position with other ranks differs between the various reserves but, in general, reservists should not have to purchase their own kit out of their own money and, if they do, they can claim under s. 336. Mess subscriptions are not allowable, as mentioned in **13.8** above.

Tax-free allowances are available for the upkeep of uniform items purchased from outfit allowances for Territorial Army, ACF, Combined Cadet Force (Army and Basic Sections) and Ulster Defence Regiment officers. Details may be obtained from the Ministry of Defence's publication, *Regulations for Army Allowances and Charges*.

13.11.1 Employee share schemes and called-up reservists

In July 2003 the Inland Revenue issued Extra Statutory Concession (ESC)A103 *Armed Forces Reservists: Revenue Approved Share Schemes and Enterprise Management Incentives (EMI)*.

Where a reservist is called up for service under the Reserve Forces Act 1996, the Inland Revenue by concession will treat the employment with the Ministry of Defence (MOD) as fulfilling the employment conditions for Inland Revenue approved employee share schemes. (For the purposes of this ESC, Inland Revenue approved employee share schemes include: Company Share Option Plans, Share Incentive Plans, Save as you Earn Schemes and Enterprise Management Incentives.)

By concession, employers and scheme providers will also be allowed to take such action as is necessary to maintain a reservist's participation in an approved employee share scheme, for the period they are away serving with the MOD, and this action will not compromise the approval of the scheme.

The concession applies from 7 January 2003.

13.12 Pensions

Forces pensions are paid following the conclusion of 22 years' service for 'other ranks' and 15 years' service for commissioned officers — when their pension should strictly be referred to as 'retired pay'. As a consequence many ex-service personnel receive pensions at a much earlier age than many other categories of employees.

All wounds and disability pensions are exempt from tax. In the case of a disability pension, the medical unfitness giving rise to the payment has to be directly attributable to military service or aggravated by it. The Government has published a list of taxable and non-taxable armed forces pensions. The following pensions paid to former members of the armed forces in respect of disability are exempt (ITEPA 2003, s. 641):

- wounds pensions granted to members of the armed forces;
- officer's disability retired pay attributable to conditions of service;
- pensions in respect of disablement or disability attributable to conditions of service granted to members of the forces other than commissioned officers;
- disablement pensions attributable to conditions of service granted to persons employed in the nursing services of the forces;
- war disability pensions administered by the Department of Work and Pensions, and
- war pensioners' mobility supplement, which introduced more flexible provisions for war pensioners with mobility needs by introducing a cash mobility supplement in place of the previous vehicle scheme (ICTA 1988, s. 617).

The Ministry of Defence confirmed in January 2002 that, due to an administrative error, a number of Armed Forces pensioners in receipt of an attributable Service Invaliding Pension (paid under the Armed Forces Pension Scheme — AFPS) had been mistakenly taxed. The Minister for Veterans' Affairs made the following statement:

> 'The Royal British Legion publicised the error to their 600,000 members in their magazine, *Legion*, in January 1999. The War Widows Association circulated their 55,000 members at around the same time. Importantly, we do believe we have identified the majority of those affected. But I have to say we are keen to find any we might have missed. These people have paid tax when there was no need. That is wrong. And we have a duty to rectify and recompense. It is not possible to give a precise estimate of the final cost of refunds until all claimants have been identified and paid. Our current assessment is that the total cost may be in the order of £30M.
>
> It is important to note that this mistake did not apply to the same category of pensioners from the Royal Navy or Royal Air Force. But in the past the administration of the different service pensions was entirely independent. There was a lack of co-ordination in addressing such matters. Policy functions are now centralised and I believe an error of this sort is significantly less likely.

The Ministry of Defence intends further publicity to ensure that those affected have the opportunity to recover the tax they have incorrectly paid. We have so far identified 1003 affected cases. Of these, refunds have been made in all but 26 cases and in these 26 cases the details are still being clarified. Any pensioner in receipt of an invalidating pension between 1952 and now who believes they may have been affected by this error, or their surviving relatives should write to the Army Pensions Office in Glasgow.

This error is deeply regretted and I look forward to informing the House when all cases have been satisfactorily settled.'

The following pensions paid to former members of the armed forces in respect of long service are taxable:

- service career pensions, and
- illness or disability pensions, other than those attributable to conditions of service.

Where members of the armed forces are invalided out of the forces on account of a disability attributable to their service, and are awarded a combined long-service and disability pension, the whole of that pension is exempt from tax because it is not possible to distinguish between the parts of the pension attributable to disability and to long service (*Hansard* Cols 654/5, 29 June 1978).

13.13 War widows' pensions

Any pension or allowance paid by the Department of Social Security which relates to death due to service in the armed forces, to wartime service in the Merchant Navy, or to war injuries, is completely exempt from tax (ITEPA 2003, s. 639). This covers war widows' pensions as well as payments for children of such widows. Similarly, any pension or allowance in respect of death due to peacetime service in the armed forces before 3 September 1939, payable by the Ministry of Defence, is exempt from tax, along with similar pensions and allowances payable by foreign governments.

Where such war widows' pensions are reduced because of the receipt of another pension, the other pension is exempt up to the extent of the reduction (ITEPA 2003, s. 640).

13.14 Employment after leaving services

In connection with retirement, bear in mind that many service personnel retire from the forces in their fifties and seek employment elsewhere, as an alternative to relying solely on their pensions. The normal Inland Revenue practice has been to aggregate benefits from the current employer's scheme with any pension already being received, and to restrict the total pension entitlement to two-thirds of the final remuneration from the employment held at the date of retirement. With an inflation-proof service pension, this could result in severe restrictions on the amount of pension that could be paid by the new employer. However, there is a concessionary practice by the Inland Revenue, under which former service personnel could receive a pension from their new employer, not exceeding one-sixtieth of final pay for each year of service in the particular employment, even though the resulting total pension, including the service pension, may exceed two-thirds of final salary. In other words, there are the alternative limits of two-thirds of final salary or, if more beneficial, the service pension plus one-sixtieth of final pay for each year of service in the new employment.

Advice should be sought on the impact (if any) of FA 2004, which comes into force from 6 April 2006.

13.15 Capital gains tax and residences

The position on residences in relation to capital gains tax exemption and relief for interest paid, is the same as for diplomats (see **8.7** above), except that job-related accommodation means, for service personnel, accommodation provided by the Ministry of Defence.

13.16 Holders of the Victoria Cross, etc.

Annuities and additional pensions paid to holders of the Victoria Cross, the George Cross, the Albert Medal and Edward Medal, are also exempt from tax. The exemption was extended from 6 April 1980 to pension additions paid with the awards to holders of the Military Cross, the Distinguished Flying Cross, the Distinguished Conduct Medal, the Conspicuous Gallantry Medal, the Distinguished Service Medal, the Military Medal and the Distinguished Flying Medal, and to pension additions paid to holders of the George Cross (ITEPA 2003, s. 638).

13.17 Death on active service

No inheritance tax is payable on the death of an individual from a wound or accident while on active service, or from a disease contracted or aggravated in the past by such a wound or accident (IHTA 1984, s. 154). By concession, the exemption also applies to the estates of members of the Police Service of Northern Ireland (formerly the Royal Ulster Constabulary) who die from injuries caused in Northern Ireland by terrorist activity.

13.18 Exemption from IHT on death: *ex gratia* payments to Britons held prisoner by the Japanese

Under ESC F20 the £10,000 *ex gratia* payments made to surviving members (or surviving spouses) of British groups held prisoner by the Japanese during the Second World War will be free from IHT on death. The payments are made to the surviving spouse where the individual concerned was not alive at 7 November 2000.

More important for many taxpayers will be the principle that the payment is to be left out of account when calculating entitlement to Income Support, Jobseeker's Allowance, Council Tax Benefit and Housing Benefit. The Social Security Amendment (Capital Disregards) Regulations 2001 (SI 2001 No. 22) provide that, in calculating entitlement to any of these benefits, a person who has received such an *ex gratia* payment can leave out of account £10,000 of any savings or capital.

A further important point is that there will be no attempt to trace the payment: therefore, even if the claimant has spent the money itself, there can still be a deduction of £10,000 from other free capital or savings when calculating entitlement to the four specified benefits. The point will also apply where the *ex gratia* payment was received by the spouse or domestic partner of the benefit claimant (because means tested benefits depend on calculation of household resources). Note, however, that if the POW was survived on 7 November 2000 not by a spouse but by a domestic partner, the *ex gratia* payment will not be made.

Chapter 14 Publicans holding tied houses, hoteliers and guest-house proprietors

14.1 Publicans: basis of assessment

Licensed victuallers who hold tied houses are assessed to tax as self-employed persons under Sch. D, Case I. They are treated as carrying on a trade at the public house of which they are the tenants.

A tenancy granted to a husband or wife, but not to both jointly, may not be effective for taxation purposes. If the wife carries on a separate business relating to the selling of the food, she can take advantage of independent taxation of husband and wife. A value added tax tribunal has also accepted that a licensee's wife's catering sales are a separate business from that carried on by the licensee (*Clark*, LON/82/338, February 1983 (1370)). This may be helpful in keeping the licensee's sales below the VAT registration limit. Customs & Excise may challenge the view that the catering is a separate business, using its powers under the Value Added Tax Act 1994 (VATA 1994), Sch. 1, para. 2. However, it is not clear whether para. 2 applies in such a case.

The effect of the trade being identified with the particular public house in question is that, if the tenant leaves the public house and takes over a new tenancy (even within the same brewery) the cessation provisions apply for income tax purposes and a new trade is treated as set up at the new public house. This treatment can also be helpful for loss relief — for example, in ICTA 1988, s. 381(1) (opening year losses) 'first carried on' refers to the specific business carried on by the trader and not to the generic category of trade. So if a publican who ran a pub in Leeds for many years sells it and buys another in York, although in the everyday sense he remains a publican throughout, the York pub is not the same trade as the Leeds pub and relief may be claimed under ICTA 1988, s. 381.

14.2 Exclusivity agreements

The Inland Revenue published the following paragraphs as Revenue Interpretation 52 in August 1993.

'The question often arises whether a lump sum payment received under an exclusivity agreement is of capital or revenue character and, if revenue, when it should be recognised as income for tax purposes.

Exclusivity agreements are a common feature of trading arrangements in various trades. They often arise, for example, between petrol suppliers and garages or between breweries and publicans. Under these agreements the trader is tied for a number of years to one supplier of goods or services and in return receives a lump sum payment. Frequently such a sum is potentially repayable but the agreement provides for the periodic waiver of the liability to repay a proportion of the sum provided the terms of the exclusivity contract are adhered to. If the agreement runs its full course, none of the lump sum will be repayable.

[The Revenue's] view is that such an 'abatable loan' should be treated in the same way as a grant, its capital or revenue nature being determined by the purpose, in the mind of the payer, for which the trader received that sum. This requires consideration of not only the particular agreement in question but also the correspondence and discussions which supplemented the terms of the agreement.

If the supplier designates the payment for a specific capital purpose, and there is evidence that the recipient has expended it in the manner specified, then it can be accepted as a capital receipt. However, if the recipient is effectively at liberty to spend the money as he or she thinks fit, the receipt is to be regarded as an undifferentiated payment and therefore a taxable revenue receipt. For tax purposes, the reduction in each accounting period of the amount that is repayable should be recognised as a trade receipt of that period. This is consistent with normal accountancy practice.'

14.3 Termination payments

Certain breweries have a policy to stop using tenants and instead to appoint managers to run their public houses. The tenancies in question usually have incorporated rights to no more than very small amounts of compensation on termination. As an inducement to leave, and in recognition of the size of the business built up, the brewery usually makes substantial *ex gratia* payments. There is now an established scale of compensation payable to tenants, agreed by the Brewers' Society (the brewers' trade body), which is based on length of service as a tenant and the rateable value of the public house.

In the case of *Murray v Goodhews* (1977) 52 TC 86, payments were made by Watneys to the tenant of a number of public houses in these circumstances. It was held that the payments were not liable to tax as income, as they were not in return for any services rendered, or by virtue of any right of compensation, but were entirely voluntary and unsolicited and in recognition of a long association between the tenant and Watneys. In that case, there was no negotiation on the amount between the parties, the amount of the payment had no connection with the profits of the public houses concerned, and was not linked to any future trading relationship between the parties. The payments therefore fell within the type of payment made in the case of *Simpson v John Reynolds & Co (Insurances) Ltd* (1975) 49 TC 693, and were exempt from income tax.

The question of whether the above payments were liable to capital gains tax was not at issue. However, they are unlikely to be regarded as liable, since they cannot be said to derive from an asset.

Similarly, it was held in *Davis v Powell* (1976) 51 TC 492 and *Drummond v Austin Brown* (1984) 58 TC 67, that payments of statutory compensation to tenants by landlords were not liable to capital gains tax, as the payments did not derive from the leases in question. The entitlement to the compensation was a statutory right.

The Inland Revenue agreed with tenants of Watneys that they would not pursue claims to capital gains tax on the special payments, except insofar as they represented extra sums for surrendering the tenancy early (in the same way as premiums to induce agricultural tenants to surrender their tenancies are liable to capital gains tax to the extent that they exceed statutory compensation).

In the Watneys case, the brewery specified a basic sum which was to be supplemented by 40 per cent if the tenant gave up his tenancy before 1 March 1974, and 20 per cent if before 1 October 1975.

It is not known whether similar agreements were reached with the tenants of other brewers over the years, but the tenant could always claim complete exemption from income tax and capital gains tax on such payments.

14.4 Expenses

If the licensee, etc. lives on the premises, much expenditure, the primary purpose of which is for the trade but which incidentally confers a personal benefit, is allowable for Sch. D, Case I purposes, on the basis of the decision in *Bentleys, Stokes and Lowless v Beeson* (1952) 33 TC 491. For instance, expenditure on newspapers available for customers qualifies under this heading.

The proportion of any rent, council tax, etc. disallowed, as relating to the private proportion of a public house, is also usually very small. Where the trade of the hotel or public house is carried on through the medium of a company, there is a potential charge on the annual value of the private part of the accommodation provided by the company, which in most cases is unlikely to have cost more than £75,000. Employees without a material interest in the company can claim they are representative occupiers, but directors with a material interest cannot claim such exemption. Similarly, in the case of the costs of heating, lighting, cleaning, repairs and furniture for the private part, these give rise to a benefit for all higher-paid employees and directors, subject to a possible restriction for representative occupiers.

An adjustment to the computations may be required in respect of meals consumed by the publican and his or her spouse. The decision in *Sharkey v Wernher* (1955) 36 TC 275, under which stock taken for own consumption is credited at market value, is not applicable in the case of eating establishments, on the basis that meals are not trading stock. However, in the case of an unincorporated business, the cost of meals falls to be disallowed because it is 'a cost of maintenance of the parties, their families or establishments' (ICTA 1988, s. 74(b)). In the case of a company, the cost should be allowed and, similarly, the benefit to the director is the cost of the meals to the company. It is also understood that, whilst cash gratuities received by licensees are taxable, free drinks bought for them by customers, even though they are in the nature of gratuities, are accepted as not ordinarily taxable, as they are not normally convertible into cash.

In the case of ordinary employees, if they are lower-paid there is no assessable benefit on free meals and, in the case of others, it is possible to use the exemption in ITEPA 2003, s. 317 for meals consumed in a canteen (see ITEPA 2003 s. 317(4), which gives this exemption where part of the restaurant or dining room is designated as being for the use of staff only).

The provision of a late night taxi home for bar and waiting staff is now common: note that ITEPA 2003, s. 248 exempts journeys made after 9pm on an irregular basis from treatment as a benefit in kind.

The general prohibition of any deduction for entertaining expenses in ICTA 1988, s. 577 is overruled for persons such as publicans and hoteliers by ICTA 1988, s. 577(10), which states that:

> 'Nothing in [s. 577] shall be taken as precluding the deduction of expenses incurred in, or any claim for capital allowances in respect of the use of an asset for, the provision of any person of anything which it is his trade to provide,

and which is provided by him in the ordinary course of that trade for payment or, with the object of advertising to the public generally, gratuitously.'

It is presumably for this reason that entertaining airline representatives and tour operators is not normally treated as disallowable, but allowed as advertising.

14.5 Hotels: own consumption adjustments

Local tax offices often propose standard adjustments to the trading profits of hotel and guest-house proprietors, and to the emoluments of managers of hotels, etc, to take account of the proprietor's private accommodation and food consumption. These adjustments are usually revised annually in accordance with increases in the retail price index. The amounts of such adjustments vary widely between districts.

Such proposals are intended to provide a convenient basis of adjustment in the majority of cases. They do not prejudice a taxpayer's statutory rights, nor do they preclude the Inland Revenue from investigating the facts where they consider that the standard figures are materially inadequate. Each case should be considered on its individual circumstances and these models should not be viewed as accepted Inland Revenue practice.

In the case of an employee, including a member of the family who is earning at the rate of less than £8,500 per annum, care should be taken to avoid the value of free board and lodging being taxed. Where a reduction is made from gross salary for board and accommodation, the Inland Revenue usually contend that the full gross amount is assessable as employment income, on the authority of *Cordy v Gordon* (1925) 9 TC 304.

14.6 Hotels: date on which trading commences

A hotel is usually regarded as starting to trade when bookings are first sought. However, it has been accepted that a hotel commences to trade when the proprietor undertakes staff training. In either event, expenses incurred within seven years of commencing to trade which, if they had been incurred after trading commenced would have been allowable, are admissible as deductions under ICTA 1988, s. 401.

14.7 Capital expenditure

Where a hotel changes hands, the allocation of a significant part of the sale proceeds to fixtures and fittings taken over from the vendors now has a twofold benefit. From the vendor's point of view, it takes a large part of the value of the property out of capital gains tax, bearing in mind the chattels exemption of £6,000 per individual item or set of items. From the purchaser's point of view, capital allowances claims are maximised in the early years of the business.

Tenants, publicans or hoteliers spend a good deal on utensils, such as glasses and crockery for use in the trade, which is allowable as a Schedule D, Case I deduction. Where capital expenditure is incurred by tenants on plant and machinery, they can claim allowances on it. If it is movable plant (for instance a television set, or tables and chairs), such allowances can be claimed in the normal way. It is possible to categorise some of the expenditure as on short-life assets which need not be pooled and on which a balancing allowance can be claimed when they are scrapped. If it consists of fixtures and fittings which become, on installation, part of the building, a claim can still be made, following an alteration in the law after the decision in *Stokes v Costain Property Investments Ltd* (1984) 57 TC 688.

Under CAA 2001, ss. 176–204, lessees who have incurred the expenditure can claim capital allowances on it, although it has become a landlord's fixture. Similarly, incoming lessees paying for such fixtures can claim capital allowances on their expenditure, with consequent balancing adjustments on the outgoing tenants. In either case, the lessor and the lessee must make a joint election to this effect. The lessor can also take over the benefit of allowances on the termination of a lease without payment by an incoming lessee.

These provisions are extremely useful for tenants of public houses. If there are loans from the brewery to carry out such improvements or for other purposes, interest on the loans ranks as a deduction against profits as an ordinary business expense, in the case of a sole trader, or as a charge on income, in the case of a company.

14.8 Plant and machinery

The Inland Revenue's view on what constitutes 'plant and machinery' on the installation of main services in new inns and hotels, was set out in a letter to the CCAB (August 1977):

'... expenditure on the provision of main services to buildings such as electrical wiring, cold water piping and gas piping is regarded as part of the cost of the building, and therefore as not qualifying for capital allowances. We do, however, regard as eligible for capital allowances expenditure on apparatus to provide electric light or power, hot water, central heating, ventilation or air-conditioning, and expenditure on alarm and sprinkler systems. Relief is also given on the cost of all hot water pipes, and on the cost of baths, wash basins, etc. although the *St John's School* case [*St John's School v Ward* (1974) 49 TC 524] suggests that the Courts might regard such expenditure as part of the cost of the building. We do not, however, propose any change of practice in this respect. Finally, to complete the picture, and since you mentioned modernisation, 1 should say that expenditure on alterations to existing buildings which is incidental to the installation of plant or machinery qualifies for relief under a separate provision (CAA 1968, s. 45) [now CAA 2001, s. 25].'

The case of *CIR v Scottish & Newcastle Breweries Ltd* (1982) 55 TC 252 broadened the scope of what can be claimed as plant and machinery in a public house or hotel. In that case it was decided that, in various hotels and restaurants owned by the taxpayer, all additions to the walls and ceilings with a certain theme (such as murals and stags' heads) qualified as plant, on the basis that they performed a function of providing the right 'atmosphere' to promote the taxpayer's trade, and were not just a passive part of the setting. However, the two decisions in favour of the Inland Revenue concerning restaurant fittings in *Wimpy International Ltd v Warland* [1988] STC 149 and *Associated Restaurants Ltd v Warland* [1989] STC 273 appear to have restricted the scope of what may be claimed as plant where an item is part of the decor of the restaurant. Specialist lighting and display objects used for this purpose should still qualify, provided that they are not clearly part of the premises. The Inland Revenue also allow expenditure on jacuzzis, squash court wall finishings and flooring, and lifts — but not lift shafts. Also, following *Cooke v Beach Station Caravans Ltd* (1974) 49 TC 514, the entire cost of excavating, concreting and lining a swimming pool with the surrounding terracing and fencing is treated as plant.

It may be of benefit to elect for short-life asset treatment for certain large items of equipment, where a limited life span is expected (CAA 2001, ss. 83–89 and Inland Revenue Statement of Practice 1/86 which covers certain practical aspects where there are large numbers of such items).

Expenditure on fire safety equipment and precautions such as fire doors and escapes is compulsory for hotels and boarding houses under SI 1972 No. 238. Such expenditure normally qualifies for capital allowances, provided that it was specified in a notice issued under the Fire Precautions Act 1971, s. 5(4) or was to avoid restrictions on the use of the premises by an order under s. 10 of that Act (CAA 2001, s. 27).

In summary, the expenditure qualifying as plant usually covers the following items:

- furniture, curtains, carpets and blinds;
- linen chutes;
- squash court wall coverings and floorings;
- jacuzzis;
- swimming pools (but not the building housing them);
- kitchen and laundry equipment;
- refuse compacters and waste disposal equipment;
- fire alarms and clocks;
- bathroom fittings;
- door locks and hinges;
- heating, ventilation and air conditioning equipment;
- public address systems;
- telephone equipment, and
- lifts (but not lift shafts).

Sometimes it is necessary to carry out extensive repairs on acquisition of a hotel. The inspector will often quote *Law Shipping Co Ltd v CIR* (1924) 12 TC 621 to disallow the repairs. However, it may be possible to argue that, as the property is very old (as many hotels are), the nature of the work done was predetermined and unavoidable by the age and type of construction of the building concerned. It should, therefore, be allowable in full as it was in the cases of *Conn v Robins Bros Ltd* (1966) 43 TC 266 and *Odeon Associated Theatres Ltd v Jones* (1973) 48 TC 257.

14.9 Furnished lettings: allowances for wear and tear

In the case of lettings which constitute furnished holiday lettings (see **14.14** below), the normal capital allowances rules apply, as the lettings constitute a trade for that and various other purposes. In the case of other furnished lettings, which do not amount to a trade and are assessable under Schedule A, inspectors are instructed to apply a uniform basis of treatment for wear and tear of furniture and fittings. Sections 15(3) and 35(1) and (2) of CAA 2001 specifically exclude a claim for capital allowances on plant or machinery let for use in a dwelling-house. Accordingly, capital allowances are not due on furniture and furnishings where the income from letting of furnished houses is assessable under Schedule A and is outside the scope of ICTA 1988, s. 503 (furnished holiday lettings).

Extra-statutory Concession B47 allows that in practice, an allowance for wear and tear may be made, where capital allowances are not due, by deducting ten per cent of the net rent received. For this purpose the rent is reduced by any part of the occupier's council tax and water rates which the landlord pays. If the rental includes payments for services which would normally be borne by a tenant and the amounts involved are material, these too should be subtracted before calculating the ten per cent deduction.

Where the ten per cent deduction is allowed, no further deduction is given for the cost of renewing furniture or furnishings, including suites, beds, carpets, curtains, linen, crockery or cutlery. Nor is a further deduction allowed for fixtures of a type which, in unfurnished accommodation, tenants would normally provide for themselves (for example, cookers, washing machines, dishwashers).

However, in addition to the ten per cent allowance, the landlord can also claim the cost of renewing fixtures which are an integral part of the buildings, and which are revenue repairs to the fabric. These are fixtures which would not normally be removed by either tenant or owner if the property were vacated or sold (for example, baths, washbasins, toilets). Expenditure on renewing such items may be treated as expenditure on repairs even though the ten per cent allowance has been claimed.

As an alternative to the ten per cent allowance, the actual cost of renewing furniture, furnishings and fixtures may be claimed as a deduction. The amount allowed is the actual cost of the replacements excluding any additions or improvements, and after deducting the scrap value or sale price of the items replaced. The cost of the original items is not expenditure on renewals and is not allowable.

Whichever basis a taxpayer chooses to adopt should be consistently applied to all furnished properties rented out.

14.10 Hotel building allowances

In the case of new hotels or additions to existing hotels a four per cent writing down allowance along the lines of industrial buildings allowances is available (CAA 2001, ss. 271 and 279). The hotel has to be open for at least four months in the season to qualify (in practice, 120 days is regarded as equivalent to four months). Hostels for workers qualify for the allowance, but not separate flats and houses provided for workers. Where the proprietor's own accommodation does not exceed 25 per cent of the total cost, no restriction is imposed on costs attributable to that part. In common with industrial buildings, the hotel receives no initial allowance.

Services provided for guests must normally include the provision of breakfast and of an evening meal if the allowances are to be given. The Inland Revenue's Statement of Practice 9/87 states that they regard this condition as satisfied where the offering of breakfast and dinner is a normal event in the hotel's conduct of its business, but not where the provision of such meals is exceptional (for example, where it is available only on request).

14.11 Dilapidations

Tenants may be required to make good any dilapidations at the end of their tenancy. Expenditure on dilapidations of a capital nature is not allowable, but expenditure on dilapidations at the end of the lease in the nature of deferred repairs is admissible, if the repairs would have been admissible if executed during the currency of the lease. A specific provision to cover such dilapidations may also be allowable in the same way as any other specific provision for a liability estimated on reasonable grounds, provided that an accurate estimate is made. A composition payment in lieu of making good dilapidations, made by the tenant at the end of the lease, is also allowable to the extent to which actual payments would have been allowed.

14.12 Residences

Managers of public houses or hotels who are employees are normally able to obtain capital gains tax exemption on a private residence other than the public house or hotel that they manage, in accordance with TCGA 1992, s. 222(8). The public house or hotel is recognised as 'job-related accommodation'.

Self-employed publicans in tied houses can also enjoy this exemption. Anti-avoidance provisions disallow relief where the trader has a material interest in the company providing the job-related accommodation, or is in partnership with the person providing it.

Where a guest-house or hotel is also used as the taxpayer's main residence, it is possible, depending on the circumstances, to obtain a measure of capital gains tax relief under TCGA 1992, ss. 222 and 223. In *Owen v Elliott* [1990] STC 469 the taxpayer also successfully claimed additional relief under TCGA 1992, s. 223(4).

The decision in *Owen v Elliott* was that the guest-house or hotel part of a property also used in part as a principal private residence constituted the letting of residential accommodation. The term residential accommodation was not to be construed narrowly as the Inland Revenue had argued, being applicable only to a flat within a house, but could cover any accommodation where people stayed and enjoyed board and lodging.

14.13 Guest-houses and roll-over relief

A possible problem arises where a guest-house, etc. is owned jointly by a husband and wife, but only one spouse is engaged in the business. If the property is owned equally on a disposal, it seems that only 50 per cent of the total gain may be rolled over. A similar problem arose (until 6 April 2003) in respect of retirement relief. In order to safeguard the reliefs, therefore, it is advisable for the husband and wife who wish to continue with joint ownership of the guest-house to carry on the business as a partnership. The husband should not necessarily be entitled to 50 per cent of the profits arising under the partnership, if he has another job and both wish to maximise the benefits of independent taxation.

14.14 Income from furnished holiday lettings

The Inland Revenue used to treat income from holiday flatlets as trading income, where some services of cleaning were provided, and to give capital gains tax roll-over relief and retirement relief where appropriate.

However, in the cases of *Gittos v Barclay* (1982) 55 TC 633, *Griffiths v Jackson* and *Griffiths v Pearman* (1982) 56 TC 583, the Inland Revenue successfully contended that such income was unearned income, and that no capital gains tax relief was available. In response to Parliamentary pressure, however, the Government announced that it would amend the law as interpreted in those cases so that, notwithstanding that the income derived from property, the source of the income would be treated as the carrying on of a trade. The Government's proposals were enacted in ICTA 1988, ss. 503 and 504.

To qualify as earned income and for capital gains tax retirement and roll-over relief, the accommodation must be available for holiday letting to the public for at least 140 days a year. It must also be actually let for at least 70 days and, within any seventh-month period, must not be occupied by the same tenant for a continuous period exceeding 31 days. There are provisions to 'average' such conditions over several properties where some properties are over or under the relevant limits. The provisions apply to income, acquisitions and disposals arising after 5 April 1982. Under this treatment as a deemed trade, losses are relieved as for trading losses, and retirement annuity premiums and personal pension premiums can be paid in respect of such earnings.

The deemed trade treatment for furnished holiday lettings given to income tax under ICTA 1988, s. 503 is extended for most capital gains tax purposes but specifically not applied for inheritance tax. Traditionally IR Capital Taxes have denied business property relief for let property and, with furnished holiday lets, one has had to work quite hard to get relief. In particular, IR Capital Taxes have traditionally required a minimum number of cottages to be included within the business, if relief is to be available at all. This aspect in particular appears to have gone, the CTO Advanced Instruction Manual stating at L.99.3 under holiday lettings:

> 'The Revenue solicitor has advised the office that in some instances the distinction between a business of furnished holiday lettings and, say, a business running an hotel or a motel may be so minimal that the courts would not regard such a business as one of 'wholly or mainly holding investments' for the purposes of IHTA 1984, s. 105(3).
>
> You should therefore normally allow relief where:
>
> - the lettings are short-term (for example, weekly or fortnightly); and
> - the owner — either himself or through an agent such as a relative or housekeeper — was substantially involved with the holidaymaker(s) in terms of their activities on and from the premises even if the lettings were for part of the year only.
>
> You should continue to refer to Litigation Group cases where relief is claimed and:
>
> - the lettings are longer-term (including Assured Shorthold Tenancies); or
> - where the owner had little involvement with the holidaymaker(s) — for example a villa or apartment abroad; or

- where the lettings were to friends and relatives only; or
- where it is clear that no services were provided to the holidaymaker(s).'

It is interesting that these instructions make no specific reference to s. 503.

14.15 PAYE

A restriction in employees' code numbers, for the estimated value of tips and gratuities that they receive and retain, can be a source of considerable irritation as, in the absence of records, amounts are estimated by the Inland Revenue. One way of avoiding the problems of recordkeeping in a large hotel is through the use of a '*tronc*' system. Here the *tronc-master* (usually the headwaiter) is responsible for deducting tax from the tips and operating a special PAYE scheme with the local inspector. Income tax is deducted at the basic rate although no National Insurance Contributions (NICs) are due, provided that the employer does not decide how the tips are to be divided among the employees (see Social Security (Contributions) Regulations 1979 (SI 1979 No. 591), reg. 19(1)(c)). However, special care is needed in order to ensure that a *tronc* system is properly established. In *Figael Ltd v Fox* [1992] STC 83, the directors who operated the system were held to be acting on behalf of the company in both organising and distributing the tips.

Chapter 15 Credit traders, hire purchase transactions, pawnbrokers, moneylenders

15.1 General

There are many forms of credit arrangement in connection with the sale of goods. In some cases traders themselves arrange the credit, although this is less common than it used to be. In other cases, the credit is arranged by an outside concern such as a hire purchase company. These arrangements operate where goods are purchased using some form of credit. Alternatively, a person who merely wants a loan and is not in a position to approach a bank for help, instead resorts to a pawnbroker or moneylender.

15.2 Credit traders

This is where the property in the goods passes to the customer on sale and traders themselves provide credit arrangements for paying for the goods. Often they arrange an agency to collect the amounts owing.

It is difficult to measure the trader's profits because the full proceeds of sale are brought into the accounts on sale and, but for any special arrangement, no allowance is due at that stage for the collection costs, which clearly reduce the value of the sale.

15.2.1 Provisions

Under an agreement between the National Federation of Credit Traders and the Inland Revenue, such traders are entitled to set up a provision for collection costs based on the direct expenses of collection and the amount collected in the year. Any increase in the provision is then deducted from profits and any decrease ranks as an addition to profits.

The provision is calculated as follows.

1. The direct expenses of collecting the book debts comprising wages, National Insurance Contributions (NICs) and travelling expenses on the trader's own staff employed for this purpose or commissions to debt collecting agencies, must be ascertained for the period in question.
2. The amount in 1 may need to be reduced to eliminate the expenses of selling the goods and other non-collection activities. It is normally agreed, where there is no more accurate figure, to reduce the direct costs by one-fifth to take account of this.
3. The amount as reduced in 2 is expressed as a percentage of the actual collections in the period.
4. This percentage is applied to the good book debts outstanding at the end of the period – that is, debts after making specific provision for any bad or doubtful items – and this is the provision carried forward at the end of the period.

Where traders have not made any provision in previous years but wish to adopt this basis, they must bring in a notional opening provision using this calculation. This is not the only basis that traders can use, however: there are variations which are accepted if consistently adhered to.

15.2.2 Valuation of debts

There is an agreed basis of debt valuation for credit traders carrying on the business of selling goods for payment by weekly instalments. Broadly, the arrangement involves writing down the value of debts, where there was no cash or goods transaction with the customer, 13 weeks before stocktaking, and reducing the value of other debts more than 13 weeks old where some transactions took place. In the latter case, the value of the debt is the lower of the amount outstanding and the total amount of cash received during the 12 months ending on the date of the stocktaking.

15.3 Hire purchase business

There are basically two types of hire purchase agreement entered into by a retailer:
1. The first, common in the motor trade, is where retailers are in effect intermediaries between the customer and finance house. They sell the goods to the finance house, from which they get the full cash price and a commission for introducing business to the finance house. The finance house

usually collects the instalments and is responsible for any bad debts, although sometimes there is a recourse clause making the retailer responsible for any amounts unrecovered after repossession and resale of the goods.

2. The second type of arrangement is more usual for the smaller hire purchase agreement. Under this, referred to as 'block discounting', retailers retain responsibility for collecting instalments and the burden of any bad debts remains with them. However, each time retailers make a sale on hire purchase, they either sell the goods to the finance company and, acting as *del credere* agent for the hire purchase company, enter into a simultaneous sale by the finance company to the customer, or alternatively enter into the hire purchase agreement direct with the customer and then assign their rights in the agreement to the finance house. There is a master agreement with the finance company under which the finance company pays a percentage (usually up to 75 per cent) of the face value of the agreements (that is, all of the amounts due under the agreements) with the balance as and when instalments are collected. The agreements are usually dealt with in batches with the finance house which the retailer has entered into as agent for the finance company or is to assign to the finance company. There is also a provision for a discount to the finance company from the total purchase price depending upon the length of the agreements included in the batch and this is the finance house's profit on the transactions.

In the case of 1 above, there is an outright cash sale. Where there is a recourse clause retailers can claim a deduction in their tax computation for any liability incurred under it as and when incurred. A provision for a possible future contingent liability under this clause is not normally allowed as it is in the nature of a general bad debt reserve (ICTA 1988, s. 74(j)).

Under 2 above the position is more complex. Strictly in law, retailers have no hire purchase debts due to them and are thus not entitled to any deduction for the gross profit in future instalments. In some cases the agreements are not assigned but are simply held as security with the right to have them assigned in certain circumstances, so that the retailer retains title to the hire purchase debt until assignment. However, in all these situations, it is established practice to treat the hire purchase debts as due to the retailer, against which provisions are made for unearned profit and bad debts. The amount paid by the finance company is then shown as a loan, and the discount given to the finance company is treated as a finance charge debited to profit and loss account. In effect, the substance of the transaction, treating it as a loan on the security of the hire purchase agreements, is followed for accounts purposes;

and provided the treatment of unearned profits and discounts is consistently adhered to, the Inland Revenue accept this for taxation purposes.

15.4 Pawnbrokers

Pawnbrokers advance money on a short-term basis in return for the deposit of articles of value as pledges. The pledge is redeemed when the loan is repaid with the appropriate amount of interest. If articles deposited as pledges are not claimed within 12 months and seven days, the pawnbroker may sell them. The only pledges which automatically become the absolute property of the pawn-broker on expiration of the redemption period are those given for loans of under £2. All other pledges can be sold only by auction and are redeemable until that takes place. Thus, if the loan is over £2, the pawnbroker can only take the loan, interest and cost of sale out of the proceeds immediately. The balance can be claimed by the pawner within a period depending upon the amount of the loan under the Pawnbrokers Act 1872. In the case of loans over £10, the Statute of Limitations applies and the balance can be reclaimed up to six years and thereafter becomes the property of the pawnbroker.

In *Jay's the Jewellers Ltd v CIR* (1947) 29 TC 274, the profit on sale of pledged goods of a pawnbroker was credited to the profit and loss account and the reserve (amounting to two-fifths of all profits on sales) was debited to an account called 'Return of Profit on Sale of Pledged Goods'. Jay's claimed that, as the property of the pawner never became their property, any profit on its sale was not taxable as part of its business profits or, on the authority of an earlier case, *Morley v Tattersall* (1938) 22 TC 51, if the profits did not belong to them at the time of sale, the expiration of the time limit for claiming the money did not convert the profits into a trading receipt. The court held that the profits were trading receipts as they arose in the ordinary course of the business but only when they became the absolute property of the pawnbroker. The profits should therefore be placed in a suspense account and be taxed only when the pawnbroker is entitled in law to retain them.

In other words, it is necessary to look at the true legal position to determine if and when such receipts are trading receipts. Thus on similar principles, deposits paid to a tailor when suits were ordered, were held to be trading receipts of the year of receipt as they belonged to the tailor at that time. If the customer did not take the garment, it was the company's policy to return the deposit to maintain goodwill but, because there was no right of recovery, *Jay's* case was distinguished (*Elson v Prices Taylors Ltd* (1963) 40 TC 671). The case for taxability and the timing of when something is taxable is best summarised by the judgement of the Lord President in *James Spencer & Co v CIR* (1950) 32 TC 111 at page 116, where he referred to:

> '... the broad working rule which emerges as a guide to the crediting or debiting in a tax computation subsequently maturing credits or debits is to inquire in which accounting period the right or liability was established and to carry the item into the account in that year. I use the vague word 'established' advisedly for we are now in the region of proper commercial and accounting practice rather than of systematic jurisprudence.'

The Inland Revenue Inspectors Manual states at IM 2920:

> 'Pawnbrokers: sales of pledges
>
> 1. Any unclaimed surplus on the sale of a pledge should be treated as a trading profit on the expiry of the borrower's right to recover the surplus (*Jay's the Jewellers Ltd v CIR*, (1947) 29 TC 274). The sale of unredeemed articles is governed by the Consumer Credit Act 1974 and SI 1983, 1566 and SI 1983, 1571. These provide that, if the article is not redeemed before the end of the redemption period, then-
>
>   a. where the redemption period is six months and the article is security for credit not exceeding £25, the property in the article passes to the pawnbroker
>
>   b. in other cases, the pawnbroker is entitled to sell the article, collect what he is owed out of the net sale proceeds and pay any balance to the borrower. The borrower's right of recovery will lapse six years after the sale.
>
> 2. Alternatively, where the practice has been to treat the surplus on a sale as arising on the date of sale and any recovery by the borrower as an expense arising on the date of payment to him, it may, if the taxpayer so requests, be continued provided that the basis is adhered to consistently.'

15.5 Moneylenders

Not everybody who makes loans is carrying on a trade of moneylending. *Prima facie*, lending money at interest is an investment and any interest received is taxable under Schedule D, Case III.

Whether the making of loans amounts to trade is essentially a question of fact and there has to be sufficient evidence of trading to displace the investment presumption. The most useful test in this context is that set out in *CIR v Livingston* (1927) 11 TC 538: 'whether the operations involved ... are of the same kind, and carried on in the same way, as those which are characteristic of ordinary trading in the line of business in which the venture was made'.

So in addition to the usual *indicia* of trade, such as the number and frequency of loan transactions, the Inland Revenue would expect to see a degree of organisation to deal with the collection of instalments from borrowers, such as debt collection agents, use of lawyers in cases of default and active pursuit of late payers.

Guidance can be found as to what sort of organisation might be involved in the description of the appellant's moneylending business at pages 313–315 in the case of *Monthly Salaries Loan Co Ltd v Furlong* (1962) 40 TC 313.

Another useful pointer in considering if someone who makes loans is trading as a moneylender is whether he or she holds a licence under the Consumer Credit Act 1974. Section 21 of this Act requires anyone who is carrying on a consumer credit business to be licensed. A consumer credit business is essentially any business so far as it relates to the provision of credit below £15,000 to individuals.

The Consumer Credit Act 1974 replaces the earlier Moneylenders Acts, and regulates the terms and conditions under which loans of £15,000 and less can be offered. Where a business only lends amounts greater than £15,000 agreements are not regulated and a licence is not needed.

15.5.1 Allocation of principal and interest

Under the predecessors to the Consumer Credit Act 1974 (the Moneylenders Act 1927 and the Moneylenders Act (Northern Ireland) 1933), where the interest on a loan was not expressed in terms of a rate per cent, any amount paid or payable to the moneylender was to be appropriated to principal, and interest in the proportion that the actual amount lent bears to the total amount of the interest. For example:

Loan	£100
Repayments 50 weekly instalments of	£3
Total repayment (50 × £3)	£150

Apportion instalments:

Interest	£1
Capital	£2

Although the Consumer Credit Act 1974 requires the lender to inform the debtor of the amount and rate of the total charge for credit, the above basis of arranging loans may still be found in practice, when it should normally be adopted in dealing with a moneylender's accounts.

15.5.2 Cessation

When a moneylender's trade ceases for tax purposes is a question of fact. In some circumstances, after the trade has ceased, a former moneylender may receive cash from the business that was not taken into account in the final accounts of the business. Where this happens, the receipts, to the extent they represent interest on loans made before the business ceased, do not fall to be dealt with under the post-cessation receipts rules because the sums are otherwise chargeable to tax, as interest under Schedule D, Case III.

Interest received by a moneylender, even if annual interest, is not treated as investment.

In fact, most moneylenders' interest is short interest which is treated as part of trading income because it is a receipt of the trade and not merely interest on an investment. Consequently, it qualifies as trading income for retirement annuity and personal pension contribution purposes. When the trade ceases, any outstanding interest becomes interest assessable under Schedule D, Case III (*Bennett v Ogston* (1930) 15 TC 374).

Note that in the case of a moneylender or person carrying on a similar sort of business, the Inland Revenue normally accept any reasonable basis of bringing in interest. However, it now appears possible for a moneylender to opt for a strict Case I basis – that is for tax purposes crediting interest on an arising basis as and when it is payable and not anticipating unrealised profits – even if that basis differs from that used in the accounts, which may employ an accruals basis. Thus in *Willingale v International Commercial Bank Ltd* [1978] STC 75, the bank claimed that discounts on treasury bills, although brought into the accounts on an accrued basis, should be assessed on a strict basis excluding unrealised profits. The court agreed with this contention. In effect, although accounting treatment is a good guide to the treatment of an item for tax purposes following *Odeon Associated Theatres Ltd v Jones* (1973) 48 TC 257, it must follow that where there is authority for treating income for tax purposes differently, it can always be followed by the Inland Revenue or the taxpayer. This principle of not bringing in unrealised profits was strengthened by the House of Lords' decision in *Pattison v Marine Midland Ltd* [1984] STC 10 where notional currency profits which had not been realised were held not to be taxable.

The distinction between the capital element of any repayments and interest, even in the case of a moneylender in considering the allowance of expenses, was illustrated in the *Monthly Salaries Loan Co Ltd case*. Here, a moneylending company claimed to deduct, in addition to normal collection costs, an estimated reserve for expenses to be incurred in the following year in the collection of outstanding loans, the amounts being calculated on a percentage basis related to the capital element in the loans. It was held that this was not allowable.

Chapter 16 Persons in receipt of foreign pensions

16.1 Remittance basis

Prior to the Finance Act 1974, foreign pensions (ie pensions arising abroad in respect of service in a foreign country), were taxed on a remittance basis under Sch. D, Case V. It was common practice therefore to accumulate such income abroad.

Under the Finance Act 1974, such pensions are taxed on an arising basis subject to a deduction of ten per cent of the pension, except where received by an individual who is either not domiciled in the UK or is a British subject or citizen of the Republic of Ireland and is not ordinarily resident in the UK. For those persons, the remittance basis continues. If all the pension were remitted in those circumstances, the person who is domiciled in the UK would therefore be better off by reason of the ten per cent deduction, which is not available where the remittance basis applies (ICTA 1988, s. 65(2) and (4)).

In *Albon v IRC* [1998] STI 1600, Mr A worked in the USA, paying Federal State and Federal Social Security taxes, and in France, paying French social security contributions. The US Federal Social Security tax was paid to obtain social security benefits and was not deductible in an individual's tax returns in the USA. One benefit purchased was a retirement pension which did not have to be declared in the individual's tax return in the USA.

Later still, A and his wife, both now resident in the UK, received pension payments from the Social Security Administration in the USA and from the equivalent authority in France. The Revenue treated the payments as income from foreign possessions and assessed the taxpayers under Schedule D, Case V in accordance with ICTA 1988, s. 18.

The taxpayers appealed, arguing that, since payments of tax in the USA had been made out of taxed income and since the pension represented a deferment of pay which had already been fully taxed, the UK assessments on the pension payments involved double taxation contrary to the double taxation agreement between the UK and the USA.

The Special Commissioner dismissed the appeals, holding that the pension payments received were liable to tax as 'income arising from possessions out of the UK, not being income consisting of emoluments of any office or employment' under Sch. D, Case V in accordance with ICTA 1988, s. 18. The Special Commissioner considered that it was irrelevant how the entitlement had been acquired. What was important was that payments had been made from the USA and from France; under the law of the UK, the taxpayers must account for tax on those sums. The taxpayers appealed further, arguing that A's pension fell within the exception to the charge to tax under Case V (income consisting of emoluments of any office or employment), and that it arose out of a contractual right originally obtained when A paid taxes in the 1960s. If tax was to be assessed, it was to be assessed in respect of that period. Further, a charge to tax under Schedule D is in respect of an annual profit or gain and a pension which had been purchased by social security contributions was not a profit or gain.

The decision of the Court of Session was that a right to a pension was not an emolument of an employment. The issue was whether the pension payments made by the US and French authorities were to be regarded as 'income arising from possessions out of the UK'. It was settled law that the right to money was a 'possession'. The right to payment of the pension was such a possession and tax fell to be charged in relation to the periods when the income was actually received even though the pension had been 'earned' years before. The whole receipts fell to be assessed to tax. The appeals were refused.

16.2 Arrears of pension

Where a foreign pension or increase of pension is granted retrospectively and that pension is chargeable under Sch. D, Case V on the arising basis then, strictly, the full amount of the award, including arrears, is assessable in one sum. Under ITEPA 2003, s. 575(2)(c), 613(3)(C) however, where it is to the benefit of the taxpayer, the tax on the pension is computed as if the arrears, after making the appropriate ICTA 1988, s. 65(2) deduction, arose in the years to which they related. This should be done by:

- deducting the amount to be spread back from the assessment for the year for which it would otherwise be chargeable, and

- adding to the tax charged for that year the tax on the amount so deducted which would have been charged on a current year basis for the year or years of assessment to which it relates. For all other years, the basis year for the purpose of the assessment is unaffected.

The agreement of the taxpayer should be obtained before assessments are made on the non-statutory basis described above. If any difficulties arise with collection of the tax, the assessments should be put on to the strict statutory basis before any proceedings for recovery of tax are taken.

Foreign pensions chargeable on the remittance basis awarded or increased retrospectively qualify for relief under ICTA 1988, s. 585(2).

16.3 Pensions paid by Crown Agents

Certain foreign pensions are payable in the UK by the Crown Agents, acting on behalf of the government of the territory to which they relate. Where the territory forms part of Her Majesty's dominions, is a country mentioned in s. 1(3) of the British Nationality Act 1981, or is under Her Majesty's protection, the pension is chargeable under ITEPA 2003, s. 615. However, although paid in the UK, provided it is not borne out of the public revenue of the UK and relates to service in one of those countries, it also qualifies for the ten per cent deduction (ITEPA 2003, s. 617).

If the liability to pay a pension has been taken over by the British Government, for instance Indian Civil Service pensions, the pension is taxed in full and does not qualify for the ten per cent deduction.

The Crown Agents again normally act as paying agents and receive instructions on what code number to operate from HM Inspector of Taxes, Public Department 1 District, Ty Glas Road, Llanishen, Cardiff CF14 5XZ, tel: (029) 2032 5048.

Where the Crown Agents pay pensions other than out of the funds of Her Majesty's Government and overseas tax is deducted on instructions from the overseas tax authority concerned, by arrangement with the Inland Revenue the UK tax code number is applied to the pension amount after any such overseas tax has been deducted. This is done to reduce any overpayment of UK tax. Note that, as with the former 25 per cent deduction in respect of overseas employments, the ten per cent deduction does not affect the amount of tax credit relief for foreign tax paid.

16.4 Pensions paid to victims of Nazi persecution

Pensions paid to victims of Nazi persecution by the law of Germany or Austria are eligible for a deduction of one-half, instead of one-tenth, if paid to a person domiciled in the UK. Attempts to claim complete exemption from UK tax on such pensions, taking advantage of the double tax treaty with Germany on the basis that the recipients were still German nationals have failed (*Nothman v Cooper* [1975] STC 91; and *Oppenheimer v Cattermole* (1975) 50 TC 159). Note, however, that there is complete exemption from income tax for annuities paid to compensate victims of Nazi persecution for any damage they suffered (ICTA 1988, s. 466). The nature of the payment received therefore needs to be checked with the authorities.

16.5 Double tax agreements

It is important in the case of any foreign pension to check the terms of the relevant double tax agreement, as the pension may be liable to tax only in the country of residence of the recipient (the position in most cases) or, in some cases, only in the country where the pension arises. For instance, certain US government pensions paid to citizens of the USA resident in the UK are exempt from UK tax under the double tax agreement (SI 1980 No. 568, Art. 18(2)). Article 18 of the 2001 Double Taxation Convention also provides relief for UK nationals who work in the US but are vested members of a UK pension scheme. Such individuals no longer need to report the imputed pension scheme income on their US tax returns.

16.6 Foreign invalidity benefits

Payments made by foreign governments which correspond to those UK Government social security benefits which are exempt from income tax under ITEPA 2003, s. 655 (which exempts such items of income as invalidity benefits and non-contributory invalidity pensions) are treated by ITEPA 2003, s. 681 as also being exempt from UK tax. Thus, an invalidity pension from a foreign government might be so exempt.

16.7 Foreign war pensions

Any pension or allowance which is payable by a foreign government to a widow, and relates to death due to war service or war injuries, is exempt from tax in the same way as comparable war widows' pensions payable by the UK Government (ITEPA 2003, s. 639).

16.8 Foreign social security payments

A pension payable under a foreign social security law arises from the pensioner's rights under that law. Those rights are a possession and the pension is assessable under Schedule D, Case V. Foreign social security pensions are not exempted from UK tax by double taxation agreements.

ITEPA 2003, s. 681 exempts from UK tax those benefits awarded to UK residents under foreign social security laws which correspond to UK social security benefits exempted from tax under ITEPA 2003, s. 677 (for example, sickness benefit, maternity benefit, attendance allowance and invalidity benefit). The exemption from tax in the UK applies whether or not the benefit is taxable in the country of origin.

ITEPA 2003, s. 681 also applies to payments corresponding to UK child benefit made by foreign governments, and to payments corresponding to the other UK social security benefits in respect of children excluded from the charge by ITEPA 2003, s. 677. In some countries, such as the United States, certain social security benefits paid in respect of children are income of the child rather than income of the parent or guardian. Such a benefit does not correspond to any non-taxable UK social security benefit paid in respect of children and it does not therefore qualify for the concession.

Any claim should be supported by evidence (preferably in the form of the documents notifying the award) to show that the benefit is paid under a foreign state scheme and corresponds to a non-taxable benefit payable under the UK social security scheme. Where a translation of foreign documents is required, the papers should be forwarded to: Foreign Intelligence Section, Duchy Rooms, Somerset House, London WC2A 1LB.

Chapter 17 Sportspeople

17.1 Basis of liability

Sportspeople, like some actors, are assessed under Sch. D, Case II as carrying on one profession, where their income does not derive from an employment. Provided that they are resident in the UK and carrying on at least part of their profession in the UK, they are assessable on their worldwide earnings under Sch. D, Case II. If a sportsperson becomes non-resident for a whole tax year, he or she can escape assessment to UK tax altogether in respect of professional earnings.

Athletes may receive all the following types of income:

- subventions;
- grants and gifts;
- sponsorship and endorsement fees, and
- appearance, participation and performance fees.

17.2 Subventions, grants and gifts

Subventions are gifts or grants to which no commercial strings are attached: Sports Aid Foundation grants are the most common. But there may be other public or semi-public sources and occasionally commercial concerns make payments akin to subventions. Most subventions are paid to athletes who cannot earn much from commercial contracts, and they are usually intended to meet specified expenses.

An athlete who receives only subventions is unlikely to be carrying on a trade or exercising a profession or vocation. Where the payment is received from a commercial concern, the facts and documentary evidence may, however, indicate that the payment is in reality a kind of sponsorship or endorsement fee.

17.3 Sponsorship and endorsement fees

Sponsorship, or product endorsement, usually involves athletes in lending their names to a promotional campaign. This may be through advertisements or through personal visits to retail outlets. The product may not, of course, have any athletic or other sporting connection. The arrangements are normally contractual, though the form of the contract may vary from a formal written agreement to an informal letter or even a telephone call. Where accounts are under enquiry it is normally useful to obtain a copy of any written agreements or other documentation.

Athletes are not permitted to wear clothes bearing sponsorship names or logos in competitions, because usually the Athletics Associations have already made agreements with manufacturers that only their kit should be worn.

17.4 Appearance, participation and performance fees

In an attempt to attract leading athletes, many competition organisers offer substantial sums for appearances or participation at meetings. Bonuses may also be paid for meritorious performances such as winning or setting records.

Athletes may also receive fees from activities not directly connected with sport, such as writing newspaper articles, making TV appearances and opening supermarkets.

17.5 Visiting sportspeople

Most double taxation agreements do not exempt visiting sportspeople from local tax, even if they have no fixed base in the country concerned. Thus, in the case of the US/UK double taxation agreement, Art. 17 specifically excludes athletes, in the widest sense, from the exemptions afforded to self-employed visitors and visiting employees of US corporations performing duties in the UK (Double Taxation Relief (Taxes on Income((United States of America) (Dividends) Regulations 1980 (SI 1980 No. 568)).

The provisions in ICTA 1988, ss. 555–558, requiring persons paying non-UK resident entertainers to deduct tax on making payments in respect of activities performed in the UK, also apply to non-resident sportspeople, in respect of activities performed in the UK (see **3.4** above in connection with entertainers).

17.6 Use of partnership or company

A sportsperson, by the very nature of the profession, normally cannot admit his or her spouse as a partner, although it is possible for them to form a partnership to deal with sponsorship and other promotional income. Another way of avoiding higher rates of income tax is to transfer the business to a company. Under TCGA 1992, s. 162, if the consideration is wholly by way of shares of the company, there is no capital gains tax liability arising from the transfer until the shares are disposed of. However, care needs to be taken to ensure that no liability arises under ICTA 1988, s. 775 (see in connection with entertainers at **3.5** above). The development of other trades in the company should overcome this.

The provisions of TCGA 1992, s. 165 offer an alternative route. It is possible to transfer at undervalue chargeable assets used in a business, such as super-earning potential (which is presumably a form of goodwill) into a company, and to hold over any gain under the hold-over provisions of TCGA 1992, s. 165. If current assets are transferred on loan account, any goodwill is transferred at undervalue and, should it ever be realised (which is extremely unlikely) the company will pay corporation tax on the gain arising from the ultimate proceeds.

17.7 Service company documentation

On any incorporation of the sportsperson's activities, take care to ensure that the documentation evidencing the transfer is correctly executed, and that future contractual relationships are entered into by the company and not the individual. The individual is contracted to the service company by a 'slavery' contract, which gives the company discretion over making the individual's services available to third parties. The contract should also define where the services are to be performed, as it may be necessary to have a separate company for overseas services. It should also indicate the rights, such as copyrights and trade marks, that the company has succeeded to.

No Inland Revenue attack on service companies under *Furniss v Dawson* (1984) 55 TC 324 has so far reached the courts. It is understood that the Inland Revenue have won a case before the Special Commissioners, but here the service company documentation was faulty.

However, consideration must be given as to whether the service company is caught by the IR35 legislation. For details of the application of this legislation, see **1.20**.

17.8 Foreign companies

In the case of UK-resident sportspeople, it is sometimes desirable to set up foreign companies in tax havens to receive income from abroad. Similar considerations apply as to those for entertainers (see **Chapter 3**).

17.9 Withholding taxes

The question of withholding taxes on payments to sportspeople by overseas countries needs to be considered. Under most double taxation agreements, independent activities carried on by those having no permanent establishment or base in a foreign country are exempt from tax in the country of payment, except in the case of payments to sportspeople. It used to be possible to avoid such withholding taxes in the case of payments from the USA by having the income paid to a UK-resident company. However, under the revised agreement, if the UK company is one which is created substantially for the benefit of one person, withholding tax still applies.

If foreign tax is withheld, it is important to ensure that maximum credit is obtained for it against UK tax. Thus, if it is withheld in the case of a payment to a company, sufficient profits should be left in charge to UK tax to cover the foreign tax.

17.10 Expenses

17.10.1 Abroad

Again, similar considerations apply as for entertainers. However, if the sportsperson is self-employed, he or she should, if possible, be treated as operating from the home, and the expenses claimed under normal Schedule D rules. In practice, this covers both travel and reasonable subsistence expenses, and no attempt is made to restrict for home saving.

17.10.2 In the UK

In the case of trips within the UK, the inspector of taxes may seek to disallow those expenses that the person would have had to incur as normal living expenses, on the basis of the decision in *Caillebotte v Quinn* (1975) 50 TC 222, although this disallowance is unlikely to be significant. In practice, a disallowance is less likely where the sportsperson has a mortgage, a spouse and family.

It has been reported that the cost of alcoholic sustenance of certain professional snooker and darts players has been successfully challenged by the Inland Revenue.

In *Ansell v Brown* 23.5.01 [2001] STI Issue 22 the question was whether, for the purposes of what is now ITEPA 2003, s. 336, the cost of dietary supplements purchased by a professional rugby player was a deductible expense. The taxpayer was a rugby player who had a contract to play with a premier division club. The contract required him to maintain at all times a high standard of physical fitness. The taxpayer purchased dietary supplements. The General Commissioners upheld the taxpayer's appeal against an amendment to his 1996–97 self assessment tax return. The commissioners found that the supplements had been taken for no other purpose than increasing his physical fitness and condition (although the Club merely gave recommendations for diet and did not insist on the purchase of particular items). The Revenue appealed.

The High Court held that the commissioners had failed to pay any regard to the statutory requirement that the expenditure had to be incurred *in* the performance of the taxpayer's duties as an employee. Clearly the supplements had been purchased with a view to achieving and maintaining the required level of fitness and the required size and physique for a back row forward. However, that did not amount to an expenditure in the performance of his duties as an employee. In particular, it was expenditure incurred to enable him to perform his duties and not in the performance itself (and indeed it was an expenditure which arose from the taxpayer's own personal circumstances, *viz* the need to increase his weight). The commissioners had misdirected themselves in law and the Revenue's appeal was allowed.

17.11 General principles on liability of various receipts

Sportspeople derive their income from many sources. In some cases, it is received in the form of prize money; in other cases, payments are made by advertisers for the use of a sportsperson's name. Bear in mind that professional footballers and cricketers are employees of their clubs, and any payments made to them by their clubs are subject to tax as employment income under ITEPA 2003. Match bonuses and payments from players' pools also form part of their earnings. Consequently, under Football League rules, earnings from the club cannot be paid to a service company as the player personally is contracted to the club. Only other income from sponsorships, etc can be paid to such a company.

Payments for international matches are paid to footballers' clubs by the Football Association and thus are passed on to them by the club as additional earnings subject to PAYE in the normal way. When footballers receive part of their transfer fee, this is also taxable in full as employment income under ITEPA 2003. It does not fall within the 'golden handshake' provisions of ITEPA 2003, s. 403 (whereby it would be completely exempt from tax up to £30,000), because it is a customary payment, even though the employee has no contractual right to it (see *Corbett v Duff* (1941) 23 TC 763). The player's share of a transfer fee paid as a signing-on fee is normally paid by instalments under Football Association rules over the length of the contract, and the tax liability can therefore be spread forward. The question of the taxation of so-called 'loyalty bonuses' paid to footballers at the end of their contracts on transfer to another club has been under discussion between the Professional Footballers' Association and the Inland Revenue. The Inland Revenue argued that these bonuses were payments as part of the deal with the club to which the player was moving, and therefore were taxable as a payment for future services. The players claimed that the bonuses were 'golden handshakes'.

The English football authorities seem to agree with the Inland Revenue's Special Compliance Office that most termination payments made by 'custom and expectation' to footballers, on a transfer to a new club by their transferring club, should be taxed as ordinary earnings.

This view was strengthened by the House of Lords' decision in *Shilton v Wilmshurst* [1991] STC 88 which confirmed that a payment by his old club to a player on a transfer was an emolument liable in full under Schedule E. The court held that the payment represented part of the contractual arrangements for the transfer, and whether it was paid for future services or not it was part of the terms of his continuing employment with the new club and therefore taxable.

Payments from other sources that are made in the ordinary course of carrying on or exercising the profession are Sch. D, Case II income of the recipient.

However, there have been exceptional payments made to individuals as marks of personal esteem, or that are peculiar to those individuals, which have been held not liable to tax. Thus, attendance money at a cricketer's benefit match paid to the cricketer was held not to be assessable to income tax (*Reed v Seymour* (1927) 11 TC 625). The basis of the decision was that the sum received showed the gratitude of the public and was in appreciation of the personal qualities of the cricketer. In contrast, in *Davis v Harrison* (1927) 11 TC 707, a footballer's benefit was held to be assessable. This was principally because the benefit accrued to the person automatically under the rules of the Football League, after a specified number of years' playing service, so that it had less of the qualities of a payment to a particular individual, than a payment by virtue of the length of service performed. In *Moorhouse v Dooland* (1954) 36 TC 1, a professional cricketer playing in the Lancashire League was assessed on the proceeds of collections from spectators that were allowed under the rules of the League where a player scored more than 50 runs. A payment for giving up amateur status was, however, held not to be assessable (*Jarrold v Boustead* (1964) 41 TC 701). In *Shilton v Wilmshurst*, as mentioned above, it was held that, in the particular circumstances, a fee of £75,000 paid to Peter Shilton, a professional footballer, by his club Nottingham Forest, as an inducement to him to consent to his transfer to a new club, was an emolument chargeable to income tax under ITEPA 2003, s. 15 (formerly Sch. E, Case I, ICTA 1988, s. 19(1)).

It is generally best to steer clear of exotic tax avoidance schemes involving sportspeople, as shown by the case of *O'Leary v McKinley* [1991] STC 42. O'Leary, who was domiciled in Ireland, had a contract with Arsenal. In addition to his basic wage and bonuses he was anxious to ensure that an additional annual sum of £28,985 was received in a tax-efficient manner. The sum of £10 was settled on a Jersey settlement by a third party for the benefit of O'Leary for life with remainder, subject to a power of advancement, to the Catholic Church in Ireland. Arsenal lent the settlement £266,000 interest-free but repayable on demand, which was invested with a Jersey bank for two years at $11\frac{1}{2}$ per cent to provide an annual sum of £28,590 for O'Leary. Based on his non-domiciled status, he would only be taxed on any interest remitted to the UK. No income was remitted. It was decided that the income arising under the settlement was an emolument of the taxpayer's employment with the club, on the basis that it was income provided by Arsenal Football Club payable only for so long as O'Leary was employed by the club. If O'Leary had had the free disposal of the £266,000 and if it had not been tied to his employment, the position might have been different. However, the case was not decided upon *Furniss v Dawson* principles but by construing all the documents together. The position on inducement payments which this case broadly followed is discussed below.

In *Sports Club (1), Evelyn (2), Jocelyn (3) (Appellants) v HMIT* [2000] SpC 00253 it was held that football players could legitimately avoid an employment income tax liability in respect of 'image' payments made to the players' offshore companies, for the commercial right for the employing club to use their names in promotional transactions.

The Arsenal football players Denis Bergkamp and David Platt (referred to in the decision as Evelyn and Jocelyn) had each arranged for £1.5 million to be paid to their offshore companies by Arsenal for the right to use their names in promotional transactions. This money was paid in instalments, in addition to the £20,000 a week under their playing contracts, when the two footballers moved from clubs in Italy. The Revenue argued that the additional sums were simply disguised earnings.

The commissioners found that it was common practice for footballers and other celebrities to arrange for consideration for 'image rights' to be paid tax-free to offshore companies. They held that the 'image' payments were for genuine commercial agreements and did not form part of the employment earnings.

For this tax treatment to follow, the individual must be resident outside the UK while the offshore company which owns the image rights is established. The two companies in this case were set up while Messrs Bergkamp and Platt lived in Italy.

Apparently the Inland Revenue have 'no plans at present to challenge the Special Commissioners' decision'.

17.12 Footballer's benefit matches

The Inland Revenue appear to have lost a case before the Commissioners concerning another footballer's benefit, and do not now argue for taxation of such benefits. However, to be safe, there must not only be no entitlement to the benefit, even in the form of verbal promises as part of the player's contract, but also neither the club nor any official of the club should be concerned in running the benefit match, which should be left to an independent committee or body of trustees. As the 'golden handshake' legislation can catch anything paid 'in connection with' the termination of an employee's contract of service, the benefit match should not take place when the player goes from one club to another or retires from the game. The receipts from the match should, if possible, be mainly on the basis of donations by spectators and only a low admission charge made for the tickets.

17.13 Operation of PAYE

There has been a crackdown on so-called expenses payments made in particular to footballers in the lower divisions, non-league clubs and amateur leagues. In addition, signing-on fees (see **17.15** below) have been abused. Following an investigation into the affairs of Swindon Town, there was an amnesty for football clubs which enabled them to declare payments which should have been subject to PAYE, without facing interest and penalties. It is believed several clubs have now had discussions with the Inland Revenue.

The Inland Revenue enquiry did not just cover signing-on fees and expenses payments to Football League contract players. Increased sponsorship of clubs has also presented a problem, as perks provided by third party sponsors should be reported by clubs and frequently are not. In addition, the payment of expenses to players where the contract is incomplete and only specifies certain payments has been the source of intense Inland Revenue enquiries, and the practice of so-called amateurs receiving round-sum payments for travelling is being attacked. If these represent genuine expenses payments, with no profit to the player, arguably the cases of *Donnelly v Williamson* [1982] STC 88 and *Pook v Owen* (1969) 45 TC 571 might mean there is nothing to assess, but this is frequently not the case.

17.14 Amateur sportspeople

In 1982 the International Amateur Athletic Federation (IAAF) amended its rules to permit 'athletes' funds'. In broad terms, amateur athletes could earn income in connection with their athletic activities without forfeiting their amateur status provided the income was paid into funds administered by the athletes' national associations. Withdrawals were permitted for specified expenses, but athletes could forfeit their amateur status if they withdrew money for other purposes.

The regulations for UK Athletics (UKA) permit two types of fund: the general fund; and the individual fund.

The general fund

1. Sometimes known as the athletic fund, this is managed for athletes by the UKA itself. All the athlete's income from grants, participation fees, sponsorship and other athletics-related activities should be paid into the fund.

Sportspeople

2. Athletes may withdraw their money from the fund at any time, but they lose their amateur status if they withdraw money other than to meet certain expenses specified by the IAAF.

3. The money is held by UKA in a general bank account in trust for the athletes, but separate records are kept of each athlete's income and withdrawals.

4. Because an athlete can take complete control over the money, a bare trust is created and, where income paid into the fund is assessable, it is regarded as the income of the athlete for income tax purposes.

5. Interest arising on the investment of the fund monies is retained by UKA and is not therefore assessable on the individual athletes.

The individual fund

1. An athlete who has more than a specified amount in the general fund may ask UKA to set up an individual trust fund. If an athlete takes this option, an individual trust deed is drawn up and three trustees are appointed, two by the BAAB and one by the athlete. The athlete does not sign the trust deed, but signs a letter acknowledging its terms.

2. All of the athlete's income from athletics or athletics-related activities should be paid into the individual trust fund. Amateur status is lost if withdrawals are made other than for expenses specified by the IAAF. Only a few leading athletes have been in a position to request their own individual funds. As well as having an individual fund, an athlete with more than the specified sum in the general fund may still remain in that fund.

3. Under the terms of the trust deed an athlete is free to withdraw money at will. Therefore a bare trust is created.

4. Usually athletes with individual trust funds are carrying on a trade, profession or vocation. If so, the income paid into the funds should be included in the computation of their profits assessable under Case I or II.

5. One of the advantages of an individual trust fund for athletes is that they are able to retain the benefit of any investment income and chargeable gains. Any such income or gains should be assessed on the athletes themselves.

The Inland Revenue's Inspectors Manual contains the following guidance on the distinction between amateur and professional status:

'That an athlete is described as an amateur is not decisive in considering whether he should be assessed under Case I or II. The leading figures in amateur athletics are likely to be assessable under Case I or II on their earnings.

But the activities of most athletes remain a purely leisure pursuit or hobby, even though money may occasionally be paid into a fund for their benefit. The distinction between a hobby on the one hand and a trade, profession or vocation on the other is very much a question of fact and degree.

Practical approach

In one or two years an athlete's earnings may have exceeded the expenses. And, perhaps, the whole of the athlete's time may be devoted substantially to sporting and associated activities. But even the presence of both those pointers is not decisive. Inspectors will need more information before deciding whether the athlete is organising the activities in a business-like manner and with a view to making a profit. In order to consider the badges of trade Inspectors will need the full facts concerning:

- the nature and scale of the activities and the way they are organised
- competitions and events entered in the relevant period, the athlete's final position in each event and any prizes received
- any subventions, grants or similar receipts from sporting or other organisations, and copies of documents setting out the terms under which they are received
- any attendance or performance fees, and sponsorship or endorsement fees, with copies of the contracts and relevant documentation
- any other income from associated activities including journalism, TV appearances, etc.
- the terms of any agreement with an agent negotiating contracts with sponsors, etc. This is usually UKA but many of the leading athletes engage their own agents
- the cost and nature of expenses.'

The point when an activity ceases to be a hobby and becomes a profession is sometimes difficult to determine, but generally it is advisable to admit Case II status early so as to claim expenses and possibly in the early days also loss relief. There may also be pre-trading expenses to claim under ICTA 1988, s. 401. Usually these are incurred before the first sponsorship is obtained and before the first appearance money or prize money is received. The athletes should be encouraged to keep detailed diaries of expenses. The most difficult areas are the loan of cars by sponsors. Whereas the benefits legislation is very comprehensive for employees, money's worth is sometimes difficult to fit into the Sch. D, Case II rules. Generally, unless someone actually receives ownership of goods in kind, so that the principle in *Gold Coast Selection Trust Ltd v Humphrey* (1948) 30 TC 209 applies to tax the payment in kind for Sch. D purposes, it is difficult to tax such benefits under Sch. D.

17.15 Signing-on fees

The decision in *Jarrold v Boustead* (see **17.11** above) does not by any means imply that all, or indeed most, signing-on fees are immune from liability as employment income under ITEPA 2003. For example, in *Riley v Coglan* (1967) 44 TC 481, a former amateur player signed professional forms with a rugby league club. In addition to the normal form of remuneration, the agreement between the individual and the club provided that, in consideration of the sum of £500, the player would serve the club for the remainder of his playing career. Ungoed-Thomas J. decided that the sum of £500 was paid for services to be rendered, and it became an emolument arising 'from' the employment properly chargeable to income tax under ITEPA 2003. The decision in *Jarrold v Boustead* was based on the conclusion that the sum paid comprised an inducement for giving up amateur status and did not reflect a reward for services rendered. This distinction indicates the extreme caution to be exercised when drafting any document or agreement including the payment of an 'inducement' or signing-on fee.

However, in the case of rugby league players, where a player genuinely relinquishes his amateur status by signing for a league club and turning professional, he will receive tax relief on the first £6,000 of any fee paid for surrendering amateur status, and the rest is taxable as income. The same rules apply to stage payments where the £6,000 limit is not exceeded on any outright payment on signing for a rugby league club provided no conditions are attached to the instalment. Inducement fees were also the subject of three other cases, *Vaughan-Neil v CIR* (1979) 54 TC 223, *Pritchard v Arundale* (1971) 47 TC 680, and *Glantre Engineering Ltd v Goodhand* (1982) 56 TC 165. The principles emerging from these cases are that, to be non-taxable, it is preferable that the sum be paid other than by the prospective employer and that the payment (whether in cash or, as in the *Arundale* case, in the form of shares) should be shown to be for giving up a valuable right, so that there is a permanent loss of a valuable asset. These decisions do not, therefore, exempt any ordinary signing-on fee paid to a player moving from one club to another.

It is understood that, in an appeal before the Special Commissioners, no tax relief was allowed to a player signing for a leading Scottish professional club in respect of his loss of amateur status on the grounds that the effects of the loss of amateur status in football are negligible these days.

17.16 Payments for winning

In the case of *Moore v Griffiths* (1972) 48 TC 338, payments to the England team for winning the World Cup – paid both by outside bodies and a special bonus paid by the Football Association – were held not to be assessable, as not being a reward for services rendered. The basis of this decision seems to be that special payments made to an individual for some unique performance or personal quality may escape assessment, particularly where the payment is unsolicited. In contrast, where it is normal for people in a sport to compete for prize money, the prizes are assessable if it can be shown that the person is carrying on his or her sport as a profession rather than as a hobby. For example, it is reported that the Inland Revenue is seeking to assess prizes in angling competitions on those who they regard as professional anglers. However, 'man of the match' awards are accepted as not taxable.

17.17 Jockeys

Racing is not a commercial activity liable to taxation and, therefore, owners receive their winnings free of tax. However, jockeys are taxable on payments from owners that are part of their earnings under their contracts. Both the Inland Revenue and Customs & Excise regard extra payments for winning as taxable, as being made for a consideration.

The Inland Revenue view, supported by the old Irish tax case of *Wing v O'Connell* [1927] IR 84, is that presents received from racehorse owners by a jockey for winning are taxable receipts of a profession.

17.18 Pension schemes

There are special company pension schemes available for footballers, whose careers are necessarily short, so that they can receive maximum benefits at age 35. Advice should be sought on this so that every advantage is taken of the facility. In particular, the Pension Schemes Office has provided sets of model rules for football club schemes. Note that no player who is member of a club scheme may have concurrent membership of the 'Football League Limited Players Retirement and Income Scheme' or any other scheme of the club. Concurrent membership of the Football League Limited Players Benefit

Sportspeople

Scheme is, however, permitted. Similar discretion is now given to the Inland Revenue to approve retirement annuity or personal pension contracts for individuals who, because of the nature of their work, are likely to retire early, such as other professional sportspeople.

The complete list is as follows:

Type of sportsperson	*Retirement age*
Athletes (appearance and prize money)	35
Badminton player	35
Boxer	35
Cricketer	40
Cyclist	35
Downhill skier	30
Footballer (excluding Football League players in pensionable employment)	35
Golfer (tournament)	40
Jockey (flat racing)	45
Jockey (national hunt)	35
Motorcycle rider (motocross or road racing)	40
Motor racing driver	40
Rugby League player	35
Rugby League referee	50
Speedway rider	40
Squash player	35
Snooker player (WPBSA)	40
Table tennis player	35
Tennis player (including real tennis)	35
Wrestler	35

Advice should be sought on the impact (if any) of FA 2004, which comes into force from 6 April 2006.

Chapter 18 Persons in receipt of gratuities

18.1 General

There are many situations in which gratuitous payments may be made, including the payment of tips and service charges, prizes and awards. The tax treatment depends on the nature of the gratuitous payment.

18.2 Tips

The most common form of gratuitous payment is a tip. It was held that a taxi driver's tips were assessable in *Calvert v Wainwright* (1947) 27 TC 475. The principle behind the decision was that voluntary payments made in the ordinary way in return for services, over and above what someone is contractually bound to pay, as opposed to exceptional gifts made on personal grounds, are liable as income. The basis of the decision was essentially the same as those relating to other voluntary payments such as Easter offerings and footballers' benefits.

18.2.1 Retirement gratuities

Sometimes the gratuity is part of the terms of service and – for instance, if it is a retirement gratuity – varies with the length of service. In such cases, it is an earned gift and taxable as such with no relief under the golden handshake provisions.

18.2.2 PAYE on tips

The employer's obligations in relation to the payment of tips in hotel and catering establishments need to be carefully checked. Ignorance of the PAYE regulations as contained the Income Tax (Pay As You Earn) Regulations 2003 (SI 2003 No. 2682) is no defence. Where there is a sharing of 'charged tips' amongst employees, but no official *tronc* (that is, pooling arrangement) exists into which the tips are paid, the establishment is deemed to be responsible for accounting for tax on the amounts paid out. Any amounts paid out where deductions should have been made are treated as net payments and the

Persons in receipt of gratuities

employer is thus liable for tax on the grossed-up value of the net amounts paid, with penalties if an incomplete declaration is made. This liability arises even if the hotel, etc. did not charge the guest in the first place or have any influence over how the amounts were shared out.

Guidance on the tax treatment of tips can be found in Inland Revenue booklet E24, *Tips, Gratuities, Service Charges and Troncs*.

Charged tips means amounts added voluntarily by a customer to a bill settled with the establishment, but not amounts paid in cash directly to an employee. Charged tips are normally accounted for as a 'paid out' either by the cashier or from the hotel front desk and are not recorded as revenue of the establishment. They do not, however, include a compulsory service charge.

There are special PAYE regulations dealing with such tips (Income Tax (Pay As You Earn) Regulations 2003 (SI 2003 No. 2682)). Broadly, where there is an established *tronc* system not operated by the company or by an employee designated by the company, no liability on the company arises unless the inspector specifically directs.

There are several different ways of dealing with charged tips which have different consequences for the establishment.

1. The employees form their own *tronc* with a designated '*tronc* master' who registers with the inspector of taxes. The *tronc* is then responsible for operating PAYE. This also applies where a service charge is distributed through the *tronc*. However, the employer must inform the Inland Revenue of the name of the *tronc* master.

2. If an employer, business partner or official of the company that operates the business performs the role of *tronc* master , the *tronc* will not be accepted by the Inland Revenue for PAYE purposes and payments made from the *tronc* are taxed under the employer's PAYE scheme.

3. If there is a *tronc* with an independent *tronc* master but the employer is involved in the distribution of monies from the *tronc*, the responsibility for PAYE rests with the employer.

4. If the employer arranges for cash tips to be collected and distributed to staff by a trusted employee in accordance with a formula set by the employer, responsibility for PAYE rests with the employer as the employee is acting on the employer's behalf.

These alternatives apply to charged tips, or charged tips and cash tips, or a combination of service charge and additional charged or cash tips paid to the establishment. Note that if PAYE is not properly operated by a *tronc*, the inspector can then direct employers to make the PAYE deductions and thus they are liable in place of the *tronc* master. Otherwise, in the absence of such a direction, the *tronc* master has personal liability for PAYE which should have been deducted.

The authority for this is in reg. 100 of the Income Tax (Pay As You Earn) Regulations 2003 (SI 2003 No. 2682) under which where there is any failure to operate PAYE the Inland Revenue may collect from the actual employer any tax on amounts paid by the employer through the *tronc* master.

The legal problems of whether the *tronc* regulation applies or whether the employer is liable to PAYE were discussed in *Figael Ltd v Fox* [1990] STC 583. The facts of the case were complex. Essentially, tips were placed in a box and at the end of each day the tips were checked by the directors and placed in an envelope. The envelopes were put into the company's safe. The box and safe were under the control of the directors. At the end of the each week, the envelopes were removed and the tips divided by the directors between themselves and the waiters. There was no formal appointment by the company of any person to take responsibility for the arrangement and no record was kept of the tips distributed. The company claimed this was a *tronc* arrangement and the persons accountable for PAYE were the directors, not the company. It was held there was no *tronc* arrangement. The regulations should be construed in context and in their ordinary and natural meaning they did not apply where the emoluments in the form of a share of tips were paid to employees by their principal employer. The fact that there was no organised arrangement to share the tips among two or more employees was not enough to attract the regulations. There had also to be a person called the *tronc* master who did the sharing out and under the regulations that person was to be regarded as the employer. If the same person who paid the wages paid out the tips, the regulations did not come into play.

18.2.3 National Insurance contributions

The relevant legislation is contained in the Social Security (Contributions) Regulations 2001 (SI 2001 No. 1004), Sch. 3, Part X, para. 5. This states that there shall be disregarded:

> 'A payment of, or in respect of, a gratuity or offering which satisfies either of the conditions in this paragraph. The first condition is that the payment:

Persons in receipt of gratuities

> (a) is not made, directly or indirectly, by the secondary contributor; and
>
> (b) does not comprise or represent sums previously paid to the secondary contributor.
>
> The alternative condition is that the secondary contributor does not allocate the payment, directly or indirectly, to the earner.'

A *tronc* master does not have to account for National Insurance Contributions (NICs). In the following circumstances where NIC liability arises on distributions from a *tronc*, the principal employer has to account for the NICs.

1. The principal employer passes all or part of a service charge made to customers to the *tronc* for distribution to employees.
2. Tips for employees are given to the principal employer who passes them to the *tronc* with instructions on their allocation or distribution.

If cash tips are received by the employee direct, that is other than via the employer's payroll or through an organised *tronc*, the employee must declare the tips personally and is liable personally on them.

An Inland Revenue press release entitled 'Tips and Tax' (28 March 1985), disclosed that certain employees of larger well-known establishments had agreed, on being challenged, that they earned tips of up to £7,500 per annum and that the lowest agreed average tips per full-time employee at any one of the establishments investigated was £750 per annum. Consequently, the Inland Revenue have increased the restriction in waiters' code numbers to collect tax on such tips at source.

The European Court of Human Rights has ruled that tips paid by cheque or credit card belong to the employer and can be used to pay employees' wages (*Nerva v United Kingdom*). Some commentators have suggested that there could therefore now be a Class 1 liability on such tips paid by a *tronc* master where none has existed up to now.

18.3 Other gifts

An example of an unsolicited gift not assessable was a payment to a professional man as a result of an introduction he had arranged, which produced a sale of some land which was entirely unsolicited and in no way in return for any services (*Bloom v Kinder* (1958) 38 TC 77). The position was well summarised in the judgment in the Court of Appeal in the case of *Simpson v John Reynolds & Co (Insurances) Ltd* [1975] STC 271, where Russell LJ. said:

> 'The facts as it seems to me on which that question is to be answered are these. First this was a wholly unexpected and unsolicited gift. Second, it was made after the business connection had ceased. Third, the gift was in recognition of past services rendered to the client company over a long period, though not because those past services were considered to have been inadequately remunerated. Fourthly, the gift was made as a consolation for the fact that those remunerative services were no longer to be performed by the taxpayer for the donor; and, fifthly, there is no suggestion that at a future date the business connection might be renewed.'

This case followed on the case of *Carnaby, Harrower, Barharn and Prykett v Walker* (1970) 46 TC 561, where a firm of auditors received a *solatium* in addition to their normal audit fee in recognition of the fact that they had been asked to resign after many years of service. The same principle was established in the case of payments to tenants of tied houses in *Murray v Goodhews* [1978] STC 207.

There are other instances where the Inland Revenue have decided that *ex gratia* compensation is not taxable as a receipt of the trade or profession, for example, payments by building societies to their former agents. Yet in none of these cases can it be said that the loss of the agency cripples the business, although the agency is usually unique in the sense that such agents act only for one society on a full agency basis.

18.4 Prizes

Prizes are received by people carrying on a variety of professions and sometimes these cause arguments with the Inland Revenue. The basic principle again is that if a person is receiving the reward for work done – for instance, a writer entering a prize competition and writing a new work for it – the prize is assessable. If, however, the prize is something that the person does not seek to win but is given in recognition of the outstanding merit of the work which is otherwise remunerated in the normal way – for instance the Nobel Prize awarded to a scientist – and is non-recurring, or the prize is given for personal qualities, it is likely to be exempt from tax. Thus a prize given by a bank to one of its employees for passing an examination was held to be not liable for income tax (*Ball v Johnson* (1971) 47 TC 155).

However, in an ICAEW press release (PR 786 March 1990), it was reported that the Inland Revenue consider in the case of those earning £8,500 per annum or more that examination prizes are taxable. The *Ball v Johnson* case does not apply to the benefits legislation, as the later *Wicks v Firth* [1983] STC 25 decision recognised that cash could be a benefit so that anyone earning £8,500 or more is chargeable to tax on the award.

18.5 Long-service awards

The Inland Revenue do not seek to tax long-service awards made to directors and employees as testimonials to mark long service which take the form of tangible articles of reasonable cost when the relevant period of service is not less than twenty years, and no similar award has been made to the recipient within the previous ten years (ITEPA 2003, s. 323). An article is taken to be of reasonable cost where the cost to the employer does not exceed £50 (£20 before 13 June 2003) for each year of service (ITEPA 2003, s. 323(2)).

18.6 Awards under suggestion schemes

Awards under suggestion schemes made to employees will be tax free under ITEPA 2003, s. 321 where the following conditions are satisfied.

1. There is a formally constituted scheme under which suggestions are made, and it is open to all employees on equal terms.

2. The suggestion for which the award is made is outside the scope of the employee's normal duties. The test is whether, taking account of his or her experience, the employee could not reasonably have been expected to put forward such a suggestion as part of the duties of the post. Where meetings of employees are held for the purpose of putting forward suggestions, they should be regarded as part of their duties, and any consequential awards would not be within the terms of this exemption.

3. Awards may be either encouragement awards or financial benefit awards. An encouragement award is an award, other than a financial benefit award, that is made for a suggestion with intrinsic merit or showing special effort. A financial benefit award is an award for a suggestion relating to an improvement in efficiency or effectiveness which the employer decides to adopt and reasonably expects to result in financial benefit.

5. The amount of a financial benefit award cannot exceed:

(a) 50 per cent of the expected net financial benefit during the first year of implementation, or

(b) 10 per cent of the expected net financial benefit over a period of up to five years,

subject to an overriding maximum of £5,000. Where an award exceeds £5,000, the excess is not covered by this concession.

6. An exempt encouragement award cannot exceed £125.

7. The maximum exempt amounts apply per suggestion, not per employee.

8. Where a suggestion is put forward by more than one employee, the exempt award is divided between them on a reasonable basis.

18.7 Third party awards

For a number of years, a third party making such an award has been able to satisfy the income tax through a Taxed Award Scheme, a non-statutory facility which allows the third party to contract with the Revenue to discharge tax due on the value of the awards at the end of the year.

From 6 April 2000 where a third party provides workers with awards in non-cash vouchers as part of an incentive scheme, the third party will be able to pay the NICs, instead of the employer having to report and pay NIC on incentives which they do not control. In such circumstances the NIC liability for non-cash vouchers changes from Class 1 (employee and employer) to Class 1A (employer only) liability.

Chapter 19 Insurance agents

19.1 Categories of agent

There are essentially two categories of insurance agent: those who work exclusively for one company but are remunerated almost wholly by commission and usually work from home; and those who are agents for any company which is prepared to pay commission and are insurance brokers bringing together the insurer and the insured.

19.1.1 Exclusive agents

Certain insurance companies do not pay commission to outside brokers and thus conduct all their business through their own employees or agents. These agents are treated as employees for tax purposes where it is only the manner of their remuneration and the fact they do not have a place of work on their employer's premises which distinguishes them from other employees.

If such employees wish to obtain an allowance for any expenses incurred by using their homes as offices, they must obtain from their employers evidence that they are required to use their homes for the purposes of the employment, and that this will apply to all agents of the company. This ensures that it is possible to show that the expenses would have to be incurred by any employee holding that position and are not peculiar to the circumstances of the individual concerned. This then satisfies the test of allowability laid down in the case of *Ricketts v Colquhoun* (1925) 10 TC 118 that the expense must be of a sort incurred by 'each and every holder of the office'.

To claim capital allowances, the same point applies, as the person must be able to show that the plant and machinery is 'necessarily provided for use in the performance of the duties' of the employment (CAA 2001, ss. 15(1)(i) and 36).

The Inland Revenue have been reviewing the tax status of insurance agents working exclusively for one company, and in many cases their status has been changed from self-employed to employed. However, in the case of several well-known life companies where agents operate very much on their own account, providing their own car, office equipment, etc, and are generally given discretion as to the manner of carrying out their agency, the Inland

Revenue accept that the agents are self-employed. Such agents have their own areas of operation within which they service their clientele and thus their operations are similar to those of general practice doctors deriving all of their income from one source but exercising a professional skill under no supervision.

19.1.2 Other agents

Insurance brokers are assessed under Sch. D. Commission is payable as to a substantial amount when the policy is taken out and a small continuing amount every year that the premiums are paid. It is generally correct to bring in commission on a receivable rather than received basis. In most cases, agents receive a commission statement from the insurance company with the amount of commission being received at the same time, but sometimes the commission is due when the policy is effected and not rescinded at the option of the policyholder. There may then be a delay which could bridge a year end before the commission is received. However, normal tax principles of bringing in income on an entitlement basis applies. Sometimes in the case of reinsurance brokers, commission may be subject to delay and difficulty of calculation, particularly where premiums are owed by the insured who may reside overseas or even be in dispute as to the amount. In such cases, it may be possible (where entitlement to an amount is difficult to quantify) to operate on a receipts basis. The business can carry with it the right to these commissions as well as all the normal goodwill of a business. This goodwill of an insurance agent was one of the examples quoted when the original capital gains legislation was being debated. It can, of course, be the subject of a roll-over claim if the person selling the goodwill does not cease to trade and reinvests the proceeds of sale in one of the classes of eligible assets (TCGA 1992, s. 152(8)). It is debatable whether goodwill arising solely out of commission on outstanding premiums is a wasting asset for capital gains purposes. If it is, it will be a depreciating asset for roll-over relief purposes and any gain rolled over into its acquisition cost can only be held over for a maximum of ten years or until the proceeds from the sale of the assets giving rise to the claim are reinvested in a non-wasting asset (TCGA 1992, s. 154).

Note that it is reported in *Taxation* (21 November 1991) that a self-employed insurance broker has succeeded in securing capital allowances and maintenance costs for expenditure on a £150 bicycle used for business purposes. Possibly the nature of an insurance broker's work, particularly in inner city areas, makes a bicycle a sensible form of transport.

19.2 Casual insurance commission

Individuals often hold agencies with one or more insurance companies and receive varying amounts of commission. If the individual is otherwise employed, the commission may well be assessed under Case VI.

The above practice is reinforced by the case of *Hugh v Rogers* (1958) 38 TC 270 where the taxpayer held a dormant agency with an insurance company. He paid reduced premiums after deduction of commission on his own policies. In addition, he introduced some pensions business from the company of which he was secretary. For that introduction, he received £750 commission. The Inland Revenue originally claimed that either the commission was taxable as an emolument of his employment, or under Sch. D, Case VI. The Inland Revenue then dropped their contentions under the old Schedule E (now tax on employment income under ITEPA 2003) and it seems this conclusion still holds good under the benefits in kind legislation in ITEPA 2003, ss. 63–69 because the commission was not received by reason of his employment but rather by reason of the agency. However, the judge said: 'There is no reason to doubt that the commission under an agency agreement is a subject matter for tax under Case VI, although it was a one-off payment with little or no services being performed by the agent'.

Sometimes the commission relates to premiums on policies effected by individuals in respect of their own insurance or agents give someone the benefit of their commission. The risks inherent in informal arrangements were under-lined in the case of *Way v Underdown (No 2)* [1975] STC 425. In that case, commissions passed on under a friendly agreement by an agent of an insurance company to the person on whose behalf he had effected the policy were held to be assessable on him as he had become entitled to them. *Obiter* even if there had been a contractually binding obligation with the policy-holder to pass on the commission, he would still have been assessable as the person receiving the commission. However, where premiums were paid net of the agent's commission, which was thus effectively waived to the insurance company by the insured, the agent was not assessable on such commission as he had never become entitled to it or received it (ICTA 1988, s. 59(1)).

In November 1997 the Inland Revenue issued revised statement of practice, SP 4/97 dealing with the tax treatment of rebated commissions and also cash-backs and discounts. The text of the statement of practice is reproduced below.

'SP 4/97 (27 November 1997) Taxation of commission, cashbacks and discounts

Introduction

1. This Statement sets out the views of the Board of Inland Revenue of the correct treatment for tax purposes of commission, cashbacks and discounts. The passing on to customers by intermediaries or agents of the whole or part of commission and the payment of cashbacks or the granting of discounts by the providers of goods or services has become increasingly common. These arrangements have given rise to considerable uncertainty about the tax consequences for both customers and intermediaries which previous Statements of Practice were unable to resolve. This Statement sets out the Revenue's practice in applying the law to these arrangements and in particular it confirms that most customers are not liable to tax on commission, cashbacks and discounts.

2. Sections A and B (paras 3–10) set out both the different types of receipt and arrangements covered by the Statement and when these receipts are not liable to tax.

Section C is concerned with the liability to tax under the different cases of Schedule D. It sets out the circumstances in which commission, cashbacks and similar inducements will be taken into account as receipts —

- in computing taxable profits from a trade or profession under Case I or II of Schedule D (paras 11–15);

- in computing other taxable annual profits under Case VI (para 19).

It also provides guidance on the deductibility of commission etc passed on to the customer

- in computing profits under Case I or II (para 17); and

- in computing profits under Case VI (para 21).

The rest of the Statement is concerned with the tax treatment of persons receiving or becoming entitled to commission or a cashback under —

- Schedule E, covered in section D (paras 23–32). (The deductibility of commission passed on to the customer and the operation of PAYE are dealt with in paras 33 and 34 respectively);

- capital gains tax, covered in section E (para 35); and

- life insurance and personal pensions, covered in section F (paras 36–41).

A Scope

3. This Statement covers —

- Commission (meaning a sum paid by the providers of goods, investments or services to agents or intermediaries as reward for the introduction of business). Sometimes, commission is passed on to the customer or to some other person by the agent or intermediary, or the customer may receive commission direct from the provider of the goods or services if that provider would normally pay commission to an agent or intermediary.

- Cashbacks (meaning lump sums received by a customer as an inducement for entering into a transaction for the purchase of goods, investments or services and received as a direct consequence of having entered into that transaction (for example a mortgage)). The payer may be either the provider of the goods, investments or services or another party with an interest in ensuring that the transaction takes place.

- Discounts (meaning that the purchaser's obligation is to pay less than the full purchase price of goods, services or investments, other than as a result of any entitlement to commission or a cashback).

4. It deals with liabilities to income or corporation tax under the rules of Schedule D, Schedule E, capital gains tax or the chargeable events legislation (that is, the rules for taxing gains on certain insurances) and with tax relief in respect of contributions to personal pension schemes.

5. It is not practicable to cover in this Statement every situation that may arise. There will be individual cases which do not fall squarely within its terms where the taxation consequences may be different. For example, where inducements or rewards offered to customers take the form of a series of payments (and are not simply capital sums calculated in advance but paid in instalments) they may be taxable as income in the recipients' hands. It is beyond the scope of the Statement to give a view on all such cases. They will have to be dealt with on an individual basis and the taxation consequences in each case will depend on the precise nature of the arrangements entered into.

B General

6. The Statement covers the main circumstances in which commission or a cashback is likely to be passed between the parties to a transaction. It deals with arrangements where:

- commission or a cashback is —
- received

- netted-off (meaning that the purchaser's entitlement to commission or a cashback is set off against the obligation to pay the full purchase price for goods or services so that only the net amount is paid); or
- invested or applied in some way for the benefit of the purchaser;
- or where
- a discounted purchase price is paid; or
- extra value is added to the goods, investments or services obtained for the purchase price where there is no entitlement to commission or a cashback. An example is the allocation of bonus units in an investment or of a different class of unit where the purchase price remains unchanged. However, where the added value represents a return on the investment, the tax treatment may differ from that dealt with in this statement.

7. In general, ordinary retail customers purchasing goods, investments or services at arm's length will not be liable to income or capital gains tax in respect of any commission, discounts or cashbacks received by them. For example, an ordinary retail customer who, when purchasing a car, negotiates to receive part of the commission earned on the sale by the salesperson will not be liable to income or capital gains tax in respect of that commission.

8. The Statement outlines some circumstances in which receipts are treated as tax-free, or in which payments qualify for tax relief. However, the legal analysis, and consequent tax treatment, will not necessarily follow that outlined in the Statement where the receipts or payments in question form part of a scheme of tax avoidance. Similarly, the treatment outlined in the Statement may not apply where the recipient of a commission, cashback or other benefit is party to an arrangement under which the purchase price for goods, investments or services has been increased.

9. The tax treatment of the person receiving or becoming entitled to the commission or cashback will be considered separately from the treatment of the person paying the commission or cashback.

10. Unless otherwise indicated, all statutory references are to the Income and Corporation Taxes Act 1988.

C Schedule D

Cases I and II — receipts

11. Where the provision of the services remunerated by commission etc. is on a sufficiently commercial, regular and organised basis to amount to a trade or profession, commission and similar sums to which the trader or professional person becomes entitled will be receipts from that source. A

Casual insurance commission

self-employed insurance or travel agent would normally be in that position.

12. The fact that some or all of the commission etc. received by a trader or professional person in the circumstances described in para 11 is passed on to customers does not cause it to cease to be a receipt of that business. See para 17 below regarding the corresponding deduction.

13. Furthermore, commission etc., which would have been taxable if it had actually been received by a trader or professional person, does not necessarily cease to be taxable merely because it goes directly to the customer without first being received by the trader. For example, commission may be passed on by way of a reduction in regular insurance or pension policy premiums or by the allocation of extra value (eg units) to the policy by the insurance company. In those circumstances, the commission remains a taxable business receipt so long as the trader or professional person had an enforceable legal right to receive that commission which he subsequently forgoes in favour of the customer (but as indicated at para 17 below a deduction may be available in respect of the amount forgone).

14. Where the trader or professional person neither receives the commission etc. nor has any such entitlement to it, there will be no taxable receipt in respect of that commission. Thus commission or a cashback payable to a trader or professional person within the first bullet of para 6 is a taxable business receipt but a discount or added value within the last two bullets of para 6 above will not be a taxable receipt.

15. Commission etc. receivable as an incident in the carrying on of any other business taxable under Cases I and II of Schedule D should be taken into account in computing the profits of the business. For example, the following items should be taken into account in computing the profits of the business —

    - insurance commission to which an accountant becomes entitled in the course of the profession;

    - commission received in respect of business insurance contracts taken out by, say, a grocer (for example, if the premium paid has been reduced by the commission, by deducting only the net sum);

    - a cashback received on a car purchased for business purposes (normally by reducing the cost of the car for the purposes of capital allowances).

16. In strict law commission earned for business introduced in the course of a trade or profession remains a taxable business receipt even where it is derived from a private transaction funded by the trader or professional person. For example, a travel agent may obtain commission for booking a package holiday for himself and his family with a tour operator whose

holidays he sells to the public. But, by concession, there may be excluded from taxable profits so much of any such commission as does not exceed the maximum amount the trader or professional person could reasonably have been expected to pass on to an arm's length customer buying the same services or product.

Case I and II — deductions

17. Commission etc. passed on to a customer, or otherwise forgone in the circumstances described in para 13 above, as an inducement to enter into a transaction is deductible if it is laid out wholly and exclusively for the purpose of the trade or profession. The statutory test is very likely to be satisfied if the customer required the commission to be passed on as a condition of entering into the transaction or if the transaction was one between independent parties acting at arm's length.

Presentation of information in tax return and/or accounts

18. This paragraph applies to commission etc. which is passed on other than by a separate payment and is to be regarded as a taxable receipt as described in para 13 above. In these circumstances, the calculation of the gross commission received and the amount passed on may not be a straightforward matter. Subject to the conditions described below, the commission applied in this way may be excluded from both commission income and commission expenses in the intermediary's tax return. Those conditions are that either the customer required the commission to be passed on as a condition of entering into the transaction or the transaction was one between independent parties acting at arm's length (see para 17 above).

Case VI — receipts

19. Commission etc. may sometimes be received by a person as consideration for introducing a customer to a supplier of goods or services, other than in circumstances where the commission would be taxable as income under Case I or II of Schedule D (see para 11 above) or under Schedule E (see para 25 below). Subject to para 20 below, if the commission arises under an enforceable contract, it should be brought into account as a taxable receipt in calculating the profit from the transaction under Case VI of Schedule D.

20. A sum, however described, which is received by an ordinary retail customer as consideration for the purchase by the customer of goods or services should not be regarded as a taxable receipt in computing profits under Case VI. This is the case whether the payer is the provider of the goods or services or another party with an economic interest in ensuring the transaction takes place.

Case VI — deductions

21. Where, in the circumstances described in para 19 above, some or all of the commission etc. in question is passed on to the customer, a deduction is due where the customer requires the commission to be passed on as a condition of entering into the transaction or where for some other reason the payment is necessary to earn the commission.

Building society distributions

22. Cashbacks received from building societies are not required as distributions in respect of investments for the purposes of the Income Tax (Building Societies) (Dividends and Interest) Regulations, SI 1990/2231. Building societies are not therefore required to deduct tax from mortgage cashbacks by virtue of those Regulations.

D Schedule E

23. The word 'employee' means office holder or an employee. The word 'emolument' defined in s 131 includes such things as salaries, fees, wages and profits.

24. It is a question of fact whether a sum within the scope of this Statement is received in the capacity of employee/office holder or in some other capacity such as the purchaser of a policy, goods or services. This part of the Statement covers only liability arising on emoluments from employment and liability under the benefits legislation (that is employees earning at the rate of £8,500 or more a year and most directors). In some circumstances liability to tax under Schedule E may arise under other provisions, such as the vouchers legislation or legislation dealing with termination and change payments. Those provisions should be considered even where there is no liability under the provisions considered here.

Commission arising from, and discounts in connection with, goods, investments or services sold to third parties

25. Employees who receive, or are entitled to receive, commission (as emoluments) from their employment in respect of goods, investments or services sold to third parties are assessable under Schedule E on the full amount of that commission. This is so whether or not the commission is passed on by them to the customer and whether the commission is paid by the employer or anyone else.

26. Where an employee consents or directs that commission which is due from his or her employment should be either paid to the customer or anyone else, or invested for his or her own benefit or the benefit of the customer or anyone else, that employee is assessable under Schedule E

on that commission (but see para 33 for circumstances where a deduction will be admissible).

27. Where the purchaser pays a discounted price, there is no Schedule E liability on the employer if —

- the purchaser is not a member of the employee's family or household; and
- neither the employee nor any member of his or her family or household receives anything (money or benefits) in consequence.

If the purchaser is a member of the employee's family or household, the provision of goods or services at a discount may constitute a taxable benefit for the employee. However, where the discounted price paid covers the cost of those goods or services to the provider, there will be no taxable benefit.

In all cases the cost of providing goods or services is a question of fact. But where the sale is of an insurance policy there will be no taxable benefit if the discount is no greater than the sum of —

- the commission that would otherwise have been paid by the insurer on selling the policy to the third party; and
- the anticipated profit on the policy.

Commission and discounts in respect of an employee's purchase of goods, investments or services from the employer

28. Paragraphs 29 and 30 below are concerned with cases of commission arising from employment. Where a commission is available to an employee on the same basis as it is available to members of the general public, it will not arise from the employment. Paragraph 31 is concerned with tax charges under the benefits legislation. Where the commission or the net or discounted amount referred to within that paragraph is available on the same basis to members of the general public, no benefit will result.

29. Employees who receive commission (from employment) in respect of their own purchase of goods, investments or services from the employer are liable to tax under Schedule E on the full amount of that commission. Where such a commission is placed at the employee's disposal but the employee requests, permits or is required to accept that the commission is applied in some way for his or her benefit, the commission remains liable to tax under Schedule E.

30. Where an employee does not receive and is not entitled to receive, or to have applied for his or her benefit, a cash commission, but does receive from employment a right which has a monetary value, a liability will arise on that value under Schedule E because that right is an emolument.

An example is the case where an additional amount is invested in an employee's investment and that investment can be disposed of or otherwise turned to account.

31. Where an employee within the scope (see para 24 above) of the benefits legislation receives a commission from, or pays a net or discounted amount to, the employer in respect of his or her purchase of goods, investments or services, the employee will be liable to tax on the benefit that has been provided. The charge to tax upon a net or discounted amount is calculated following the principles described in para 27 above. The charge upon a commission, not otherwise chargeable to tax, is calculated by reference to the cost of its provision and will typically be the amount paid.

Services etc. provided by persons other than the employer in return for commission, or for a net or discounted purchase price, may give rise to a charge calculated in the same way if the benefit is provided by reason of the employment.

Cashbacks

32. Where an employee receives a cashback from his or her employer or a third party on the same basis as is available to members of the general public, Schedule E liability will not arise if the cashback is received under a contract with the employer or third party dissociated from the contract of employment, and the employee gives fair value for the cashback under that contract or by entering into some other contract with the employer or third party. The cashback will then be neither an emolument from employment (within s 19) nor a benefit (within s 154).

However, if in such circumstances the cashback is provided gratuitously and is received from the employee's employer, liability under the benefits legislation must be considered.

Deductions

33. Where commission etc. within the scope of this Statement is assessable under Schedule E, a claim for deduction in respect of commission shared with, passed on to, or invested for the benefit of, some other party will be admissible if the employee is obliged to expend the sum wholly, exclusively and necessarily in performing the duties of the office or employment. Such an obligation is likely to exist when the transaction falls within the normal framework of the employer's business and is a transaction between independent parties acting at arm's length.

PAYE

34. PAYE applies where commission etc. is paid to an employee or on his or her behalf if it is assessable under Schedule E. This includes amounts relating to commission invested on behalf of the employee if the amount of the commission is taxable. Where commission or other taxable income is provided in the form of tradable assets rather than cash, PAYE applies under s 203F.

E Capital gains tax

35. A cashback does not derive from a chargeable asset for capital gains tax purposes. No chargeable gain therefore arises on receipt of the payment. (A cashback does not include a cash payment by a building society to members etc. on take-over by, or conversion to, a bank; or by other mutual organisations such as insurance companies or friendly societies on demutualisation.)

F Life insurance and personal pensions

Qualifying life insurance policies

36. Where commission in respect of a policy holder's own qualifying life insurance policy is received, netted off or invested, that policy will not be disqualified as a result of entitlement to that commission if the contract under which commission arises is separate from the contract of insurance. In practice, the Revenue will not seek to read two contracts as one in a way that would lead to the loss of qualifying policy status.

37. Where a policy holder pays a discounted premium in respect of his or her own policy, the premium payable under the policy will be the discounted premium. It is this amount that must be used for the purposes of establishing whether the relevant qualifying rules are met.

Calculation of chargeable event gains in respect of life insurance policies, capital redemption policies and life annuity contracts

38. Chargeable event gains are computed by reference to the premiums or lump sum consideration paid. The amount paid will be interpreted as follows —

    - where a policy holder pays a gross premium and receives commission in respect of that policy, the chargeable event gain is calculated using the gross amount paid without taking the commission received into account;

    - where an amount of commission is received or due under an enforceable legal right and subsequently invested in the policy, that amount is included as a premium paid when calculating the chargeable event gain;

- where a policy holder nets off commission from an insurer in respect of his or her own policy from the gross amount of premium payable and the commission is not taxable as income on the policy holder, the chargeable event gain is calculated using the net amount paid to the insurer;

- where a policy holder pays a discounted premium, the chargeable event gain is calculated using the discounted amount of premium paid;

- where extra value is added to the policy by the insurer (for example by allocation of bonus units), the premium for the purpose of calculating the chargeable event gain is the amount paid by the policy holder without taking the extra value into account.

Tax relief in respect of personal pension contributions

39. Tax relief for contributions to personal pension schemes is due in respect of 'a contribution paid by an individual'. The amount of the contribution will be interpreted as follows where the contract under which the commission arises is separate from the personal pension scheme contract —

    - where a contributor pays a gross contribution and receives commission in respect of that contribution, tax relief is given on the gross amount paid without taking the commission received into account;

    - where an amount of commission is received by, or is due under an enforceable legal right to, the contributor and subsequently invested in the personal pension that gave rise to the commission, tax relief is given on that amount;

    - where a contributor deducts commission in respect of his or her own pension contribution from the gross amount payable, relief is due on the net amount paid;

    - where a contributor pays discounted contributions, tax relief is due on the discounted amount paid;

    - where extra value is added to the policy by the insurer (for example by allocation of bonus units), relief is due on the amount paid by the contributor without taking the extra value into account.

40. If commission were to be rebated to the contributor under the same contract as the personal pension contract, this would be an unapprovable benefit (since it would involve leakage of the pension fund to the

member) which would jeopardise the tax-approved status of the arrangement.

41. The consequences of paying commission on transfers between tax-approved pension schemes may be different from those outlined if such payment is effectively a benefit not authorised by the rules of the pension scheme. Alternatively, the misrepresentation as an annual premium of any premium applied to new pensions business so that a higher rate of rebated commission is generated will call into question the bona fides of the pension arrangement and jeopardise its approval from inception.

19.3 Commission receivable on indemnity terms

In November 1992 the Inland Revenue issued Revenue Interpretation 30 *Insurance agents' commission receivable on indemnity terms* the text of which is reproduced below.

> 'Frequently, when an insurance company accepts a new policy the selling agent becomes immediately entitled to most or all of the total commission due on the policy. That commission is calculated on the assumption that the policy will not be allowed to lapse at an early date. If, however, the policy lapses within a specified period the agent may have to repay part of the initial commission received. When should commission which is potentially repayable be recognised as income for tax purposes? And is a provision in respect of the potential liability to repay allowable?
>
> The time at which such commission is recognised as income for tax purposes depends on the agency contract terms. Under most contracts, however, the agent has done substantially all the work required by the contract when the policy is sold. For instance, the agent is usually entitled at that point to retain the initial commission should the policy run the required term even if the agency is terminated. In all such cases the full initial commission receivable should be recognised as income in the accounting period in which the policy is sold (*IRC v Gardner Mountain and D'Ambrumenil* [(1945) 29 TC 69]).
>
> Where the commission is recognised as income at the outset, a reasonably accurate provision will be accepted for the contingent liability to repay the commission should the policy lapse. A proper valuation rather than a "speculative estimate" is required (*Owen v Southern Railway of Peru* [36 TC 602, 634]). For instance the calculation of the provision should take into account the lapse rate amongst customers and the proportion of commission that usually has to be repaid on the relevant policy.'

The accounting treatment of indemnity commissions was considered in *Robertson v CIR* (SpC 309), [1997] SSCD 282. R was a self-employed insurance agent for Allied Dunbar. His agency contract provided for the payment of initial commission on each policy sold by him at a percentage rate of the premiums payable on each policy. His right to full initial commission depended on the policies being maintained for up to four years but a proportion of the initial commission was not repayable even if the policy lapsed. In common with other life offices Allied Dunbar operated a scheme whereby certain of its agents could apply to be paid on a basis known as 'indemnity terms'. Under indemnity terms, all or part of the initial commission was paid to the agent before the periodic premiums were received from the assured from which the agent's entitlement would normally accrue. The taxpayer applied for indemnity terms on 14 June 1988 and was paid on that basis between 1 July 1988 and 1 January 1993. The advances in 1992–93 were sought and paid at a rate of 50 per cent discounted at 19 per cent per month and made on the basis that the appropriate proportion would be repaid if the policy lapsed. In R's accounts for the years ended 10 April 1989 and 1990 the advances made to him were treated as taxable in the year of receipt. R's accounts for the year ended 10 April 1991, however, excluded that part of the advances of initial commission which related to premiums which had not been received by Allied Dunbar by the year end. R was assessed under Schedule D, Case I for the year of assessment 1992–93 on the basis that the advances should be brought into account in full in the year of receipt. R appealed, contending that the advances should only be brought into account to the extent that his entitlement to them was vested with no potential liability to repay. The Revenue contended that the full advances were to be brought into account, since R had performed the work to earn the commission in the year of receipt and on average only 13 per cent of the policies lapsed. R's expert considered, *inter alia*, that R, as a sole trader with a single source of income, was justified in preparing his accounts for the year ended 10 April 1991 on the deferred accruals basis by the prudence concept in Statement of Standard Accounting Practice (SSAP) 2, which provided that revenue and profits were recognised by inclusion in the profit and loss account only when realised in the form of cash or other assets the ultimate realisation of which could be assessed with reasonable certainty. The Revenue's expert agreed that the deferred accruals basis adopted by R was acceptable, but he preferred the 'up-front' method of accounting for agent's commission based on the fundamental accounting concept of accrual that revenue and costs should be matched so far as possible, such that advances were recognised when received subject to any necessary provision for the lapses of policies.

The High Court held that there was no rule of law as to when receipts should be brought into account. It was well settled that, in relation to the framing of a profit and loss account for tax purposes, the ordinary principles of commercial accounting had to be used except insofar as any specific statutory provision otherwise required. Since both the up-front method and the deferred accruals method were acceptable, it was necessary to determine the correct principle of commercial accountancy to be applied in the instant case. The payments by Allied Dunbar to R on indemnity terms were advances of commission, which R had received as consideration for his services, subject to a discount because payment had been accelerated. R had adopted an acceptable method of accounting in full for the advance payments in the years of receipt prior to the year ended 10 April 1991, since it had been unnecessary to include a provision for lapsed policies in view of the wide margin between the 50 per cent of initial commission advanced and the 87 per cent of policies expected not to lapse. In the year ended 10 April 1991, in the light of the evidence, it could have been assessed with reasonable certainty at the time of the advances whether the 50 per cent of commission advanced had been realised. The prudence concept did not therefore preclude the use of the up-front method in the instant case, although R was a sole trader. Moreover, since most of R's expenditure in relation to policies issued had been incurred prior to issue, the up-front method matched revenue and costs more closely than the deferred accruals method in accordance with the accruals concept as stated in SSAP 2. The correct principle of commercial accounting practice to be applied in the light of the facts and circumstances of the instant case was therefore the 'up-front' method, whereby advances were recognised in full in the accounts for the period in which they were received (see p 291 d, and p 292 f, *post*). Dictum of Lord Reid in *BSC Footwear Ltd (formerly Freeman, Hardy & Willis Ltd) v Ridgway (Inspector of Taxes)* (1969) 47 TC 495 at 524, Sir John Pennycuick V-C in *Odeon Associated Theatres Ltd v Jones (Inspector of Taxes)* (1970) 48 TC 257 at 273 and Warner J in *Symons (Inspector of Taxes) v Weeks* [1983] STC 195 at 237 applied. *IRC v Gardner Mountain & D'Ambrumenil* (1945) 29 TC 69 considered.

Accordingly, R's appeal would be dismissed.

Chapter 20 Trawler crew, river and sea pilots

20.1 Introduction

Trawlers from such ports as Hull, Grimsby, Fleetwood and Aberdeen used to form the bulk of the UK fishing industry, and the inshore vessels operating from smaller ports were relatively insignificant. Nowadays, the picture is very different. With Icelandic waters closed to British fishers, and many other countries imposing strict territorial limits, the distant-water trawler fleet has declined dramatically, while the inshore fleet has expanded to form the greater part of the UK fishing industry.

20.2 Employed or self-employed?

20.2.1 Trawler crew

Generally, trawlers used to be owned by fishing companies or sometimes a partnership of fishing company and skipper. Where skippers had a capital stake in the fishing vessel, they were regarded as being self-employed. Crew usually had the status of employees (see *Boyd Line v Pitts* [1986] ICR 244).

20.2.2 Share fishing

Share fishing is the pattern most commonly found in Scotland. Boats are owned by partnerships consisting typically of the skipper and one or two of the crew. The fishing companies may help to finance the purchase of the vessel and often have shares in the vessel, but this is usually a minority interest.

The modern fishing vessel operating from Scottish ports has a crew of between six and ten, all of whom are engaged as share fishers. The proceeds of each fishing trip are first shared between the vessel and the crew so that if the net proceeds of the trip are, for example, £32,000, a crew of eight would receive £2,000 each, regardless of any other interest in the vessel they may have, with the remaining £16,000 going to the boat's account. It is presumably because of these mutual arrangements that the Inland Revenue accept that share fishers are self-employed.

299

Share fishers are treated as self-employed for National Insurance (NI) purposes, but any Class 4 National Insurance Contributions (NICs) for which they are liable are recorded on a deduction working sheet and treated for accounting purposes as Class 1 NICs. Share fishers are often paid jobseeker's allowance for odd days ashore at whatever port the vessel may be berthed. Normal commencing or ceasing of a claim does not usually apply, nor does lay-off or short-time working. A share fisher's taxable benefit is reported on Form P181 either at 5 April or earlier if the claim closes.

Share fishermen pay a special rate of Class 2 NICs. The weekly rate is £2.70 for 2004–05. The special rate of Class 2 NICs (different from the standard rate generally paid by the self-employed – £2.05 for 2004–05.), takes into account the fact that (on top of state retirement pension, widow's benefits, incapacity benefit and maternity allowance) share fishers can claim jobseeker's allowance which is not available to those who pay standard rate Class 2 NICs. Share fishers may also of course have to pay Class 4 NICs if the taxable profits of their business exceed a certain level.

A special voluntary savings scheme with Barclays has been launched by the fishing industry, with help from the Revenue. A fisher can decide to have money deducted from earnings and paid directly into a special interest-bearing account with Barclays. That money will be used to pay his or her tax and Class 4 NI liability. The fisher will still have to pay Class 2 NI contributions separately. This is a scheme similar to one that has been working successfully in Scotland for about ten years, involving 98 per cent of Scottish share fishers.

PAYE under Scheme A is adopted on the rare occasions a share fisher produces a Form P45(3).

There are other aspects of a share fisher's working arrangements which are not usually characteristic of the self-employed. For example, while at sea, share fishers work entirely under the direction of the skipper and/or mate and, unless they have a share in the vessel, risk no capital. However, the level of their income depends entirely on the results of the fishing venture, and there is authority for their self-employed status in the case of *CIR v Francis West* (1950) 31 TC 402.

20.2.3 English ports

Following the Anglo-Icelandic 'cod war', English fishing ports became severely depressed. The remaining industry consists mainly of smaller vessels suitable for inshore fishing, most of which are probably crewed by their owners.

Note that a Press Release of 29 October 1987 confirmed that UK fishing licences qualify for roll-over relief. These licences (granted to enable the UK to conform with European Community legislation) represent the right to catch a certain quantity of fish. They are treated as goodwill for capital gains tax purposes and hence qualify for roll-over relief and, in appropriate circumstances, retirement relief.

Following representations from fishing organisations and others for capital gains tax roll-over relief to be given for fish quota, in March 1999 the Inland Revenue announced a relaxation of the capital gains tax rules. The sale of a fishing vessel can include the vessel, the waiver of a licence entitlement, a 'track record' and the fish quota. Roll-over relief is already available for the vessel and the licence. It is proposed that the track record be treated as if it were goodwill. To complete the picture, fish quota, which is not, and never has been, treated as goodwill, is now a qualifying asset.

20.3 Retirement age

The normal retirement age for employees in company schemes and for the purposes of retirement annuity contracts is 55 for both distant water and inshore fishers. However, the personal pension provisions in ICTA 1988, s. 634(2) bring the general lower retirement age down to 50.

Advice should be sought on the impact (if any) of FA 2004, which comes into force from 6 April 2006.

20.4 Special clothing

The Inland Revenue recognise that it is impracticable to determine a flat-rate expenses deduction for clothing and tools applicable to all fishers, mainly because conditions vary from port to port and there is no trade union representing the majority of such fishers. Where appropriate, a flat-rate expenses deduction for these fishers may be negotiated with their local association or trade union.

20.5 Capital allowances

20.5.1 Free depreciation

Free depreciation is the facility available to ship owners either to claim the full writing-down allowance due for the period in question or to postpone all or part of it to a later period. This facility used to be available only in respect of first-year allowances on new ships. However, following the abolition of first-year allowances from 1 April 1986, and the introduction of the short-life asset provisions, the option of free depreciation was extended to writing down allowances and to expenditure on second-hand ships (CAA 2001, ss. 127 and 128). The Inland Revenue seem to accept that any vessel that can propel itself, as opposed to being towed, is regarded as a 'ship' for the purposes of free depreciation.

Where free depreciation is claimed, the amount of the allowance to be given must be specified by the person to whom the allowance is made. Where fishers act in partnership, the Inland Revenue regard their boat as an asset of the trade carried on by that partnership. As it is the partnership, therefore, that has an entitlement to capital allowances, the partnership must make a joint decision regarding capital allowances and free depreciation. The total allowances claimed are then allocated among the partners by reference to their individual shares in the boat. This also applies to any corporate members of a partnership.

Those wishing to defer claiming any part of the allowance must specify in a notice to the inspector of taxes, not later than two years after the end of the chargeable period, the amount that they wish to defer. The deferred allowance, when claimed, then ranks as an allowance for the period in which it is given, and is thus available to create a loss in that period for the purposes of set-off against other income of the same or the following year.

The amount of free depreciation claimed should be decided by reference to the trader's income for the year. It is possible to defer claiming all of it on a ship, even until after the ship has been sold and replaced with another ship, as the allowance may be claimed for any subsequent period in which the person carries on the trade. The allowances postponed have, however, to be brought in calculating the balancing adjustment. If there is little income in the period of sale, it may be better to reserve claiming any balance of the free depreciation on the ship sold until later, when income is higher.

20.5.2 'Depooling'

The legislation provides for the 'depooling' of expenditure on ships as well as for the postponement (by election) of writing-down allowances on ships. This does not apply in certain leasing situations.

Each ship is assumed to be used for a separate notional trade. The effect of this is that a balancing charge on one ship cannot be offset directly against the written-down value of another ship. When a ship is sold or scrapped, a balancing allowance or charge is calculated but is not actually allowed or charged unless the actual trade ceases. Instead it is added to or deducted from the shipowner's main pool of expenditure qualifying for capital allowances.

Further options available to the shipowner are as follows.

1. Include any expenditure on the ship in the pool from the outset.
2. Transfer the ship to the pool part way through its life.
3. Transfer part of any expenditure (or part of the written-down value) to the pool.

In the case of 1 above, no election to postpone allowances can be made and the normal capital allowances rules apply.

20.5.3 Roll-over claims

The legislation in CAA 2001, ss. 135–136 allows a shipowner to defer the balancing charge in the main pool which arises from the disposal of a qualifying ship. Not all balancing charges on ships can be deferred — only balancing charges arising on qualifying ships as defined in s. 33E. This is known as roll-over and the balancing charge is rolled over into the cost of new shipping the shipowner acquires. The legislation was introduced by FA 1995 and amended by FA 1996 to let a shipowner which is a member of a group and which disposes of a qualifying ship, roll over the balancing charge which arises on that ship into the cost of new shipping acquired by other members of the group.

When a balancing charge is rolled over it is not assessed when it arises, but is deferred. This is how the deferral is done. An amount equal to the part of the balancing charge in the general pool which arises from the disposal of the old ship is treated as qualifying expenditure in the general pool. This cancels out the balancing charge when it arises. When a new ship against whose cost the balancing charge is rolled over is acquired the same amount (the part of the balancing charge in the general pool arising from the disposal of the old ship) is treated as a disposal value in the single ship pool for that new ship. This reduces the expenditure qualifying for allowances in the single ship pool for the new ship so that the balancing charge is collected as reduced allowances are given on the new ship. For example, suppose that a balancing charge of £60,000 is rolled over against a new ship costing £100,000. The £100,000 cost of the new ship is put into a single ship pool in the usual way. The balancing charge of £60,000 is treated as a disposal value in that single ship pool and is deducted from the qualifying expenditure of £100,000. This means that writing-down allowances are given on £40,000 rather than £100,000.

When there is a disposal event, CAA 2001, s. 62 restricts the disposal value to the capital expenditure incurred. If the ship against which a balancing charge has been rolled over is sold, the s. 62 restriction on disposal value is based on the original cost of the ship and not the cost less the balancing charge rolled over. For example, if a balancing charge of £60,000 is rolled over against a new ship costing £100,000, the disposal value restriction in s. 62 is £100,000 not £40,000.

20.6 Partnerships

20.6.1 Partnership changes

Where there is a change in the shares in a vessel or a change of boat but no change in partners, it is the Inland Revenue's view that there is no cessation for the purposes of ICTA 1988, s. 113. In such circumstances, any payments made or received in respect of shares changing hands are ignored for capital allowances purposes, but the allocation of written-down value between the partners is revised. No balancing charge arises.

However, where a change in vessel involves a change in the method of fishing, it is sometimes possible to claim that a new trade has commenced. This may make possible a claim under ICTA 1988, s. 381, which can include the capital allowances available on the new vessel. As such new vessels can cost anything up to £2 million, even writing-down allowances can create a substantial loss claim and a worthwhile repayment with supplement.

It is therefore advisable to ensure that changes in partnership and vessel do not occur simultaneously where continuation treatment is being sought. There should be a period of trading between the changes to establish continuity.

20.6.2 Partnerships including a company

The Inland Revenue follows the guidelines listed below in dealing with a partnership that includes a company.

1. Capital allowances due to the company are computed by reference to the accounting period of the boat partnership, and should be allocated on a strictly *pro rata* basis in accordance with the company's share in the partnership, following the case of *Lewis v CIR* (1933) 18 TC 174, ie the company cannot claim the capital allowances at a different rate from that of the individual partners.
2. Changes in the individual members of the partnership will be dealt with as at **20.6.1** above, without reference to the position of the company.
3. If a company sells part of its share in the boat, the sale price is set against the written-down value and either a balancing charge raised or a reduced allowance given.
4. If the company leaves the partnership, there is a balancing adjustment by reference to the sale price and the written-down value of its share.

20.7 River and sea pilots

20.7.1 General

Such pilots can be self-employed. However, following ICTA 1988, s. 607, all contributions to a pilot's benevolent fund established under s. 15(1)(i) of the Pilotage Act 1983 (or any scheme supplementing or replacing any such fund) may, if the Board approves the fund, count as contributions under an approved pension scheme as if the pilot were an employee. Consequently all contributions, from the time that approval is given by the Pension Schemes Office, are, subject (presumably) to the usual limits laid down for employees' contributions, allowed as a trading expense for tax purposes in the same way as the contributions of general medical practitioners and dentists. The pilots are then treated as holding a pensionable office or employment for the purposes of the retirement annuity and personal pension scheme rules, and thus are no longer able to make such payments.

Advice should be sought on the impact (if any) of FA 2004, which comes into force from 6 April 2006.

20.7.2 Compensation payments by Trinity House

Some freelance sea pilots in certain areas have had their earnings from Trinity House reduced or terminated, following the increasing use of its own boats and pilots by Trinity House, and *ex gratia* compensation payments have been made by Trinity House to such pilots. Where the Trinity House business accounted for a large proportion of the pilot's business, it is likely that the payments are exempt from tax, following the principles outlined in *Simpson v John Reynolds & Co (Insurances) Ltd* (1975) 49 TC 693 and *Murray v Goodhews* (1977) 52 TC 86.

Chapter 21 Private schools, higher education institutions, teachers, etc

21.1 Definition of a charity

Many schools and university colleges are recognised as charities. In *CIR v Pemsel* (1891) 3 TC 53 a charity was defined as including a body existing for the furtherance of education. In general, where the education is available to children generally and is not confined to particular categories of children or is not of a specialist kind (for instance in a narrow field of technical education), charitable status is given for tax purposes.

21.2 Public schools

If a school is a public school, that is in the original sense of the term open to all entrants, it will be accepted as a charity. It need not be wholly supported by charity to rank as a public school. A number of factors have been held to be indicative that a school is a public school and thus a charity. These are the following.

1. Part of the income is used for providing scholarships.
2. The foundation of the school is perpetual. Although the absence of such a foundation proved fatal in *Birkenhead School Ltd v Dring* (1926) 11 TC 273, in the later case of *Ereaut v Girls' Public Day School Trust Ltd* (1963) 15 TC 529, it was stated that this was not decisive.
3. The managers are a public body.
4. No individual is financially interested in the school.
5. The school does not aim primarily to make a profit from its activities but to provide a public school education for its pupils. Therefore, although money was paid to shareholders, as education was the primary object in *Ereaut v Girls' Public Day School Trust Ltd* (above), the trust was regarded as charitable.
6. The objects of the school are to provide an education for a large class of Her Majesty's subjects and are not confined to a small group of

individuals (*Blake v London Corporation* (1887) 2 TC 209; and *Cardinal Vaughan Memorial School Trustees v Ryall* (1920) 7 TC 611).

21.3 Effect of charitable status

Charitable status does not confer automatic exemption from tax on all forms of income and capital gains but, if a school is a charity, it is exempt from income tax or corporation tax (ICTA 1988, s. 505) on the following specific types of income.

1. Rents assessable under Sch. A or Sch. D.
2. Income from which tax is deducted under Sch. C (mainly interest on British Government securities).
3. Interest or annual payments falling within Sch. D (this includes deeds of covenant).
4. Dividends from UK companies.
5. Profits from a trade if either:
    (a) the trade is exercised in the course of the actual carrying-on of the primary purpose of the charity. Thus old cases such as *Brighton College v Marriott* (1925) 10 TC 213 where the college, although accepted as a charity, made a profit from charging fees and was assessed on the profit although it was exempt on other sources of income, should not now be relevant, or
    (b) the work in connection with the trade is mainly carried out by beneficiaries of the charity. Examples of such trades in the case of a school would be carrying on such peripheral trades as charging visitors to see historical buildings of the school or charging members of the public to see dramatic performances by members of the school.

Where the profits from bazaars, jumble sales, etc in aid of a charity, such as occasional fund raising by a school which is a charity, fall within the tax definition of a trade (ICTA 1988, s. 832(1)) and are outside the scope of these statutory exemptions for certain trading activities, Extra-statutory Concession (ESC) C4 exempts the profits from tax. The text of the concession, which was revised with effect from 31 March 2000, is as follows:

> 'Certain events arranged by voluntary organisations or charities for the purpose of raising funds for charity may fall within the definition of "trade" in

Effect of charitable status

Section 832 ICTA 1988, with the result that any profits will be liable to income tax or corporation tax. Tax will not be charged on such profits provided:

- the event is of a kind which falls within the exemption from VAT under Group 12 of Schedule 9 to the VAT Act 1994 and
- the profits are transferred to charities or otherwise applied for charitable purposes.'.

Activities that fall under VATA 1994, Sch. 9, Grp. 12 are the supply of goods and services by a charity in connection with an event:

- that is organised for charitable purposes by a charity or jointly by more than one charity;
- whose primary purpose is the raising of money, and
- that is promoted as being primarily for raising money.

Also covered by Sch. 19, Grp. 12 is the supply of goods and services by a qualifying body in connection with an event:

- that is organised exclusively for the body's own benefit,
- whose primary purpose is the raising of money, and
- that is promoted as being primarily for the raising of money.

The Grp. 9 exemption also extends to the supply of goods and services by a charity or a qualifying body in connection with an event:

- that is organised jointly by a charity, or two or more charities, and the qualifying body;
- that is so organised exclusively for charitable purposes, or exclusively for the body's own benefit or exclusively for a combination of those purposes and that benefit;
- whose primary purpose is the raising of money, and
- that is promoted as being primarily for the raising of money.

Where the school is trading and cannot claim statutory exemption from tax on its trading profits or claim the benefit of the Extra-statutory Concession, it is allowed to make a deduction in its trading accounts of such running expenses as it might have incurred if the trade had been on a normal commercial basis. Thus a price can be put on voluntary help, rent-free premises, and any other things that would normally qualify as allowable business expenses (*British Legion, Peterhead Branch Remembrance and Welcome Home*

Fund v CIR (1953) 35 TC 509). Schools often allow their premises to be used for leisure holidays, summer schools and conferences to add to their income.

In such a situation, it might be preferable to form a separate company to carry on the above activities. Any profits can then be paid under Gift Aid to the charity.

All these exemptions are given on the basis that the income will be applied for charitable purposes; that is in defraying the general running expenses of the school.

Public schools are similarly exempt from capital gains tax (TCGA 1992, s. 256), provided again that the chargeable gains are applied for charitable purposes.

It appears that schools which rank as charities cannot claim exemption from tax on profits chargeable as income from land under ITCA 1988, s. 776 (artificial transactions in land). Therefore, if there is any risk that this section may apply, it is best to make an application for clearance.

21.4 Investment income

Most schools have been endowed with investments, some of which are subject to special trusts to provide scholarships (for instance, for pupils from a particular preparatory school). The income from such special scholarship funds falling under one of the categories of income mentioned above are normally exempt from tax, provided that the class of potential beneficiaries is sufficiently wide to come within the ambit of a charitable purpose.

21.5 Gift Aid

Appeals for carrying out improvements to school buildings, etc, used to take the form of invitations to make payments under deeds of covenant. Since April 2000 tax relief has been withdrawn for covenanted payments and such payments are now made under the Gift Aid scheme.

The procedure should involve only writing a letter evidencing the gift and the deduction of tax from the gift.

21.6 Payment of school fees in the case of separated parents

It used to be possible for a divorced parent to obtain tax relief on the payment of school fees.

In the case of new obligations entered into after 14 March 1988, the maintaining parent has simply been entitled to the special allowance or the amount of the maintenance whichever is the lesser, the former being the same as the married couples' allowance for all maintenance payments to or for the benefit of all his or her children (ICTA 1988, s. 347B).

However, since 6 April 2000 no tax relief has been available for maintenance payments irrespective of the date of the court order.

21.7 Capital allowances

Should it be necessary for a school to prepare tax computations – for instance, because it is not a charitable body – the accounts and computations proceed on the normal basis for an unincorporated business or a limited company as appropriate. In this connection, the importance of keeping records sufficient to enable claims to be made for capital allowances on items ranking as plant and machinery was illustrated in the case of *St John's School (Mountford and Knibbs) v Ward* [1975] STC 7. In that case, a claim that a prefabricated school gymnasium and its contents was plant in its entirety was rejected, and it appears from the facts of the case that the school put forward this claim partly because it had not been able to segregate satisfactorily costs relating to items which were admitted as plant — such as gymnasium equipment.

21.8 Academics, teachers, etc

Guidance on the employment status of teachers, lecturers and tutors is found in the Inland Revenue Employment Status Manual at ESM 4500ff and is reproduced below:

> 'In determining whether a particular lecturing or teaching engagement amounts to employment or self-employment it is necessary to consider all the terms, conditions and facts surrounding that engagement (see *ESM1000* onwards). The following paragraphs refer to lecturing engagements but similar considerations will apply to teaching engagements.

It is important in all cases to consider any written contract or letters of appointment/acceptance in establishing the terms and conditions that apply for a particular engagement.

There are special regulations governing the status of teachers/lecturers for National Insurance Contributions (NICs) purposes (see *ESM4503* below).

A full-time lecturer is likely to be an employee — particularly where engaged by a university, college, school/local authority, etc. This follows from the terms and conditions of engagement which will usually include many of the following features — all of which point towards employment although none are likely to be decisive on their own

- payment of a salary;
- paid holidays and sick leave;
- availability of pension scheme membership;
- no financial risk for the lecturer;
- control (or right of control) over matters such as conduct and discipline, hours of attendance, where and when lectures are given and, possibly, detailed control over what is taught (for example course to follow a set syllabus), etc;
- the bulk of the equipment needed will be supplied by the engager.

A part-time lecturer whose engagement covers a complete academic term or longer may well have similar terms and conditions to a full-time lecturer. Many such part-time lecturers will be employees. See *ESM4503* below for the NICs position.

A visiting lecturer who gives an occasional talk or short series of talks on a subject about which he has specialist knowledge and which is not part of the core curriculum will normally have rather different terms and conditions and is likely to be self- employed.

Between those extremes engagements should be considered on their own facts – taking into account such matters as:

- control (or right of control) over conduct and discipline, hours of attendance, where and when lectures are given, course content, etc. (the more extensive control the more indicative it is of employment);
- whether the lecturer must undertake the lecturing personally or whether a substitute can be sent (see *ESM1051* onwards);
- who is to supply the equipment necessary (where the contractual terms require the lecturer to supply his own equipment [for example, overhead projector and handouts] at his own expense this would point towards self- employment);

- whether any financial risk attaches to the engagement (financial risk would be a pointer towards self-employment – but most engagements will lack any element of financial risk);
- the intention of the parties to the contract (see below).

In assessing the importance of the factors see *ESM1000* onwards and, in particular the sections on personal factors at *ESM1091* onwards concerning personal factors where a lecturer has many short-term lecturing engagements with a variety of engagers.

Exceptionally, fees chargeable under Schedule E as employment income may be regarded as assessable under Schedule D Case II where the conditions at SE03002/EIM03002 are met.'

Guidance was issued to the universities in March 1996 by the Committee of Vice Chancellors and Principals (CVCP) concerning the employment status of lecturers and the tax treatment of expense payments made to employed lecturers. These notes have been approved by the Revenue and should be followed when dealing with the affairs of both universities and, where appropriate, lecturers. The full text of the notes is as follows:

'Tax Guidance Notes: Lecturers engaged by universities

Introduction

These guidance notes are intended to help universities and lecturers with two issues that sometimes cause difficulty:

- whether lecturers are employed or self-employed
- the tax treatment of fees and expenses paid to lecturers who are employed.

The guidance has been prepared in consultation with the Inland Revenue and is based on the law in force at 6 April 1996. It has no binding force and does not affect the right of appeal on any point concerning liability to tax.

These notes apply only to lecturers. The tax treatment of external examiners engaged by universities is currently under review by the CVCP and Inland Revenue. In the meantime, examiners up to and including first degree level should be treated as employees of the university. Tax should be deducted from fees paid to employed examiners whereas their reimbursed expenses may normally be paid gross, including payments for travel from home.

Further information

There is general guidance on employment status in the Inland Revenue/ Contributions Agency leaflet IR56/NI39 (available in any tax/Contributions

Private schools, higher education institutions, teachers, etc.

Agency office). Inland Revenue booklet 480 is a guide to the tax treatment of expenses and benefits. You can also ask your Tax Office for further advice.

Employed or self-employed?

1. General

Different tax rules apply to employees and to people who are self-employed. So whenever you engage a lecturer you need to decide at the outset whether the contract is one of employment or self-employment. If the lecturer is an employee then you must, by law, operate PAYE.

You must also account for Class 1 National Insurance Contributions (NICs) for the amounts paid to lecturers who are within the Department of Social Security's special regulations. This applies irrespective of whether the lecturer is employed or self-employed for tax purposes. The DSS regulations are explained in paragraph 7 below.

Customs and Excise have agreed that this guidance will also apply for the purposes of deciding whether VAT is payable in respect of a particular engagement. (Where individual lecturers are in any doubt about whether they need to register for VAT they should contact their local VAT office.)

2. The difference between employment and self-employment

Employment status is not a matter of choice but follows from the terms and conditions of the engagement. There is no statutory definition of 'employment' or 'self-employment' so the decision depends a number of criteria derived from case law. In deciding whether a particular lecturing engagement amounts to employment or self employment you need to look at the terms, conditions and facts surrounding that engagement. The following notes are intended to help both universities and lecturers in deciding status for a particular engagement for tax purposes. Where doubt remains you should get advice from your Tax Office as early as possible.

3. Full-time lecturers

A full-time lecturer will normally be an employee. This follows from the terms and conditions of engagement which usually include some or all of the following features that point towards employment:

- payment of a salary
- paid holidays and sick leave
- availability of pension scheme membership
- no financial risk for the lecturer

- control (or right of control) over matters such as conduct and discipline, hours of attendance, where and when lectures are given and, possibly, detailed control over what is taught (for example, course to follow a set syllabus), etc.

4. Part-time Lecturers

A part-time lecturer whose engagement covers a complete academic term or longer and who has similar terms and conditions to a full-time lecturer is likely to be an employee. But someone who is taken on for a whole academic term or year but only for say two or three hours a week, and on different terms and conditions to full-time lecturers, is more likely to fall within the guidance given for occasional lecturers below.

5. Visiting Lecturers

A visiting lecturer who gives a one-off talk or short series of talks on a subject about which he or she has specialist knowledge and which is not part of the core curriculum will normally be engaged on rather different terms and conditions and is likely to be self-employed.

6. Occasional Lecturers

Sometimes lecturers are engaged on a less formal basis to give, for example, a series of lectures on a particular topic. They are the group whose employment status for tax purposes is often the most difficult to decide. In each case it is necessary to consider all the circumstances, including:

(a) The terms and conditions of the engagement:

- Control (or right of control) over conduct and discipline, hours of attendance, where and when lectures are given, course content, etc (Generally the more extensive control the more indicative it is of employment.) For example a lecturer required to teach in accordance with a set syllabus would be more indicative of employment than if the lecturer was engaged to talk about a specific subject but was left to determine the content of the lecture.

- Whether the individual must undertake the lecturing personally or whether a substitute can be sent. (On the lecturer's part, to send a substitute is a strong pointer towards self-employment although the absence of such a right is not a particularly strong indicator the other way.)

- Who is to supply the equipment necessary (where the contractual terms require the lecturer to supply his own equipment [for example, overhead projector and handouts] at his own expense this would point towards self-employment).

Private schools, higher education institutions, teachers, etc.

- Whether any financial risk attaches to the engagement (financial risk would be a pointer towards self-employment — but most engagements will lack any element of financial risk).

(b) Factors personal to the lecturer:

The following factors point towards self-employment. But they are only relevant where both university and lecturer intend that the terms of the engagement amount to self-employment:

- Many short-term lecturing engagements with different institutions.
- A business approach to obtaining and organising his/her engagements and expenditure in this area of a type not normally associated with employment (for example, provision of office accommodation, office equipment, etc.).
- Self-employment in a related full-time (or substantial) profession or business where occasional lectures are regarded as part of the individual's profession or business.

(c) The intention of the parties to the contract:

- A university that wishes to take on an occasional lecturer as an employee has that right. Where a contract, freely signed by both parties, specifically states that the engagement amounts to a contract of service (employment) — and the terms and conditions are consistent with that — then that will conclude the matter.
- Where a review of other factors indicates that the engagement is on the borderline between employment and self-employment a common intention expressed in the contract, whether for employment or self-employment, will decide the issue.

7. National Insurance Contributions — employment status

As explained above, for tax purposes whether a particular lecturer is employed or self-employed depends upon the particular circumstances. For NICs the position is slightly different. The Department of Social Security has special regulations which apply to lecturers for the purposes of determining the charge to NICs. If a lecturer is employed under a contract of service he or she will be an employee and liable to pay Class 1 NICs. If a lecturer is employed under a contract of service, the Social Security Regulations mean that Class 1 NIC will be due unless:

- the lecturer is engaged to lecture on not more than three days in three consecutive months; or;
- the instruction is given as a public lecture which anyone can attend.

More details about the National Insurance rules are in the Contributions Agency leaflet CA26.

Fees and expenses

This part of the guidance outlines how fees and travelling and subsistence expenses paid by universities, colleges, language schools, etc. to lecturers who are employees for tax purposes.

8. General

Under general income tax law employees who are earning at the rate of £8,500 a year or more are liable to tax on the full amount of their remuneration. This includes all fees, wages, salaries and expenses payments etc. They may have a deduction from their earnings for any travelling and subsistence costs 'necessarily' incurred in travelling in the performance of their work. They can also claim a deduction for any other expenses 'wholly, exclusively and necessarily' incurred in the actual performance of their work.

For employees earning below the £8,500 a year limit, a reimbursement of actual expenses incurred is not treated as remuneration provided the expense to which it relates is deductible by the employee.

9. Fees

Fees paid to lecturers who are employees are taxable under Schedule E.

What action must the employer take?

The university, college etc., must operate PAYE and pay any NICs which are due.

10. Travelling and Subsistence Expenses

When lecture fees are taxable under the Schedule E rules, any reimbursed travelling and subsistence expenses would normally be treated in the same way unless paid in respect of travel undertaken in the performance of the lecturer's duties. The term 'in the performance of' means that the expenses must be incurred in actually carrying out the duties of employment. It is not sufficient that an expense is simply relevant to, or incurred in connection with, the duties of employment, or if the expense is to put the employee in a position to perform his or her duties. So if a university reimburses an employed lecturer for the costs of travelling from home to the university the payment is chargeable to tax. This is because the journey is not in the actual performance of the lecturer's duties.

What action must the employer take?

The university, college etc. must operate PAYE and pay any NICs which are due.

When is travel in the performance of the lecturer's duties?

Necessary travel from one place of work to another for the same employer is in the performance of the lecturer's duties, but not travel from home to any of those places So, for example, if a lecturer has a single employment requiring teaching at various centres, and the expenses of travelling between the centres are reimbursed, the travelling would normally be in the performance of the duties and the reimbursed expenses deductible. If a lecturer is in any doubt about this he or she should check with his or her Tax Office.

What about travel from one place of work for one employer to the place or work from another employer?

Reimbursed travelling expenses for journeys between places of work of different employers are taxable and PAYE should be operated because the travelling is not in the performance of the duties of the employment.'

Guidance on the treatment of expenses incurred by teachers, lecturers and tutors can also be found in the Inland Revenue Employment Income Manual at EIM 70700ff.

21.8.1 National Insurance contributions

Special rules apply to teachers and lecturers for National Insurance purposes under the Social Security Contributions and Benefits Act 1992 (SSCBA 1992), s. 2(2)(b), and reg. 2(2) and Sch. 1, Pt. I, para. 4 of the Categorisation Regulations 1978 (SI 1978 No. 1689) as amended by reg. 2 of the Categorisation Amendment Regulations 1984 (SI 1984 No. 350). Guidance can be found in Inland Revenue booklet CA 26, *National Insurance contributions for examiners, moderators, invigilators, lecturers, teachers and instructors.*

People who, on or after 6 April 1978, are employed as lecturers, teachers, instructors or in any similar capacity in an educational establishment by any person providing education, are to be treated as falling within the category of employed earners provided:

- they are not agency workers; and
- the instruction is not given as public lectures; and

- the number of days on which the instruction is given has not been limited, by prior agreement, to three days or less in three consecutive months; and
- they give the instruction in the presence of the person to whom the instruction is given, except where the employment is in the Open University, and
- their earnings are paid by, or on behalf of, the person providing the education.

Where the person is an agency worker he or she is still categorised as an employed earner, but under the special categorisation rules and not under these rules.

A lecture is regarded as 'public' if members of the public may attend whether they do or not and whether or not they are charged for admission. A lecture that is part of a course or that is only open to a particular group of persons or to the members of a particular society is not regarded as 'public'.

An 'educational establishment' includes any place where instruction is provided in any course or part of a course designed to lead to a certificate, diploma, degree or professional qualification, or any like place where courses are substantially similar but do not lead to a certificate, etc. The term therefore includes universities, colleges and schools of all kinds including schools of arts and crafts and languages (see DSS Leaflet CA 26 — updated October 2002).

The Contributions Agency has used the regulations recently in relation to self-employed peripatetic music teachers giving instruction in non-local authority schools. If the teacher is paid by or on behalf of the school, Class 1 contributions are due from both the individual and the school. However, if the teacher contracts directly with the parents of the children in question and receives payment directly from the parents, the arrangement is outside the scope of the regulations.

The position is similar in relation to university lecturers, etc. whose employers have also been subject to recent special interest by the Agency.

The person falling to be treated as the secondary contributor in a case falling within these provisions is the person providing the education (reg. 5, Sch. 6, para. 3 of the Categorisation Regulations, as amended by reg. 4 of the Categorisation Amendment Regulations 1984).

Employees of non-trading bodies, including charities, are potentially brought within the scope of the benefits provisions for directors and employees earning at a rate of £8,500 per annum or more (hereafter called higher-paid employees) (see especially ICTA 1988, ss. 153–168). Equally, all employees are potentially liable to tax on the value of living accommodation provided for them by reason of their employment, and directors and higher-paid employees are also potentially liable on any expenses of upkeep of such accommodation borne by the employer (ICTA 1988, ss. 145, 146, 155(2) and 163).

The Inland Revenue Employment Status Manual contains the following guidance at *ESM 4504*:

> 'Most teachers etc. are engaged either part-time or full-time under a contract of service.
>
> Where they are not, the above Regulations make provision for treating teachers, who are not employed under a contract of service, as employees.
>
> They provide for a teacher who teaches in an educational establishment to be treated as an employed earner if they
>
> - teach in the presence of their students unless they are working for the Open University; and
> - are paid by the Education Authority or the person who provides the education, not by the individual student.
>
> *Exceptions*
>
> Do not treat a teacher as an employed earner if:
>
> - prior to giving the instruction, they have agreed to give it on not more than 3 days in 3 consecutive months; or
> - the instruction is given as public lectures. A public lecture is regarded as one which any one can attend; that is, it is not part of a course or confined to a particular group or society.
>
> *What is an educational establishment?*
>
> An educational establishment is defined in Regulation 1(2) as including
>
> - a place where instruction is given leading to a certificate, diploma, degree or professional qualification; or
> - a place where instruction is given which follows substantially the same type of syllabus but which is not designed to lead to such a certificate, diploma, degree or professional qualification.

Usually, it will be fairly easy to decide whether the place at which instruction is provided is an educational establishment — for instance, a school, university or college. However, less obvious places may also be an educational establishment. For example, a local town hall will be an educational establishment on occasions when it is used by a visiting instructor to give evening classes designed to lead to a diploma. The case of *St. John's School, Cambridge v Secretary of State for Social Security* gives further guidance on this point — see ESM7230.

Who pays the teacher?

If the school takes on the teacher, guarantees their payment of fees and is responsible for ensuring that the fees are paid by the parents, the school is paying the teacher.

If the teacher receives his/her fees, either via the school or direct from the parents, and has to personally pursue non-payment of fees with the parents, the teacher is not paid by the school. So the condition in paragraph 4(c) is not satisfied and the teacher retains self-employed status.

If it is alleged that the previous paragraph applies, confirm the facts carefully and check for evidence before accepting that the provisions are not satisfied. Do not assume that the school is liable because it includes the particular instruction in its syllabus or sets the fees.'

21.8.2 Taxation of bursaries, scholarships, etc.

Income in the form of a 'scholarship or bursary' is specifically exempt from tax, although no guidance is given as to what is meant by those terms in the legislation (ICTA 1988, s. 331).

In some cases, this includes income from fellowships, etc. which have been agreed by the Inland Revenue to be tax-free where, broadly, the income is designed to enable the recipient to do research towards a higher degree rather than to teach. In most cases, the college will have agreed the position with the Inland Revenue.

Generally, research grants are taxable where people are engaged in other professional work for which they are or have been paid, as the research grant usually enables them to do the research without undue loss of income (see *Duff v Williamson* [1973] STC 434).

Exemption or relief from tax may also be available under Statement of Practice 4/86 and ITEPA 2003, s. 250.

Under SP 4/86 where certain qualifying conditions are met, payments for attendance on a full-time educational course (including a sandwich course) at a university, technical college or similar educational establishment open to the public at large are exempt from tax. The period of enrolment must be at least one academic year and actual full-time attendance during that period must average at least 20 weeks a year. The rate of payment including lodging, subsistence and travelling allowances, but excluding any university, etc fees, must not exceed the higher of £7,000 a year (or the equivalent monthly or weekly rates) or the grant which would have been payable in similar circumstances by a public awarding body. Where payments exceed the above limits, they are taxable in full (see also Inland Revenue Press Release dated 12 April 1989).

Similarly, exemption from tax for course fees paid or reimbursed by an employer and a deduction for the cost of essential books may be available under ESC A63 and A64.

ITEPA 2003, s. 250 grants an employee exemption from tax for certain expenses borne by the employer in respect of course fees and the cost of essential books in connection with work-related training.

21.8.3 Meals and entertaining

The provision of meals in any canteen in which meals are provided for the staff generally is not taxable (ITEPA 2003, s. 317), and this includes refectories. Also, expenditure on festive occasions when members of the school, etc. entertain guests of the school and parents will not, in practice, give rise to a charge to tax on higher-paid employees, provided the expenditure is modest and the occasion is open to the staff generally. The usual limits of £150 given by ITEPA 2003, s. 264 apply. The legislation contains the following paragraphs:

> 'This section applies to an annual party or similar annual function provided for an employer's employees and available to them generally or available generally to those at a particular location.
>
> Where in the tax year only one annual party or similar annual function to which this section applies is provided for the employer's employees, or the employees in question, no liability to income tax arises in respect of its provision if the cost per head of the party or function does not exceed £150.
>
> Where in the tax year two or more such parties or functions are so provided, no liability to income tax arises in respect of the provision of one or more of them ("the exempt party or parties") if the cost per head of the exempt party or parties does not exceed £150 or £150 in aggregate.

For the purposes of this section, the cost per head of a party or function is the total cost of providing —

(a) the party or function, and

(b) any transport or accommodation incidentally provided for persons attending it (whether or not they are the employer's employees),

divided by the number of those persons.

That total cost includes any value added tax on the expenses incurred in providing the party, function, transport or accommodation.'

Where a university teacher is reimbursed for entertaining expenses directly connected with the employment, such as those arising from tutorial duties or on the occasion of official visits, he or she generally is not assessed to tax, even if 'higher-paid'. It is also likely that modest round-sum allowances will not be taxed, provided that the inspector is satisfied that the allowance does not exceed the actual expenditure so incurred. According to the Association of University Teachers, expenses incurred out of a teacher's own remuneration on such entertaining are allowed, although not strictly within ITEPA 2003, s. 336. However, the safest course is probably to seek to have the expenses reimbursed. The Inland Revenue are likely to look more kindly on expenditure that has first satisfied an employer's scrutiny.

21.8.4 Capital allowances

The Inland Revenue Memorandum TS40/1990 deals with capital allowances claims by ministers of religion who are employees, and CAA 2001, s. 36 enables capital allowances to be given to employees where they incur expenditure on machinery or plant which is 'necessarily provided for use in the performance of the duties'. Two conditions must be satisfied:

1. The duties must objectively require the use of the equipment.
2. The employee must be obliged to incur the expense of providing the equipment.

For ministers of religion the conditions are satisfied where the minister has incurred expenditure on equipment which is used to perform tasks arising from normal ministerial duties. The use of a computer or word processor to produce parish records, parish magazines and the like is acceptable. The fact that a more up-to-date method of keeping records is being adopted than before does not prevent allowances from being given.

The same argument should apply for teachers.

21.8.5 Remission of school fees

The whole issue of the tax impact of the remission of school fees was squarely raised in *Pepper v Hart* (1993) 65 TC 421.

In that case the taxpayers were the bursar and assistant master at Malvern College, who were entitled under a concessionary fees scheme to educate their children at the college on payment of one-fifth of the ordinary fees. The Inland Revenue took the view that since the employees were higher-paid, the concessionary education was a benefit which fell within the provisions of ICTA 1988, s. 154. Further, the measure of the charge (the 'cash equivalent' of the benefit) was a proportionate part of the total cost of running the school less the sums made good by the taxpayers in question. This view was rejected by the Special Commissioner but accepted by Vinelott J. in the High Court. Under ICTA 1988, s. 156 the cost of providing the benefit of a cheap education for the sons of employees of Malvern College was, insofar as the facilities used were those used by other boys in the school, a rateable proportion of the expenses incurred by the school in providing those facilities, less the sums made good by the parent. Vinelott J. described this as 'the inescapable effect of the legislation'. The interpretation of the legislation taken by the taxpayers and agreed by the Special Commissioner, that the value of the benefit was equivalent only to the direct additional costs referable to educating those pupils in addition to others, is the view which has historically been adopted. The decision was upheld in the Court of Appeal but rejected by the House of Lords.

The House of Lords decided the value for tax purposes of in-house benefits in kind is only the marginal or additional cost to the employer.

The marginal cost of in-house benefits depends on each employer's particular circumstances. But, as a general guide, the Inland Revenue accept that where teachers pay 15 per cent or more of a school's normal fees there is no net benefit.

If the teacher's salary is adjusted downwards in return for the free education of the child, this reduction constitutes a taxable benefit on the principle decided in *Heaton v Bell* (1969) 46 TC 211, whether the employee is higher-paid or not.

21.8.6 Research costs

Sometimes, school teachers undertake research projects as part of their duties. Where research costs are reimbursed in whole or in part by the school, the reimbursement is not taxed in the hands of a higher-paid employee, as the assessable income could be covered by an expense claim under ITEPA 2003, s. 336. Where it is not reimbursed, the inspector may, in practice, consider an expense claim where it is reasonable in nature and not unduly large (see also **21.8.10** below).

Similar considerations apply to university teachers. The AUT advises that deductions may be claimed for research expenses that are directly related to the teacher's subject and that are moderate in amount, if reimbursement is not available.

A claim is less likely to be successful to the extent that the research is voluntary on the teacher's part. Expenses incurred in preparing a thesis to secure advanced qualifications are not allowable for income tax purposes.

21.8.7 Conference and course expenses

Reimbursed conference expenses are not taxed. However, a claim for allowance of unreimbursed conference expenses is likely to be challenged as not having been incurred wholly, exclusively and necessarily in the performance of the duties of the employment because there may be duality of purpose involved (see *Bowden v Russell and Russell* (1965) 42 TC 301 and *Edwards v Warmsley Henshall & Co* (1967) 44 TC 431).

A teacher seconded on full salary to attend a full-time course of training lasting at least four weeks may claim concessional relief on expenses necessarily incurred in attending the course, including the costs of accommodation, course fees, essential books and travelling (notes circulated by the Association of Teachers in Further and Higher Education and the Association of University and College Lecturers).

21.8.8 Travel expenses

Most travelling expenses of academics on official business are reimbursed and, where the academic is higher-paid and taxed on the reimbursed expenses, an equivalent ITEPA 2003, s. 281 claim should be allowed or not on normal principles (*Ricketts v Colquhoun* (1925) 10 TC 118 and *Pook v Owen* (1969) 45 TC 571). However, it is reported that, where teachers or lecturers have to incur expenses of travelling between different places of work in the same town, the Inland Revenue have been reluctant to allow the expenses if they are not reimbursed by the school, college, etc., on the basis that they cannot have been necessarily incurred in the performance of the duties if the school does not reimburse them.

In *Warner v Prior* SpC 353 30.1.03 [2003] STI issue 7, the issue was whether the travelling expenses of a supply teacher were necessarily expended on travelling in the performance of the duties of the employment; whether the taxpayer had two places of work, one at home, so that travel expenses between them were allowable.

Ms Warner was employed by Kent County Council as a supply teacher. She was required to perform two types of duty: 'directed time', which covered actual teaching time, and 'additional time', which included marking work, writing reports and preparing lessons.

In the school where she worked as a supply teacher, she had in practice fewer facilities than permanent teachers, through having no place of her own at which to work or keep papers. She carried out the bulk of her 'additional time' in an office she maintained at home. She travelled between her home and the various schools in which she worked in her own car. In her self assessment for 1999–2000, Ms Warner claimed a deduction in computing her emoluments for expenses of travel from her home to the schools. On the Revenue's adjustment of her self assessment, she appealed, contending that:

- she had two places of work, at her home and at whichever school she was sent to;
- the place of work at home was objectively necessary to the performance of her duties, and
- accordingly, the expenses of travel between them was allowable.

The Revenue argued that, even if she did have two places of work, that alone was insufficient to establish entitlement to deductibility of the travel expenses between them, since that deduction was allowable only when the duties were required to be performed in two specific locations.

The Special Commissioner found that Ms Warner did have a place of work outside the schools and that it was objectively necessary, having regard to her duties, for her to have a place of work somewhere other than the schools, which was in fact at her home. He then asked whether that fact of itself meant that she was entitled to deduct travelling expenses between her two places of work. The location of her other place of work at her home had no bearing on her appointment to her job or her ability to perform it. If Ms Warner were to move house, at least within Kent, there was no evidence to suggest that Kent County Council would have any objections. She might have further to travel to some schools and less far to others, but it would make no difference to her ability to do her job. The significant factor was that her secondary place of work at home was dictated by where she lived and not by the requirements of the job itself. She had not brought herself within the exception to the rule that travel from home to work was not allowable. Therefore her appeal would be dismissed.

The Inland Revenue are prepared to give some measure of relief to college lecturers in respect of the cost of travelling between different parts of a college. Sessional lecturers employed at colleges of further education under typical county council contracts are not entitled to claim travel expenses for distances under ten miles. Full-time lecturers normally receive reimbursement. The Inland Revenue had argued against allowance on the basis that a college, albeit on two sites, was one place of employment, so that a person was not temporarily away from his or her normal place of employment. It is reported that the Inland Revenue have granted relief where the campuses in question are in different towns that were only 2.8 miles apart. It appears that in this situation, expenses of travelling can be claimed by teachers, lecturers and other part-time employees who work on the same day at different sites for the same employer.

The reimbursement of expenses incurred in going to the school from home are taxable or not on normal principles. However, where no 'profit' has been made from the reimbursement, it appears that a lower-paid employee is not taxable on the reimbursement, following the case of *Donnelly v Williamson* [1982] STC 88, which concerned a lower-paid teacher who was reimbursed in respect of her expenses of voluntarily attending parents' evenings. In view of the small amount involved, the payment could not have been a contribution towards the overhead expenses of putting her car on the road. Thus the court followed the principle in *Pook v Owen* that no taxable profit can arise from a pure reimbursement of an actual outlay. In practice, *Donnelly v Williamson* has only a limited application to small amounts of reimbursed expenditure. Reimbursed expenses of higher-paid teachers are treated as emoluments, subject to any claim for deductions under ITEPA 2003, s. 336.

In any event the revised employee travel expense rules, effective from 6 April 1998, allow tax relief for the actual cost of any journey that is not ordinary commuting, and it may be that teachers or lecturers are better able to claim relief for such journeys if travelling between different college premises within the same town than they have been in the past.

21.8.9 Books, subscriptions and special clothing

Where there is an obligation for teachers to provide their own text books for use in class or in the preparation of lectures, a deduction may be claimed for their cost. This would normally be relevant only in higher education.

The inspector may ask for a list of titles. Where substantial reference books are purchased, a claim for capital allowances may be accepted, unless the books are available in university or departmental libraries.

A deduction may be claimed for annual subscriptions to learned societies, so far as they are paid to secure professional literature for use in lectures or for research. No deduction is available for payments for life membership. The annual subscriptions to the following, as subscriptions to professional bodies, are allowable in full:

- the Association of Teachers and Lecturers;
- the Society of Assistants Teaching in Preparatory Schools;
- the British Association of Advisers and Lecturers in Physical Education;
- the National Union of Teachers;
- the Guild of Lecturers;
- the Association of Lecturers in Accountancy;
- the Association of Lecturers in Colleges of Education in Scotland;
- the Association of Lecturers for Teachers' Certificates in Business Studies;
- the Association for Religious Education for Teachers and Lecturers;
- the National Association of Teachers in Further and Higher Education, and
- the Association of University and College Lecturers.

Academic dress, protective clothing (such as is used in laboratories) and gymnastic dress are examples of special clothing for which a deduction may be claimed on a 'renewals' basis.

21.8.10 Study allowances

The position is different for university lecturers and those dealing with degree courses on the one hand, and ordinary teachers on the other.

The National Association of Teachers in Further and Higher Education have circulated to all their members notes for guidance on deductible expenses. In connection with the use of accommodation at home, the Inland Revenue are prepared to grant a concessionary allowance to those teachers involved in higher education (ie degree level work) who can show that a study is required by the nature of their duties and is not used merely as a matter of convenience. It is unlikely that this concessionary allowance will be granted to any teacher who is not obliged to engage in research.

Factors that such a teacher might bring to the attention of the inspector of taxes when seeking an allowance are the need to consult journals and reference books for the preparation of lectures as well as for research (where such material cannot reasonably be kept in a college room), and the overcrowding of staff accommodation at the college. The amount of any allowance depends upon all relevant facts and, because of the exceptional nature of the concessionary treatment, there can be no question of a flat-rate allowance. Where a room is set aside at home for exclusive use as a study, a broad guideline is to compare the floor space covered by the study with total floor space, excluding common areas such as entrance halls and bathrooms, and then apply this ratio to expenses such as heat and light, and cleaning and rent (but not water rates).

It has further been agreed that, where a study allowance is given under ITEPA 2003, no liability to capital gains tax is incurred on the sale of the dwelling, as regards the proportion of the sale price attributable to the study, provided that the dwelling is the teacher's only or main residence under the normal rules (TCGA 1992, s. 222).

This nationally negotiated concession is not normally available to teachers at the primary or secondary level, who therefore have to rely on proving that the terms of their employment require them to work at home, not merely on research, but directly on school work. Otherwise, even if the availability of private study facilities at home improves the teacher's academic knowledge, the expenses of providing it are likely to be disallowed by the Inland Revenue on the basis of *Humbles v Brooks* (1962) 40 TC 500 where, as stated above, the court refused to allow a school teacher's expenses of attending weekend lectures to improve his knowledge of the subjects he taught.

21.8.11 Living accommodation

In most cases, employees such as wardens of halls of residence, head teachers, housemasters, chaplains and caretakers escape a charge in respect of the provision of accommodation, by virtue of the exemptions for representative occupiers. If the employer pays the council tax as well, this is included in the exemption (ITEPA 2003, s. 314). Furthermore, the additional charge under ITEPA 2003, s. 106 cannot apply where the warden, etc is exempt from any charge on the annual value of the property as a representative occupier.

If, in addition, directors or higher-paid employees are provided by reason of their employment with other services (including heating, lighting, cleaning and repairs, the provision of furniture and other effects normal for domestic occupation), they are liable to income tax on the cost of those services (less any amount made good by employees). However, if they are exempt from income tax on the value of the accommodation, because they are in representative occupation, their liability is limited to ten per cent of their net emoluments after deducting expenses, capital allowances and payments to any superannuation scheme (ITEPA 2003, s. 315). The amount of the benefit excludes any proportion of the cost of the services that is referable to professional use of the accommodation as a study, or for meetings connected with school matters.

21.8.12 Other services

In addition, the cost of other services such as gardeners and domestic services other than cleaning, are treated as emoluments of directors or higher-paid employees and are taxable (without limit) under the benefits code (ITEPA 2003, s. 203), to the extent that they have not been made good by the director or employee. Lower-paid employees escape being charged, provided that the costs incurred are not their own liability that have been met by the employer. In regard to gardeners it is understood that, if the garden is not completely private but is open to the public or staff and pupils (for instance an Oxford college garden), the cost of upkeep is not regarded as a benefit.

21.8.13 Residences

Someone who lives in job-related accommodation can obtain capital gains tax exemption on the sale of that residence (TCGA 1992, s. 222(8)).

21.8.14 Other income of teachers

As part of an attempt to reclassify certain earnings as falling within the employment income rules rather than Sch. D, and thus to apply PAYE to them, one of the Inland Revenue Special Offices has issued instructions that all fees paid by local examination boards to GCSE and other examiners should be subject to PAYE. Most examiners have, in the past, been assessed to tax on such fees under Sch. D, Case II or sometimes Case VI. It is possible for examiners still to receive the fees gross, where they can prove that they are not liable to tax by virtue of available personal allowances, and they complete a signed statement obtainable from the examining board in question, enabling that board to pay the fees gross.

The Inland Revenue also require that basic rate income tax be deducted from payments to university teachers for setting, marking and invigilating examinations. An exception is again made for those who can demonstrate that no tax liability arises on the income. There is also an exception for payments for occasional examining for an individual higher degree. Where expenses of travelling to examiners' meetings are reimbursed, the reimbursement may be made without deduction of income tax. Fees received for extra-mural lecturing, etc should also be paid under deduction of tax. Payments for travel expenses in connection with such lecturing are likely to be in respect of travel from home and should be made under deduction of tax. Generally, reference should be made to the cases of *Walls v Sinnett* [1987] STC 236 and *Sidey v Phillips* [1987] STC 87, in which part-time lecture fees paid by local authorities were held to be within ITEPA 2003.

There is no special treatment for royalties received by academics. Some universities give a 'loan in aid' to a member of staff publishing a book and stipulate that the first charge on any royalties be the repayment of the loan. This can lead to authors being liable to income tax on income that they do not actually receive. Careful attention must be given to the wording of the contract with the publisher.

21.8.15 Director of non-profit-making company

Note that a director of a non-profit-making company, or a company established for charitable purposes only, who does not hold a material interest in the company (that is, who does not own with his or her associates more than five per cent of the ordinary share capital of the company), will not be treated as taxable on benefits within ITEPA 2003, unless also higher-paid (see ITEPA 2003, s. 216). This could cover a head teacher who is also a director of the company running the school, if his or her emoluments (including benefits and assessable expenses) do not exceed £8,500 in any tax year.

21.8.16 Study leave overseas

Where teachers continue to be paid while on study leave overseas, it might be argued that their remuneration arose from duties performed in the UK. However, by concession, it has been agreed between the teachers' associations and the Inland Revenue that an individual on such study leave will be treated as performing his or her duties wholly overseas.

Chapter 22 Inventors and persons holding patent rights

22.1 Expenses: general

Unless an inventor is carrying on a wider trade, of which devising a particular invention is the natural development or extension, the costs incurred in carrying out this work are not allowable as a deduction from any income unless a patent is obtained in respect of the invention. If the inventor is carrying on such a trade, then the allowance of the costs is given on the basis of the normal test of whether they are incurred wholly and exclusively for the purposes of the trade.

22.2 The law of patents

To appreciate the means by which allowances are given to inventors, it is necessary to know something of UK patent law. To ensure that no one pirates an invention, inventors apply to the Patent Office for Letters Patent, for which they pay certain fees and usually employ the services of an experienced patent agent. A brief specification of the invention is lodged first in case anyone subsequently applies for a patent for a similar invention. Then a complete specification is filed and, if it is found acceptable, formal acceptance is notified by the Patent Office, which also publishes details of the invention. The date of acceptance for filing is the date on which the patent rights commence, although the actual Letters Patent are not issued until some time afterwards. The acceptance of the specification gives the inventor the exclusive right for 20 years from the date the rights commence to make or exploit in any way the invention in the UK under the Patents Act 1977. Formerly, before the introduction of that Act, the period was 16 years.

The rights lapse after four years unless annual renewal fees are paid and only exceptionally are the rights extended beyond 20 years. The rights so granted protect the invention only within the UK; other countries have similar provisions controlling the exploitation of inventions within their boundaries.

Unless otherwise stated, the tax provisions relating to patents cover patent rights acquired under the laws of any country.

Patent rights are thus defined (ICTA 1988, s. 533(1)) as 'the right to do or authorise the doing of anything which would but for that right be an infringement of a patent'.

The legal position has been further modified in the Copyrights, Designs and Patents Act 1988, but not so as to affect the tax treatment described below.

22.3 Income tax position on expenses

The income tax position on expenses of devising an invention is as follows.

1. Where an individual or individuals have devised an invention and the expenditure incurred on it cannot be deducted in computing Case I profits (that is, there is no existing trade out of which the work flows naturally), an allowance is given for the amount of the expenditure by discharge or repayment against patent income of the year of assessment in which the expenditure was incurred (ICTA 1988, s. 526(2)), and any balance unrelieved can be carried forward and set against patent income of subsequent years. It cannot be allowed against other income in any year (ICTA 1988, s. 528(2)). Note also that this allowance is available only to individuals. Where the individual carries on a trade, and the patent rights are to be used for the purposes of the trade, the allowance is given for the year in which the expenditure was incurred.

2. Where any person incurs expenses on applying for or maintaining a patent, they are deductible in arriving at the Case I profit if the application is to obtain a patent for the purposes of a trade (ICTA 1988, s. 83). Otherwise they are allowed by discharge or repayment against patent income, any balance unabsorbed being carried forward against future patent income only (ICTA 1988, ss. 526(1) and 528(2)). These fees and expenses are allowed whether or not patent rights are granted in respect of the invention concerned. A similar allowance is given for expenses incurred in maintaining or obtaining an extension of the term of a patent.

22.4 Treatment of receipts

22.4.1 Capital sums

Where patent rights are sold for a capital sum (that is, where the person selling them is not carrying on a trade of dealing in patent rights and the sum can be classed as capital on the tests mentioned below), that sum is still charged to tax as income. The sale of patent rights includes, for this purpose, the sale of part of patent rights, the sale of a right to purchase patent rights, and the grant of a licence in respect of the patent in question (ICTA 1988, s. 533(2) and (3)).

Where the person selling the rights acquired them for a capital sum, only the profit is assessable.

The sum received is assessed under Sch. D, Case VI in six equal instalments spread over the six years commencing with the year in which the sum is received, with the option to have the whole sum assessed in one year (ICTA 1988, s. 524(1) and (2)). This ranks as earned income where the invention in respect of which the rights are sold was devised by the recipient of the capital sum (ICTA 1988, s. 529).

22.4.2 Death

If the seller dies before the beginning of the sixth year of assessment, the unassessed balance of the capital sum is assessed in the year of death, unless the personal representatives claim that the extra tax payable in the year of death should be reduced to the tax that would have been payable if the unassessed balance had been taxed by equal instalments in each of the years to the year of death. The time limit for making such a claim is 30 days after receiving the notice of assessment relating to the year of death (ICTA 1988, s. 525(1) and (2)).

22.4.3 Non-residents

A person resident in the UK is liable on the sale of any patent right. A non-resident is liable in respect of the sale of UK patents and, in that event, the payer is liable to deduct tax at the basic rate on the sum paid on account of the liability of the recipient unless exempt from UK tax under a double tax treaty (ICTA 1988, s. 524(3) and (4)), and the Inland Revenue have authorised the payer to make the payment gross.

22.5 Incorporation of business

Difficulties could arise in relation to patent rights on the incorporation of a business, as a capital sum for the sale of patent rights could include shares issued by the new company in exchange for the patent rights. Depending on the value of the shares, which in turn would depend on the value of the rights, a substantial income tax liability could arise to the inventor although the purchasing company could claim capital allowances as described below. For

Inventors and persons holding patent rights

patents sold between persons who are under common control, the sale price sticks provided it does not exceed the original capital expenditure. In addition, if there is no original expenditure on purchase, as is frequently the case with an inventor, but sellers receive a capital sum on which they are charged to income tax, the amount of that sum is brought into charge to tax (ICTA 1988, s. 521(6)(b)). Therefore, if a nominal amount is paid by the company for the patents, that is effective for income tax purposes. The shares could be issued to the individual and subsequently the nominal amount paid by the company for the invention. If nothing is paid, the sum brought in for capital allowances purposes is the smallest of:

- the market value of the rights;
- the capital expenditure incurred by the seller, or
- where capital expenditure was incurred by any person connected with the seller, that amount.

Therefore, if there was no capital expenditure, there is no disposal value for capital allowances purposes, and the vendor is free to minimise the capital amount in order to avoid an income tax liability.

So far as capital gains tax is concerned, the difference between the price paid and the market value can be held over if the transaction represents the disposal of an asset used in a trade to the company (TCGA 1992, s. 165). However, if there is no use in the trade by a professional inventor, the Inland Revenue would probably not argue for capital gains treatment on the basis that ultimately all the capital proceeds received by the company would be taxed as income.

Although the facility to transfer assets at tax written-down value between persons under the same control does not apply to patents, the provisions concerning assets qualifying for capital allowances and successions to trades between connected persons do apparently apply. Therefore, if the inventor carries on a trade, an election to transfer the patents at tax written-down value should be possible, whatever the price paid, but only if they qualify on the basis of having been purchased in the first place. If the inventor has paid nothing for the patents, as is usually the case, the election (under CAA 2001, s. 266) cannot be made.

22.6 Capital allowances

Capital allowances are given broadly on the same basis as for plant and machinery, ie 25 per cent of the balance in the pool of expenditure after allowing for sales.

An allowance is made only in respect of expenditure where the person is carrying on a trade, or where income receivable in respect of the rights is liable to tax. Any pre-trading expenditure is treated for this purpose as incurred on the commencement of trading.

The allowance is based on 25 per cent of the excess of any expenditure over any disposal value to be taken into account. There is a proportionately reduced percentage if the period does not cover a complete year. If the trade ceases, there is a balancing allowance equal to all the excess. Alternatively, if the last of the relevant patent rights lapses in the period without being renewed, there is a balancing allowance equal to the excess.

Where the whole or any part of the rights are sold, and on earlier purchase the vendor incurred capital expenditure qualifying for capital allowances, the disposal value is brought into account in calculating the writing-down allowance or balancing adjustment. The disposal value will usually be the sale proceeds, subject to it not being in excess of cost, with the modifications mentioned above for special circumstances.

As with the previous system, allowances and charges are made in taxing the trade or given against patent income only in the case of a non-trader.

22.7 Royalties

The distinction between income and capital sums from the exploitation of patents has to some extent lost its significance with the taxation of capital sums as income in the manner described. However, there may be situations where payer and payee are materially affected by the fact that they are paying and receiving a royalty; for instance, the incidence of tax may be higher in the case of a royalty in a particular year. A royalty covers payment in respect of past or future limited use restricted as to amount or quantity where there is no acquisition of a defined portion of the property in the patent. Other payments in respect of patents – for example, for outright acquisition, for exclusive use during the whole of the unexpired life, or for future unlimited use within a defined area or for a term of years – are generally treated as capital. If the Crown pays a lump sum to a patentee for the acquisition of a defined

Inventors and persons holding patent rights

portion of the property in a patent, the transaction is treated as a capital sum (ICTA 1988, s. 533(1) and (4)).

A patent royalty is thus a sum paid for the use of a patent which ranks as income rather than capital. For this purpose, sums paid for rights incidental to the use of such a patent are to be regarded as sums paid in respect of the use of a patent.

Whether a sum derived from patents is income rather than capital has been before the courts several times. In *Constantinesco v R* (1927) 11 TC 730, Mr Constantinesco and another person patented a mechanism used in many fighter planes. A Royal Commission appointed to consider claims for use of inventions by the Crown in war awarded them £70,000, from which tax was deducted. It was held that the £70,000 was not a capital sum but a payment for successive uses of the patent in the past. Rowlatt J. remarked: 'What ground is there for saying that this is not the total sum for the actual use as opposed to a lump sum to abolish the payment for the actual use and capitalise it?' In *CIR v British Salmson Aero Engines Ltd* (1938) 22 TC 29, the company obtained a licence for exclusive use for ten years in the UK and certain other areas of an invention and in return paid for the licence a lump sum payable in instalments and, in addition, a royalty of so much per annum. It was held that the lump sum was capital.

In other words the sum paid must have the character of income to be treated as a royalty. The consequence is that, if the patent is a UK patent, the payer should deduct tax from the payment and account for it (ICTA 1988, ss. 348(2)(a) and 349(1)(b)) and no deduction is allowed for Case I purposes in respect of such a payment (ICTA 1988, s. 74(p)). A company can of course claim the payment as a charge on income deductible from total profits (ICTA 1988, s. 338(3)(a)).

22.8 Deduction of tax

Note that deduction of tax can take place only where the patent is protected by a UK patent, as there is no machinery for deducting UK tax from an agreement made outside the UK. However, under some double tax agreements patent royalties paid by a UK resident to a resident of the other country, which would otherwise be subject to deduction of UK tax, are exempt from UK tax if the Inland Revenue are satisfied that the provisions of the treaty apply.

22.9 Foreign patents

Royalties received from foreign patents by a UK resident are taxed under Sch. D, Case V. Royalties received under deduction of income tax are income of the year for which the deduction of income tax is made (ICTA 1988, s. 835(6)), for the purposes of any liability to higher rates. Royalties from foreign patents follow the normal Case V rules of assessment.

22.10 Earned income

All royalties rank as earned income if received by the inventor of the patented device (ICTA 1988, s. 529) and should thus qualify as relevant earnings for retirement annuity and personal pension purposes.

22.11 Spreading provisions

To prevent the bunching of income in one year in respect of a royalty, there are provisions for spreading patent royalties over several years (ICTA 1988, s. 527). If the use extends to six years or more, and tax is deducted, then recipients may claim to have their liability computed as if they had received one-sixth of the sum annually for the six years ending with the year in which the payment is made. Where the period of use is two complete years or more but less than six, the payment may be spread over the years of use.

22.12 Know-how

An inventor is unlikely in most cases to be the possessor of know-how in the taxation sense. This is defined as 'any industrial information and techniques likely to assist in the manufacture or processing of goods or materials' (ICTA 1988, s. 533(7)).

Specific legislation was introduced in 1968 relating to dealings in such know-how as a result of a series of cases involving the sale of know-how for what were claimed to be capital sums. In some cases this was upheld by the court usually on the basis that the sale also involved effectively the sale of part of the vendor's business and the capital assets of the business were permanently reduced (see *Evans Medical Supplies Ltd v Moriarty* (1957) 37 TC 540; *Jeffrey v Rolls-Royce Ltd* (1962) 40 TC 443; *Wolf Electric Tools Ltd v Wilson* (1969) 45 TC 326; and *Thomsons (Carron) Ltd v CIR* [1976] STC 317). Where shares were issued as consideration for the know-how, and the shares were issued in instalments, the know-how was taxed in the year of receipt of the shares (*John & E Sturge v Hessel* [1975] STC 573).

Where exceptionally inventors do generate such know-how, if they are able to exploit it by selling it without selling a trade or part of a trade, and it would otherwise still be treated as capital, they are now charged on any profit they make (after deducting any expenses on the acquisition or disposal of the know-how) under Case VI: this is then treated as earned income if they devised the know-how in question (ICTA 1988, s. 531(4), (5) and (6)). This provision does not apply if the sale is to a person under their control, for instance their own company, in which event the sale is treated as the sale of goodwill chargeable to capital gains tax.

It is important to avoid this charge to income tax on a sale of know-how as there are no spreading provisions. It might be sensible, if practicable, to arrange a prior sale to a company controlled by the inventor and for that company to sell on at no profit so that the sale to the company is liable only to capital gains tax depending on base values of the know-how for capital gains tax purposes.

Revenue Interpretation 46 published in August 1993 reads as follows:

> '[The Revenue] are sometimes asked whether capital allowances are available for capital expenditure incurred on the acquisition of commercial know-how.
>
> In [their] view there are no capital allowances available for such expenditure because of the statutory definition of know-how.
>
> TA 1988 s530 permits capital allowances to be given on capital expenditure incurred on the acquisition of know-how. 'Know-how' is defined for s530 purposes at TA 1988 s 533(7) as '... any industrial information and techniques likely to assist in the manufacture or processing of goods or materials ...' (or in mining, agricultural, forestry or fishing operations).
>
> The terms of this definition accordingly restrict allowances to capital expenditure incurred in acquiring information relevant only to industrial or technical processes. Information relevant to commercial processes is not included.
>
> [The Revenue's] view is that know-how which does not assist directly in the manufacturing and processing operations is commercial know-how. Examples include information about marketing, packaging or distributing a manufactured product. Such information does not assist directly in the manufacture of that product. Rather it is concerned with selling the product once it has been manufactured. As such it is not in [the Revenue's] view

within the definition of know-how in TA 1988 s533(7) and so cannot qualify for allowances under s 530. ...'

The other provisions on know-how are unlikely to be relevant in the case of an individual inventor and therefore are not dealt with in this book.

In the case of capital allowances where capital sums are paid for the acquisition of know-how, the rules similarly have been changed depending upon whether the acquisition is after 31 March 1986. From that date the rules follow closely those for patents. Similarly, there is no longer the facility to elect for tax written-down value in the case of controlled sales (ICTA 1988, s. 532(5)).

22.13 Trade marks and designs

A design 'right' is an original non-commonplace design of shape or configuration of articles which is now covered by the Copyright, Designs and Patents Act 1988, ss. 213–216. Protection for a design right is an exclusive right of marketing for five years with extensions to 10–15 years, although others are allowed licences in this period.

The inventor may wish to register a trade mark or design. The registration of trade marks or designs protects the goods and also offers opportunities for exploitation of the mark or design as with a patent by licensing or straightforward assignment of the rights.

The Registered Designs Act 1949 (as amended by the Copyright, Designs and Patents Act 1988, s. 265) defines designs (s. 3) as 'features of shape, configuration, pattern or ornament applied to an article by any industrial process or means being features which, in the finished article, appeal to and are judged solely by the eye'. Trade marks, defined under the Trade Marks Act 1938 as marks 'distinctive of' or 'capable of distinguishing' the product, acquire permanent protection.

Unlike patents and copyrights there is practically no mention of trade marks or registered designs in the Taxes Acts. Licensing to manufacture a product involves patent licences, copyright drawings and licensed use of trade marks and designs of the inventor. Royalties for the use of a design or trade mark are not normally subject to deduction of tax by the payer and are taxable when receivable as trading income in the hands of the inventor. The inventor will want relatively more attached by way of royalty to trade marks than designs or patents which have limited lives but the Inland Revenue can challenge the allocation if it is totally artificial (see *Paterson Engineering Co Ltd v Duff* (1943) 25 TC 43).

However, under ICTA 1988, ss. 537A and 537B, the designer who assigns or grants a licence for that design which has taken more than 12 months to create, may claim to have the lump sum or periodic payments taxed over a period of two years, in two equal instalments: one instalment being assessed on the date of receipt and the second being assessed 12 months previously (ICTA 1988, s. 537A(1) and (2)).

If the creation of the design has taken more than two years then an election can be made to have the receipts assessed in three equal amounts: on the date of receipt, 12 months prior to that date and 24 months prior to the date of receipt (ICTA 1988, s. 537A(1) and (3)).

If the owner of the design in respect of which royalties are paid lives abroad, then tax must be deducted under ICTA 1988, s. 349 and accounted for to the Inland Revenue after taking into account agents' commissions in respect of royalties.

22.14 Case III and trade marks

If the registered trade marks and designs were hived off from the inventor's trade, for instance into a company, they would be held as an investment so that the income is probably assessable under Case III, with formerly all the problems of apportionment in the case of a close company and deduction of tax at source. In this situation it appears that, as the royalties are pure income profit in the hands of the recipient, they would be regarded as an annual payment of the payer and subject to deduction of tax under ICTA 1988, ss. 349 and 350 in the same way as patent royalties.

22.15 Capital or income

If the inventor sold an invention and with it the trade mark or design for a lump sum, and nothing was left of his or her business as a result, the parts of the proceeds attributable to the trade mark or design should be capital as being for the total loss of the sub-stratum of the business (see *Handley Page Ltd v Butterworth* (1935) 19 TC 328). It also seems from that case that an outright sale of one of several designs or trade marks by an inventor is a capital receipt if the capital asset concerned ceased to be owned. However, if the lump sum was paid for a licence, it is normally treated as income on general principles on the basis that the asset was retained.

Any capital receipt is, of course, liable as a chargeable gain under TCGA 1992, s. 21. The same principles apply if the inventor is unable to register the design.

22.16 Fees and expenses

It is specifically provided that the fees or expenses incurred in the registration of a design or trade mark, or in an extension of the period of copyright in a design or a renewal of the registration of a trade mark, can be treated as a trading expense by virtue of ICTA 1988, s. 83. This is so even if they give rise to a capital asset and would otherwise be disallowed under ICTA 1988, s. 74(1)(f).

Chapter 23 Subcontractors

23.1 Tax deduction scheme

A tax deduction scheme for subcontractors in the construction and building industry was first introduced in 1971. Under the scheme in its original form, a contractor making a payment to a self-employed subcontractor had to deduct tax at the current standard rate and pay it to the Inland Revenue, unless the subcontractor had an exemption certificate or was a limited company.

The subcontractor scheme has been subject to much change. It was substantially revised with effect from 1 August 1999, and a new scheme is to be introduced from April 2006. The commentary relates to the scheme as it applies for 2004–05, and is substantially based on the Inland Revenue Manuals.

The new scheme applying from 6 April 2006 is outlined at **23.14**.

Guidance for non-UK resident contractors and subcontractors operating in the construction industry scheme (CIS) can be found in Inland Revenue leaflet IR 180 (CIS – *Construction Industry Scheme – A guide for non-residents*) which gives advice on the scheme and also provides details of a central point of contact at the Centre for Non-Residents (CNR), Fitz Roy House, PO Box 46, Nottingham NG2 1BD, tel: (0151) 210 2222.

From 10 March 2003, non-UK resident companies which do not have a permanent establishment in the UK can register for CIS with the CNR rather than with a local tax office. Companies which have a permanent establishment in the UK should continue to deal with the office which holds their corporation tax records.

Also in March 2003 the Inland Revenue published a revised Code of Practice 3 (*Reviews of Employers' and Contractors' Records*), which covers their routine visits to employers and also to contractors within the construction industry scheme. This version updates the April 2000 edition.

Subcontractors

23.2 Background

The special tax deduction scheme in the construction industry applies to payments made by contractors to subcontractors for work involving construction, installation, repairs, fitting, decorating and demolition. The terms 'contractor' and 'subcontractor' are widely defined. In essence, the scheme requires a contractor to make tax deductions at a prescribed rate from amounts payable to subcontractors for services unless the subcontractor holds a valid subcontractor's certificate issued by the Revenue. There are various classes of certificates that a subcontractor may hold.

Subcontractors whose tax is deducted at source by contractors receive a deduction certificate and settle up their tax and Class 4 National Insurance liabilities with their inspector at the end of the year. Those holding a subcontractor's certificate issued by the Revenue pay directly to the Revenue under self assessment.

Some businesses may act solely as contractors or as subcontractors, but many act as both. This means that they both pay businesses below them and are paid by businesses above them in a chain. Thus, for some of their transactions they will have to follow the rules for contractors and for others the rules for subcontractors.

As from 6 April 2000, the deduction rate applying to payments under CIS was reduced from basic rate to 18 per cent. There are over 500,000 sub-contractors who are paid after deduction of tax. The reason for the reduction is to take account of personal allowances and the lower rate band, with a view to getting closer to the final tax liability which is likely to fall on sub-contractors.

23.3 IR35 and the construction industry: ESC C32

The IR35 rules require people using service companies to have to account for tax and NIC by 19 April on a minimum amount of salary, based on the money received during the tax year from engagements which would have counted as employment apart from the existence of the company. A worker in the construction industry may also have suffered deduction of tax from the same income under CIS. Although these deductions can be repaid once the company has submitted its accounts, the timing of the repayment may create cash flow difficulties.

Extra-statutory Concession (ESC) C32 allows a company to avoid paying tax twice on the same money, if repayment of CIS deductions is claimed before 31 January following the end of the tax year for which the deemed salary payment has been calculated. If a service company informs the Revenue, when it sends in the end-of-year employer's return, that it wants to defer paying the tax due under IR35, it will be able to set the CIS repayment against the PAYE and NIC due, so that payment of two amounts of tax is avoided.

Where such a claim is accepted, interest will not be charged on any late-paid tax and NIC due under IR35, to the extent that late-paid tax and NIC is matched by the CT repayment due to the company, up to the date of repayment of the CT.

A company will need to include enough information in its claim to identify the amounts to be matched.

Claims under ESC C32 in respect of tax and NIC due on 19 April 2001 under IR35 had to be made by 31 January 2002. Although the concession states that it will be reviewed for years after 2000–01, it thus far has continued into 2004–05.

23.4 What is a 'contractor'?

The term 'contractor' has a wide meaning. It includes the following.

1. Any person carrying on a business which includes construction operations and who pays others for work carried out within the scheme.
2. A property developer or speculative builder, erecting and altering buildings in order to make a profit.
3. A labour agency or staff bureau supplying self-employed workers to perform construction operations. Such an agency or bureau may also be a subcontractor.
4. A gang-leader.
5. A foreign business if it carries out construction operations in the UK or within UK territorial waters (up to the 12-mile limit).
6. Any of the following which spends on average more than £1 million a year on construction operations:
    (a) a public office or Department of the Crown (including Northern Ireland);

Subcontractors

  (b) a local authority;
  (c) a development corporation;
  (d) the Commission for the New Towns;
  (e) the Housing Corporation, Housing for Wales, a housing trust, a housing society, Scottish Homes and the Northern Ireland Housing Executive;
  (f) certain public bodies named in the regulations, such as National Health Trusts, and
  (g) non-construction businesses.

Private householders having work done on their own premises (for example, redecoration, repairs or an extension), or a business where the trading activities do not include construction operations and the average annual expenditure on construction work on its own premises in recent years has been less than £1 million a year, are *not* contractors for the purposes of the scheme.

23.5 What is a subcontractor?

A subcontractor is any business which has agreed to carry out construction operations for another business or public body which is a contractor – whether by doing the operations itself, or by having them done by its own employees, or in any other way. Subcontractors include concerns normally known as main contractors, where they are engaged by a client who is a contractor, for example, a local authority.

The term encompasses the following.

1. A company, any corporate body or public body, as well as any individual self-employed person(s) running a business or partnership.

2. A labour agency or staff bureau which contracts either to get work done with its own workforce, or to supply workers to a contractor.

3. A foreign business if the construction operations for which it is being paid take place in the UK or within UK territorial waters (up to the 12-mile limit).

4. A local authority (and its Direct Service or Labour Organisation) or public body (or its subsidiaries) if they are engaged on construction operations for someone else.

5. A gang-leader who agrees with a contractor on the work to be done, and in turn receives payment for the work of the gang.

Where a worker is supplied to a contractor by or through an agency, and the worker carries out construction operations under the terms of a contract he or she has with the agency, the agency supplying the worker is a subcontractor as far as the contractor is concerned. In all cases the contractor should apply the scheme when paying the agency. If the agency does not hold a valid certificate, the contractor must ask to see the agency's registration card before making payment under deduction.

Special rules applying to agency workers normally treat the worker as an employee for income tax and National Insurance contribution (NIC) purposes. The person paying the worker should therefore normally deduct income tax under PAYE and account for Class 1 NICs. Where, very exceptionally, the special rules for agency workers do not apply (ie where the worker's contract is established to be one of self-employment), the agency is a contractor, and should apply CIS when making payments to the worker.

However, where a worker is merely introduced to the contractor by an agency and carries out construction operations under the terms of a contract he or she has with the contractor, the scheme does not apply to the agency.

23.6 What type of 'construction' is within the scheme?

The phrase 'construction operations' covers almost anything that is done to a permanent or temporary building, structure, civil engineering work or installation, including site preparation, alteration, dismantling, construction, repair and demolition.

Anything done on a construction site in the UK or within its territorial waters (up to the 12-mile limit) in connection with construction work and under contract to the owner, client, main contractor or a subcontractor is likely to be a construction operation. The only exceptions are things that are clearly not construction work, such as the running of canteen, hostel, medical, safety, security or temporary office facilities.

Booklet IR14/15 (CIS) contains a detailed list of construction operations and shows which types of construction work are within the scheme and which are not. The list cannot include every possible construction job, and where areas of doubt arise, it is prudent to check the position with the Revenue.

Subcontractors

It is, however, clear that where a single contract relates to a mixture of jobs, all payments due under the contract are within the scheme, even if only one of the jobs is within the meaning of construction operations.

23.7 Who qualifies for a 'gross certificate'?

Three tests must be satisfied before a business can hold a tax certificate enabling it to be paid without deductions at source:

- the *business* test;
- the *compliance* test, and
- the *turnover* test.

23.7.1 The business test

Booklet IR40 states that the business must be:

- carrying out construction work in the UK, or providing labour for such work;
- run through a bank account;
- run with proper records, and
- run from proper premises with proper stock, equipment and other facilities.

The last is dependent on the nature of the business.

23.7.2 The compliance test

Taxpayers must establish a 'qualifying period' of three years ending with the date of the application. For all periods ending within the qualifying period, the taxpayer must have:

- completed all returns issued;
- supplied any information requested to the Revenue;
- paid all tax due;
- paid all NICs due;

- paid all tax and NICs due as an employer, and
- paid any deductions due as a contractor in the construction industry.

It is made clear that the compliance obligations must have been met on time, and applications are not considered where taxpayers have merely brought their affairs up to date just before the application.

The test *may* still be satisfied where the failure to comply has been 'minor and technical'; a phrase which is defined at length in Booklet IR40.

23.7.3 The turnover test

Having satisfied the above two tests, a business qualifies for a tax certificate only where it can further meet the turnover test. Over a given period this measures the turnover of the business net of the cost of materials supplied.

The Revenue set out the various tests in the following table.

	Sole Traders	Partnerships	Companies
Standard test			
3 years within the 4 years to date of application. Averaging applies.	£30,000 per year	£30,000 × number of partners	£30,000 × number of 'relevant persons'
Six month test			
6 consecutive months within the 12 months to date of application, or shorter period	£21,000 per 6 months	£21,000 × number of partners	£21,000 × number of 'relevant persons'
Alternative test			
3 years within the 4 years to date of application. Averaging applies.		£200,000 per year	£200,000 per year

Partnerships and companies may count *all* their construction income, net of materials, whether or not it arises within the construction industry scheme, as 'turnover' for the purpose of meeting the threshold. Legislation has been introduced in Finance Act 1999 to extend this test to individuals, subject to there being no abuse.

Where the multiple partnership and company turnover tests are used on the three-year basis, the thresholds are arrived at by multiplying the maximum number of partners or directors (and shareholders of close companies) in each of the three years by the individual turnover threshold of £30,000.

Example 23.1

A construction partnership makes an application on 1.6.99. The year end is 30 April; the period chosen for the test is the three years ended 30.4.99.

Partners A, B and C are in the firm throughout the period. Partner D is with the firm at the start of the period but leaves on 31.10.98. The individual threshold set in the regulations for the whole of this period is £30,000.

The partnership's construction turnover, net of the cost of materials, is £92,000, £95,000 and £100,000 in the years ended in 1997, 1998 and 1999 respectively.

The strict multiple thresholds (based on the maximum number of partners at any point in each of the three years) are £120,000 in each case.

However, concessionally (as the application was made before 1.8.01), the thresholds for each of the years can be based on the maximum number of partners in the last six months from 1.11.98 — 30.4.99, ie £90,000 for each period.

The partnership meets this threshold in each year and thus passes the turnover test.

A concession (published on 23 October 1998) has been made to allow the multiple turnover thresholds for all three years in such cases to be based on the maximum number of partners or directors and shareholders at any point in the last six months of the three-year period, if that results in lower thresholds. The concession applied to applications for gross payment certificates made before 1 August 2001.

23.8 Certificates and procedures

From commencement of the current scheme on 1 August 1999, contractors making payments to subcontractors for work within CIS must examine the new gross payment certificates and registration cards presented to them by subcontractors. Payments to those holding registration cards are subject to deductions on account of tax and Class 4 NICs. All payments made under the scheme must be accompanied by vouchers, prepared and transmitted either in paper or electronic form.

23.9 Registration cards (CIS4)

Even if someone holds a registration card it is the contractor's responsibility to establish whether or not the person is employed or self-employed. If he or she is employed, the PAYE system must be operated. The contractor should consult the Tax Office if there is any doubt.

Before making any payment under deduction, the contractor must see and ensure that the subcontractor's registration card is genuine and the person producing it is the user of that card. The contractor should establish whether the card is a permanent or temporary one.

Where the contractor has previously seen the subcontractor's permanent registration card and has no reason to doubt that the person who produced it remains the user of that card, he or she need not ask to see it again.

The following should be excluded when working out the amount of payment from which the deduction should be made:

- value added tax (VAT);
- what the subcontractor actually paid for materials, consumable stores, fuel (except fuel for travelling), plant hire used in the construction operations;
- the cost of manufacture or prefabrication of materials used in the construction operations, and
- any Construction Industry Training Board levy.

Any travelling expenses (including fuel costs) and subsistence paid to the sub-contractor should be included in the payment from which the deduction is made.

Subcontractors should supply the contractor with evidence of the actual cost to them of materials. Where this is not done, the contractor should make a fair estimate of the actual cost of materials. A contractor must always check, as far as possible, that the part of the payment for materials supplied is not over-stated.

The contractor must supply the subcontractor with a CIS25 voucher to evidence payments made under deduction in the previous month.

23.10 Subcontractor's tax certificate (CIS6)

If the contractor is not satisfied that a certificate is valid, a deduction from the payment must be made. Payment can only be made on sight of either a valid tax certificate or registration card.

Failure to operate the rules correctly may cause a contractor to be liable for the deductions that should have been made and could result in the withdrawal of the contractor's own tax certificate.

Even if someone holds a subcontractor's tax certificate, it is the contractor's responsibility to establish whether or not the person is employed or self-employed. If he or she is employed, the PAYE system must be operated. The contractor should consult the Tax Office if there is any doubt.

Before the first payment is made the contractor must inspect the certificate and make the following checks.

1. Is it genuine? Always see the original certificate — not a copy. Check that it is one issued by the Inland Revenue.
2. Is it in date? Check that the 'valid from' date has passed and that the 'expires end' date has not been reached.
3. Is this the certificate holder? Check that the photograph on the certificate is of the person presenting it. Ask for a specimen signature and check it matches the signature on the certificate. If there is still some doubt the contractor should ask for further proof of identity.
4. Do the vouchers match? On making payment, check that the name and National Insurance number (NINO) on the certificate (or registration number in the case of a company holding a CIS5 certificate) match the details shown on the voucher.

Only if the contractor is satisfied, as a result of these checks, can payment be made without deduction, but where it is requested that the payment is made to anyone other than the holder of a valid certificate, the holder of a CIS6 certificate must use it only for payments to the business named on the certificate. If the holder has another business, payments without deduction can only be obtained with a separate certificate relating to that business.

Further payments may continue to be made gross to the subcontractor without further inspection of the certificate provided that the certificate has not expired, and there is no reason to doubt that the certificate is still valid. This is referred to as the 'run-on' rule.

The subcontractor is responsible for supplying a CIS24 voucher for each/all payments received on a monthly basis, to the contractor making those payments.

23.11 Construction tax certificate (CIS5)

Under the CIS, which was introduced in August 1999, a subcontractor may qualify for either a CIS5 or CIS6 certificate.

Although the CIS5 certificate is easier to use, since it does not have to be personally presented to the contractor, it poses a greater security risk. For this reason, CIS5 certificates should be given only to companies which have a very good tax history, can demonstrate a genuine need to hold them, and would have great difficulty trading with CIS6 certificates.

A CIS5 will be issued to a company or partnership which fulfils one or more of the following three conditions. The business must:

- be a plc, or subsidiary of a plc, or a partnership;
- have a turnover of at least £1 million, or
- show that operating with a CIS6 would cause substantial difficulties.

An applicant relying only on the last condition listed has to supply with the application form a detailed 'business case', setting out evidence of either an administrative or commercial need for a CIS5. An administrative need arises where using CIS6s would involve a high volume of vouchers each year – something in the order of 300 a year – or an excessive amount of travelling specifically to present a CIS6 (at least 200 hours over a three-year period, or

Subcontractors

100 hours in any one of those years). A commercial need would normally arise where the applicant's trade is largely based on work for contractors who give work only to CIS5 holders.

Two methods are available to subcontractors to evidence they hold a valid certificate:

- the *certificate method* whereby the certificate is produced to the contractor for inspection, and
- the *certifying document method* where a special certifying document signed by the secretary or a director is given to the contractor certifying that a valid certificate is held, and certifying the details on it.

Similar checks to those outlined above must be made by the contractor before making a payment without deduction.

The contractor must complete a CIS23 voucher, one copy of which is retained for the contractor's records, in respect of each payment made to a subcontractor holding a CIS5 certificate.

23.12 Employment status

A contractor needs to consider whether or not a particular worker is in fact an employee rather than a self-employed subcontractor. The Inland Revenue published guidance in *Tax Bulletin* issue 28 as follows.

> 'How does a contractor decide if a worker is employed or self-employed? There is no statutory definition of 'employment'. However, the question of employment status has come before the Courts on many occasions over the years. The approach taken by the Courts has been to identify the factors which help to determine if a particular contract amounts to employment or self-employment. It is important to note, though, that the contract does not necessarily have to be in writing. It can be written, or oral, or it may be implied by the way in which the parties deal with each other. It may even be a combination of all three.
>
> The relevant factors are:
>
> *Control*
>
> It is a feature of employment that the engager has the right to tell the worker what to do, or where or when to do it, or how it is to be done. The extent of

control may vary from one case to another — a contractor will probably exercise more control over an unskilled labourer than over a skilled craftsman. However, a working relationship which involves no control at all is unlikely to be an employment *(Ready Mixed Concrete (South East) Ltd v Minister of Pensions and National Insurance* [1968] 2 QB 497).

The right to get a substitute or helper to do the job

Personal service is an essential element of a contract of employment. A person who has the freedom to choose whether to do the job himself or hire somebody else to do it for him, or who can hire someone else to provide substantial help, is probably self-employed (*Australian Mutual Provident Society v Chaplin* (1978) 18 ALR 385).

Provision of equipment

A self-employed contractor generally provides whatever equipment is needed to do the job (though in many trades, such as carpentry, it is common for employees, as well as self-employed workers, to provide their own hand tools). Provision by the engager of the major items of equipment and/or the materials necessary to do the job will point towards employment (*Ready Mixed Concrete (South East) Ltd v Minister of Pensions and National Insurance*).

Financial risk

An individual who risks his own money by, for example, buying assets and bearing their running costs and paying for overheads and large quantities of materials, is almost certainly self-employed. Financial risk could also take the form of quoting a fixed price for a job, with the consequent risk of bearing the additional costs if the job overruns. However, this will not necessarily mean that the worker is self-employed unless there is a real risk of financial loss (*Market Investigations Ltd v The Minister of Social Security* [1968] 2 QB 173).

Basis of payment

Employees tend to be paid a fixed wage or salary by the week or month and often qualify for additional payments such as overtime, long service bonus or profit share. Independent contractors, on the other hand, tend to be paid a fixed sum for a particular job. Payment 'by the piece' (where the worker is paid according to the amount of work actually done) can be a feature of both employment and self-employment (see Example 2 below).

Opportunity to profit from sound management

A person whose profit or loss depends on his capacity to reduce overheads and organise his work effectively may well be self-employed (*Market Investigations Ltd v The Minister of Social Security*). People who are paid by the job will often be in this position.

Right of dismissal

A right to terminate an engagement by giving notice of a specified length is a common feature of employment. It is less common in a contract for services, which usually ends only on completion of the task, or if the terms of the contract are breached.

Employee benefits

Employees are often entitled to sick pay, holiday pay, pensions, expenses and so on. However, the absence of those features does not necessarily mean that the worker is self-employed — especially in the case of short-term engagements (see Example 1).

Length of engagement

Long periods working for one contractor may be typical of an employment but are not conclusive. It is still necessary to consider all the terms and conditions of each engagement. Regular working for the same contractor may indicate that there is a single and continuing contract of employment (*Nethermere (St Neots) Ltd v Gardiner* (1984) ICR 612). See also Question 5 below.

Personal factors

In deciding a person's employment status it may sometimes be necessary to take into account factors which are personal to the worker and which have little to do with the terms of the particular engagement being considered. For example, if a skilled craftsman works for a number of contractors throughout the year and has a business-like approach to obtaining his engagement (perhaps involving expenditure on office accommodation, office equipment, etc) this will point towards self-employment (*Hall v Lorimer*, 66 TC 349). Personal factors will usually carry less weight in the case of an unskilled worker, where other factors such as the high level of control exercised by the contractor are likely to be conclusive of employment.

Employment status

Intention

It is the reality of the relationship that matters. It is not enough to call a person 'self-employed' if all the terms and conditions of the engagement point towards employment. However, if other factors are neutral the intention of the parties will then be the decisive factor in deciding employment status (*Massey v Crown Life Insurance Co* [1978] ICR 590).

When the detailed facts have been established the right approach is to stand back and look at the picture as a whole, to see if the overall effect is that of a person in business on his own account or a person working as an employee in somebody else's business. If the evidence is evenly balanced the intention of the parties may then decide the issue (*Massey v Crown Life Insurance Co*).

Example 1 — General labourer

Facts	Comments
(1) Job description/control Undertakes a variety of unskilled and semi-skilled work (eg digging footings assisting craftsmen, etc). Engager moves him from task to task as necessary. Can be told how to do a particular task but this is generally unnecessary in view of his experience.	Strong control exists here. The more important features are the engager's ability to move the worker from job to job as priorities change and to have the ultimate say in how the work should be carried out.
(2) Payment basis/risk Paid a weekly wage plus overtime.	No financial risk or opportunity to profit from sound management. Points to employment.
(3) Holiday/sick pay No sick pay paid (has been sick twice over last 12 months). No holiday pay but has been allowed to take three weeks off (unpaid) for holidays during engagements over the last 12 months.	The engagements run to some months and holiday pay/sick pay might be expected. But both parties think the engagement is self-employment and this is probably why no such payments are made. A minor pointer towards self-employment.

Subcontractors

(4) Length of engagement and personal factors Taken on for the expected duration of the engager's building project — usually weeks or months with the actual length depending on how well the project progresses. Has worked for the same engager almost exclusively for three years — but with two periods of 'unemployment' of three weeks and two months during that time.	Not a 'permanent' employment, but a series of fairly lengthy separate engagements with one engager. No evidence of working for several engagers. Overall, the pattern of work suggests employment.
Does odd jobs for private householders at weekends with payment 'by the task'. Earned £600 from this over the last 12 months.	Is to this extent 'in business'. But small part-time earnings of this nature will not be a key factor when measured against a full time engagement running to weeks or months.
Worker keeps an 'office' at home. He has a home computer which he uses to record income and expenses. He also has a phone which he uses to arrange weekend work and new contracts.	Has an office and is fairly business-like in the way he organises and runs his engagements. This point towards self-employment.
Other factors All equipment and materials provided by the engager except for working clothes and boots.	}
Hired personally to do the work.	}All point to employment
Engagement can be terminated by either side on one week's notice	}
Both parties clearly intend that the engagements amount to self-employment	Pointer towards self-employment and important in borderline situations. Not conclusive where — overall — other factors point to employment.

Employment status

> **Overall picture**
>
> The picture which emerges is of a weekly-paid worker carrying out unskilled and semi-skilled work with the engager having strong control. These are strong pointers towards employment. Other factors also point to employment (equipment, lack of financial risk, period of notice). Although some personal factors point to self-employment taking ALL factors into account the engagements amount to employment.
>
> The mutual intention for self-employment would only be decisive where the other factors were borderline — and here they point to employment.
>
> The result would be similar even if personal factors were stronger (eg regular working for many engagers). Other factors (particularly the strong right of control) would outweigh such factors.

Example 2 — Plasterer

Facts	Comments
(1) Job description/control Contracted to plaster walls and ceilings of a two classroom school extension. Cannot be told 'how' to do the work but it must be completed satisfactorily. Work to be done during normal working hours at the site.	Little or no control over 'what' is to be done and 'where' (fixed by the contract) or how it is to be done. Limited control over when the work is to be done. Points to self-employment.
(2) Substitution May choose to pay and send a substitute or use assistants. Engaged and used an assistant to help throughout the contract.	Strong pointer towards self-employment.
(3) Equipment and materials Provides only equipment needed (hand tools and shovel/container for mixing). Materials supplied by engager.	No significant equipment required. The fact that the engager supplies materials points towards employment.

Subcontractors

(4) Payment basis/risk Paid per square metre plastered. Worker is responsible for completing entire job within time allotted.	There is opportunity to maximise profit from the sound management of the task. Worker must complete the contract so this is not pure piecework and there is real financial risk. Eg, were the worker to fall ill he would be responsible for hiring others to complete the contract (even at a loss).
Three week deadline for completion with a penalty of £100 per day for failure to complete the work on time.	Further risks arise from the penalty clause for failing to meet the deadline and the requirement to rectify work at his own cost (including materials).
Must rectify faulty work in own time and at own cost (including supplying extra materials needed).	All pointers to self-employment.
Other factors Length of contract — three weeks	A minor pointer to self-employment.
Works for many engagers (20 in past 12 months). All contracts of less than six weeks' duration.	Has a pattern of working under short-term contracts for many different engagers. Pointer to self-employment.
No holiday or sick pay. No right to end contract unless serious breach of terms.	Not significant in the context of a three week engagement.
No office at home. Prepares accounts from record book recording all receipts and expenditure. Has a phone which he uses to arrange new contracts.	Little in the way of a 'business organisation' (eg yard or office, etc). Not a significant pointer either way.
Both parties intend that the engagements amount to self-employment.	Pointer towards self-employment in borderline situations.

> *Overall picture*
> The picture painted is of a self-employed individual carrying out skilled work and genuinely accepting the risks of being in business on his own account. The worker:
>
> - is subject to little control
> - faces real financial risk
> - engages and pays an assistant to help perform the contract
> - works for a variety of engagers on fairly short-term contracts.

Example 3 — Bricklayer

Facts	Comments
(1) Job description/control Engaged solely as a bricklayer. Engager moves him from task to task as necessary. He is provided with helpers who mix mortar carry bricks, etc. Engager cannot tell him 'how' he wants the work done but expects competent workmanship and a reasonable level of output.	Control over 'what" is to be done — but limited to the extent of what bricks should be laid and cannot be diverted to quite different work. Little control over the manner in which the work is to be done. An employment pointer but not as strong as in Example 1.
(2) Substitution Hired personally to do the work.	Points toward employment.
(3) Equipment All provided by engager except for working clothes, boots and trowel.	Workers providing own 'small tools'. Engager supplies other equipment and all materials. Pointer to employment.
(4) Payment basis/risk Paid a weekly wage plus overtime	No financial risk or opportunity to profit from sound management. Points to employment.

Subcontractors

(5) Length of contract Taken on for the expected duration of the engager's building project (usually weeks or months at a time). Has worked for the same engager almost exclusively for three years but with three periods of 'unemployment' of one week, three weeks and one month during that time.	Not a 'permanent' employment but a series of fairly lengthy separate engagements with one engager. No evidence of working for several engagers. Overall, the pattern of working suggests employment.
(6) Right of dismissal Engagement can be terminated by either side on one week's notice.	Pointer towards employment.
(7) Holiday/sick pay No sick pay paid (has been sick once over last 12 months). No holiday pay but has been allowed to take a total of three weeks off for holidays (unpaid) during engagements over the last 12 months.	The engagements run to some months and holiday/sick pay might be expected. But both parties think the engagements are self-employment and this is probably why no such payments are made. A minor pointer towards self-employment.
(8) Intention Both parties clearly intend that the engagements amount to self-employment.	Pointer towards self-employment and important in borderline situations. Not conclusive where overall other factors point to employment.
(9) Personal factors No office at home. Records income and expenditure in a notebook. Has a phone which he uses to arrange weekend work and new contracts.	Little in the way of a 'business organisation' (eg yard or office, etc). Not a significant pointer either way.

Does odd jobs for private householders at weekends with payment 'by the task' — earned £600 from this over the last 12 months.	Is to this extent 'in business'. But small part-time earnings of this nature will not be a key factor when measured against a full-time engagement running to weeks or months.
Prior to first working for this engager had been an apprentice bricklayer with another firm.	No evidence of existing full-time business prior to working for this engager.
Has had a 714 certificate for the last three years — which expires in two years time.	Not a relevant factor.

Overall picture
The picture painted is of a skilled worker who is told what is to be done at any particular time but with little control over how it is to be done. 'Control' points towards employment but not as strongly as in the Example 1. Other factors also point towards employment (eg weekly wage, lack of financial risk, period of notice). Of those factors pointing to self employment:

— Lack of holiday and sick pay are not conclusive.

— Mutual intention will only be decisive where other factors put the engagement near the borderline.

— There are no significant personal factors pointing to self-employment. There is not, for example, a clear pattern of regular working for many engagers or regular working under very short-term contracts. Further there is no evidence of an established pattern of working and business prior to the series of engagements with this engager.

Overall, the terms and conditions alone point towards employment and personal factors do not significantly affect this. The contracts are therefore considered to be contracts of employment.

But the case is not far from the point where mutual intention would be decisive. If there had been a single ongoing contract or holiday pay/sick pay had been paid the argument for employment would be much stronger. On the other hand, if significant personal factors had existed (eg regular working for many engagers under short-term contracts), or there had been task-based payment, the picture overall would probably be sufficiently borderline for mutual intention to decide that these SEPARATE engagements amounted to self-employment.

23.13 Expenses

If subcontractors are treated as self-employed, operating from home, and can be said to move around frequently from contract to contract so that the only fixed place from which they work is their home, they can claim to deduct an allowance of part of the costs of running their house, the payment of a secretarial wage to their spouse, if applicable, and travelling expenses to and from the sites. The allowability of such expenses was confirmed in the test case of *Horton v Young* (1971) 47 TC 69.

The new Sch. E expenses regime that came into effect on 6 April 1998 provides more generous relief for travelling and subsistence expenses for site-based employees.

The cost of lunch on the site and other living rather than working expenses are not allowable (*Caillebotte v Quinn* [1975] STC 265). To this extent, therefore, the self-employed subcontractor is worse off than employees in the construction and allied industries who are not taxed on allowances towards travelling, subsistence and lodging made by their employers if they fall within the working rule agreements ((1981) STI p. 64), and who in any event are more notably treated under the new expenses regime referred to above.

In *Phillips v Hamilton and Macken v Hamilton* SpC 366 19.5.03 [2003] STI Issue 23, the issue was whether travel expenditure was deductible from emoluments insofar as relating to travel between 'temporary workplaces' or whether it was non-deductible as 'ordinary commuting'.

P was a construction worker registered with an agency P Ltd, which was a subsidiary of C plc, a construction company. In 2000–01, P had three separate assignments, each with a separate contract with C plc and two other construction companies. The three assignments were geographically spread.

M was also registered with P Ltd. His permanent address was in Birmingham. In tax year 1998–99, he had an assignment with C plc at a site in Bristol. During the year he became directly employed by C plc and continued to work at the Bristol site. In total he worked at that site from March 1998 to May 2000.

ICTA 1988, s. 198(1) (now ITEPA 2003, s. 337) provides for the deduction of qualifying travel expenses. Section 198(1A) (ITEPA 2003, s. 338(2)) excludes expenses of ordinary commuting, defined by Sch. 12A, para. 2(1) (s. 338(3)) as travel between home and a permanent workplace. Para. 4 (s. 339(2)) defines a permanent workplace as a place which an employee regularly attends in the performance of the duties of the employment and which is not a temporary workplace. A 'temporary workplace' means a place which the employee attends in the performance of the duties of the employment for the purpose of performing a task of limited duration or for some other temporary purpose. Para. 5(1)(a), (b) (s. 339(5)) provides that a place is not regarded as a temporary workplace if the employee's attendance is in the course of a period of continuous work at that place lasting more than 24 months or comprising all or almost all of the period for which the employee is likely to hold the employment.

P and M both submitted self assessments deducting their travelling expenses. The Revenue amended the assessments. P and M appealed, contending that the expenses of travelling from their homes to the building sites were qualifying travelling expenses and not ordinary commuting.

The Special Commissioner decided that commuting to and from work at a temporary job was ordinary commuting because the *locus in quo* was a permanent workplace within para. 4 and not a temporary one. In the relevant year of assessment P had had three assignments and signed a separate contract for each. They were with three different clients and were at three different places. They were therefore three separate employments or temporary jobs. P's attendance at each place of work was in the course of a period of continuous work at that place which comprised all of the period for which he held that employment. Thus under Sch. 12A, para. 5(1)(b) each workplace was a permanent workplace. Travel from his home to each workplace was ordinary commuting. Therefore the expenses were not qualifying expenses and were not deductible.

In the relevant year of assessment M was originally an agency worker working for C plc in Bristol and had then become employed by C plc while continuing to work at Bristol. Although he had therefore had one temporary job and one permanent job in that year, he had nevertheless worked continuously at the same site in Bristol for more than 24 months, beginning before that year of assessment and ending after it. Under Sch. 12A, para. 5(1)(a) the Bristol site could not be regarded as a temporary workplace, from which it followed that it had to be a permanent workplace. M's travel from home to the Bristol site was therefore ordinary commuting and so the expenses were not qualifying expenses and not deductible.

23.14 New scheme from 6 April 2006

A new subcontractor scheme is planned to cone into effect from April 2006. The necessary legislation to implement the new scheme is contained within the FA 2004, Ch. 3.

The new scheme aims to:

- reduce the regulatory burden of the scheme on the construction industry;
- improve the level of compliance by construction businesses with their tax obligations; and
- to help the construction industry to get the employment status of its workers correct.

Under the new scheme, the current registration card system will be replaced with a verification service that can be accessed by telephone or over the internet. This will remove the need for subcontractors holding a CIS4 registration card or a CIS6 tax certificate to present these in person. The new scheme will also feature an employment status declaration, which is designed to ensure that all those engaging subcontractors take the responsibility of determining employment status seriously.

The new scheme will feature periodic returns in place of the current system of vouchers. The voucher system places a large administrative burden on contractors and is incompatible with the move towards electronic communication. The new returns-based system will be compatible with electronic delivery and should reduce the administrative burden placed on contractors.

Chapter 24 Local councillors and members of Government boards

24.1 Reimbursed expenses

Holders of an unpaid office are not liable to tax on any amount reimbursed to them as expenses. This position has been accepted by the Inland Revenue for many years and includes members of the House of Lords, local authority councillors, justices of the peace, etc in receipt of expenses allowances only, and members of Government committees in the same position.

24.2 Attendance allowances

Under Part 7, Ch. 1 of the Income Tax (Pay As You Earn) Regulations 2003 (SI 2003 No. 2682) attendance allowances paid to local councillors under the various UK Local Government Acts may, at the taxpayer's option, be paid under deduction of basic rate income tax where the taxpayer is unhappy with the manner in which his or her coding is determined. In such a case, however, part of any attendance allowance may be paid gross, to the extent that the councillor can show that he or she has to incur expenses allowable under normal employment income rules.

Allowances taxable as employment income under ITEPA 2003 include the following:

- basic allowance;
- attendance allowance;
- special responsibility allowance, and
- conference attendance allowance.

Special rules apply where an individual receives a financial loss allowance. This is not an emolument and cannot therefore be taxed as employment income.

24.3 Expenses

Councillors and civic dignitaries who receive an allowance taxable as employment income under ITEPA 2003 may be entitled to claim a deduction for qualifying travelling expenses and other expenses incurred wholly exclusively and necessarily in the performance of their duties to the extent that they are not already reimbursed for these costs by the council.

The most common types of allowable expenditure are likely to be telephone calls, postage, stationery, travelling expenses on non-approved duties and use of home. Local authorities differ in their definition of approved duties for which travelling and subsistence allowances are payable and in the other assistance provided for councillors. The level of expenses claimed may, therefore, vary not only because of the weight of work undertaken by a councillor but because of the local authority's policy on the reimbursement of expenses. It is accepted that councillors normally have two places of work. This means that travelling allowances are not taxable provided that the councillor undertakes duties on behalf of the authority at home and is paid for travel between home and the authority's offices, or the councillor is paid for travel between home or the authority's office and some other place on council business and the mileage allowance paid does not include any element of profit.

24.4 Guidance note prepared by the Association of Local Councillors

'Local councillors – expenses under Section 198 ICTA 1988 (now ITEPA 2003, s. 336)

Attendance allowances, with travelling and subsistence allowances where appropriate, paid by the local authority in connection with approved duties, are assessable to Income Tax under the rules of Schedule E.

In addition to the expenses covered by the travelling and subsistence allowances which councillors receive from the local authority in connection with approved duties certain items of expenditure may also be incurred in their capacity as councillors other than in connection with approved duties. A deduction for tax purposes may be claimed by councillors for such expenses provided they are incurred wholly and exclusively and necessarily in the performance of their duties as councillors and are met from their taxable allowances.

No deduction can be given:

- where reimbursement has been or could be claimed from the local authority
- where a councillor could use services provided by the local authority, for example, postage, stationery, but incurs expenses because he chooses not to do so
- where expenses are incurred for political purposes, for example electioneering
- for an amount in excess of the total taxable allowances received in respect of the councillor's duties
- where a councillor receives a non-taxable allowance (financial loss allowance).

The following notes set out, as a result of discussion with the Inland Revenue, the various types of expenditure concerned, with guidance as to the basis of claim under each individual head. These notes have no legal force and do not affect your rights of appeal on points concerning your own liability to tax. You should remember that the Inspector may require evidence of the amount spent on all or any of the items listed below.

Categories of expenditure

Travel

Councillors may incur expenses on necessary travelling in the performance of their duties as a councillor for which they do not receive an allowance from the local authority (because the authority does not regard that particular travel as part of the councillor's "authorised duties"). In such a case, the councillor may claim expenses as below:

a. Car. In the case of a privately owned car used by a councillor: an allowance calculated using Inland Revenue authorised mileage rates.

Councillors will need to keep records of their mileage on non-approved duties which will attract this relief.

b. Public transport/other. The actual costs incurred for which no allowance can be obtained from the local authority.

Postage and stationery

The amount of claims should be limited to the actual cost incurred.

Telephone

A claim may be made for the cost of calls made in respect of approved and non-approved duties. No deduction can be given for any part of the rental of the telephone. Any claim should be reduced by any non-taxable reimbursement made by the local authority and where that reimbursement covers the cost of the calls no claim should be made.

Secretarial assistance

A deduction may be given for payments for necessary secretarial assistance involving for example drafting replies to letters, typing and filing where such assistance is not provided by the local authority. Any amounts claimed should be reasonable in relation to the councillor's allowances and to the assistance given. The amounts must actually have been paid to the assistant on a regular basis; the Inspector may wish to see evidence of such payments.

Hire of rooms

The expenditure to be claimed should be limited to the amount incurred and should relate to hire for "surgeries" or protest meetings such as objections to planning applications. A claim will not be admitted in respect of the hire of rooms for party political purposes.

Household expenses

Where it is necessary for a councillor to provide facilities at home, to do some of his or her work as a councillor, a deduction can be given for the additional costs incurred such as heating and lighting. Following discussions it has been agreed with the Inland Revenue that a standard deduction of £65 per annum up to 1991–92, and £120 thereafter can be given.

If a room is used exclusively for council business, a claim may be made for the proportion of Council Tax, heat and light relative to that room.'

24.5 Office or profession

Practitioners in a particular professional field undertake special assignments for Government departments and other similar bodies for a fee. Is such an appointment part of the exercise of the profession, taxable under Schedule D, or is it an office taxable under ITEPA 2003? This was the point at issue in *Edwards v Clinch* (1981) 56 TC 367.

The question that the court had to decide was whether certain fees of a professional man were emoluments of an 'office' in the sense of ITEPA 2003, s. 5 (formerly ICTA 1988, s. 19). The taxpayer was a chartered civil engineer, who had for some years been one of a panel of persons invited by the Department of the Environment to conduct independent public inquiries and to make reports thereon. The Crown maintained that each appointment was a separate 'office'. However, in the Court of Appeal, Buckley LJ did not accept that the statutory, public character of the appointed inspector's duties was sufficient to make the appointment an office. An office had to have a sufficient degree of continuance to admit of its being held by successive incumbents, an existence not necessarily prolonged or indefinite, but not an existence limited to the tenure of one man. This requirement for continuance was supported by authority. On this basis, it was decided that the taxpayer was exercising his profession and not holding an office when being remunerated for each appointment. This decision was upheld by the House of Lords.

Chapter 25 Farmers (including market gardeners) and owners of commercial woodlands

25.1 One trade

All farming is treated as the carrying on of a trade, and all farming carried on in the UK by the same person or partnership is treated as one trade (ICTA 1988, s. 53(1) and (2)). This is particularly useful in relation to the carry forward of losses as it is possible, for instance, for the same person to give up farming in one area and recommence elsewhere, and carry forward any unabsorbed losses against future profits from the new farm. The Inland Revenue also allow a gap between the sale of one farm and the purchase of another, and do not insist on applying the cessation provisions in those circumstances, provided that the gap (generally) is not more than 12 months and that there is a genuine intention to continue to carry on farming.

Where there is a change in the person's carrying on a business, extra care is needed to ensure that maximum loss relief is obtained as early as possible. For example, where a business is transferred from a sole trader to a partnership, any trading losses of the sole trader are available to carry forward only against the trader's share of the partnership's subsequent profits. If, therefore, the sole trader has very substantial trading losses brought forward, it is wise to draft the partnership agreement carefully so that initially, if possible, the former sole trader receives the greater part of any profits arising.

The position regarding unused capital allowances depends upon whether or not the business is deemed to be continuing.

If the business continues, unused capital allowances are carried forward and deducted from future profits of the business. If there is a cessation, all unused capital allowances lapse, except for those applicable to the continuing partners and attributable to the part of the year before the change.

Note that where there is a succession between connected persons, the rules are now contained in CAA 2001, s. 266 An election, with a two-year time limit is available to persons chargeable to UK tax on the profits of the trade. The trade is not deemed to be continuing, but the successors can take over the plant and machinery at tax written-down value. However, there is an extended definition of 'connected persons' to include partnerships.

The ability to carry forward losses from one farm to another was the subject of the decision in *Bispham v Eardiston Farming Co (1919) Ltd* (1962) 40 TC 322. In that case, unrelieved losses of one farm sold were allowed against another farm's subsequent profits. The point is particularly relevant in a company situation where there is a change in ownership, as ICTA 1988, s. 768 might otherwise restrict the carry forward of losses. Such a challenge is less easy for the Inland Revenue in the case of a farming company, as all farming is specifically deemed to be one trade.

25.2 Losses

The following provisions are relevant to farming losses.

1. *ICTA 1988, s. 397*, known as the 'hobby farming' provisions. Section 397 prevents the set-off of losses against general income or total profits, under ICTA 1988, ss. 380 (individuals) or 393A(1) (companies), including related capital allowances given in taxing the trade, where there have been five years of continuous losses by the same person. Any revenue loss is computed on normal Sch. D, Case I principles, without regard to capital allowances. In giving income tax relief for losses, it is normally possible to use the loss incurred in the accounting period ending in the year of assessment to establish whether there has been a loss or a profit. For hobby farming purposes, however, the Inland Revenue generally insist on apportioning profits and losses on a fiscal year basis. The farmer must, therefore, make a profit in one of the five years of assessment preceding that for which a loss relief claim is made.

    There are anti-avoidance provisions (ICTA 1988, s. 397(10)), to prevent husband-and-wife partnerships being formed or dissolved in order to recommence another cycle of five years' losses. Generally, where at least one person is involved in carrying on a trade both before and after a deemed discontinuance, the discontinuance is ignored in reckoning whether there have been five years' losses.

    There is a 'let-out' from these provisions if the farmer can prove that no competent farmer could have made a profit in the sixth year if he or she had undertaken the farming at the beginning of the five years concerned. The Inland Revenue also make a concession concerning the rearing of certain forms of livestock — for instance, deer farming or other long-term breeding projects.

As the losses are based on the ordinary adjusted loss, it is best where possible to minimise revenue expenditure (such as repairs) in the fifth year. Equally, where there is a choice of structuring interest as an expense, or as a deduction from total income, the latter course should be taken as this will not then enter into the calculation of the loss. Thus, if a partnership wishes to buy more land, the partners should borrow and inject their personal borrowings into the partnership as capital or interest-free loans, in order to purchase the land as partnership property. The interest is then a charge against their total incomes. The Inland Revenue do not operate any concession where the high cost of borrowing is the cause of the loss.

2. *ICTA 1988, ss. 384 (individuals) and 393A(3) (companies)*. These sections have the effect of denying relief under ICTA 1988, ss. 380 and 393A(1) where a trade is not carried on on a commercial basis and with a view to the realisation of profits.

3. *FA 1991, s. 72.* Where a trading loss has been incurred any excess that cannot be relieved against income may be set against capital gains of the same or following year.

Where owners of farms make a loss, but are debarred from making a claim under ICTA 1988, ss. 380 or 393A(1) by virtue of one of the above sections, Inland Revenue ESC (ESC) B5 allows them to claim the same relief, against general income, for the cost of maintenance, insurance and repairs of agricultural land (including a third of the relevant expenditure on a farmhouse), that an agricultural landlord could claim under ICTA 1988, s. 33 against rents.

Where the Inland Revenue contend that a trade is not carried on on a commercial basis, this also poses a threat to any relief claimed by an individual under ICTA 1988, s. 381. Where an individual carries on a trade and sustains a loss in the first year of assessment or in any of the next three years, he or she may claim to carry back the losses to the period before that trade was commenced. However, ICTA 1988, s. 381(4) denies this relief where the trade is not conducted on a commercial basis and: 'in such a way that profits . . . could reasonably be expected to be realised in [the period in which the loss arose] or within a reasonable time thereafter'.

An inspector may mount a challenge under both ICTA 1988, s. 381(4) and ICTA 1988, s. 384, where relief has been claimed under both ICTA 1988, s. 381, and ICTA 1988, ss. 380 and 383.

Farmers (including market gardeners) and owners of commercial woodlands

Cases have been known where an inspector appears to have been convinced, in part, that a farm is run on a commercial basis because some of the improvements, the costs of which gave rise to the losses, have received approval from the Ministry of Agriculture.

ESC B55 (now obsolete) temporarily relaxed this rule in ICTA 1988, s. 397 for the years 2000–01 and 2001–02 (or, for companies, the accounting period ending in the years ended 31 March 2001 and 31 March 2002) where:

- 2000–01 (or the accounting period ending in the year ended 31 March 2001) is the sixth consecutive year of losses or for 2001–02 (or the accounting period ending in the year ended 31 March 2002) it is the sixth or seventh consecutive year;

- the six year period (or the six or seven-year period for 2001–02) is immediately preceded by one year of profit, and

- there was at least one other year of profit in the three years immediately preceding that one year of profit.

The test of a year of profit before the six (or seven) years of losses ensures that genuine farming businesses which had previously been profitable will benefit, though those who had never made profits will not. The second test, that there be at least one other year of profit in the three years immediately preceding that year of profit, ensures that the relaxation applies only to businesses with a history of profitability before the present difficult time.

> ### *Example 25.1*
>
> A farmer has six loss-making years from 1995–96 to 2000–01, but had a year of profit in 1994–95 and at least one year of profit in 1991–92, 1992–93 or 1993–94. In this case sideways relief would continue to be available in 2000–01. Similarly, if the loss-making years continued into 2001–02, sideways relief would still be available if the conditions were met.

25.3 Stocks

All animals for farming are treated as trading stock for tax purposes (ICTA 1988, Sch. 5, para. 1(1)) unless the 'herd basis' applies (see **25.4** below). This means that the animals should each theoretically be valued at the lower of cost or net realisable value. In March 1993 the Inland Revenue published Business Economic Note 19 *Farming — stock valuation for income tax purposes*. The contents of BEN 19 are reproduced below.

'1. INTRODUCTION

1.1. This statement explains the basis of valuation of farm stock at the end of periods of account which is acceptable to Inspectors of Taxes. It has been prepared to assist farmers and their professional advisers. It has been prepared after consultation between the Inland Revenue, the Central Association of Agricultural Valuers, the Institute of Chartered Accountants in England and Wales, the Institute of Taxation, the Royal Institution of Chartered Surveyors, the Country Landowners Association and the NFU. It supersedes all previous arrangements made by the Inland Revenue and the NFU. It does not affect rights of appeal in individual cases.

1.2. Other methods of valuation may also be acceptable to Inspectors of Taxes in particular cases provided they are recognised by the accountancy profession as a whole as giving a true and fair view of the results for the period concerned and do not violate the taxing statutes as interpreted by the Courts.

1.3. A valuation which, although in form made on a recognised basis, pays insufficient attention to the facts will not be acceptable.

2. GENERAL PRINCIPLES

2.1. The reason for valuing stock at the end of an accounting period is to identify and carry forward those costs which were incurred before that date but will not give rise to income until a later period. By carrying forward those costs they can be matched with the income when it arises. Profit will be understated if stock is not brought in.

2.2. However, if there is no reasonable expectation that the proceeds from the sale of the stock in a future period will be enough to cover the costs, then relief for the expected loss may be obtained in the period for which the accounts are being prepared by valuing the stock at what it is expected to realise when sold in the normal course of trade.

2.3. For tax purposes we are looking for a figure (commonly referred to as a valuation) which represents the cost, or, if lower, the net realisable value of the stock.

2.4. In some circumstances there may be more than one acceptable method of computing the value of stock but the basis of valuation in a particular case should be consistent. If it is decided to change the basis of valuation the Inspector of Taxes should be advised when the accounts are submitted. The Revenue's practice on changes of basis in valuation is set out in Statement of Practice 3/90.

2.5. Occasionally Inspectors discover that the stock figure in the accounts is net of a provision (reserve), for example, for dilapidations. If the creation of such a provision is considered appropriate the Inspector should be made fully aware of it. Provisions are only allowable for tax purposes if profits would not be properly stated in their absence and the amount referable to the year can be quantified with reasonable accuracy. Even if these conditions are met tax law provides that some provisions are not allowable for tax purposes (for example, for repairs to premises which are not allowable unless expended).

2.6. The value of stock is primarily a matter of fact which is ultimately to be decided by the Commissioners in the absence of agreement.

2.7. Valuation problems can be complex, and farmers normally seek the assistance of accountants and agricultural valuers and surveyors. But this is not compulsory and some farmers prepare their own valuations.

2.8. Although strictly livestock should be valued on an animal by animal basis, it is acceptable for farmers to value animals of a similar type and quality together on a global or average basis classified according to age. If deemed cost is used (see paragraph 7 below) home bred animals should be distinguished from animals which have been bought in.

2.9. If tax is lost or delayed as a result of incorrect valuation of stock then interest and penalties may be due in addition to the tax.

3. LIVESTOCK, GROWING AND HARVESTED CROPS

3.1. Production Cost

Production cost is the actual cost of getting the stock into its condition and location at the balance sheet date. Farm stock valuations should include the costs directly attributable to producing or rearing the stock in question. From an accountancy point of view it is preferable but not mandatory, except in the case of certain limited companies, also to include a reasonable proportion of the costs which are only indirectly attributable to the production of the stock to the extent that those costs relate to the period of production as this will result in a more accurate matching of costs with related sales income. Either method, if applied consistently, is acceptable to Inspectors of Taxes.

3.1.1. Direct Costs

3.1.1.1. Costs which are directly attributable to buying, producing and growing the livestock or crops should be included. Such costs will consist not only of the expenses of acquiring the 'raw materials' for example, seeds, but also of any expenses which directly relate to producing or rearing the stock in question. There can be no definitive list, but the following are examples of direct costs:

3.1.2. Livestock

- purchase costs, or
- insemination costs plus additional maternal feed costs in excess of maintenance;

PLUS costs of rearing to the valuation date or maturity if earlier including:

- feed costs including forage;
- vets' fees including drugs;
- drenches and other medicines;
- ringing, cutting and dehorning;
- supervisory employee or contract labour costs.

3.1.3. Growing and Harvested Crops

- seeds;
- fertilisers;
- beneficial sprays (the term beneficial sprays includes preventative sprays and means any sprays which are not applied to remedy a particular infestation or crop deficiency);
- seasonal licence payments (for example, short term hire of land to grow a particular crop) but not normal farm rents;
- drying;
- storage;
- employee (including director) or contract labour and direct machinery costs (for example, fuel, servicing, rental, spares and the reduction in value due to wear and tear caused by actual usage for the activity concerned) incurred on:
    - cultivations,
    - crop working,
    - harvesting.

3.1.4. Indirect costs

3.1.4.1. Once again there can be no definitive list of indirect items, but examples of such costs are:—

- depreciation and maintenance of farm buildings;

Farmers (including market gardeners) and owners of commercial woodlands

- rent and rates (excluding licence payments added under 3.1.3 above);
- general employee (including director) or contract labour and machinery costs.

3.1.5. Cost to be based on expenditure incurred

3.1.5.1. Except where the deemed cost method is used (see 3.2) cost must represent the actual costs incurred by the particular farmer on producing the stock as established from his own records. Larger and specialised businesses, such as intensive pig rearing units, will usually have adequate records to compute cost. The current Guide to Costings as issued by the Central Association of Agricultural Valuers and figures produced by other independent institutions provide useful models to help farmers establish their own costs.

3.1.5.2. Labour costs should not include anything for the notional cost of own labour for sole proprietors or partners.

3.2. Deemed cost acceptable in some circumstances

3.2.1. If it is not possible to ascertain actual costs from the farmer's records, Inspectors will accept deemed cost valuations (see paragraph 7 below).

3.3. Net Realisable Value

3.3.1. If there is no reasonable expectation that the net realisable value of stock will cover costs incurred then the stock should be stated at net realisable value.

3.3.2. Net realisable value consists of:

- The sale proceeds that it is anticipated will be received from the eventual disposal of the stock in the condition in which the farmer intended at his balance sheet date subsequently to market it. It is important to note that the valuation should be made on a normal commercial basis, for instance, it is not acceptable to value stock on the basis that it would have been sold in a forced sale on the balance sheet date in its then possibly immature state.

PLUS

- Grants and subsidies intended to augment the sale prices of stocks (see 5.2).
- For breeding/production animals the ancillary stream of income from the sale of their progeny and produce.

LESS

- The further costs to be incurred in getting the stock into marketable condition and then marketing, selling and distributing that stock. Where the proceeds from the sale of progeny/produce are brought in then the costs relating to their production and marketing should also be deducted.

3.3.3. It is not acceptable to treat cull value as the only future revenue from production animals as this does not recognise the value of the future income stream from the produce and/or progeny.

3.3.4. The Revenue recognises, however, that farmers may not have the extensive records necessary to calculate net realisable value with reasonable accuracy, therefore:

- For production animals such as laying hens and breeding sows which are not usually sold except for slaughter at the end of their productive lives, the Revenue will accept that a reasonable approximation of the net realisable value is the value at the balance sheet date arrived at by consistently writing off the cost, down to anticipated cull value, on a straight line or other appropriate basis over the animal's expected productive life.

- For other production animals the Revenue will accept the use of the open market value of animals of the same kind, quality and condition based on the assumption that there is a willing buyer and a willing seller of the particular animal as a production animal at the balance sheet date.

3.3.5. Where net realisable value is used as being less than cost the Inspector may want to establish the basis of valuation.

4. CO–OPERATIVES

4.1. In the same way as any other stock held by a farmer, stock marketed through co-operatives acting as agent for the farmer must be included in the valuation unless it has been sold.

4.2. Stock held off the farm which is identifiable as belonging to the farmer must also be included.

4.3. Where stock held off the farm has been pooled and cannot be identified as belonging to a particular farmer the unsold proportion must be included. This may be computed by taking $A \times B/C$ where A is the amount in the pool which came from the farmer, B is the amount in the pool not sold at the valuation date and C is the amount in the pool not sold at the valuation date plus the amount sold from it up to that date.

4.4. Where a co-operative acts as agent for the farmer but the relevant stock can be identified as not being part of a pool, no apportionment is necessary.

It should be included in the valuation (see 4.2 above).

4.5. Stock which has been sold to a co-operative which does not act as agent should not be included in the valuation.

5. GRANTS AND SUBSIDIES — EFFECT ON STOCK VALUATIONS

5.1. Grants and subsidies towards specific expenses should be regarded as reducing those expenses. If those expenses are included in the cost for stock valuation then the figure used should be the net cost after deducting the related grants.

5.2. Grants and subsidies intended to augment the sale prices of stocks should be taken into account in calculating their net realisable values.

6. CONSUMABLES

6.1. Consumables include spares for plant and equipment, oil, diesel, sprays, fertilisers, feedstuffs and bags. For any stock of unused, but usable consumables held at the balance sheet date, normally the valuation should be made at cost.

6.2. If, however, the consumables have deteriorated or become obsolete then their net realisable value should be used if it is lower than cost.

7. DEEMED COST VALUATION

7.1. When deemed cost is acceptable

7.1.1. Valuations should only be based on deemed cost where it is not possible to ascertain actual costs from the farmer's records. Deemed cost should not be used for purchased animals if it is less than the original purchase price plus, if the animal was immature when purchased, the costs of rearing from the date of purchase to the valuation date or, if earlier, to maturity.

7.1.2. In such situations Inspectors will accept that a reasonable estimate of cost, 'deemed cost', is given by a specific percentage of open market value. It may be necessary, from time to time, to review the percentages if the relationship between costs and market value changes. Current percentages are set out in paragraphs 7.2.1 and 7.3.1 below.

7.1.3. For production animals open market value should be based on the assumption that there is a willing buyer and a willing seller of the animal as a production animal free from, for example, movement restrictions. It is not acceptable to treat cull value as the open market value of production animals as this does not recognise the value of the future income stream from produce and/or progeny.

7.2. Livestock

7.2.1. The percentages in the case of livestock are

- cattle — 60% of open market value
- sheep and pigs — 75% of open market value

7.2.2. The following points should be noted:

7.2.3. Deemed cost valuations are only valid for home-bred or home-reared stock or stock acquired some time before maturity and matured on the farm. (See also 7.1.1 above in the case of stock other than home bred stock.)

7.2.4. It is preferable for deemed cost to be fixed at maturity but Inspectors will accept valuations at deemed costs based on open market value at the balance sheet date if that method has been used consistently. Farmers should be aware that using deemed cost at each balance sheet date may result in profits coming into tax earlier.

7.2.5. The valuation of immature and unweaned animals using deemed cost methods based on the open market value of animals of a similar age and type is acceptable to the Inland Revenue except in the situation described in paragraph 7.2.6 below. If it is appropriate to value mother and progeny together because that is the market unit, this should be done.

7.2.6. The method at 7.2.5 above is not appropriate where the mother is on the herd basis and where there is no market or a very limited market in unweaned progeny (for example unweaned lambs at foot). In this situation failure to recognise the young stock at all in the valuation is not acceptable. The costs of producing the progeny (see 3.1 above) should be carried forward to be set against the eventual sale price.

7.3. Deadstock (that is, harvested crops)

7.3.1. Deemed cost based on 75% (85% for valuations as at dates before 31 March 1993) of open market value at the balance sheet date will be accepted by Inspectors.'

25.4 Herd basis

It is possible to elect for the 'herd basis' to apply, as an alternative to the usual trading stock basis (see **25.3** above), in respect of production herds – such as a dairy herd or a ewe flock – kept only for the sale of milk, wool, eggs, young animals or other produce. The herd basis cannot apply to animals kept for only a short time, such as steers for fattening or a 'flying flock' of ewes (see ICTA 1988, Sch. 5).

Farmers (including market gardeners) and owners of commercial woodlands

A herd basis election is useful in times of high inflation and where numbers in the herd or flock are stable. By contrast, such an election is not much use where the numbers in the initial herd are likely to be increased. Where numbers are likely to fluctuate, averaging may be a more appropriate strategy to adopt.

An election has to be made to adopt the herd basis, and normally it should be made within 12 months following 31 January after the relevant tax year in which the farmer first keeps the production herd of the class in question. The election, once made by the farmer, is irrevocable. As the election has to be made by the farmer, a fresh election has to be made on a change of partners or on an incorporation of the farming business. If an election has not been made previously, such a change would provide a fresh opportunity to make one.

It is also possible to make an election if a farmer's production herd, or a substantial part of it (normally 20 per cent or more), has had to be slaughtered compulsorily on account of disease. In this case the election should be made within two years of the end of the year of assessment that is based on the accounts for the year in which the compensation is receivable. Similarly, if farmers cease to keep a production herd of the class in question for a period of at least five years, they may make an election in respect of such herds after the end of that period, if they reacquire such a herd.

Generally, the effect of making an election is that, if the whole herd is sold without being replaced or if a substantial part of it is sold (normally 20 per cent or more), any profit on the sale is free of all tax, as profits from the animals are also exempt from capital gains tax because the animals are wasting assets. If the numbers in the herd increase within five years of such a substantial reduction, a proportion of the previously 'tax-free' profit is brought back into account. Any profit on a lesser reduction of the herd is brought into account as income, whilst replacements (provided that they are not home-bred) are written off to the profit and loss account as the cost of rearing new home-bred animals will already have been deducted as part of the expense of labour, foodstuffs, etc. Any extra cost due to any improvement element in the replacement animal is not deducted. Immature animals are generally not treated as part of the herd, with a few exceptions, such as hill sheep. It is clear from the above that, where an election is made and numbers in the herd are likely to fluctuate, accurate records of herd transactions must be kept.

Note that making an election for the herd basis to apply, other than on first keeping a herd, does not mean that the animals are appropriated from stock at market value. If that were the case, the farmer would lose the benefit of the election. Rather, the animals are treated as never having been part of the stock in the period in question, and are thus removed at their book value from stock for tax purposes, with no income or corporation tax charge resulting from this change.

Generally, the legislation is unclear as to whether, where there are sales and replacements spanning the end of an accounting period, the sale proceeds have to be brought in and taxed when received and relief only given for the replacement when incurred, or whether some other basis be adopted. In practice, provided that the replacement occurs within 12 months, the Inland Revenue have allowed the sale proceeds to be carried forward to be credited against the cost of replacement. There seems to be no particular time limit for replacement, provided that there is a clear intention to replace the animal. An attempt to ignore this practice by one inspector has been rejected by the commissioners. In some cases, farmers have not replaced animals for several years. This is especially likely to occur with pedigree herds, where replacements are found from home-bred stock. However, the position is far from clear and a cautious approach should be adopted.

Note that in a share farming arrangement, each part-owner has to elect for the herd basis to apply for the election to be valid.

Following representations the Revenue have reconsidered their interpretation of the herd basis legislation. In *Tax Bulletin* Issue 64 April 2003, the Inland Revenue state that it is no longer considered necessary or appropriate to compute the profit on a minor disposal from the herd, without replacement, using what the Revenue have previously described as the 'herd basis cost' (which consisted of the initial cost of the herd and the cost of any improvement or increase in herd size). Such costs were not and still are not deductible in the farm trading account. When an animal replaced another of the same quality, it took on the 'herd basis cost' of its predecessor.

The Revenue consider a disposal amounting to less than 20 per cent of the herd to be minor. Profits on these disposals are taxable (para. 3(10)). In the past this profit was computed by reference to 'herd basis cost'. In older established herds the original animals would have been replaced, perhaps several times, and this brought into charge a profit largely due to inflation. On the Revenue's revised view, where a farmer sells without replacement a small part of the herd, the Revenue accept that the profit should be computed by reference to the actual cost of the animal or animals disposed of. The fact that an animal taken from the herd replaced an earlier one is no longer relevant.

The following example illustrates the practical effect.

Farmers (including market gardeners) and owners of commercial woodlands

> **Example 25.2**
>
> Jim has been a dairy farmer since 1950. He started his herd with an initial purchase of 60 cows costing £100 each. Over the years he has maintained his herd by regularly replacing his stock with animals of the same quality.
>
> In 2004, at the age of 70, he decided to sell 10 of his most recently purchased cattle without replacement. The sale proceeds were £5,500 in total. As this disposal amounted to less than 20 per cent of the herd the profit needs to be included in the trading account of the farm by virtue of paragraph 3(10). The 'herd basis cost' of these animals would have been £100 each, but they actually cost him £450 each.
>
> Using the 'herd basis cost' the profit would have been:
>
> £5,500 – (10 × £100) = £4,500.
>
> Using actual cost the profit becomes:
>
> £5,500 – (10 × £450) = £1,000.
>
> The computation of the profit at £1,000 accords with the current Inland Revenue interpretation of paragraph 3(10).
>
> In a situation where the farmer's records are simply so bad that this identification is not possible, the Inland Revenue will accept that the cost of the animals removed be computed by reference to the BEN 19 formula applied to the sale price. In this case it would work out at £3,300 (60 per cent of £5,500). The chargeable profit would then be £2,200.

This revised interpretation will be accepted both in returns received from the date of the *Tax Bulletin* article and for returns already received where the liability can be recomputed under the normal self assessment provisions.

25.5 Partnership changes and the herd basis

Following the introduction of the current year basis the Inland Revenue published Revenue Interpretation 173 in June 1997. The text is reproduced below.

> **'Partnership changes and the herd basis**
>
> Schedule D, Case I — Partnership changes and the herd basis — TA 1988 s. 113, Sch. 5

Averaging

[The Revenue] explained in Tax Bulletin Issue 3 (May 1992) that a fresh herd basis election is required after a change in the membership of a partnership if herd basis treatment is to continue. [They] have been asked whether the changes to TA 1988 s 113 introduced as part of the preparation for self-assessment remove this requirement.

TA 1988 Sch 5 (the herd basis) applies to 'animals kept by a farmer'. It is clear from paragraphs 2(3), [and] 5 that in this context, where the farming is carried on in partnership, the partnership is the farmer. Moreover, a partnership before a change in its membership is not the same partnership as that after the change. An election applies to all production herds of the class concerned kept 'by the farmer making the election'.

Under the new Self Assessment rules, TA 1988 s 113(2) disapplies s 113(1) so that a change in the membership of a partnership does not trigger a cessation and recommencement of the trade. But this does not alter the fact that the farmer carrying on the trade before the change is not the same as the farmer after the change. So the herd is no longer kept by the farmer making the election. It follows that a fresh herd basis election by the new farmer is still required after a partnership change, if the new partnership wants the herd basis to apply. Thus there is no change from the view of the law set out [by the Revenue] in the May 1992 article.

There is no special form for making a herd basis election, nor is there a requirement that the election be signed by the farmer. Where it is clear from material submitted to the Revenue within the time limit that a farmer has applied the herd basis, then [the Revenue] would regard an election as having been made. For example, the Help Sheet IR 224 which assists farmers in completing the self-employed pages of their returns, suggests that the additional information space on the return is used to record an analysis of herds on the herd basis and details of any adjustments. If this information is provided [the Revenue] would not need a separate election. But if the new partnership wants the herd basis to apply and this is not obvious from the return or other information routinely submitted, a written election stating the class of herd should be made.'

25.6 Averaging

It is possible for unincorporated farmers to average profits for income tax purposes, to remove themselves from the effect of high marginal rates of income tax caused by severe fluctuations in their farming income. An individual or partnership may thus claim to average the profits of the business for any two consecutive years of assessment. The profits are the profits as adjusted for Sch. D, Case I purposes, before any deduction for losses or adjustments for capital allowances, balancing charges or stock relief. The relief does not apply to profits subject to corporation tax (eg profits of UK-resident companies) (see ICTA 1988, s. 96).

Averaging can be claimed if the profits for either of the two years do not exceed 70 per cent of the profits of the other year or are nil. A loss is treated as a nil profit for this purpose. There is a marginal relief where the profits of one year exceed 70 per cent of the other but are less than 75 per cent. If the profits have been revised under an averaging claim, it is the revised figure that is then used in any averaging claim for the second year and the next year.

A claim must be made within 12 months after 31 January following the end of the second year to which the claim relates, and is irrevocable.

No claim is possible in respect of the year in which a trade commences or is discontinued. This includes a year where a partnership change is treated as a discontinuance. A claim does not affect relief for losses, and is ignored in deciding whether the profits of the two years prior to a cessation are to be increased. If such profits are increased, the original claim becomes invalid, but a fresh claim can then be made using the revised profits, thus spreading back profits outside the two years.

Note that averaging can create profits against which losses can be set, and time limits for loss claims are, therefore, extended to the end of the period during which the averaging claim must be made.

A stand-alone averaging claim cannot be made. The claim must be made on the tax return for the second year. Therefore a claim to reduce the payments on account in respect of the second year's liability (where profits are falling) cannot be validly made. The date of submission of the tax return claiming the relief is treated as the date of payment of the credit arising as a result of a claim for overpaid tax for earlier years. Interest runs from the due date of the payments on account until the date of the submission of the tax return. This is of course unfair, as repayment supplement is not received on the overpaid tax. The moral is to prepare the client's accounts and submit the self-assessment return as soon as possible.

Under self-assessment averaging no longer relates to a partnership assessment as a whole and each individual partner can decide whether or not to make a claim. Note that, once an averaging claim has been made for two consecutive years, it cannot be made for any years preceding those years, and the effect on retirement annuity premium and personal pension payment relief needs to be considered in all cases. Advice should be sought on the impact (if any) of FA 2004, which comes into force from 6 April 2006.

Under Inland Revenue ESC A29, farming for averaging purposes also includes the intensive rearing of livestock or fish on a commercial basis for the production of food for human consumption.

The Inland Revenue Manual says (at IM 2322a):

> 'Averaging is not available where the trade is not farming or market gardening (as extended by extra-statutory concession A29). For example, averaging is not available where:
>
> - the trade is agricultural contracting since this trade does not involve the occupation of farmland (see IM 2254 onwards); or
>
> - the trade includes substantial non-farming activities such as haulage or a caravan site as well as farming.'

Also, at IM 2258:

> 'Contract farming is an arrangement whereby a contractor carries out operations of husbandry as agent for the landowner. Even where the contractor carries out all, or substantially all, the operations of husbandry on a particular farm, the arrangement should not be confused with share farming (see IM 2257a onwards). In contract farming cases, the landowner is likely to be the occupier of the land and therefore farming.
>
> The contractor is not farming and is chargeable under Schedule D Case I on his or her profits as a contractor.'

All this is a matter of degree and depends on the particular facts. There should not be any problem with averaging in a case where the contracting income is small. Consider, under self-assessment, what element of disclosure is required.

25.6.1 Tax credits

The computation of income for tax credits purposes (from 6 April 2003) ignores the income tax averaging of farming profits. For example the farming profits for 2003–04 may have been £75,000 and for 2004–05 £13,000. An averaging election will result in 2004–05 taxable income of £44,000, but income for that year for tax credit purposes will still be just £13,000.

25.7 Capital allowances

There may be difficulty in determining whether an item of farm capital expenditure is 'plant' or is a building qualifying only for agricultural buildings allowances. Where a Ministry of Agriculture grant has been claimed, the problem is usually readily resolved, as machinery and plant attracts a lower rate of grant than building work. For chargeable periods, or basis periods, ending on or after 27 July 1989, a person may elect for one allowance or the other, if expenditure can qualify for different types of allowances (CAA 2001, s. 7 and IR Capital Allowances Manual, para. 31800).

Some of the main problems in this area concern dairy houses or purpose-built structures for intensive rearing of livestock, where the equipment element is so integrated with the rest of the structure that the building works can be regarded almost as no more than cladding for the plant and machinery, and thus the whole structure should qualify as plant. The Inland Revenue resist this approach except in the case of mobile poultry houses, pig units or similar items.

Also, whilst Land Rovers qualify for writing down allowances without restriction, note that a Range Rover is regarded as a private car, subject to the £12,000 limit. The Inland Revenue have been known to argue that personal choice may restrict capital allowances on a car in the case of a farmer (following the case of *GH Chambers (Northiam Farms) Ltd v Watmough* (1956) 36 TC 711), although the earlier £8,000 limit for writing-down allowance has, in general, meant that this point is not often raised.

25.8 Agricultural buildings allowances

The whole scheme of agricultural buildings allowances was recast for expenditure incurred on or after 1 April 1986. Broadly, for expenditure incurred before that date, allowances were given to the person incurring the expenditure, provided that he or she had an interest in the land. The allowances were given primarily against agricultural or forestry income of the year following the year to 31 March, or the end of the accounting period in which the expenditure was incurred. The balance of the expenditure was available against other income of that year and of the next following year. Thereafter, any remaining balance was available only against agricultural or forestry income. There was no system of balancing adjustments, and the successor took over any balance of allowances due.

With the abolition of the initial allowance and the reduction of the writing-down allowances to four per cent per annum, the allowances would not have taken account of the short life of some agricultural buildings. The current system, therefore, introduced a system of balancing adjustments, at the option of the taxpayer, on the disposal of buildings, including where they are pulled down or otherwise destroyed. The scheme (CAA 2001, ss. 361–390) is now broadly similar to that for industrial buildings. In particular, allowances are given on the cost of any buildings, cottages, fences or other works incurred for the purposes of agriculture, including one-third of the expenditure on a farmhouse or, if the farmhouse is relatively large in relation to the farm, such lesser fraction as is reasonable. What is a 'farmhouse' for this purpose was discussed in *Lindsay v CIR* (1953) 34 TC 289. Generally, it is the house from which the farming operations are controlled and managed, even if it is occupied by an employee.

The terms 'works' includes such things as demolition, drainage and sewerage works, water and electricity installations, walls, shelter belts of trees, glasshouses on market garden land, and the reclamation of former agricultural land.

The allowances belong to the person having the 'relevant interest' at the time the expenditure was incurred (ie the freehold or leasehold interest). When that interest is transferred, the allowances pass to the transferee, with a division of the allowance where the transfer occurs partway through a year.

If an agricultural building is purchased unused, no allowance is given to the vendor, but the purchaser obtains allowances based only on the lower of the costs of construction or the price he or she paid.

If no election is made for a balancing adjustment to apply on a sale of the relevant interest, the purchaser takes over the vendor's entitlement to the allowances for the remainder of the 25 years. Otherwise, on either a disposal of the relevant interest, or if a building is demolished, destroyed or otherwise ceases to exist, a balancing adjustment is made. Where appropriate on a sale, future writing-down allowances are calculated in the same way as for industrial buildings allowances for the remainder of the 25 years. For example, the demolition of a short-life building probably gives rise to a balancing allowance in the year in which it is demolished, equal to the balance of any allowances due.

It appears that, as with industrial buildings allowances, if an inferior interest is granted out of the relevant interest on sale (for instance, a long lease out of a freehold), vendors retain the allowances, although they would not now do so on a sale and lease-back.

Agricultural land and buildings allowances are given in taxing the farming trade. This means that allowances can, in certain circumstances, figure in loss claims under ICTA 1988, s. 383. In the case of landlords, as before, such allowances are given primarily against agricultural income such as rents.

The Inland Revenue did not use to be particularly concerned as to whether farmers had an interest in the relevant land, provided that they had incurred the qualifying expenditure. There were fears that this might no longer be true under the current system, where the concept of a 'relevant interest' was introduced. It was thought that it might be necessary, for instance, for a partnership to own a lease of property granted by the partner owning the freehold in order for the partnership to qualify for allowances in respect of any expenditure that it incurred on agricultural buildings on that land. However, the Inland Revenue have confirmed that they will not interpret the current legislation more restrictively than the previous legislation. Therefore, a lease could include a licence for this purpose.

The landlord's consent must be obtained for any improvements made to tenanted farm land. If approval is not obtained, no compensation can subsequently be claimed. Furthermore, under the Law of Property Act 1925, unless approval has been granted, any benefit of the improvement reverts to the landlord upon cessation of the lease.

25.9 Revenue receipts and payments

There are a number of special points concerning revenue receipts and payments. Where compensation is paid for compulsorily slaughtered stock for which a herd basis election cannot be made, the profits arising, being the excess of the compensation over the book value of the animal (or over cost in the case of animals bred or purchased during the current year) can, under ESC B11, be taken out of the accounts for the current year and spread over the next three years in equal amounts. As mentioned in **25.4** above, there is a right of election for the herd basis where a substantial part (normally 20 per cent or more) of a production herd is compulsorily slaughtered. In such a case, this spreading relief cannot be claimed for the mature animals in the herd, even if the farmer chooses not to elect for the herd basis thereafter. The relief normally, therefore, applies only to young stock and followers, flying flocks and animals kept for fattening, and to mature animals where less than one-fifth of the herd is slaughtered.

Revenue receipts and payments

The special tax treatment for compensation for compulsory slaughter referred to in the previous paragraph applies to compensation under:

- the BSE Suspects Schemes, and
- the BSE Selective Cull where the animal slaughtered was born on or after 15 October 1990.

The special tax treatment for compensation for compulsory slaughter does not apply to sums paid under:

- the Calf Processing Scheme;
- the Over Thirty Month Scheme, or
- the BSE Selective Cull where the animal slaughtered was born before 15 October 1990.

Payments under these schemes should be dealt with in the same way as if the compensation was received from the ordinary commercial sale of the animal(s) concerned.

Grants and subsidies have to be analysed to determine whether they are capital or revenue receipts. Land set-aside payments are treated as trading income under the normal principles of taxation for such receipts, to the extent that the payments are made for keeping land out of production for a period of five years on a 'care and maintenance' basis, and thus compensate for lost trading income.

The regulations (Statutory Instruments 1988 No. 1352; 1989 No. 1042; 1990 No. 1716) made under the European Communities Act 1972 provide the land must be set aside for a period of five years for one of the following purposes.

1. Permanent fallow where the same parcels of land are set aside for the full five years.
2. Rotational fallow whereby different parcels of land are set aside each year as part of a rotation with land which was in arable cropping during the year to 30 June 1988.
3. Grazed fallow whereby livestock can be grazed on the fallow at 1 and 2 above provided the livestock units do not exceed the numbers held in the year ended 30 June 1988.
4. Non-agricultural use which allows, for example, tourist or recreational activities but no form of agricultural production, mineral extraction or permanent buildings unless for approved farm diversification activities.

5. Woodlands for which payments available depend on whether or not the set-aside is integrated with the farm woodland scheme.

Payments under 4, although of an income nature on the principles outlined in *White v G and M Davies* [1979] STC 415 and *CIR v Biggar* [1982] STC 677, may not be agricultural income if the existing farming trade does not continue on other land. It is submitted they are not Schedule A income as they do not derive from an interest in land. As the payments are arguably pure income profit, a charge under Schedule D, Case III might be appropriate, or failing that Case VI.

Payments under 5, as they are integrated into the regulations with the farm woodland scheme, arise from the commercial occupation of woodland and, following the FA 1988, are tax-free.

Where the land is treated as continuing to be farmed, retirement, roll-over and hold-over reliefs will are available without restriction. If the set-aside period represents an interruption in the trade which then resumes, there is a restriction to retirement, roll-over and hold-over relief by reference to the period of non-trading use.

If the trade does not resume, retirement relief is lost but, as confirmed in the Court of Appeal decision in *Richart v Lyons & Co Ltd* [1989] STC 665, this does not apply to roll-over and hold-over reliefs where proportionate relief continues.

In some cases, receipts can be of a mixed nature, as in the case of the Farm and Horticulture Development Scheme. Price-guarantee payments, subsidies and grants of a non-capital nature (such as cereals deficiency payments) constitute income. Certain deficiency payments in respect of home-grown cereals could, under Inland Revenue ESC B6, be brought in on a notified basis, rather than by reference to the date of harvesting, except in the opening and closing years. Any grant of a capital nature towards buildings or equipment, unlike certain regional development grants for industry, has to be deducted from the cost of the assets, in order to establish the expenditure qualifying for capital allowances.

Note in this connection, however, that it is specifically provided that grants for relinquishing occupation of uncommercial agricultural units (by virtue of a scheme under the Agriculture Act 1967, s. 27) are not to be taken into account for capital gains tax purposes (TCGA 1992, s. 249).

On the expenses side, usually only up to one-third of the cost of the repairs to a farmhouse are allowed as an expense. However, it is understood that some inspectors have sought to challenge this long-established practice.

Under Inland Revenue Statement of Practice 5/81 necessary net expenditure incurred, after crediting any grants receivable, in order to restore efficient draining or on redraining (the land having become waterlogged), are admitted as revenue expenditure, provided that it excludes:

- any substantial element of improvement, and
- the capital element (where the current owner is known to have acquired the land at a depressed price because of its swampy condition).

Generally, 'wages' paid to minors are not allowed, but are regarded as no more than pocket money, as the case of *Dollar (t/a I J Dollar) v Lyon* (1981) 54 TC 459 illustrated. The operation of PAYE also has to be watched, and details of exceptions for casual workers such as harvest workers, and workers genuinely engaged for no more than a day, are contained in the special *Farmers' Guide to PAYE*, available free of charge from local tax offices.

Note, however, that a change of practice for casual harvest workers was announced in a Press Release dated 29 May 1991. Under the 1984 agreement between the NFU and the Inland Revenue, PAYE need not be applied to wages paid to a daily casual worker. These workers are defined as employed for a period not exceeding a day whose employment ends on that day with no agreement for further employment and who are paid cash at the end of the day. The Inland Revenue used to regard the words 'agreement for further employment' as including both contractual arrangements and cases where the farmer and employee expected there to be further employment. Now, however, any such expectation will be ignored and it is only where there is a contract (not necessarily in writing) that the concession is not applicable. This interpretation applies to existing cases which have not been settled. The farmer must still inform the Inland Revenue of details if the amount exceeds £100 in total for the year per worker.

The 1984 agreement also says that PAYE need not be applied to harvest workers who are not daily casuals but are taken on for two weeks or less (this concession can be applied only once a year for any particular worker by any one employer).

There are also special arrangements exempting from PAYE foreign students coming to work in the vacation on UK farms.

Farmers (including market gardeners) and owners of commercial woodlands

The Inland Revenue have a special unit based in Sheffield to deal with tax compliance by agricultural gang-masters (middlemen who supply casual labour for farmers at peak times). Its functions are to ensure that gang-masters deduct and account for PAYE and National Insurance Contributions (NICs) from the earnings of their workers, and that they make proper returns of their profits. The Inland Revenue have insisted that farmers, being the principal employer, should be responsible for PAYE in respect of payments to their casual workers, notwithstanding the presence of a gang-master.

In the case of *Andrews v King* [1991] STC 481 the taxpayer was engaged by a firm of potato merchants in connection with potato picking and grading. The potato merchant informed him how many men were required and he selected the men, although they were not obliged to accept the work he offered them. The Inland Revenue argued that he was self-employed and also that he was responsible for PAYE on the workers selected as a gang-master and made nine determinations on him under what was then the Income Tax (Employments) Regulations 1993 (SI 1993 No. 744), reg. 48. The court held he was not self-employed as apart from selecting the workers, he took no financial risk and was not in business on his own account. Applying the regulations, the taxpayer and other workers worked under the general control and management of the merchant who was, therefore, the principal employer and as such was the employer for the purposes of the regulations. The taxpayer did not employ the workers or pay them wages. Accordingly, the determination under reg. 49 was invalid.

In ESC A60, the Inland Revenue confirmed that they will follow past practice and will not seek to tax the provision of free board and lodging for lower-paid agricultural employees, even if off the farm, provided that, in the latter case, the employer has a contract with a third party for its provision, and that payments under the contract are made direct to the third party. Strictly, because under the Agricultural Wages Acts workers are entitled to take a higher wage on which they would be taxed and to pay their own board and lodging, they are taxable on the value of the board and lodging supplied (under the principles laid down in *Heaton v Bell* (1969) 46 TC 211). However, provided that workers are not directors or higher-paid, and that their contract of employment provides for a net cash wage with free board and lodging, they are not taxed on such free board and lodging. Where agricultural workers are entitled to a gross cash wage, they are assessable on the gross amount, even if their contract of employment provides for their employer to deduct a sum to pay for board and lodging.

The whole (formerly seven-eighths) of the membership subscription to the National Farmers' Union is allowed under an agreement with the Inland Revenue.

Interest on business loans is allowed in the normal way. If a partner borrows to buy farmland, which is then used by the partnership, the interest payable can effectively be treated as a partnership expense, provided that the partnership pays the partner an amount equal to the interest that he or she has to pay. Under Inland Revenue Statement of Practice 4/85, the partner is treated as being paid a rent by the partnership equal to the amount of the interest that he or she has to pay. However, the effect of receiving rent on capital gains tax retirement relief should not be overlooked (see **25.11.4** below). Furthermore, the partner may be denied the higher rate of agricultural property relief, now 100 per cent, for inheritance tax purposes. It is usually more tax-efficient for the farmer to transfer the land to the partnership. A special capital account could then be set up for the partner to which any surpluses on disposal or revaluation could be credited. The farmer would then be entitled to claim a deduction for loan interest, would not be denied capital gains tax retirement relief, and would be entitled to the higher rate of agricultural property relief.

25.10 Partnerships and joint ventures

If a partnership is to be set up from a certain time, it is necessary to ensure that the facts support the existence of the partnership from that time, irrespective of what any partnership agreement says. This point was emphasised in the farming case of *Dickenson v Gross* (1927) 11 TC 614, and in the cases of *Waddington v O'Callaghan* (1931) 16 TC 187 and *Saywell v Pope* (1979) 53 TC 40. It is thus not possible to make a partnership retrospective. Similarly, a partnership agreement of itself is not conclusive evidence of a partnership if it conflicts with the realities of the situation, eg where the children are not really acting as partners but are employees.

There are numerous forms of joint ventures in farming. Usually one party supplies the land as capital, and the other supplies the rest of the fixed and working capital and manages the farming operations on the land. Such arrangements are usually entered into to ensure that the landowner continues to trade for tax purposes – particularly where there are unabsorbed losses – and also to avoid the grant of a tenancy. However, the letting of land on a 364-day grazing licence for grass keep might not be regarded as trading. Also, any arrangement under which the profit share of the landowner is guaranteed, whatever the outcome of the venture, might also not be treated as a trading activity. The share of the landowner should, therefore, fluctuate, so that a claim to loss relief can be sustained.

The Inland Revenue appear to have contended that many share farming agreements did not give trading income to the owner. They maintained that only the operator is farming, the owner merely receiving a form of income derived from the land and assessable under Sch. A. The Inland Revenue were apparently arguing that where persons do not have qualitatively the same occupation rights, only one can be treated as occupier of the land in receipt of farming income for tax purposes.

The person in receipt of farming income on this basis was deemed to be the one with the greater presence and control over the land and occupation rights, and on this analysis only the operator would be in receipt of farming income.

The Inland Revenue contentions were based on decisions in certain old cases relating to the occupation of land for Sch. D purposes. As farming was brought within s. D only in FA 1948, it was argued that these cases are irrelevant and that the question of occupation may be disregarded in determining who is carrying on the trade. At stake are:

- averaging of profits;
- sct off of trading losses;
- roll-over and (until April 2003) retirement relief, and
- agricultural property relief for inheritance tax at formerly 50 per cent, now 100 per cent.

This view was, therefore, vigorously contested by the CLA and similar bodies, and resulted in a change of heart by the Inland Revenue. They now accept that both parties to a share farming agreement may be considered to be carrying on farming. Landowners in an agreement based upon the CLA model may be regarded as trading provided they take an active part in the share farming venture, at least to the extent of concerning themselves with details of farming policy and exercising their right to enter on to their land for some material purpose, even if only for inspection and policy making. Where a new share farming agreement does not amount to a partnership landowners should, for tax purposes, continue to carry on any existing farming trade, so that any unabsorbed losses are available to set off against their share of any profits. From the agreed proportion of the outputs of the venture there is deducted the agreed inputs, in order to arrive at the profit assessable on the landowner only.

Stocks sometimes cause complications in share farming arrangements. If they are transferred from one party to the other when mature, 60 per cent or 75 per cent of their market value is accepted as cost in the normal way for home-bred animals. However, if there are joint interests in the animals, each party must account for a proportionate share of 'cost' in the profit and loss account. Such joint ownership, if the joint venturers also share in the ultimate results for the year, can be construed as a partnership, with consequential 'one assessment' implications. Instead, therefore, shares of inputs and outputs should be different, so that one joint venturer can make a loss and the other a profit.

Companies sometimes enter into joint-farming ventures with individuals or other companies. A company, even if it is a partner, is assessed separately on its share of profits, capital allowances, etc as if it were carrying on the trade on its own (under the special rules for partnerships involving companies in ICTA 1988, ss. 114 and 115). It appears therefore that, where it has sustained losses in the past in its farming trade, these can be set against future profits from the joint venture.

Institutions, in particular pension funds, have invested in agricultural land. Typically, the pension fund owns the land and the farmer is the fund's own subsidiary or a third party in partnership with such a subsidiary. The pension fund can then receive its share of profits in the form of rents which can be geared partly to profits. These rents are exempt from tax in its own hands, unlike trading income. Provided that the rents paid do not exceed the highest possible tender rent, they should be deductible by the subsidiary or the third party, on the authority of the case of *Union Cold Storage Co Ltd v Adamson* (1931) 16 TC 293. Because the pension fund will not want normally to grant an agricultural tenancy to a third party, its own trading subsidiary usually shares occupation of the land in partnership with the outside operator. Consequently, any expenditure generating tax allowances should be incurred in the trading company rather than in the pension fund, which receives only exempt income.

25.11 Capital gains tax

25.11.1 Hold-over relief

Note that all land which qualifies for agricultural relief for inheritance tax purposes, whether at the 100 per cent or 50 per cent (previously 50 per cent or 30 per cent) rate, continues to qualify for hold-over relief where, for instance, it is given by a parent to a child, or where a trust comes to an end and a person becomes absolutely entitled to trust assets (see TCGA 1992, Sch. 7).

The Inland Revenue have also confirmed that even if the land has development value which does not qualify for agricultural relief for inheritance tax purposes, holdover relief still applies.

25.11.2 Roll-over relief

Roll-over relief is often especially useful for farmers. In this connection, improvements to land and buildings are accepted by the Inland Revenue as 'new assets'. Such improvements can include, for example, drainage channels and other building work that cannot rank as 'fixed plant', eg sprinkler systems. In addition, if a tenant farmer purchases the freehold reversion, that is also accepted as a new asset. However, if a farmer has to sell part of the land to which the freehold relates, for example, in order to meet the cost of the freehold, the sale proceeds of that part cannot be rolled over against the cost of the freehold. In that situation, the proceeds would derive from the same asset as the 'replacement' asset, and thus there would be no new asset. The farmer can only roll over the sale proceeds of other land already owned against such an acquisition (see ESC D22).

There is no territorial limitation to roll-over relief (subject to restrictions in connection with dual resident companies). Farmers who remain UK-resident can sell a farm in the UK and roll over the gain into the acquisition of a farm, say in the USA, provided that where the UK trading operations cease, they carry on the new trade successively. This means, in practice, not more than three years from the cessation of the old trade — the same period as that normally allowed for purchasing new assets.

Agricultural cottages should qualify as eligible assets, provided that they can be said to be used in the farm business. This means that they must be in the representative occupation of a farm worker. Following the case of *Anderton v Lamb* (1980) 55 TC 1, it is not clear whether a house occupied by a partner, other than the farmhouse, would qualify. However, if such a house were partnership property and restricted as to occupation to someone engaged in agriculture, it might rank as a business asset for roll-over relief.

Land that is in joint ownership often has to be partitioned to enable, say, two brothers to farm separately. A partition is also accepted as qualifying for roll-over relief. Provided that there is equality of exchange, full relief is given for the gain, with restriction on relief where there is a partial gift or where the land includes or becomes a dwelling-house (see ESC D26). This concession is now extended to include exchanges of joint interests in milk and potato quota, where these accompany exchanging joint interests in land to which the quota is attached.

The proceeds on small part-disposals can be deducted from the cost rather than be assessed. This can help farmers who have to sell land to repay borrowings. However, for the relief to apply, the value of the land being disposed of cannot exceed one-fifth of the whole. There is also a monetary limit of £20,000. If the transferor makes any other disposals of land in the same year of assessment, the relief does not apply if the total value of the consideration for all disposals exceeds £20,000 (TCGA 1992, s. 242).

Where land has been held for a long time and has a relatively low base cost compared with its market value, it may be to the owner's benefit to use the part-disposal, or a 'just and reasonable' formula, to compute the gain (see below).

In general, it is not necessary to apply the strict part-disposal formula where part of an estate is disposed of. Instead, the Inland Revenue accept that the part disposed of can be treated as a separate asset and any just or reasonable method of apportioning part of the total cost of it is accepted, for instance, by reference to the value of that part at acquisition. Similar treatment applies where an election is made for market value as at 6 April 1965 to be treated as cost. The cost identified is then deducted from the total cost for future part disposals. Consistency should, in general, be followed and, once the taxpayer has opted for this basis, it should be adhered to. This basis means that it is possible to choose whether to elect for 6 April 1965 value on each disposal, unlike the situation where the normal part-disposal formula is used.

Presumably, in the absence of an election under TCGA 1992, s. 120(5) for all relevant disposals to be based on the value of the asset at 31 March 1982, this practice has to be adapted to allow either original cost or the market value at 31 March 1982 to apply on each disposal, whichever is the more favourable.

25.11.3 Tenancies

It was held in *Henderson v Karmel's Executors* [1984] 58 TC 201 that, even where land is let to a company controlled by the owner of the land, the freehold should still be valued for capital gains tax purposes having regard to the tenancy, ie without vacant possession. In that case, the existence of the tenancy depressed the value at 6 April 1965.

However, unlike a tenancy in favour of an individual, a tenancy granted to a company can effectively be assigned by the transfer of shares in the company. Hence, both for capital gains tax and inheritance tax purposes, the Inland Revenue may argue that a company tenancy has a value in assessing the value of the company's shares.

The Capital Taxes Office have successfully argued in a case before the Scottish Lands Tribunal (*Executors of George A Baird v CIR — see Country Landowner*, September 1990) that a share in a tenancy formed by a Scottish partnership had a very substantial value for capital transfer tax purposes on death because it was transferred on death to the wife and son of the deceased.

A similar decision was given by the Lands Tribunal on 31 July 1991 in the case of *Executors of the Honourable Myra Alice Lady Fox (Deceased)* where a share in a partnership tenancy was held to have a significant value for capital transfer tax purposes (45 per cent of vacant possession premium), although it had to be valued separately from the reversion, and not as a single unit of property with the reversion as the Inland Revenue contended.

A sum paid to a tenant to give up a tenancy, insofar as it is statutory compensation for disturbance (usually measured by reference to five times the annual rent under the Agricultural Holdings Act 1986, s. 60, which replaced the Agricultural Holdings Act 1948 and the Agriculture (Miscellaneous Provisions) Act 1968) is free of capital gains tax, following the case of *Davis v Powell* (1976) 51 TC 492. It had been accepted by the Inland Revenue, before that case, that payments under the 1968 Act were free of capital gains tax, but the case established that a payment under the 1948 Act was not derived from an asset and was thus free of capital gains tax.

Where there is no notice to quit, or where there is a negotiated payment to induce the tenant to surrender the lease, the Inland Revenue argue that no part of the compensation is free of tax, on the basis that the payment is derived from the lease.

All such payments should be deductible by the landlord as enhancement expenditure in computing capital gains tax liability.

Note that all surrenders of leases are now standard-rated for VAT purposes, provided the person makes the surrender in the course of business (VATA 1994, Sch. 9, Part II, Group 1, Note 1). However, the surrender of a leasehold interest in a residential property by the person who actually lives in the property is outside the scope of VAT. Therefore, the surrender consideration attributable to a farmhouse is outside the scope of VAT.

Capital gains tax

25.11.4 Retirement relief

Retirement relief for farmers applied to disposals on or before 5 April 2003 and followed the normal rules. However, if a farm was run by a partnership, one of the partners owned the farmland, and the partnership paid rent, TCGA 1992, Sch. 6, para. 10 operated to restrict the amount of the relief available. The land is treated as an investment, except to the extent of the owner's own share of the rent paid. If the rent is below a market rent, a larger proportion of the gain may have qualified.

Thus, if an individual is entitled to a 50 per cent profit share and the rent paid is one-half of a market rent throughout the period of ownership, the restriction is 50 per cent $\times$ 1/2 or 25 per cent of the gain qualifying for relief. As has been mentioned, interest paid by a partnership for this purpose is treated as rent. It is also a matter of argument as to whether a prior profit share is considered to be rent in these circumstances. Probably it depends upon the extent to which the prior profit share is in return for the partner's extra efforts or seniority, rather than consideration for the use of the land (see **25.9** above for a more tax-efficient way to approach this in order not to lose capital tax reliefs).

Although the analysis above has been accepted wisdom for many years, a recent case has cast doubt on the restriction of retirement relief when rent has been paid by the partnership. The case concerned a farmer who let land to his farming company, but the same principles would apply had there been a partnership.

Plumbly v Spencer [1996] STI 1079: the facts

H was a full-time director and shareholder of SC Harbour (Besthorpe) Ltd, a trading company. He owned 163 acres of land which he let to the company, which was a family company for the purposes of (what is now) TCGA 1992, s. 163. On 29 January 1988 H sold the land. The company ceased to carry on its business at the same time. H died and the Revenue assessed to capital gains tax the gain arising on the sale of the land. H's personal representatives appealed on the ground that retirement relief was available under s. 163(2)(b), which provided that retirement relief was available where there had been a disposal of business assets which, at the time when the business had ceased to be carried on, were in use for the purposes of that business.

The Revenue argued that the whole scheme of the legislation should be considered. Section 163(2)(b) was confined to the assets of the business which were used for the purposes of that business, ie the assets had to be owned by the business. The Revenue argued that if H had, for example, sold his shares, he could have chosen whether to claim relief under s. 163 or under s. 164 in respect of the land as an associated disposal. Under s. 164, however, the rent paid by the company would have been taken into account, whereas under s. 163 no account would be so taken.

The taxpayer's appeal was dismissed both by the Special Commissioners and by the High Court. While the High Court acknowledged that s. 163(2)(b) required only a disposal of an asset used for the purposes of 'a business' not of 'a business of the individual making the disposal', this interpretation was reached by looking at the statutory provision in isolation. On a true construction of s. 163(2)(b), read in the context with the rest of s. 163, s. 164 and Sch. 6, it was clear that the reference was to the business of the individual making the disposal. The taxpayer appealed further.

The decision (CA)

Section 163(2)(a) and (b) were concerned with two alternative situations, namely:

- the sale of a business as a going concern, and
- the sale of assets formerly used in a discontinued business.

While quite clearly a sole trader selling a business as a going concern owned the business which was sold, it was not so obvious that the taxpayer selling assets formerly used in a discontinued business had to be the owner of the business. Unless the sale and cessation were absolutely simultaneous (which was improbable in practice and did not fit well with the statutory language), the business did not belong to anyone when the assets were disposed of, since it had ceased to exist. It was the assets which would necessarily belong to the person disposing of them.

The court acknowledged that there were oddities and anomalies within the statute, though questions of statutory construction should not be resolved by balancing competing anomalies.

Of central importance to the present case were s. 163(2) and (4). Section 163(2)(b) raised, though it did not conclusively answer, the question to whom, where there was a disposal of assets formerly used in a discontinued business, the business had to have belonged if there was to be retirement relief. The question was answered by s. 163(4)(a), read with s. 163(3)(a). The court did not consider that s. 163(4)(a) read with s. 163(3)(a) could be read as imposing one strict condition (namely individual ownership at the moment of cessation) and another less strict condition (individual or family company ownership during the preceding period of at least a year). The Revenue had argued that it was improbable that there should be some overlap between s. 163(2)(b) and s. 164(6), though this could not overcome the clear language of s. 163(4)(a), which was clear, specific and directly in point.

Retirement relief was therefore given to the taxpayer. This was not an absurd or anomalous result; it might have been more anomalous if the taxpayer had been denied retirement relief following a period of 40 years during which the company had been farming, simply because he had failed either to transfer the farming business to himself just before it came to an end or to sell the shares in his dormant company. The appeal was therefore allowed.

Other cases

The availability of the relief depends, except in the case of a cessation of the business followed by a sale of the assets formerly used in the business, on the disposal not just of a business asset but also of the whole or a part of the business or, in the case of a sale of an asset held outside the business, withdrawal from the business. What constitutes part of a business was considered in *McGregor v Adcock* (1977) 51 TC 692, where it was held that a farmer merely selling farmland was not entitled to the relief. There was no evidence, in that case, that the nature and extent of the farming after the disposal of the land was any different from what it had been before, as there had been a disposal of only 4.8 acres out of a total holding of 35 acres, with no diminution in the scale of the farming activities following the sale. Similar decisions in favour of the Inland Revenue were given in the cases of *Mannion v Johnston* (1988) 61 TC 598 and *Atkinson v Dancer* [1988] 61 TC 598.

It is understood that the Inland Revenue normally accepts that there has been a disposal of part of a business where more than one-half of an area of farmland is disposed of, provided that there is reasonable evidence of a diminution in the scale, or of a change in the nature, of the farming carried on on the remainder of the farm.

25.12 'One estate' election (up to 2001–02)

A special relief for the owners of estates managed as one unit at the end of the tax year 1962–63 operates for years before 2001–02 where the estate owner made the relevant election within the stipulated time limit, but not later than 5 April 1965. A new owner can renew the election, provided that the original election was validly made and successive owners have all made the election. Once made, the election cannot be revoked (ICTA 1988, s. 26).

The effect of the election is that, in return for bringing in the annual value of property occupied by the landowner, repairs and maintenance costs of that property can be set off against that annual value and against other rents from tenanted farms on the estate. In the case of property let at less than a full rent, an amount must be added to increase the actual rent to the full annual value. This is not required, however, for an estate office or tied cottages occupied rent-free.

By pooling rents and such notional rents in this way and offsetting all repairs and maintenance expenditure, surplus relief is transferred from one property to the other. If the result of the computation is a loss, that loss can be set against other Sch. A income, except where it arises from a tenant's full repairing leases.

The properties in the election can be augmented by additional properties, provided that they are managed as part of the estate, although certain conditions have to be fulfilled where they are not let at a full rent.

To the extent there is no agricultural income against which any such excess expenditure can be set, it can be set against other income of the same and the following year of assessment as if it comprised excess capital allowances (under CAA 1990, s. 141).

The one estate provisions are repealed for 2001–02 and later tax years by FA 1998, s. 39.

25.13 Quotas

25.13.1 Milk

From 30 October 1987, roll-over relief is available where there is a disposal or an acquisition of a milk quota (Inland Revenue Press Release, 29 October 1987 and TCGA 1992, s. 155). In a press release dated 11 July 1988 (1988) STI 578, the Inland Revenue confirmed that roll-over relief is available if either:
- the milk quota was disposed of before 30 October 1987, and the replacement asset was acquired on or after that date, or

- the milk quota was acquired before 30 October 1987 and another asset was sold on or after that date, but within one year after the acquisition of the milk quota.

As the proceeds from the sale of the cows is a separate matter from the compensation, it was possible for a farmer to elect for the herd basis under FA 1984, s. 48(6), make a tax-free profit on the sale of the herd, and then to receive the compensation under one of the options available.

As the compensation arises from a quota allocation operative from 2 April 1984, there is no time-apportionment, or March 1982 value for indexation.

If the farmer applied for compensation for loss of profits, the sums received are treated as trading receipts of the farming business for as long as the farmer continues to trade. If the farmer ceases trading, or the trade is treated as discontinued for tax purposes, payments made after the discontinuance are annual income chargeable under Case VI of Sch. D. If he applied for compensation for the withdrawal of the quota, he is treated as disposing of a capital asset.

The quota should qualify for retirement relief as a chargeable business asset if the other conditions for the relief are met, for instance, if the compensation is received as an element in the disposal of part of the farmer's business.

Reductions in milk quotas have resulted in the selling of existing quotas on the sale of the herds with which they are associated. This is usually done by the seller granting to the buyer temporary grazing rights over the land to which the quota attaches. A lump sum is paid for the benefit of the quota. Under a separate agreement, the seller agrees to cooperate with the buyer in securing the identification of the quota with land belonging to the buyer, following the transfer of the cattle to his or her land. In some cases, the quota is 'leased' to a neighbour. It seems that a sale of the quota is a chargeable occasion for capital gains tax purposes, whilst leasing the quota would generate receipts assessable under Sch. D, Case VI or, alternatively, under Sch. D, Case III. There are provisions in the regulations for a straightforward transfer of the quota on a change of occupation of the farm. If no part of the sale price of the farm is allocated to the quota, it is arguable that the Inland Revenue cannot apportion a notional value for tax purposes to the quota. It is also possible for a direct sales quota to be exchanged for a wholesale quota, on terms agreed with the Ministry. Roll-over relief would now be due on such an exchange.

The Inland Revenue published an article in *Tax Bulletin 6* (February 1993) which is reproduced below.

'There has been comment in the technical and farming press suggesting that a recent non-tax case, *Faulks v Faulks* [1992] 15 EG 15, has affected the treatment of milk quota for capital gains tax purposes. In our view the case does not affect it and this article sets out our position on the point.

Milk quota was introduced by EEC Regulations in 1984. Quota is a scheme which allows wholesale milk producers to produce milk up to their quota without attracting a supplementary levy. If production exceeds the quota a levy is payable. Quota is allocated in respect of a particular holding of land, but in our view this is only a means of identification and not an indication that quota is an interest in land. Our view is that quota and land are separate assets for capital gains tax purposes. We have been asked whether the decision in the *Faulks* case alters that view.

FAULKS v FAULKS

The *Faulks* case concerned a dispute between the surviving partner and the widow of the deceased partner over the amount of compensation due to the widow. This was calculated by reference to the assets of the partnership. The Court had to decide whether milk quota which was registered in the partners' names should be included in valuing those assets, it having been agreed already that the tenancy of the farm concerned was not to be included. The issue was therefore the interpretation of the partnership deed and the Partnership Act 1890. The case is not a tax case and the roll-over provisions of TCGA 1992, Section 155 were not central to the case although they were touched on.

In the course of his judgement Chadwick J was clearly inclined to the view that quota was indistinguishable from land for CGT purposes but this was not the question he was addressing. He himself commented that 'these are not questions which I need to decide.' In the circumstances his comments were not essential to his decision and are therefore without binding authority.

Additionally we do not find any compelling reasoning in his judgement to alter our long-held view that quota and land are separate assets for capital gains tax purposes.

COMPUTATIONS INVOLVING QUOTA

We are aware that, following the *Faulks v Faulks* decision some computations may be submitted on the basis that quota is part of the land. The following points set out our view of the correct position:

- Where quota was acquired by allotment in 1984 nothing has been paid for it. It was acquired in a non-arm's length transaction and there was no corresponding disposal. The allowable acquisition cost (Section 38(1)(a) TCGA) is therefore nil since the market value rule is disapplied by Section 17(2) TCGA.

- Where quota has been acquired in a later transaction the normal rules apply. If it was acquired in an arm's length transaction the allowable cost is the amount paid, and if acquired in a non-arm's length transaction the allowable cost is market value.

In neither circumstance, on a disposal of quota, is any deduction allowable which relates to the cost of the land to which quota is 'attached.'

- Indexation allowance (Section 53 *et seq* TCGA) is given on each item of acquisition and enhancement expenditure. It follows from what is said above that where quota was acquired in 1984 by allotment there can be no indexation allowance as there is no acquisition cost. For quota acquired in later transactions indexation allowance will be due in the usual way. If acquired with other assets (eg land) any necessary apportionments of the purchase price are to be made on a 'just and reasonable' basis (Section 52(4) TCGA).

If there is no allowable deduction for the cost of quota it follows that no indexation allowance is due.

- The rebasing provisions in Section 35 TCGA and the indexation provisions in Section 55 TCGA only apply to disposals of assets which existed at 31 March 1982. Quota was introduced in 1984 and so cannot have had a market value at 31 March 1982. As the quota and the land are separate assets, the 31 March 1982 market value of the land is only relevant in computing the gain or loss on any land which has also been disposed of.

Computations on quota disposal should not show a 31 March 1982 value (either of quota or land).

- A disposal of quota on its own does not represent a part disposal of the land within Section 42 TCGA since they are separate assets. The part disposal formula A / A + B in subsection (2) which allocates part of the acquisition cost to the part and where it was originally acquired by purchase. It may be necessary to apportion the cost between quota and land before applying Section 42(2).

Computations on a part disposal basis are only appropriate where it is part of quota which is disposed of.

- Quota only became a qualifying asset for the purposes of roll-over relief (Sections 152–158 TCGA) with effect from 30 October 1987. Relief is *only* available where:
  — both transactions (acquisition and disposal) occurred *on or after* 30 October 1987; or
  — the transaction involving quota occurred *on or after* 30 October 1987 and the other occurred *before* that date; or

— the transaction involving quota occurred *before* 30 October 1987 and the other occurred *on or after* that date.

Where both transactions occurred before 30 October 1987 roll-over relief is not due in respect of either the acquisition or the disposal of quota.

QUOTA AND INHERITANCE TAX

For inheritance tax purposes, where agricultural land, or an interest in agricultural land, is valued and the valuation of the land reflects the benefit of milk quota, agricultural relief is given on that value.

Where milk quota is valued separately, it will normally constitute an asset used in the business, within IHTA 1984, Section 110, so that business relief under Section 105(1)(a) IHTA may be available.'

The Inland Revenue view was subsequently upheld by the Special Commissioners in *Cottle v Coldicott* [1995] SSCD 239 (Sp C 40).

25.13.2 Potatoes

In the case of potato quotas, it is possible for there to be a transfer of the basic area for 1985 between registered producers. Where the basic quota is permanently transferred, the Inland Revenue consider it to be a capital transaction that is liable to capital gains tax in the hands of the vendor. The only cost that can be set against the sale proceeds is the acquisition of any basic quota purchased in the past. It is considered that a March 1982 value is probably minimal. A quota is considered to be an asset separate from the land itself. From 30 October 1987, roll-over relief is available on a disposal or acquisition of a potato quota (Inland Revenue Press Release, 29 October 1987 and TCGA 1992, s. 155). See the comments in **25.13.1** above for disposals and acquisitions available for relief. Retirement relief may be due in appropriate circumstances.

More recently, the removal of control over the acreage for growing potatoes means that potato quota has become worthless, and it is thus eligible for a negligible value claim.

25.13.3 Hops

A basic hop quota no longer has a value whereas, when the right to grow hops was acquired, whether alone or on a purchase of the land, it presumably had one. The Inland Revenue have agreed that it is possible to claim an allowable capital loss on the basis that the quota is now an asset of negligible value. The basic quota was not transferable before 1 April 1956, the date on which the Hops Marketing Board was established. Thereafter, it could be transferred at a price and, where a farm is sold with a quota, it is necessary to apportion the part of the price applicable to the quota. The Inland Revenue have agreed that, where the cost is not known (such as where a quota was not purchased on its own), the records of the Hops Marketing Board can be used by taking the average price of the basic quota for the year in question to find the cost. The Board has records of the quantities of basic quota belonging to each member and, by using this average, the cost can be determined.

A claim can be made on the basis that the quota was of negligible value in respect of any date after 5 April 1981. The usual two-year time limit applies in respect of a claim.

25.14 Ostrich 'farming'

The Inland Revenue published the following article in *Tax Bulletin 23* in June 1996.

> 'We have been asked about the tax consequences for taxpayers who purchase ostriches with the intention of making money out of the birds and their products. There are a number of schemes on offer to the public at present and the detailed arrangements vary from scheme to scheme. This article is inevitably in fairly general terms. It does not cover taxpayers who farm ostriches on their own land; such taxpayers are covered by the same tax rules as all other farmers. The taxpayers covered by this article are described for convenience as 'investors'. The use of that term is not intended to prejudge their tax treatment.
>
> The key question is whether the activities of investors amount to the carrying on of a trade. The Taxes Act requires 'farming', as the statute defines it, to be regarded as a trade for tax purposes, but the activities of investors do not constitute 'farming' because they do not take place on land occupied by the investor. For the same reason their activities are not 'share farming' for tax purposes. The question therefore has to be determined by applying general principles to the facts of each case.
>
> ### Is it a trade?
>
> In general, investors who have acquired one or more ostriches, which are being looked after on their behalf in a business-like way, are likely to be carrying on a trade. It follows that investors who, for example, cannot establish that they have acquired an ostrich, may not be able to demonstrate that they were carrying on a trade. It makes little difference whether the care of the

ostrich is entrusted to an agent; in determining whether there is a trade, the acts of the agent will normally be regarded as if they were the acts of the investor. Likewise, the intentions of the investor are less important than what actually happens, even if what actually happens is the responsibility of an agent.

Consequences of trading

Investors whose ostrich-managing activities amount to a trade are subject to the same tax provisions as any other trader. Again, the fact that the trade is being carried on through an agent makes no difference. This means they must keep records in the same way as other traders, including details of all amounts received and expended and of all purchases and sales made in the course of the trade. They must (unless they already receive a tax return) notify their tax office that they are carrying on a trade and after the end of the tax year enter the results of their trade on their tax return.

The results should be worked out using normal accounting principles; in particular, adjustments should be made for all trading stock (that is, ostriches, chicks, eggs and any unsold ostrich products) in the same way that a farmer would. The cost of ostriches cannot be deducted immediately (the stock valuation rules for farmers are summarised in Business Economics Note 19 [see **25.3**]).

Alternatively, a 'herd basis' election may be made in respect of mature ostriches kept not for sale or killing but for the eggs, chicks or feathers which they produce. The herd basis rules are complex and investors considering such an election are urged to take professional advice. Inspectors of Taxes cannot advise on whether a herd basis election might benefit a taxpayer.

Losses

If the investor's results for a year show a loss, it may be possible for the loss to be set against the investor's other taxable income, either for that year or another year. The necessary conditions for set-off are that the investor is carrying on a trade and that the trade is conducted 'on a commercial basis'. Investors whose activities do not amount to a trade cannot set any losses against their taxable income.

Whether a trade is carried on a commercial basis will be a question of fact in each case. Inspectors will, in general, wish to look at the commerciality of the arrangements made by the investor with or through any managing agent. For example, has the investor paid the same amount for the ostrich as someone farming personally might pay? Do the charges made by the managing agent represent a commercial rate for the services provided? If the managing agent takes a proportion of the eggs or chicks, or a proportion of the sale proceeds of these, does this represent a commercial reward for the agent's services? The 'commercial basis' test is objective and does not depend on the investor's intention.

Where investors whose activities amount to a trade incur a loss, then to the extent that the loss is not (or cannot be) set against other taxable income of any year it can be carried forward and deducted from profits of the same trade in subsequent years until it is used up.

Capital gains tax

There are unlikely to be any Capital Gains Tax consequences of investments in ostrich farming schemes where an investor's only interest is in the birds and their products. If, however, they acquire an interest in any other assets used in the scheme, such as buildings or plant, the normal Capital Gains Tax rules will apply.'

25.15 Foot and mouth disease

The outbreak of foot and mouth disease (FMD) in February 2001 led to a number of tax-related concessions for those businesses (not just farmers) affected.

25.15.1 Interest

Under FA 2001, s. 107 businesses did not have to pay interest on tax deferred as a result of financial difficulty caused by the foot and mouth outbreak (further to a report on the joint Customs and Revenue hotline).

The interest charged is removed where the Revenue have agreed to defer payment of tax in the circumstances of foot and mouth. This ensures that the Revenue can waive interest charges in all the circumstances of the foot and mouth outbreak.

Regulations also ensure that interest is not charged on NIC deferred in the same circumstances.

25.15.2 Stocktaking valuations

It was not always possible for valuers to visit some clients at their usual valuation dates (especially as 31 March is a common date for farmers who keep livestock). Where valuers had to report provisional figures to accountants, they were required to make it clear that the valuation was provisional and firm up valuations when restrictions were lifted.

Where stocktaking valuations were based on deemed cost in accordance with para. 7 of BEN 19 and markets were closed because of foot and mouth, so that market values on which to base deemed costs were not readily available, valuations were required to take into account:

- market values prevailing before the outbreak of foot and mouth disease;
- levels of compensation being paid in respect of animals slaughtered, and
- prices being offered to farmers who are able to deliver animals to abattoirs.

25.15.3 Compensation for slaughter of animals

Compensation paid to farmers for destruction of their animals is treated just as the proceeds would have been if the animals had been sold. The precise treatment depended on whether the farmer:

- had made a herd basis election or made one following compulsory slaughter, or
- chose to make use of ESC B11, which allows forward spreading of profits deriving from compensation where the herd basis does not apply.

25.15.4 Herd basis

Farmers who had not elected for the herd basis in respect of the production animals or their young have a fresh opportunity to do so under ICTA 1988, Sch. 5, para. 6 where the whole or substantial part of their herd is compulsorily slaughtered. 'Substantial' means 20 per cent or more (see Inspectors' Manual IM2303b and IM2316c).

To help farmers thinking of making an election, the Revenue regard slaughter resulting from the outbreak as being compulsory whether the animals were slaughtered because:

- they were in contact with, foot and mouth disease;
- they were in firebreak zones surrounding outbreaks, or
- they were slaughtered under the Welfare Scheme.

Under the herd basis the compensation following slaughter of the whole or a substantial part of a herd is tax-free until replacement of the herd. The compensation then becomes taxable, though the cost of the replacement animals is an allowable deduction.

25.15.5 Extra Statutory Concession B11

Farmers who suffer the slaughter of animals treated as trading stock because they are not on the herd basis may realise unexpectedly high profits in the year concerned, with consequent liability to higher rate tax. This can cause problems when they want to restock. To help this situation ESC B11 allows farmers to remove profits arising from the compulsory slaughter of animals which are not on the herd basis and could not be following a late election, from the profits of the period in which the slaughter took place, and to spread them over the following three years.

In 2001 the Revenue did not seek to enforce the condition that animals which could be on the herd basis following a late election are excluded. The Revenue will extend the term 'compulsory slaughter' to include the same circumstances as mentioned above.

Those who wish to claim the benefit of ESC B11 should enter the amount of the reduction in box 3.71 of the self-employment pages of their SA tax return and put a note in box 3.116 (additional information). Where farmers' averaging is also claimed, it applies to the profits after the claim to relief under ESC B11.

25.15.6 Increases in the number of mature animals caused by foot and mouth

Where there is a substantial disposal from the production herd the profit is tax-free unless the animals are replaced within five years. If they are replaced the profit becomes taxable. Will this rule cause unexpected tax liabilities for farmers who have made a substantial disposal within the last five years and involuntarily increase the number of mature animals they hold because of foot and mouth? The Revenue do not think it will.

> **Example 25.3**
>
> A dairy farmer usually rears female progeny and sells them before they give birth to their first offspring. The movement restrictions resulting from foot and mouth prevented him from doing so and the animals gave birth on his holding.
>
> There are two possible scenarios.
>
> First, he does not intend to increase the size of his herd. When the movement restrictions were lifted he would sell or dispose of some older animals or he would sell the animals he was forced to hang on to.
>
> If he decided to keep the animals he would have sold as part of the herd and dispose of some older animals when circumstances permit, then the situation is covered by IM2307. The new animals could reasonably be viewed as substitutes for animals awaiting disposal.
>
> If he decided to sell the young animals when circumstances permit, then they have always been for sale and it is likely that they never became part of the production herd as defined by the herd basis. So they would not count as replacements for the herd basis computation and cause the earlier tax-free gain to become taxable. This is because they were not kept (ICTA 1988, Sch. 5, para. 8(5)) wholly or mainly for the sake of the products which they produce for him to sell. Rather they were kept for sale and products were incidental. They would fall within the second category of animals excluded at IM2313a, 'animals added temporarily to a herd and then sold'. So they would remain trading stock throughout, despite giving birth.

So in either case the earlier profit remains tax-free if the farmer never decides to increase the size of his herd. Second, if the farmer decides that he will increase the size of his herd then the normal clawback would apply.

25.15.7 MAFF aid package

Various forms of assistance to farmers were announced by MAFF (now DEFRA) in addition to compensation for compulsory slaughter. Under the Pig Industry Restructuring Scheme, payments are part of the farmer's income. The time at which payment should be recognised as income will follow the accounting treatment. Under Agrimonetary Compensation, the amounts would on average be worth £2,750 to the average dairy farmer, £650 to sheep farmers, £650 to suckler cow premium claimants and £450 to beef special premium claimants. These payments are liable to income tax and should be recognised in farm accounts in accordance with normal accountancy principles.

The tax treatment of other aspects of aid to those affected by foot and mouth will be explained by the Revenue as soon as they can and if possible by including guidance in the material available to claimants.

25.15.8 Agricultural buildings allowances

ABAs are available where relevant expenditure is incurred for purposes of husbandry on agricultural land. The claimant must have a major interest in the land, which includes a freehold or leasehold interest. Relief is given over 25 years at a rate of four per cent per annum.

Foot and mouth may cause some farmers to cease to trade. Where a farmer gives up farming but retains the major interest in the farm he continues to be entitled to ABAs. The allowances and charges are made in taxing any other trade he or she may carry on. If no trade is carried on in a chargeable period, the allowances and charges are treated as expenses and receipts of any Sch. A business carried on. If there is no Sch. A business, then a notional Sch. A business is deemed to exist and the appropriate relief is given.

If the farmer decides to sell all or part of the farm the remaining allowance is passed to the new owner. In the chargeable period in which the disposal takes place the allowance is apportioned between the seller and the purchaser on a time basis. Alternatively, both parties may elect within two years of the chargeable period to have the transaction treated as a balancing event. Full details of ABAs are given in the Revenue Capital Allowances Manual at paras. 4500 onwards.

25.15.9 Furnished holiday letting

FHL is treated as a trade for loss purposes, provided the activity satisfies the tests of occupation, letting and availability for letting, explained in paras. 415–422 of booklet IR 150 *Taxation of rents*. Where the foot and mouth restrictions prevented an established FHL business from satisfying these conditions, any loss would normally have had to be dealt with under the less advantageous Sch. A rules.

The tests were relaxed for tax years 2000–01 and 2001–02. If the FHL business satisfied the tests in 1999–00 or 2000–01 but was prevented from doing so, by foot and mouth, in 2000–01 or 2001–02, the failure was disregarded and the FHL rules were deemed to be satisfied. This concession enabled the offset against other income.

Farmers (including market gardeners) and owners of commercial woodlands

25.15.10 Access to IHT/CGT exempt properties

Heritage land and buildings can be exempted from IHT and CGT on condition that the public are allowed access to them, either at any time or by visiting on specified days. If property fell in an exclusion zone at a time when access should be given, or in other cases where local conditions or Government guidelines made it impractical for access or visits, the Revenue did not regard it as a breach of the owner's undertaking where he or she decided, after judging the risks, that access or visits had to be suspended. Where owners are committed to visits on a number of pre-arranged days each year, the Revenue did not insist for tax-compliance purposes that missed days were made up later in the year.

25.15.11 Waivers of rent

In 2001, some landlords waived all or part of their rents to assist their tenants. The Revenue understand that excluding the rent waived from the income included in the landlord's accounts would be in accordance with generally accepted accountancy practice, even though there may be a strict legal entitlement. Provided the waiver was made as a direct result of foot and mouth, the Revenue did not argue that the property was let uncommercially.

However, where the collection of the rent was simply delayed, the Revenue understand that in accordance with generally accepted accountancy practice the full amount of the rent should be included in the accounts. In that case relief was given only if the debt was bad or doubtful under ICTA 1988, s. 74.

The current guidance on this subject, in booklet IR 150 at para. 169, should be read as amended above for purposes of waivers made as a direct result of foot and mouth. Landlords who waived rents should include a note in the box for additional information on their SA tax return.

25.15.12 Appeal funds

A person experiencing hardship may have received payments from special appeal funds launched by national newspapers and other arrangements set up to provide financial help. A payment will not be taxable if unconnected with the trade (for example, if made purely to alleviate personal hardship being suffered by the trader and the family). However, if the trader received money from such a fund to be used in the business, eg to supplement trading income or to help meet business expenses, it is likely to be taxable under normal

Sch. D, Case I principles. The tax treatment of such payments depended on the precise facts of each case. The Revenue and Customs published guidance for those setting up appeals, giving information on the tax and VAT issues involved.

Index

academics *see* lecturers; teachers
actors *see* entertainers
agents *see* insurance agents; land agents
agricultural buildings allowances
        25.8, 25.15.8
agricultural land, pension investment
        25.10
aircrew 12.1, 12.16
    expenses 12.16.2
    free or reduced-price travel 12.16.3
    residence 12.16.1
    travel expenses 12.16.2
    uniform allowance 12.16.2
Alternative Investment Market 4.19
anti-avoidance legislation
    entertainers 3.6
    stockbrokers and market makers
        4.16
armed forces
    annual subscriptions to headquarters
        mess central fund 13.8
    capital gains tax and residences
        13.15
    death on active service 13.17
    employment after leaving services
        13.14
    entertaining expenses 13.5
    exemptions in respect of allowances
        13.6
    extra cost of living abroad 13.3
    foreign war pensions 16.7
    hotel expenses 13.7
    inheritance tax exemption 13.17,
        13.18
    PAYE 13.10
    pensions 13.12
    place of performance of duties 13.1
    prisoners of Japanese, *ex gratia*
        payments to 13.18
    reserve and auxiliary forces 13.11
        employee share schemes and
            called-up reservists 13.11.1
    residence position 13.2
    residences, capital gains tax and
        13.15
    travel facilities 13.4

    uniform allowances 13.9
    Victoria Cross, holders of 13.16
    war widows' pensions 13.13
        foreign 16.7
artists *see* authors; copyright; painters;
    sculptors
Arts Council awards and bursaries
    2.14.2
artworks *see* works of art
Ash cash 9.8.6
assessment
    cash basis 1.1, 1.12
        abolition of 1.13
    authors 2.2
    barristers 1.1, 1.12, 1.13.1, 1.13.3,
        10.1.1
    catching-up charge 1.13.1, 1.13
    current year basis 1.11
    earnings basis 1.12
    generally accepted accounting
        practice basis 1.13
    new barristers 1.13.4
    partnerships 1.13.5
    relief for any initial double charge
        1.13.3
    spread and cap 1.13.2
    true and fair view basis 1.13
    valuation of work in progress
        1.13.6
    work in progress valuations 1.13.6
    Tax Faculty guidance 1.14
authors
    awards 2.14
    Booker Prize 2.14.1
    cash basis assessment 2.2
    casual 2.4.2
    categories of 2.4
    copyright *see* copyright
    deductions 2.6
    income averaging provisions 2.10
    income spreading provisions 2.9
    literary earnings 2.6
    losses 2.7
    Nobel Prize for literature 2.14.1
    non-professional 2.4.1
        pre-trading expenditure 2.4.1

Index

authors — *cont.*
    sale of copyright for lump sum 2.4.1
    pension scheme 2.14
    post-cessation receipts 2.5
    professional 2.4.3
        advance royalties 2.4.3, 2.9
        deductions 2.6
        losses 2.7
    public lending right 2.11
    residence, change of 2.8
    royalties 2.1
        advance royalties 2.4.3, 2.9
        assignment of rights to 2.2
        income spreading provisions 2.9
        public lending right 2.11
        residence abroad and 2.8
    Whitbread Award 2.14.1
awards, taxation of 2.14
    Arts Council awards and bursaries 2.14.2
    Booker Prize 2.14.1
    general principles 2.14.1
    Nobel prizes 2.14.1, 18.4
    prizes 18.4
    Whitbread Award 2.14.1

barristers 10.1
    adjustment charge election 10.1.1
    books, replacement of 10.1.3
    cash basis assessment 1.1, 1.12, 1.13.1, 1.13.3, 10.1.1
    catching-up charge
        new barristers 1.13.4
        relief for any initial double charge 1.13.3
    childcare costs 10.1.3
    clerks 10.2
    cost of chambers 10.1.3
    court apparel 10.1.3
    earnings basis of assessment 1.13.4, 10.1.1
    expenses 10.1.3
    inducement receipts 10.1.2
    new 1.13.1, 1.13.4, 10.1.1
    patent fee 10.1.3
    Queen's Counsel 1.1, 10.1
    Scotland 1.13.1
    secretarial assistance 10.1.3
    taking silk 1.1, 10.1
    travel expenses 10.1.3
bear excess 4.5

beneficial loans *see* loans
benefits in kind, clergy *see* clergy
bond washing 4.16.2
Booker Prize 2.14.1
bookmakers 1.2
bull excess 4.5
business property relief
    bank guarantees and 5.13.1
    Lloyd's underwriters 5.13.1–5.13.2
    secured assets and 5.13.2
butlers 1.10

cannabis growing 1.1
capital allowances
    clergy 7.6.3, 21.8.4
    entertainers 3.8
    farmers 25.1, 25.7
    fishing industry
        depooling 20.5.2
        free depreciation 20.5.1
        roll-over claims 20.5.3
    inventions and patents 22.6
    musicians 3.8
    schools 21.7, 21.8.4
    teachers 21.8.4
capital gains tax
    armed forces, residences of members 13.15
    copyright
        gift of 2.2
        sale of 2.2.1
    Crown servants, UK residence of 8.7.1
    farmers
        hold-over relief 25.9, 25.11.1
        retirement relief 25.9, 25.11.4
        roll-over relief 25.9, 25.11.2
        tenancies 25.11.3
    Lloyd's underwriters 5.9, 5.12
    professions 1.2
    residence, change of 1.8.2
    temporary visitors to UK 6.14, 6.15
    vocations 1.2
    works of art, disposals of 2.13
car allowances
    consultants 9.4.1
    Members of Parliaments and Assemblies 11.3
cars and car fuel, clergy 7.6.3, 7.8.1, 7.8.2
cash basis assessment 1.1, 1.12
    abolition of 1.13

Index

authors 2.2
barristers 1.1, 1.12, 1.13.1, 1.13.3, 10.1.1
catching-up charge 13.1, 1.13.1
  barristers
    new barristers 1.13.4
    relief for any initial double charge 1.13.3
  partnerships 1.13.1, 1.13.5
  spread and cap 1.13.2
children, share income 1.19
clergy
  beneficial loans 7.8.3
  benefits in kind 7.8
    beneficial loans 7.8.3
    car fuel 7.8.2
    cars 7.8.1
  books, purchase of 7.6.3
  capital allowances 7.6.3, 21.8.4
  car
    benefit in kind 7.8.1
    expenses 7.6.3
    fuel 7.8.2
  contemplative religious communities, income of 7.9
  domestic help 7.6.3
  evangelists 1.2, 7.10
    income of vocation 7.11
  expenses
    general 7.6.3
    maintenance 7.6.2
    property expenses 7.5.2–7.5.5
    removal 7.6.5
    rent 7.6.1
    unpaid appointments 7.6.4
  fees 7.1
  general principles 7.1
  heating costs 7.6.3
  income tax
    exemptions 7.5
    other property expenses 7.5.3
    property expenses 7.5.2–7.5.5
    statutory property expenses 7.5.2
    taxable income 7.4
    vicarage, manse or other church property occupied by clergy 7.5.1
  income of vocation 7.11
  lighting costs 7.6.3
  loans to 7.8.3
  maintenance expenditure 7.6.2
  missionaries 7.11
  National Insurance contributions 7.3
  office holders, as 7.1
  PAYE 7.2
  plant and machinery 7.6.3
  procurations 7.6.3
  property expenses
    directors of church charities, of 7.5.4
    higher paid clergy, of 7.5.4
    other 7.5.3
    reimbursement 7.5.5
    statutory 7.5.2
  removal expenses 7.6.5
  rent 7.6.1
  repair costs 7.6.3
  robes, cost of repair or replacement 7.6.3
  second residences 7.7
  secretarial assistance 7.6.3
  self-assessment 7.2
  synodals 7.6.3
  travel expenses 7.6.3
  unpaid appointments, expenses of 7.6.4
  vicarage or manse, treatment of 7.5.1
  vocation, income of 7.11
clothing
  clergy 7.6.3
  consultants 9.4.8
  entertainers 3.18
  fishing industry 12.9.2, 20.4
  lecturers 21.8.9
  merchant navy personnel 12.9.2
  teachers 21.8.9
  trawler crew 12.9.2
commercial woodlands, owners of *see* farmers
companies
  overseas work 1.21
  pension provision 1.19
  profession carried on by 1.19
  purchase of own shares by 4.9
  service companies 1.20
    entertainers 3.5
    personal service companies 1.10
    sportspeople 17.6, 17.7
  tax liability of shareholders 1.19

Index

construction industry scheme (CIS) 23.1, 23.3
  see also subcontractors
consultants *see* doctors
contemplative religious communities, income of 7.9
contractor
  meaning 23.4
  see also subcontractors
conventional basis assessment *see* cash basis assessment
copyright 2.1
  accumulation and maintenance trust, settlement as 2.2
  assignment 2.1
  capital gains tax 2.2.1, 2.2
  duration of 2.2.1
  gifts of 2.2
  interest in, grant of 2.1
  licensing 2.1
  nature of 2.1
  royalties *see* royalties
  sale of
    by estate 2.2.1
    lump sum for outright sale 2.4.1, 2.9
  works of art, disposals of 2.11
councillors *see* local councillors and members of Government boards
creative artists *see* authors; painters; sculptors
credit traders 15.1, 15.2
  provisions 15.2.1
  valuation of debts 15.2.2
Crown servants, working abroad *see* diplomatic service members and other Crown servants working abroad
current year basis of assessment 1.11

dentists 9.11
  associates 9.11.1
  case law 9.12
  goodwill 9.11.3
  partnerships 9.11.2
  superannuation deductions 9.10
  see also consultants
designs 22.13
  capital receipts 22.15
  fees and expenses 22.16
  sale for lump sum 22.15

  see also inventions and patents
diplomatic service members and other Crown servants working abroad
  capital gains 8.3
  European Union Office in Brussels, employment in 8.8
  exempt allowances 8.2
  other income 8.3
  personal allowances 8.5
  place of performance of duties 8.1
  tax credits 8.6
  tax-free investments 8.4
  UK residences
    capital gains tax 8.7.1
    job-related accommodation 8.7.2
director
  fees for professional services 1.15
  non-profit making companies 21.8.15
  pensions 1.19
  spouse as 1.19
divers 6.11.3
dividend income 4.7
dividend stripping 4.16.1
doctors 9.1
  Ash cash 9.8.6
  case law 9.12
  consultants 9.2
    assisted travel scheme 9.4.5
    car allowances 9.4.1
    clothing 9.4.8
    conference expenses 9.5.1
    emergency call-out expenses 9.4.4
    employment and self-employment income 9.2
    excess travelling expenses 9.4.3
    expenses 9.3
    fees and subscriptions 9.4.10
    in-house bridging loans 9.4.2
    journey between home and headquarters 9.4.6
    late night duties 9.4.7
    motor expenses 9.3.2, 9.4.1
    practice accounts 9.5
    property expenses 9.3.1
    removal and associated expenses 9.4.2
    telephone expenses 9.4.9
    travel expenses 9.4.3

Index

uniforms 9.4.8
general practice 9.6
  best accounting date 9.8.8
  cremation certificates 9.8.6
  group practice 9.6
  hospital appointments 9.8.5
  notional rent allowances 9.8.3
  partnership changes 9.8.2
  personal awards 9.8.4
  personal expenses claim 9.8.9
  practice accounts 9.5
  retired doctors 9.8.10
  salaried partners 9.8.7
  self-assessment guidance 9.7
  sundry fees 9.8.6
  superannuation 9.8.1, 9.10
pro bono work, expenses in connection with 9.9
domestic help, for clergy 7.6.3
domestic workers 1.10
domicile
  meaning 6.5
  temporary visitors to UK 6.5
double tax agreements
  foreign pensions 16.5
  with Hungary 6.12
  with Norway 6.11.5
  overseas partnerships 1.4
  with USA 1.6, 3.3
  withholding of foreign tax at source 3.3

earnings basis assessment 1.12
education *see* schools; universities
employments, professional employments 1.9, 1.15
entertainers
  accommodation *see* subsistence *below*
  angels 3.22
  anti-avoidance legislation 3.6
  basis of assessment 3.1
  capital allowances 3.8
  capital sums received by 3.7
  casual 3.1
  clothing 3.18
  contracts 3.9.1
  employment status
    National Insurance purposes 3.9.2
    tax purposes 3.9.1
  expenses 3.1, 3.14

  clothing 3.18
  medical expenses 3.19
  other expenses 3.20
  subsistence 3.15, 3.17
  travelling abroad 3.15
  travelling in UK 3.16
  film and allied industries, freelance workers in 3.10
  foreign entertainers in UK 1.6, 3.4
  groups' tax treatment 3.21
  Inland Revenue investigations 3.11
  loans 3.12
  medical expenses 3.19
  musicians
    capital allowances 3.8
    sale of instruments 3.24
  non-resident company, use of 3.2
  non-resident entertainers 1.6, 3.4
  overseas work 3.2
    withholding of foreign tax at source 3.3
  pensions 3.23
  residence, change of 3.1
  retirement 3.23
  self-assessment 3.1
  service companies 3.5
  'slavery' contracts 3.5
  subsistence 3.15
    in UK 3.17
  tax returns 3.13
  theatre angels 3.22
  travel expenses
    abroad 3.15
    in UK 3.16
  uncommercial professional activity 3.1
  unpaid 3.1
  vocation 3.1
European Parliament, Members of *see* Members of Parliaments and Assemblies
European Union, officials employed by, in Brussels 8.8
evangelists 1.2, 7.10
  income of vocation 7.11

farmers
  agricultural buildings allowances 25.8, 25.15.8
  averaging 25.6
    tax credits 25.6.1
  capital allowances 25.1, 25.7

farmers — *cont.*
  capital gains tax
    hold-over relief 25.9, 25.11.1
    retirement relief 25.9, 25.11.4
    roll-over relief 25.9, 25.11.2
    tenancies 25.11.3
  casual workers 25.9
  change in person carrying on business 25.1
  Farm and Horticulture Development Scheme 25.9
  farm woodland scheme 25.9
  foot and mouth disease 25.15
    access to IHT/CGT exempt properties 25.15.10
    agricultural buildings allowances 25.15.8
    appeal funds 25.15.12
    compensation for slaughter of animals 25.9, 25.15.3
    compulsory slaughter 25.15.3, 25.15.5
    Extra Statutory Concession B11 25.15.5
    furnished holiday letting 25.15.9
    herd basis election 25.15.4
    increases in number of mature animals 25.15.6
    interest 25.15.1
    MAFF aid package 25.15.7
    stocktaking valuations 25.15.2
    waivers of rent 25.15.11
  foreign students 25.9
  free board and lodging for lower-paid employees 25.9
  gang-masters 25.9
  grants 25.9
  harvest workers 25.9
  herd basis election 25.4
    foot and mouth disease and 25.15.4
    partnership changes and 25.5
  hop quotas 25.13.3
  joint ventures 25.10
  loans, interest on 25.9
  losses 25.2
    carrying forward 25.1
    hobby farming provisions 25.2
  milk quotas 25.13.1
  minors, wages paid to 25.9
  'one estate' election 25.12
  ostrich farming 25.14
  partnerships 25.1, 25.9, 25.10
    changes 25.5
  PAYE 25.9
  potato quotas 25.13.2
  price-guarantee payments 25.9
  quotas
    hops 25.13.3
    milk 25.13.1
    potatoes 25.13.2
  revenue receipts and payments 25.9
  set aside 25.9
  share farming arrangements 25.10
  slaughter of animals
    compensation for 25.9, 25.15.3
    compulsory 25.9, 25.15.3, 25.15.5
  stocks 25.3
    foot and mouth disease and 25.15.2
    herd basis election 25.4, 25.5, 25.15.4
    share farming arrangements 25.10
    valuation 25.3
  subscriptions 25.9
  subsidies 25.9
  succession between connected persons 25.1
  tax credits 25,6.1
  trade, as 25.1
film and allied industries
  freelance workers in 3.10
  see also entertainers
financial futures market 4.17.2
  capital gains treatment 4.18
fishing industry 20.1
  bedding, provision of 12.9.2
  capital allowances
    depooling 20.5.2
    free depreciation 20.5.1
    roll-over claims 20.5.3
  clothing
    allowances 20.4
    protective 12.9.2
  employment status 20.2.1
    share fishing 20.2.2
    trawler crew 20.2.1
  English ports 20.2.3
  partnerships
    changes in 20.6.1
    company, including 20.6.2
  retirement age 20.3

Index

roll-over relief for fishing licences
and fish quota 20.2.3
share fishing 20.2.2
trawler crew 20.2.1
foreign pensions *see* pensions
foresters *see* farmers
freelance workers, film and allied
industries 3.10
furnished holiday lettings
foot and mouth restrictions and
25.15.9
income from 14.14
wear and tear 14.9
see also hotels

gamblers 1.2
gang-masters 25.9
gardeners *see* farmers
**generally accepted accounting practice
basis** 1.13
Gift Aid 21.5
gifts
copyright 2.2
sportspeople, to 17.2
unsolicited 18.3
golden handcuffs, stockbrokers and
market makers 4.3
golden handshakes, sportspeople
17.11
golf professionals 1.2
Government boards, members of *see*
local councillors and
members of Government
boards
grants
European Parliament, terminal
grants 11.12.4
farmers, to 25.9
sportspeople, to 17.2
see also awards
gratuities 18.1
gifts, unsolicited 18.3
long service awards 18.5
National Insurance contributions
18.2.3
prizes 18.4
retirement, on 18.2.1
suggestion schemes, awards under
18.6
third party awards 18.7
tips 18.2
National Insurance contributions
18.2.3
PAYE 14.15, 18.2.2
tronc system 14.15, 18.2.2
guest-houses
residences 14.12
roll-over relief 14.13

harvest workers 25.9
higher education *see* universities
hire purchase business 15.1, 15.3
holiday lettings *see* furnished holiday
lettings
hop quotas 25.13.3
hotels
army officers 13.7
building allowances 14.10
capital expenditure 14.7
date on which trading commences
14.6
dilapidations 14.11
own consumption adjustments 14.5
PAYE, tips 14.15, 18.2.2
plant and machinery 14.8
residences 14.12
roll-over relief 14.13
tips
PAYE 14.15, 18.2.2
tronc system 14.15, 18.2.2
see also furnished holiday lettings
House of Lords, members of 11.13

illegal business 1.1
income averaging provisions 2.10
income spreading provisions 2.9, 22.11
inheritance tax
armed forces, death on active service
13.17, 13.18
Lloyd's underwriters 5.13
business property relief
5.13.1–5.13.2
temporary visitors to UK 6.16
works of art, disposal of 2.13
insurance agents
brokers 19.1.2
categories of 19.1
commission 19.1.2
casual 19.2
indemnity terms, on 19.3
employment status 19.1.1
exclusive agents 19.1.1
intellectual property *see* copyright;
inventions and patents

Index

interest
  earned income, as 1.22
  foot and mouth disease and 25.15.1
  relief for 4.10, 4.11
  solicitors
    bank interest etc received 10.4.1
    interest paid by or through 10.4.3
    interest received on behalf of clients 10.4.2
invalidity benefits, foreign 16.6
inventions and patents
  capital allowances 22.6
  death 22.4.2
  deduction of tax 22.8
  designs 22.13
    capital receipts 22.15
    fees and expenses 22.16
    sale for lump sum 22.15
  earned income 22.10
  expenses 22.1
    income tax position 22.3
    trade marks and designs 22.16
  foreign patents 22.9
  incorporation of business 22.5
  know-how 22.12
  law of patents 22.2
  non-residents 22.4.3
  receipts, treatment of 22.4
    capital sums 22.4.1
    death 22.4.2
    non-residents 22.4.3
  royalties 22.7
    spreading provisions 22.11
  trade marks 22.13
    capital receipts 22.15
    Case III and 22.14
    fees and expenses 22.16
    sale for lump sum 22.15
investment income
  earned income, as 1.22, 4.10
  non-resident Crown employees 8.4
  schools 21.4
  temporary visitors to UK 6.14, 6.17

jockeys 1.2, 17.17
judges 10.3
  assistant recorders 10.3.1
  circuit judges 10.3.1
  deputy circuit judges 10.3.1
  deputy district judges 10.3.1
  Deputy High Court judges 10.3.1
  recorders 10.3.1

know-how 22.12
  see also inventions and patents

land agents 1.2
lecturers 21.8
  books 21.8.9
  clothing, special 21.8.9
  conference and course expenses 21.8.7
  directors of non-profit-making companies 21.8.15
  domestic services 21.8.12
  employment status 21.8
  full-time 21.8
  living accommodation 21.8.11
  National Insurance contributions 21.8.1
  occasional 21.8
  other income 21.8.14
  part-time 21.8
  research costs 21.8.6
  residences 21.8.13
  study allowances 21.8.10
  study leave overseas 21.8.16
  subscriptions 21.8.9
  temporary visitors to UK 6.12
  travel expenses 21.8.8
  visiting 21.8
legal profession *see* barristers; judges; solicitors
limited liability partnerships 1.1
limited partnerships 1.1
Lloyd's underwriters 5.1
  accrued income scheme 5.19
  business property relief
    bank guarantees and 5.13.1
    secured assets and 5.13.2
  capital gains 5.9
  capital gains tax 5.9
    retirement or death 5.12
  corporate membership 5.22
  death, capital gains tax position on 5.12
  double taxation relief 5.17
  earned income 5.4
  expenses 5.16
  foreign taxes paid 5.17
    US taxes 5.17.1
  gains, sources of 5.2

430

Index

husband and wife, taxation of 5.21
income
    earned or unearned 5.4
    sources of 5.2
    inheritance tax 5.13
business property relief 5.13.1–5.13.2
    interest paid 5.8
    losses 5.6
        PAYE relief 5.6.1
        terminal loss relief 5.6
    Member's Agent Pooling
        Arrangements 5.11
    non-resident names 5.18
    personal pensions premiums 5.15
    premiums trust funds 5.20
    reinsurance to close 5.5
    reinsurance policies 5.7
    retirement annuity 5.15
    retirement, capital gains tax position on 5.12
    special reserve fund 5.14
    stakeholder pensions premiums 5.15
    stock lending 5.20
    stop-loss policies 5.7
    subscriptions 5.16
    syndicate capacity auctions 5.10
    underwriting account 5.3
    unearned income 5.4
    US tax 5.17.1
    wife and husband, taxation of 5.21

loans
    clergy, to 7.8.3
    consultants, in-house bridging loans to 9.4.2
    entertainers, to 3.12
    farmers, to 25.9
    temporary loans by solicitors 10.4.4

local councillors and members of Government boards
    attendance allowances 24.2, 24.4
    expenses 24.3
        guidance note on 24.4
        hire of rooms 24.4
        household expenses 24.4
        reimbursed 24.1
        secretarial assistance 24.4
        telephone 24.4
        travel 24.4
    office or profession 24.5

long service awards 18.5

manse *see* clergy
market makers *see* stockbrokers and market makers
Member's Agent Pooling Arrangements 5.11
members of the diplomatic service *see* diplomatic service members and other Crown servants working abroad
Members of Parliaments and Assemblies
    additional costs allowance 11.2
    car allowance 11.3
    European Parliament
        deductions for expenses 11.12.3
        salaries 11.12.1
        subsistence allowances 11.12.2
        terminal grants 11.12.4
        travel allowances 11.12.2
    European travel expenses 11.5
    general taxation position 11.1
    House of Lords 11.13
    other incidental expenses 11.7
    other income 11.10
    overnight expense allowances 11.6
    pension arrangements 11.9
    research assistants 11.11
    retirement 11.9
    secretaries 11.11
    staffing allowance 11.7
    travel costs 11.4
        European travel expenses 11.5
merchant navy personnel 12.1
    administration 12.6
    definitions 12.5
    employment outside UK territorial waters 12.11
    flat rate deduction of expenses 12.13
    foreign seafarers 12.3
    non-resident seafarers 12.2
        not resident but ordinarily resident 12.2.2
        not resident and not ordinarily resident 12.2.1
    PAYE 12.14
    place of performance of duties 12.12
    reservists 12.15
    residence of seafarers 12.10
    salvage awards 12.7
    subsistence allowance 12.9

Index

merchant navy personnel — *cont.*
    bedding and protective clothing 12.9.2
    deduction for provision of own food 12.9.1
    travelling allowance 12.9
    UK residents 12.4
        100 per cent deduction 12.4.1
    uniform allowances 12.8
milk quotas 25.13.1
ministers of religion *see* clergy
missionaries 7.11
moneylenders 15.1, 15.5
    allocation of principal and interest 15.5.1
    cessation 15.5.2
musicians
    awards 2.14
    capital allowances 3.8
    instruments
        capital allowances 3.8
        sale of 3.24
    see also entertainers

nannies 1.10
National Insurance contributions
    clergy 7.3
    education 21.8.1
    entertainers 3.9.2
    gratuities 18.2.3
    lecturers 21.8.1
    teachers 21.8.1
    temporary visitors to UK 6.18
        reciprocal arrangements 6.18.1–6.18.3
    tips 18.2.3
Nobel prizes 2.14.1, 18.4
non-residents
    authors' royalties and 2.8
    construction industry scheme (CIS) 23.1
    foreign entertainers in UK 1.6, 3.4
    non-resident company, use of 3.2
    representatives of *see* UK representatives
    seafarers 12.2
    tax liability of 1.5
    see also residence
Northern Ireland Legislative Assembly, Members of *see* Members of Parliaments and Assemblies

North Sea
    Clark v Oceanic Contractors Inc. 6.11.2
    divers 6.11.3
    employers, returns by 6.11.1
    expenses 6.11.4
    Norwegian sector 6.11.5
    PAYE 6.11.2

ostrich farming 25.14
overseas income
    companies 1.21
    double tax agreements 1.4
    entertainers 3.2
        withholding of foreign tax at source 3.3
    non-resident company, use of 3.2
    partnerships 1.4
    study leave 21.8.16

painters
    awards 2.14
    disposals 2.13
    income averaging provisions 2.10
    income spreading provisions 2.9
    tax relief 2.12
    see also works of art
partnerships
    catching-up charge 1.13.1, 1.13.5
    current year basis of assessment 1.11
    dentists 9.11.2
    doctors, changes 9.8.2
    earnings basis assessment 1.12
    expenses 1.18
    farmers 25.1, 25.9, 25.10
        changes 25.5
    fishing industry
        changes 20.6.1
        partnerships including a company 20.6.2
    limited liability partnerships 1.1
    limited partnerships 1.1
    overseas partnerships 1.4
    sportspeople 17.6
    UK representative, as 1.7.5
patents *see* inventions and patents
pawnbrokers 15.1, 15.4
PAYE
    armed forces 13.10
    clergy 7.2
    farmers 25.9

Lloyd's underwriters, relief for losses 5.6.1
merchant navy personnel 12.14
North Sea, workers in 6.11.2
publicans and hoteliers 14.15
seafarers 12.14
sportspeople 17.13
tips 14.15, 18.2.2
pensions
agricultural land, investment in 25.10
armed forces 13.12
authors 2.14
entertainers 3.23
foreign
　arrears of pension 16.2
　Crown Agents, paid by 16.3
　double tax agreements 16.5
　invalidity benefits 16.6
　pensions paid to victims of Nazi persecution 16.4
　remittance basis 16.1
　social security payments 16.8
　war pensions 16.7
Lloyd's underwriters 5.15
Members of Parliaments and Assemblies 11.9
sportspeople 17.18
trading companies and 1.19
war widows' pensions 13.13
　foreign 16.7
personal service companies 1.10
plant and machinery
clergy 7.6.3
hotels 14.8
publicans 14.8
potato quotas 25.13.2
priests *see* clergy
prisoners of Japanese, *ex gratia* payments to 13.18
prizes 2.14.1, 18.4
see also awards
profession
carried on abroad 1.3
carried on in UK 1.6
company carrying on 1.19
meaning 1.1
professional employments 1.9, 1.15
trade distinguished 1.1
property expenses, clergy 7.5.2–7.5.5
prostitution 1.1

publicans
basis of assessment 14.1
dilapidations 14.11
exclusivity agreements 14.2
expenses 14.4
PAYE, tips 14.15, 18.2.2
plant and machinery 14.8
residences 14.12
tenancies 14.3
termination payments 14.3
tips
　PAYE 14.15, 18.2.2
　tronc system 14.15, 18.2.2
public lending right 2.11
public schools, charitable status 21.2

Queen's Counsel *see* barristers

recorders 10.3.1
assistant recorders 10.3.1
religious communities, income of 7.9
removal expenses
clergy 7.6.5
consultants 9.4.2
rent
clergy 7.6.1
doctors 9.8.3
farmers 25.15.11
repair costs, clergy 7.6.3
reserve and auxiliary forces 13.11
employee share schemes and called-up reservists 13.11.1
residence
aircrew 12.16.1
armed forces 13.2
　capital gains tax 13.15
effect of change
　authors 2.8
　capital gains tax 1.8.2
　entertainers 3.1
　income tax 1.8.1
seafarers 12.10
temporary visitors to UK 6.2.1
see also non-residents
retirement
entertainers 3.23
farmers 25.9, 25.11.4
fishing industry 20.3
gratuities on 18.2.1
Lloyd's underwriters 5.12, 5.15

433

Index

retirement — *cont.*
    Members of Parliaments and Assemblies 11.9
river pilots 20.8.1
royalties 2.1
    advance royalties 2.4.3, 2.9
    annual payments, as 2.2
    assignment of rights to 2.2
    income spreading provisions 2.9
    patents, exploitation of 22.7
    public lending right 2.11
    residence abroad and 2.8
    service companies 3.5

Schedule D Cases I and II
    expenses 1.18
    payment of tax under 1.17
scholarships, taxation of 21.8.2
schools
    bursaries, taxation of 21.8.2
    capital allowances 21.7, 21.8.4
    charitable status
        definition of charity 21.1
        effect of 21.3
        public schools 21.2
    entertaining 21.8.3
    fees
        payment where parents separated 21.6
        remission of 21.8.5
    Gift Aid 21.5
    investment income 21.4
    meals, provision of 21.8.3
    research costs 21.8.6
    scholarships, taxation of 21.8.2
    teachers 21.8
        books 21.8.9
        capital allowances 21.8.4
        clothing, special 21.8.9
        conference and course expenses 21.8.7
        directors of non-profit-making companies 21.8.15
        domestic services 21.8.12
        living accommodation 21.8.11
        National Insurance contributions 21.8.1
        other income 21.8.14
        research costs 21.8.6
        residences 21.8.13
        study allowances 21.8.10
        study leave overseas 21.8.16

    subscriptions 21.8.9
    temporary visitors to UK 6.12
    see also lecturers; teachers
Scottish Parliament, Members of *see* Members of Parliaments and Assemblies
sculptors
    awards 2.14
    disposals 2.13
    income averaging provisions 2.10
    income spreading provisions 2.9
    tax relief 2.12
    see also works of art
seafarers *see* fishing industry; merchant navy personnel
sea pilots 20.8.1
    compensation payments by Trinity House 20.8.2
secretarial assistance
    barristers 10.1.3
    clergy 7.6.3
    local councillors and members of Government boards 24.4
    Members of Parliaments and Assemblies 11.11
self-assessment
    clergy 7.2
    doctors 9.7
    entertainers 3.1
    expenses 1.18
    income spreading, claim for 2.9
    payment of tax under Schedule D cases I and II 1.17
service companies 1.20
    entertainers 3.5
    personal service companies 1.10
    sportspeople 17.6
        documentation 17.7
share farming arrangements 25.10
share fishing 20.2.2
    employment status 20.2.2
    see also fishing industry
shareholders, tax liability 1.19
'slavery' contracts 3.5
small companies' rate 1.19, 2.2
social security payments, foreign 16.8
solicitors 10.4
    interest
        bank interest etc received 10.4.1
        paid by or through a solicitor 10.4.3

Index

received on behalf of clients 10.4.2
office holders 10.4.5
  engagement in related area 10.4.6
  public tribunals and trusts, membership of 10.4.6
  temporary loans and guarantees 10.4.4
sportspeople
  amateurs 17.14
  appearance fees 17.4
  basis of liability 17.1
  benefit matches 17.11, 17.12
  endorsement fees 17.3
  expenses
    abroad 17.10.1
    in the UK 17.10.2
  foreign companies 17.8
  general principles on liability of various receipts 17.11
  gifts 17.2
  golden handshakes 17.11
  golf professionals 1.2
  grants 17.2
  'image' payments 17.11
  inducement payments 17.11
  international matches, payments for 17.11
  jockeys 1.2, 17.17
  offshore companies 17.11
  participation fees 17.4
  partnership, use of 17.6
  PAYE 17.13
  pension schemes 17.18
  performance fees 17.4
  service company
    documentation 17.7
    use of 17.6
  signing on fees 17.15
  sponsorship 17.3
  subventions 17.2
  transfer fees 17.11
  visiting sportspeople 1.6, 17.5
  winning, payment for 17.16
  withholding taxes 17.9
spouse
  director, as 1.19
  Lloyd's underwriters, taxation of husband and wife 5.21
stockbrokers and market makers
  accounts, period of 4.4

Alternative Investment Market 4.19
anti-avoidance provisions 4.16
  bond washing 4.16.2
  dividend stripping 4.16.1
attachés 4.13
bear excess 4.5
bond washing 4.16.2
bull excess 4.5
capital gains returns 4.15
clerks 4.13
dividend income 4.7
dividend stripping 4.16.1
dividends unclaimed 4.12
expenses 4.14
financial futures market 4.17.2
  capital gains treatment 4.18
golden handcuffs 4.3
incorporation 4.2
interest paid 4.11
interest received 4.10
period of accounts 4.4
purchase of own shares by company 4.9
returns 4.6
securities
  borrowing and lending 4.8
  profits and losses on sale 4.7
Stock Exchange rules 4.1
traded options 4.17.1
  capital gains treatment 4.18
unclaimed dividends 4.12
subcontractors
  certificates 23.2, 23.8
  construction industry scheme 23.1, 23.3
  construction operations, meaning 23.6
  contractor, meaning 23.4
  deduction certificate 23.2
  employment status 23.12
  expenses 23.13
  extra-statutory concession C32 23.3
  gross certificate 23.7
    business test 23.7.1
    compliance test 23.7.2
    turnover test 23.7.3
  IR35 rules 23.3
  meaning 23.5
  new scheme from 6 April 2006 23.14
  procedures 23.8
  registration cards 23.9, 23.14

435

Index

subcontractors — *cont.*
  tax certificates
    CIS5 23.11
    CIS6 23.10, 23.14
  tax deduction scheme 23.1
subventions, sportspeople, to 17.2
suggestion schemes, awards under 18.6
synodals 7.6.3

teachers 21.8
  books 21.8.9
  capital allowances 21.8.4
  clothing, special 21.8.9
  conference and course expenses 21.8.7
  directors of non-profit-making companies 21.8.15
  domestic services 21.8.12
  living accommodation 21.8.11
  National Insurance contributions 21.8.1
  other income 21.8.14
  research costs 21.8.6
  residences 21.8.13
  study allowances 21.8.10
  study leave overseas 21.8.16
  subscriptions 21.8.9
  temporary visitors to UK 6.12
  travel expenses 21.8.8
television, freelance workers in 3.10
temporary visitors to UK
  capital gains 6.14, 6.15
  corresponding payments relief 6.8
  departure from UK 6.17
  domicile 6.5
  dual employment contracts 6.7
  education, for 6.13
  employees 6.1
    requirements of 6.10
  employer, requirements of 6.10
  foreign entertainers 1.6, 3.4
  inheritance tax 6.16
  investment income 6.14, 6.17
  National Insurance contributions 6.18
    reciprocal arrangements 6.18.1–6.18.3
  North Sea
    divers 6.11.3
    expenses 6.11.4
    individuals working on 6.11

    Norwegian sector 6.11.5
    PAYE 6.11.2
    returns by employers 6.11.1
  payer of income 6.6
  place of performance of duties 6.4
  professors 6.12
  remittance 6.3
  residence position 6.2.1
  teachers 6.12
  travel expenses 6.9
third party awards 18.7
tips 18.2
  National Insurance contributions 18.2.3
  PAYE 14.15, 18.2.2
  tronc system 14.15, 18.2.2
  see also gratuities
trade
  carried on abroad 1.3
  company carrying on a profession 1.19
  meaning 1.1
  profession distinguished 1.1
traded options 4.17.1
  capital gains treatment 4.18
trade marks 22.13
  capital receipts 22.15
  Case III and 22.14
  fees and expenses 22.16
  sale for lump sum 22.15
  see also inventions and patents
travel expenses
  aircrew 12.16.2
  barristers 10.1.3
  clergy 7.6.3
  consultants 9.4.3
  education 21.8.8
  entertainers
    travelling abroad 3.15
    travelling in UK 3.16
  lecturers 21.8.8
  local councillors 24.4
  Members of Parliaments and Assemblies 11.4, 11.12.2
    European travel expenses 11.5
  teachers 21.8.8
  temporary visitors to UK 6.9
trawler crew 20.2.1
  bedding and protective clothing 12.9.2
  employment status 20.2.1
  see also fishing industry

Index

Trinity House, compensation payments 20.8.2
tronc system 14.15, 18.2.2
true and fair view basis of assessment 1.13
trust, copyright, settlement of 2.2
trusteeships 1.16

UK representatives 1.7
  definition 1.7.1
  independent agents
    definition 1.7.3
    obligations and liabilities 1.7.3
    retention and recovery of monies due 1.7.4
  obligations and liabilities 1.7.2
    limitation 1.7.3
  partnership as 1.7.5
universities
  bursaries, taxation of 21.8.2
  charity, definition of 21.1
  entertaining 21.8.3
  lecturers 21.8
    books 21.8.9
    clothing, special 21.8.9
    conference and course expenses 21.8.7
    directors of non-profit-making companies 21.8.15
    domestic services 21.8.12
    living accommodation 21.8.11
    other income 21.8.14
    research costs 21.8.6
    residences 21.8.13
    study allowances 21.8.10
    study leave overseas 21.8.16
    subscriptions 21.8.9
    temporary visitors to UK 6.12
    travel expenses 21.8.8
  meals, provision of 21.8.3
  research costs 21.8.6
  scholarships, taxation of 21.8.2

vicars *see* clergy
Victoria Cross, holders of 13.16
visitors *see* temporary visitors to UK
vocation, meaning 1.2

war widows' pensions 13.13
  foreign 16.7
Welsh Assembly, Members of *see* Members of Parliaments and Assemblies
Whitbread Award 2.14.1
winnings 1.2
woodlands, owners of *see* farmers
work in progress valuations 1.13.6
  Tax Faculty guidance 1.14
works of art
  copyright *see* copyright
  disposals of 2.11
  donations of 2.13
  gifts of 2.13
  money received in connection with, capital or income 2.3
  national importance, of 2.13
writers *see* authors